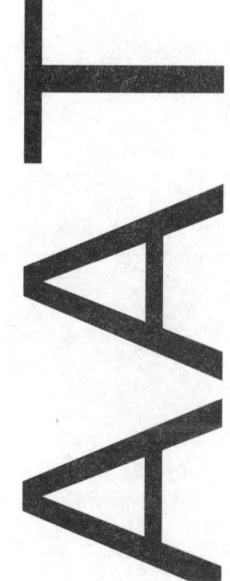

Payroll Administration
Technical Units 71 to 73

Payroll Administration
(Finance Act 2004)
NVQ/SVQ Level 2

Tutorial Text

In this August 2004 second edition

- Everything you need to get you through the 2003 Standards at NVQ/SVQ Level 2
- New uncluttered format, with plenty of space for your own notes
- Material up to date at 1 August 2004 including Finance Act 2004 and taking into account all AAT guidance issued

FOR DECEMBER 2004 AND JUNE 2005 EXAMS AND SKILLS TESTING

First edition September 2003
Second edition August 2004

ISBN 0 7517 1716 9 (Previous edition 0 7517 1220 5)

British Library Cataloguing-in-Publication Data
A catalogue record for this book
is available from the British Library

Published by

BPP Professional Education
Aldine House, Aldine Place
London W12 8AW

www.bpp.com

Printed in Great Britain by W M Print
45-47 Frederick Street
Walsall, West Midlands
WS2 9NE

All our rights reserved. No part of this publication may be reproduced, stored in a retrieval system or transmitted, in any form or by any means, electronic, mechanical, photocopying, recording or otherwise, without the prior written permission of BPP Professional Education.

We are grateful to the QCA for permission to reproduce extracts from the Standards of Competence for Accounting, and to the AAT for permission to reproduce extracts from the mapping and Guidance Notes.

©
BPP Professional Education
2004

Contents

Introduction
How to use this Tutorial Text – Payroll Administration Structure – Level 2
Standards of Competence – Assessment Strategy – Building your portfolio

		Page	Answers to activities

PART A Maintaining employee records

1	Starters and leavers	3	313
2	Instructions from external agencies	47	317
3	Recording permanent payroll variations	59	318

PART B Ascertaining gross pay

| 4 | Calculation of gross pay | 73 | 319 |
| 5 | Statutory pay entitlements | 115 | 322 |

PART C Determining net pay

6	Income tax: simple cases	165	323
7	Income tax: more complex cases	205	328
8	National Insurance: basic NICs	231	332
9	National insurance: advanced NICs	251	334
10	Other deductions	261	336
11	Net pay and aggregate payroll totals	289	340

INTRODUCTION

	Page
Answers to activities	313
Tax tables	345
Index	421

Order forms

Review form & free prize draw

Contents

Introduction
How to use this Tutorial Text – Payroll Administration Structure – Level 2 Standards of Competence – Assessment Strategy – Building your portfolio

		Page	Answers to activities

PART A Maintaining employee records

1	Starters and leavers	3	313
2	Instructions from external agencies	47	317
3	Recording permanent payroll variations	59	318

PART B Ascertaining gross pay

| 4 | Calculation of gross pay | 73 | 319 |
| 5 | Statutory pay entitlements | 115 | 322 |

PART C Determining net pay

6	Income tax: simple cases	165	323
7	Income tax: more complex cases	205	328
8	National Insurance: basic NICs	231	332
9	National insurance: advanced NICs	251	334
10	Other deductions	261	336
11	Net pay and aggregate payroll totals	289	340

Page

Answers to activities 313

Tax tables 345

Index 421

Order forms

Review form & free prize draw

Introduction

How to use this Tutorial Text

Aims of this Tutorial Text

> To provide the knowledge and practice to help you succeed in the exam and skills testing for Payroll Administration Technical Units 71 to 73.

To pass the exam and skills tests you need a thorough understanding in all areas covered by the standards of competence.

> To tie in with the other components of the BPP Effective Study Package to ensure you have the best possible chance of success.

Tutorial Text

This covers all you need to know for the exam and skills tests for Payroll Administration Technical Units 71 to 73. Numerous activities throughout the text help you practise what you have just learnt.

Assessment Kit

When you have understood and practised the material in the Tutorial Text, you will have the knowledge and experience to tackle the Assessment Kit for Units 71 to 73. This aims to get you through the exam and skills tests, whether in the form of the AAT simulation or in the workplace.

INTRODUCTION

Recommended approach to this Tutorial Text

(a) To achieve competence in Payroll Administration, you need to be able to do **everything** specified by the standards. Study the Tutorial Text carefully and do not skip any of it.

(b) Learning is an **active** process. Do **all** the activities as you work through the Tutorial Text so you can be sure you really understand what you have read. There is a checklist at the end of each chapter, detailing the performance criteria, range statement and knowledge and understanding covered by each activity.

(c) After you have covered the material in the Tutorial Text, work through the **Assessment Kit**.

(d) Before you take the exam or skills tests, check that you still remember the material using the following quick revision plan for each chapter.

    (i) Read through the chapter contents list. Are there any gaps in your knowledge? If so, study the section again.

    (ii) Read and learn the key learning points, which are a summary of the chapter.

    (iii) Do the quick quiz again. If you know what you're doing, it shouldn't take long.

This approach is only a suggestion. Your college may well adapt it to suit your needs.

Quick quizzes

> These include true/false and other formats not used by the AAT. However, these types of questions are usually very familiar to students and are used to help students adjust to otherwise unfamiliar material.

Remember this is a **practical** course.

(a) Try to relate the material to your experience in the workplace or any other work experience you may have had.

(b) Try to make as many links as you can to your study of the other Units at NVQ/SVQ Level 2.

(c) Keep this text, (hopefully) you will find it invaluable in your everyday work too!

Payroll administration structure

The competence-based Education and Training Scheme of the Association of Accounting Technicians is based on an analysis of the work of accounting staff in a wide range of industries and types of organisation. The Standards of Competence for Payroll Administration which students are expected to meet are based on this analysis.

The Standards identify the key purpose of the payroll administration occupation, which is to operate, maintain and improve systems to record, plan, monitor and report on the payroll activities of an organisation, and a number of key roles of the occupation. Each key role is subdivided into units of competence, which are further divided into elements of competences. By successfully completing assessments in specified units of competence, students can gain qualifications at NVQ/SVQ Levels 2 and 3.

Whether you are competent in a Unit is demonstrated by means of:

- *Either* an exam (set and marked by AAT assessors)
- *Or* a skills test (where competence is judged by an Approved Assessment Centre to whom responsibility for this is devolved)
- Or *both* an exam *and* a skills test

Below we set out the overall structure of the NVQ/SVQ Level 2 stage, indicating how competence in each Unit is assessed. There is more detail about the exam and skills test on page (xxi).

About the qualification

This qualification is for people already working within, or wishing to pursue a career in, payroll administration. It develops a mixture of specialist payroll skills, as well as essential IT, communication and management skills. **This Tutorial Text covers only the specialist payroll skills.** Other BPP Study Texts are available for the IT, communication and management skills, as these are common to other AAT qualifications in Accounting, Business Administration or Management.

The target audience

The qualification will be relevant for those who already work in the payroll function of a large organisation or a small business, who work in payroll bureaux, who are self-employed, or who aspire to become payroll administrators.

INTRODUCTION

NVQ/SVQ Level 2

All units are mandatory

Unit of competence	Elements of competence
Unit 71 Maintaining employee records	Element 71.1 Verify and process personal data for starters and leavers
	Element 71.2 Implement instructions from external agencies
	Element 71.3 Evaluate and process permanent organisational variations to payroll

Skills testing *only*

Unit 72 Ascertaining gross pay	Element 72.1 Determine entitlements
	Element 72.2 Determine statutory pay entitlements

Skills testing *only*

Unit 73 Determining net pay	Element 73.1 Calculate and verify net pay
	Element 73.2 Ascertain and reconcile aggregate payroll totals

Exam *and* skills testing

Unit 21* Working with computers	Element 21.1 Use computer systems and software
	Element 21.2 Maintain the security of data

Skills testing *only*

Unit 22* Contribute to the maintenance of a healthy, safe and protective working environment	Element 22.1 Monitor and maintain a safe, healthy and secure working environment
	Element 22.2 Monitor and maintain an effective and efficient working environment

Skills testing *only*

Unit 23 Achieving personal effectiveness	Element 23.1 Plan and organise your own work
	Element 23.2 Maintain good working relationships
	Element 23.3 Improve your own performance

Skills testing *only*

*This unit can be completed at either NVQ/SVQ Level 2 or Level 3.

Level 2 Standards of competence

The structure of the Standards for Level 2

Each Unit commences with a statement of the **knowledge and understanding** which underpin competence in the Unit's elements.

The Unit of Competence is then divided into **elements of competence** describing activities which the individual should be able to perform.

Each element includes:

(a) A set of **performance criteria.** This defines what constitutes competent performance.

(b) A **range statement.** This defines the situations, contexts, methods etc in which competence should be displayed.

(c) **Evidence requirements.** These state that competence must be demonstrated consistently, over an appropriate time scale with evidence of performance being provided from the appropriate sources.

(d) **Sources of evidence.** These are suggestions of ways in which you can find evidence to demonstrate that competence. These fall under the headings: 'observed performance; work produced by the candidate; authenticated testimonies from relevant witnesses; personal account of competence; other sources of evidence.' They are reproduced in full in our Assessment Kit for Level 2.

The elements of competence for NVQ/SVQ Level 2 are set out below. Knowledge and understanding required for the unit as a whole are listed first, followed by the performance criteria and range statements for each element. Performance criteria are cross-referenced below to chapters in this NVQ/SVQ Level 2 Tutorial Text.

Unit 71 Maintaining Employee Records

What is the unit about?

This unit is about setting up and amending basic employee records within a computerised payroll administration system. Throughout the unit you need to show that you maintain confidentiality of employees' personal details and that you meet organisational and statutory deadlines.

The first element requires you to input new employees' personal data as well as the termination dates of employees who are leaving. You need to show that you input only those details that have been properly authorised, and that you know whether or not particular details are required by statute.

The second element is concerned with the implementation of instructions from external agencies such as the Inland Revenue and trades unions. You need to show that you verify all such instructions and obtain employees' authorisation for non-statutory deductions. You also need to show that you identify discrepancies in instructions and resolve them either directly or by referring them to the appropriate person.

The final element requires you to process permanent changes that your organisation requires you to make to individual employees' payroll records, such as increases in their basic rate of pay. You need to show that you identify inaccurate or unusual instructions and query these promptly with the right person, as well as inputting data to the payroll system accurately.

Elements contained within this unit are:

Element 71.1 Verify and process personal data for starters and leavers
Element 71.2 Implement instructions from external agencies
Element 71.3 Evaluate and process permanent organisational variations to payroll

INTRODUCTION

Knowledge and understanding

The Statutory framework

1. Tax and Social Security legislation affecting:

    Starters and leavers (Element 71.1)
    Tax code changes (Element 71.2)
    Student Loan Deductions (Element 71.2)
    Tax Credits (Element 71.2)
    National Insurance category letters (Elements 71.1 & 71.2)

2. Employment Rights legislation (Elements 71.1, 71.2 & 71.3)

3. Data Protection legislation (Element 71.1)

4. Asylum and Immigration legislation (Element 71.1)

5. Legislation relating to attachments of earnings (Elements 71.1, 71.2, & 71.3)

The Organisation

6. Procedures for keeping data confidential and secure (Elements 71.1, 71.2 & 71.3)

7. Dealing with instructions from external agencies (Element 71.2)

8. Who to refer discrepancies to (Elements 71.1, 71.2 & 71.3)

9. How to record and store data (Elements 71.1, 71.2 & 71.3)

10. Types of information input from external agencies (Element 71.2)

11. Signatories and authorisations (Elements 71.1, 71.2 & 71.3)

12. Timescales and schedules for updating, presenting and despatching data (Elements 71.1, 71.2 & 71.3)

13. Information flows within the organisation (Elements 71.1, 71.2 & 71.3)

INTRODUCTION

Element 71.1 Verify and process personal data for starters and leavers

Performance criteria	Chapters in this Text
A Ensure proper authorised **documentation** of every appointment and cessation of employment is obtained before payroll is amended	1
B Input accurately statutory and **non-statutory** personal and contract details, including allowances and deductions, onto new employee records	1
C Amend leavers' records to ensure that leavers will not be paid in future pay runs	1
D Accurately complete and despatch **statutory documentation.**	1
E Identify and document all discrepancies and either resolve directly or by reference to the appropriate organisation or person	1
F Comply with all organisational and statutory timescales	1
G File source **documentation** in accordance with statutory and organisational requirements and in a logical and orderly manner	1
H Maintain confidentiality and security of data at all times	1

Range statement

1	**Non-statutory data:** marital status; employee number; rates of variable elements of pay; details of fixed deductions; bank or building society details; pay frequency; eligibility for occupational sick or maternity pay; duration of contract	1
2	**Source documentation:** form P45; form P46; evidence of appointment; evidence of termination of employment; communications in relation to queries	1

Element 71.2 Implement instructions from external agencies

Performance criteria	Chapters in this Text
A Verify all payment and deduction instructions for accuracy, completeness and correct **documentation**	2
B Process instructions from **statutory agencies** or **non-statutory bodies** in accordance with statutory and organisational requirements and within the timescale specified	2
C Ensure all non-statutory deductions are authorised by the employee concerned	2
D Identify and resolve all discrepancies directly or by reference to the appropriate organisation or person	2

Range statement

1	**Documentation:** court orders; Inland Revenue documentation; Child Support Agency instructions; local authority attachment of earnings; individual mandates	2
2	**Statutory agencies:** Inland Revenue; Inland Revenue Contributions Office; Child Support Agency; courts; local authorities	2
3	**Non-statutory bodies:** pension funds; trades unions and associations; financial institutions; charities	2

INTRODUCTION

Element 71.3 Evaluate and process permanent organisational variations to payroll

Performance criteria		Chapters in this Text
A	Evaluate all data relating to **permanent variations** for accuracy and reasonableness	3
B	Check all data and documentation received for proper **authorisation**	3
C	Identify and resolve all discrepancies directly or by reference to the appropriate person	3
D	Process permanent variations accurately and in a timely manner	3

Range statement

1	**Permanent variations:** changes of grade; changes of employment status; variation in voluntary deductions; changes to pay rates for fixed and variable pay; changes in personal details	3
2	**Authorisation:** authorised signatory list; authority from the employee; organisational instructions	3

Unit 72 Ascertaining gross pay

What is the unit about?

This unit is about ensuring that employees' gross pay takes into account temporary variations including statutory entitlements. You need to demonstrate that you input these details accurately into a computerised system and you also need to show that you calculate statutory pay manually when this is necessary, for example where a query has been raised.

The first element requires you to process temporary variations to gross pay, where these are authorised by the employer. You are expected to verify the authorisation for such payments and check that the instructions are reasonable. You also need to show that you identify the appropriate tax and National Insurance treatment for temporary variations to gross pay as well as any effect they may have on pension contributions.

The second element is concerned with processing statutory entitlements in the payroll, such as Statutory Maternity Pay. You need to ensure that you respond correctly to the regulatory forms and that employees receive their entitlements at the right time. You also need to ensure that these payments cease when the employee is no longer eligible to them.

Throughout the unit you need to show that you maintain confidentiality of employees' personal details and that you meet organisational and statutory deadlines.

Elements contained within this unit are:

Element 72.1 Determine entitlements
Element 72.2 Determine statutory pay entitlements

INTRODUCTION

Knowledge and understanding

General Information

1. Positive payrolls (those payrolls where employees will not get paid unless input is submitted such as hourly paid employees)
2. Negative payrolls (those payrolls where employees will be paid automatically unless action is taken to prevent payment such as salaried employees)

Statutory Framework

3. Employment Rights legislation (Elements 72.1 & 72.2)
4. Statutory Maternity Pay – including the rules relating to entitlement, earnings, evidence of pregnancy, start date for payment, stopping payments (Element 72.2)
5. Statutory Sick Pay – including the rules relating to period of incapacity for work, qualifying days, waiting days, linking, earnings test, changeover to state responsibility, stopping payments (Element 72.2)
6. Statutory Adoption Pay – including the rules relating to entitlement, earnings, evidence of adoption, start date for payment, stopping payments (Element 72.2)
7. Statutory Paternity Pay including the rules relating to entitlement, earnings, evidence of parenthood, start date for payment, stopping payments (Element 72.2)
8. Parental Leave including the rules relating to entitlement, earnings, evidence of parental responsibility, payment (Element 72.2)
9. Time off for Dependents including the rules relating to entitlement, evidence of emergency, payment and their interaction with occupational schemes (Element 72.2)

The organisation

10. The security and confidentiality of information (Elements 72.1 & 72.2)
11. Dealing with instructions from external agencies (Element 72.2)
12. The resolution of discrepancies (Elements 72.1 & 72.2)
13. How to record and store data (Elements 72.1 & 72.2)
14. Types of information input from external agencies (Element 72.2)
15. Signatories and authorisations (Elements 72.1 & 72.2)
16. Timescales and schedules for updating, presenting and despatching data (Elements 72.1 & 72.2)
17. Information flows within the organisation (Elements 72.1 & 72.2)

Techniques and Methods

18. How to use Statutory Sick Pay, Statutory Maternity Pay tables to perform manual calculations of statutory additions to gross pay
19. How to set up and use spreadsheets for the manual calculation of gross pay

INTRODUCTION

Element 72.1 Determine entitlements

	Performance criteria	Chapters in this Text
A	Evaluate all data relating to **temporary variations** for accuracy and reasonableness	4
B	Ensure **documentation** relating to temporary variations is verified for authorisation	4
C	Identify employees where input is required in order to ensure payment and ensure relevant details are correctly inserted	4
D	Check rates for overtime payments against agreed scales for each type of employee affected	4
E	Identify all payments in respect of their tax, National Insurance and pension liability	4, 6, 8, 10
F	Take appropriate action to apply the terms of statutory and organisational payment schemes, where variations arise as a result of sickness, maternity leave or holidays	4, 5
G	Identify and resolve all discrepancies directly or by reference to the appropriate person	4
H	Process temporary payments and deductions accurately	4
I	File source **documentation** in accordance with statutory and organisational requirements and in a logical and orderly manner	4
J	Maintain security and confidentiality of sensitive information at all times	4

Range statement

1	**Temporary variations:** payments; deductions	4
2	**Documentation:** authorised time recording documentation; authorised instructions from management	4

INTRODUCTION

Element 72.2 Determine statutory pay entitlements

Performance criteria		Chapters in this Text
A	Determine entitlement to Statutory Sick Pay when entitlement to occupational sick pay expires or is not paid	5
B	Process Statutory Sick Pay payments accurately on receipt of regulatory forms	5
C	Determine entitlement to Ordinary and Additional Maternity Leave, Adoption Leave and Paternity Leave	5
D	Determine entitlement to Statutory Maternity Pay, Statutory Adoption Pay, Statutory Paternity Pay, when entitlement to occupational payments are not made.	5
E	Process Statutory Maternity Pay, Statutory Adoption Pay, Statutory Paternity Pay payments accurately on receipt of regulatory forms	5
F	Process Tax Credit payments on receipt of regulatory forms	5
G	Contribute to the resolution of individual employees' queries by checking statutory pay entitlements manually, using the appropriate tables	5
H	Identify and resolve all discrepancies directly or by reference to the appropriate person	5
I	Issue the correct **regulatory documentation** where entitlement to statutory payments does not arise or ceases	5
Range statement		
1	**Regulatory documentation:** SSP1; SMP1; stop notice and certificates of payment	5

Unit 73 Determining Net Pay

What is the unit about?

This unit is about determining the net pay that employees should receive. You need to demonstrate that you input deductions from net pay accurately into a computerised system and you also need to show that you calculate net pay manually when this is necessary, for example where a query has been raised.

The first element is about calculating and verifying net pay. You need to show that you ensure that only those employees who are entitled to receive pay in the current pay period are included. You are required to input all relevant pre- and post-tax deductions, produce and distribute payslips and check net pay totals.

The second element is about reconciling aggregate payroll totals against control totals. This includes calculating sums recoverable from the National Insurance Contributions and netting them off against payments due.

Throughout the unit you need to show that you maintain confidentiality of employees' personal details and that you meet organisational and statutory deadlines.

Elements contained within this unit are:

Element 73.1 Calculate and verify net pay
Element 73.2 Ascertain and reconcile aggregate payroll totals

INTRODUCTION

Knowledge and understanding

The Statutory Framework

1. Data Protection legislation (Elements 73.1 & 73.2)
2. PAYE regulations in respect of the manual calculation of gross to net pay (Element 73.1)
3. PAYE regulations in respect of charitable giving (Element 73.1)
4. Social Security regulations governing contributions in particular the manual calculation of gross to net pay (Element 73.1)
5. Pension legislation in respect of tax relief (Element 73.1)

The Organisation

6. Checking validity of all employees (Element 73.1)
7. Timescales and schedules for despatching payslips (Element 73.1)
8. Information flows within the organisation (Element 73.2)
9. Procedures for the security and confidentiality of information (Elements 73.1 & 73.2)
10. Procedures for initiating and monitoring payments (Element 73.1)
11. Methods of disbursement (Element 73.2)
12. Information and timescale requirements of systems for transmission of disbursements to employees (Element 73.1)

Techniques and Methods

13. How to use tax and National Insurance tables to perform manual calculations of net pay
14. How to set up and use spreadsheets for reconciliations and the manual calculation of net pay

Element 73.1 Calculate and verify net pay

Performance criteria		Chapters in this Text
A	Check the payroll status of all employees for validity for the pay period	10
B	Input any applicable **pre-tax deductions**	10
C	Input all relevant **statutory** and **non-statutory deductions**	10
D	Produce and distribute accurate and legible payslips in accordance with statutory and organisational requirements	10
E	Contribute to the resolution of individual employees' queries by checking net pay calculations manually, using the appropriate tax and National Insurance tables	6–10
F	Check net pay totals to ensure that the full range of applicable allowances and deductions has been made	10
G	Check net pay figures against the parameters for the payroll concerned and resolve any discrepancies or refer them to the appropriate person for resolution	10

Range statement

1	**Pre-tax deductions:** contributions to occupational pension schemes; charitable giving	10
2	**Statutory deductions:** attachment of earnings; student loans	10
3	**Non-statutory deductions:** pensions contributions; recovery of overpayments; repayment of loans and advances; voluntary deductions	10

INTRODUCTION

Element 73.2 Ascertain and reconcile aggregate payroll totals

Performance criteria		Chapters in this Text
A	Reconcile actual payroll totals against authorised totals for all pay periods	11
B	Reconcile the number of no pays and actual pays promptly with the number of employees on the payroll	11
C	Ensure that aggregate **statutory payments** and **non-statutory deductions** are correctly calculated and reconciled against control totals.	11
D	Check aggregate **statutory payments** against control totals	11
E	Calculate sums recoverable from the National Insurance Contributions Office in respect of **statutory payments** and net them off against payments due	11
F	Calculate and reconcile aggregate amounts payable to **statutory and non-statutory bodies,** in respect of **statutory and non-statutory deductions** against control totals	11
G	Resolve discrepancies and where they cannot be resolved, refer them to the appropriate supervisor(s)	11
H	Meet all organisational and statutory timescales	11

Range statement

1	**Statutory payments:** Statutory Sick Pay; Statutory Maternity Pay; Statutory Adoption Pay; Statutory Paternity Pay	11
2	**Non-statutory deductions:** employee and employer pension contributions; charitable giving; recovery of overpayments; repayment of loans and advances; voluntary deductions	11
3	**Statutory bodies:** Inland Revenue; courts; Child Support Agency; local authorities	11
4	**Non-statutory bodies:** pension provider; bodies responsible for miscellaneous deductions; trade unions; social clubs	11
5	**Statutory deductions:** tax; Employee and Employer National Insurance contributions; student loan deductions; earnings attachments; Scottish arrestments of earnings; child support orders and attachment of earnings orders	11

Assessment strategy

Units 71 and 72 are assessed by skills testing. Unit 73 is assessed by exam *and* skills testing.

Skills Testing *(More detail can be found in the Assessment Kit)*

Skills testing is a means of collecting evidence of your ability to carry out practical activities and to operate effectively in the conditions of the workplace to the standards required. Evidence may be collected at your place of work or at an Approved Assessment Centre by means of simulations of workplace activity, or by a combination of these methods.

If the Approved Assessment Centre is a workplace you may be observed carrying out accounting activities as part of your normal work routine. You should collect documentary evidence of the work you have done, or contributed, in an accounting portfolio. Evidence collected in a portfolio can be assessed in addition to observed performance or where it is not possible to assess by observation.

Where the Approved Assessment Centre is a college or training organisation, skills testing will be by means of a combination of the following.

(a)   Documentary evidence of activities carried out at the workplace, collected by you in an accounting portfolio

(b)   Realistic simulations of workplace activities; these simulations may take the form of case studies and in-tray exercises and involve the use of primary documents and reference sources

(c)   Projects and assignments designed to assess the Standards of Competence

If you are unable to provide workplace evidence, you will be able to complete the assessment requirements by the alternative methods listed above.

Exam *(More detail can be found in the Assessment Kit)*

The exam is set and marked by the AAT and consists of a short case study and a number of short answer questions. The exam is undertaken under controlled conditions at specific times.

Exams are designed to collect supplementary evidence that you have the necessary knowledge and understanding which underpins competence and that you can apply your skills to a range of contexts. Exams test the application of knowledge and understanding, not the recall of facts and figures.

INTRODUCTION

Building your portfolio

What is a portfolio?

A portfolio is a collection of work that demonstrates what the owner can do. In AAT language the portfolio demonstrates **competence**.

A painter will have a collection of his paintings to exhibit in a gallery, an advertising executive will have a range of advertisements and ideas that she has produced to show to a prospective client. Both the collection of paintings and the advertisements form the portfolio of that artist or advertising executive.

Your portfolio will be unique to you just as the portfolio of the artist will be unique because no one will paint the same range of pictures in the same way. It is a very personal collection of your work and should be treated as a **confidential** record.

What evidence should a portfolio include?

No two portfolios will be the same but by following some simple guidelines you can decide which of the following suggestions will be appropriate in your case.

(a) **Your current CV**

This should be at the front. It will give your personal details as well as brief descriptions of posts you have held with the most recent one shown first.

(b) **References and testimonials**

References from previous employers may be included especially those of which you are particularly proud.

(c) **Your current job description**

You should emphasise financial **responsibilities and duties**.

(d) **Your student record sheets**

These should be supplied by AAT when you begin your studies, and your training provider should also have some if necessary.

(e) **Evidence from your current workplace**

This could take many forms including **letters, memos, reports** you have written, **copies of accounts** or **reconciliations** you have prepared, **discrepancies** you have investigated etc. Remember to obtain permission to include the evidence from your line manager because some records may be sensitive. Discuss the performance criteria that are listed in your Student Record Sheets with your training provider and employer, and think of other evidence that could be appropriate to you.

(f) **Evidence from your social activities**

For example you may be the treasurer of a club in which case examples of your cash and banking records could be appropriate.

(g) **Evidence from your studies**

Few students are able to satisfy all the requirements of competence by workplace evidence alone. They therefore rely on simulations to provide the remaining evidence to complete a unit. If you are not working or not working in a relevant post, then you may need to rely more heavily on simulations as a source of evidence.

(h) **Additional work**

Your training provider may give you work that specifically targets one or a group of performance criteria in order to complete a unit. It could take the form of questions, presentations or demonstrations. Each training provider will approach this in a different way.

(i) **Evidence from a previous workplace**

This evidence may be difficult to obtain and should be used with caution because it must satisfy the 'rules' of evidence, that is it must be current. Only rely on this as evidence if you have changed jobs recently.

(j) **Prior achievements**

For example you may have already completed the health and safety unit during a previous course of study, and therefore there is no need to repeat this work. Advise your training provider who will check to ensure that it is the same unit and record it as complete if appropriate.

How should it be presented?

As you assemble the evidence remember to **make a note** of it on your Student Record Sheet in the space provided and **cross reference** it. In this way it is easy to check to see if your evidence is **appropriate**. Remember one piece of evidence may satisfy a number of performance criteria so remember to check this thoroughly and discuss it with your training provider if in doubt.

To keep all your evidence together a ring binder or lever arch file is a good means of storage.

When should evidence be assembled?

You should begin to assemble evidence **as soon as you have registered as a student**. **Don't leave it all** until the last few weeks of your studies, because you may miss vital deadlines and your resulting certificate sent by the AAT may not include all the units you have completed. Give yourself and your training provider time to examine your portfolio and report your results to AAT at regular intervals. In this way the task of assembling the portfolio will be spread out over a longer period of time and will be presented in a more professional manner.

What are the key criteria that the portfolio must fulfil?

As you assemble your evidence bear in mind that it must be:

- **Valid**. It must relate to the Standards.
- **Authentic**. It must be your own work.
- **Current**. It must refer to your current or most recent job.
- **Sufficient**. It must meet all the performance criteria by the time you have completed your portfolio.

What are the most important elements in a portfolio that covers Level 2?

You should remember that the unit is about **payroll administration**. Therefore you need to produce evidence not only demonstrating that you can carry out certain tasks, but also you must show that you can exercise control.

For Unit 71, *Maintaining employee records* you not only need to show that you can prepare employee records, you also need to demonstrate that you can maintain the records. Reports or memos can provide the necessary evidence. The main evidence needed is detail of starters and leavers and how you have prepared forms P45. You only need evidence of checking variations for validity.

To fulfil the requirements of Unit 72 *Ascertaining gross pay* you need to demonstrate that you have used various sources of evidence to prepare the wages records, including calculation of tax credits, SSP, SMP, SAP and SPP.

For Unit 73 *Determining net pay* you need to demonstrate that you can calculate tax and NIC deductions, as well as other statutory and non-statutory deductions.

Finally

Remember that the portfolio is **your property** and **your responsibility**. Not only could it be presented to the external verifier before your award can be confirmed; it could be used when you are seeking **promotion** or applying for a more senior and better paid post elsewhere. How your portfolio is presented can say as much about you as the evidence inside.

> For further information on portfolio building, see the BPP Text *Building Your Portfolio*. This can be ordered using the form at the back of this Text or via the Internet: www.bpp.com/aat

PART A

Maintaining employee records

chapter 1

Starters and leavers

Contents

1. The problem
2. The solution
3. What is an employee?
4. Statutory data
5. Non-statutory data
6. Outline of payroll procedures for leavers
7. Filling in a P45 for a leaver
8. Outline of payroll procedures for starters
9. Completing a P45 for a starter
10. Starters without a P45
11. Tax refunds for new employees
12. Storage of data

Performance criteria

71.1.A Ensure proper authorised documentation of every appointment and cessation of employment is obtained before payroll is amended

71.1.B Input accurately statutory and non-statutory personal and contract details, including allowances and deductions, onto new employee records

71.1.C Amend leavers' records to ensure that leavers will not be paid in future pay runs

71.1.D Accurately complete and despatch statutory documentation.

71.1.E Identify and document all discrepancies and either resolve directly or by reference to the appropriate organisation or person

71.1.F Comply with all organisational and statutory timescales

71.1.G File source documentation in accordance with statutory and organisational requirements and in a logical and orderly manner

71.1.H Maintain confidentiality and security of data at all times

PART A   MAINTAINING EMPLOYEE RECORDS

Range statement

71.1.1 Non-statutory data: marital status; employee number; rates of variable elements of pay; details of fixed deductions; bank or building society details; pay frequency; eligibility for occupational sick or maternity pay; duration of contract

71.1.2 Source documentation: form P45; form P46; evidence of appointment; evidence of termination of employment; communications in relation to queries

Knowledge and understanding

1   Tax and Social Security legislation affecting:
       Starters and leavers (Element 71.1)
       National Insurance category letters (Elements 71.1 & 71.2)

2   Employment Rights legislation (Elements 71.1, 71.2 & 71.3)

3   Data Protection legislation (Element 71.1)

4   Asylum and Immigration legislation (Element 71.1)

6   Procedures for keeping data confidential and secure (Elements 71.1, 71.2 & 71.3)

8   Who to refer discrepancies to (Elements 71.1, 71.2 & 71.3)

9   How to record and store data (Elements 71.1, 71.2 & 71.3)

11   Signatories and authorisations (Elements 71.1, 71.2 & 71.3)

12   Timescales and schedules for updating, presenting and despatching data (Elements 71.1, 71.2 & 71.3)

13   Information flows within the organisation (Elements 71.1, 71.2 & 71.3)

> **Signpost**
>
> Unit 71, under the 2003 standards, concentrates on setting up the payroll records, and ensuring all entitlements and deductions are correctly **authorised** and entered **accurately**. Although attachment of earnings, court orders and similar items are mentioned in the range statement, the emphasis is on putting the orders onto the payroll. The detailed operation of these orders is dealt with at Level 3.

1 The problem

How does a business ensure that only genuine employees are paid? How does a new employee get on the payroll? How does a business ensure that leavers are removed from the payroll?

2 The solution

Whether an employee is a starter or leaver, you will need to update the **employee record cards** accordingly. Note that all changes must be **verified** and **authorised**.

In this chapter, we will look at the documentation needed by the business, the Inland Revenue and NICO (National Insurance Contributions Office) in respect of starters and leavers.

But first, we need to decide who is an employee. Section 3 deals with this.

Sections 4 and 5 look at the information needed on employee record cards.

Section 6 will outline procedures in respect of leavers, while Section 7 deals with the statutory form required, form P45.

Section 8 deals with the outline procedures for starters, and Section 9 shows you what to do with statutory form P45 received from the previous employer.

Section 10 then deals with what happens if a starter does not have a form P45 and Section 11 looks at the position where a tax refund is due to a new employee.

Finally it is important to store payroll records safely. This is dealt with in Section 12.

3 What is an employee?

This may seem a silly question. We all think we know what it means to work for someone or an organisation. However, a legal definition is needed as employee status affects people in different ways.

- **Tax status** within the payroll system.
- **Rights under employment legislation.**

Example: employee status

Think about the following people working at Sorrento Ceramics Ltd.

(a) Anna Muti is a payroll clerk for Sorrento Ceramics Ltd. She works from 9 am to 5 pm, and receives no income from any activity other than her work for Sorrento Ceramics Ltd.

(b) Sorrento Ceramics Ltd uses Katz Klean Ltd to sweep its floors and empty its bins. Mr Capri empties Anna's bin every evening at 6 pm.

(c) Sorrento Ceramics Ltd is investing in a new computer system, and has asked Yasmin Zabit to design and install the system. Yasmin has an office at Sorrento Ceramics Ltd and she regularly asks Anna about the payroll system. However, she has a number of other clients so she is not always at Sorrento Ceramics Ltd. She has her own office and advertises her services as a management consultant.

Which of them are employees of Sorrento Ceramics Ltd?

Solution

The only employee of Sorrento Ceramics Ltd is Anna Muti. She works exclusively for Sorrento Ceramics Ltd. Even if she did some bookkeeping for a friend's business, the bulk of her work is for Sorrento Ceramics Ltd and so she is an employee.

Mr Capri is an employee of Katz Klean Ltd. He is paid by Katz Klean Ltd, and they set his terms and conditions of employment. Katz Klean Ltd will have a contract with Sorrento Ceramics Ltd; but as a **trade supplier**, not an employee.

Yasmin Zabit is not an employee of Sorrento Ceramics Ltd. She is a **self-employed** management consultant, as she has a number of clients and her own place of business.

PART A MAINTAINING EMPLOYEE RECORDS

The distinction between employment and self-employment is an important one.

- The **tax status** of Anna and Mr Capri on the one hand, and Yasmin on the other, are different.
- Employees have a number of **legal rights** which the self-employed do not have.

The Inland Revenue publish a leaflet IR 56 Employed or Self Employed? If in doubt you should refer to this leaflet. It can be downloaded from the Inland Revenue website: www.inlandrevenue.gov.uk/leaflets/c6.htm, if your employer does not have a copy.

3.1 Taxation of the self-employed

Whether a person is an employee or is self-employed is not always as clear as in the example above.

The **tax advantages of self-employment** mean that self-employed people like Yasmin pay less tax and National Insurance than employees like Anna or Mr Capri. So the Inland Revenue is generally quite suspicious of people who claim to be self-employed but act as employees.

The **disadvantages of self-employment** include far fewer rights under **employment legislation**. Also, the self-employed are responsible for the payment of their own tax and National Insurance and are entitled to **fewer State benefits**.

Whatever is decided privately between the employee and the employer, the Inland Revenue will decide for itself by looking at the **substance of the relationship**.

If the Inland Revenue decides that a person claiming to be self-employed is actually an employee, they can **reclaim** the tax (PAYE) and National Insurance contributions (NICs) that should have been paid by the employer, **not the employee**, going back at least six years. This can be *very* expensive!

Therefore it is highly important that employers keep good records, both of their employees and their contracts with the self-employed. These records need to be kept for **at least six years**.

3.2 Are you self-employed?

'Yes' answers to the following questions indicate **self-employment**.

Self-employment questions	Yes or no?
Do I work from home?	
Do I use my own equipment?	
Am I unable to claim holiday or sick pay?	
Am I excluded from the company's pension scheme?	
Do I offer my services to a number of people?	
Do I control my working schedule?	
Can I refuse to accept a particular job?	
Have I employees of my own?	

Self-employment questions	Yes or no?
Must I correct defective work myself in my own time?	
Can I send someone else if I can't go myself?	

If you are not sure whether a person working for your organisation is employed or self-employed, you need to make sure **before** paying him or her. Your organisation won't benefit financially in the long-term from a failure to deduct income tax and National Insurance that the Inland Revenue thinks is due. The Inland Revenue can be contacted to give a ruling if necessary.

3.3 Advantages of employment

An employee is protected by employment rights legislation.

- Working time regulations
- National minimum wage
- Flexible working hours
- Protection from discrimination

3.3.1 Working time regulations

- Average maximum of 48 hours worked per week (excluding lunch and other breaks)
- A break of 20 minutes away from work station, if daily working time exceeds 6 hours
- Daily rest period of not less than 11 consecutive hours in every 24 hours
- Weekly rest period of not less than 24 consecutive hours in every 7 days or 48 hours in every 14 days
- All staff entitled to four weeks paid annual holiday (inclusive of paid bank holidays)
- Special provision for night workers

Note that some workers were exempt from the original legislation. However, extensions applied from 1 August 2003, eg to road haulage workers, and from 1 August 2004 to junior doctors.

3.3.2 National minimum wage

- From 1 October 2003, £4.50 per hour (18 to 21 year olds £3.80)
- From 1 October 2004 £4.85 per hour (18 to 21 year olds £4.10)

From 1 October 2004, there will also be a new young workers' rate for 16 and 17 year olds of £3.00 per hour.

The Government is also proposing to introduce fair piece rates for output workers, including homeworkers. This will be set at 100% of the minimum wage from 1 October 2004 and will increase to 120% of the minimum wage in April 2005.

> **Important!**
>
> These are proposals. Check the DTI website (www.dti.gov.uk/er/nmw/index.htm) nearer the time for the final legislation.

3.3.3 Flexible working hours

From 6 April 2003, employees have the right to request a variation in their contract of employment to enable them to care for a child.

The employee must have 26 weeks' qualifying service and be the mother, father, adoptive parent, guardian or foster parent of a child aged under six (18 if disabled). The rules also apply to the partner or spouse of these relatives, with responsibility for bringing up the child.

3.3.4 Protection from discrimination

As at 6 April 2004, employees are protected from discrimination on the following grounds.

- Sex
- Race
- Disability
- Sexual orientation
- Religion and belief

Discrimination includes:

- Direct discrimination, eg less favourable treatment
- Indirect discrimination, eg applying business rules to disadvantage certain types of people
- Harassment
- Victimisation

4 Statutory data

4.1 Employment law

There are a number of statutes affecting payrolls. For your studies, you need to know about the following Acts.

- Employment Rights Act 1996
- The Employment Relations Act 1999
- Data Protection Act 1998
- Asylum and Immigration Act 1996

The first three are understandable, as the first two cover employment rights and the third storage and use of data. The fourth law may come as a surprise to you. However, you will see why this is included below.

4.2 Employment Rights Act 1996

The Employment Rights Act 1996 covers all aspects of employment, including the following.

- (a) The right of the employee to receive a contract of employment, or details of the employment's particulars.
- (b) The right of an employee to receive an itemised pay statement (payslip) giving details of all deductions from pay.
- (c) The right of an employee not to suffer unauthorised deductions.
- (d) Health and Safety aspects of employment are covered.
- (e) The rights of employees for time off work to carry out public duties (eg as a magistrate) or for ante-natal care.
- (f) The right of an employer to suspend an employee from work on medical grounds.
- (g) Maternity rights.
- (h) The rights of employer and employee on termination of employment.

This act is the most important piece of legislation to do with employment. As an employee yourself, it is important to you as it sets out your rights.

However, from the point of view of your studies, you only need to know its general outline; the most important rules for payroll being (b), (c), (g) and (h). These and other points will be dealt with as they arise in the course of your studies.

4.3 The Employment Relations Act 1999

The Employment Relations Act 1999 governs maternity leave. These regulations came into force from 15 December 1999. It was amended from 6 April 2003 under the Employment Act 2002.

4.3.1 Maternity leave

Maternity leave is divided into three categories.

- Ordinary maternity leave
- Additional maternity leave
- Compulsory maternity leave

Ordinary maternity leave is 26 weeks. All women are entitled to this leave regardless of how long they have been with their employer. During this period, the woman does not lose any accrual of seniority or pension rights.

Additional maternity leave is for a further period of 26 weeks. It begins when ordinary maternity leave ends. The qualifying period is 26 weeks' service with the employer prior to the 15th week before the baby is due. Seniority is suspended during this period and pension rights continue to accrue only if she is receiving maternity pay from her employer.

Compulsory maternity leave is usually covered by the 26 week ordinary maternity leave. Women are **forbidden** to return to work for the two week period immediately following birth. In the case of female factory workers, the period is extended to four weeks.

Paternity leave is one or two weeks' leave at the time of birth. It is available to partners that qualify to receive Statutory Paternity Pay (see Chapter 5).

Adoption leave is also available for adoptive parents (see Chapter 5). It consists of 26 weeks' ordinary leave and 26 weeks' additional leave.

4.3.2 Other leave

A new right to leave called **parental leave** commenced on 15 December 1999.

Parental leave is available for both men and women, and is an entitlement to thirteen weeks' **unpaid** leave in total from the day of birth up to the child's fifth birthday.

Employees must have at least one year's full service to qualify and the leave must be taken in blocks of at least a full week, with a maximum of four weeks in one year.

Parents of a disabled child can take parental leave in single days and at any time up to the child's eighteenth birthday.

An employer is entitled to at least 21 days' prior notice of parental leave. Employers are not legally required to keep records of maternity or parental leave. However an employer would be wise to do so, in order to avoid abuse of the system.

Employees also have the right to **short term unpaid leave** to deal with domestic incidents or to look after a sick dependent.

4.4 Data Protection Act 1998

You will deal with this in more detail in your Unit 21 studies. However, an outline of the main Act is given below.

The Data Protection Act 1998 is an attempt to protect the **individual**.

In order to understand the Act it is necessary to know some of the technical terms used in it.

(a) **Personal data** is information about a living individual, including expressions of opinion about him or her. Data about other organisations (eg suppliers or customers) is not personal data, unless it contains data about individuals who belong to those other organisations.

(b) **Data users** are organisations or individuals who control the contents of files of personal data and the use of personal data which is processed (or intended to be processed) automatically - ie who use personal data which is covered by the terms of the Act.

(c) A **data subject** is an individual who is the subject of personal data.

Data users must comply with the Data Protection Principles contained in the Act. These are shown in the following table.

DATA PROTECTION PRINCIPLES

1. Personal data shall be processed fairly and lawfully and, in particular, shall not be processed unless certain conditions are met.

2. Personal data shall be obtained only for one or more specified and lawful purposes, and shall not be further processed in any manner incompatible with that purpose or those purposes.

3. Personal data shall be adequate, relevant and not excessive in relation to the purpose or purposes for which they are processed.

4. Personal data shall be accurate and, where necessary, kept up to date.

5. Personal data processed for any purpose or purposes shall not be kept for longer than is necessary for that purpose or those purposes.

6. Personal data shall be processed in accordance with the rights of data subjects under this Act.

7. Appropriate technical and organisational measures shall be taken against unauthorised or unlawful processing of personal data and against accidental loss or destruction of, or damage to, personal data.

8. Personal data shall not be transferred to a country or territory outside the European Economic Area unless that country or territory ensures an adequate level of protection for the rights and freedoms of data subjects in relation to the processing of personal data.

Features of the 1998 legislation are:

(a) Everyone now has the right to go to court to seek redress for **any breach** of data protection law, rather than just for certain aspects of it.

(b) Filing systems that are structured so as to facilitate access to information about a particular person now fall within the legislation. This includes systems that are **paper-based** or on **microfilm** or **microfiche**. Personnel records meet this classification.

(c) Processing of personal data is **forbidden** except in the following circumstances.

   (i) With the **consent** of the subject (person).
   (ii) As a result of a **contractual arrangement.**
   (iii) Because of a **legal obligation** (eg payroll).
   (iv) To **protect the vital interests** of the subject.
   (v) Where processing is in the **public interest.**
   (vi) Where processing is required to exercise **official authority.**

(d) The processing of **'sensitive data'** is forbidden, unless express consent has been obtained or there are conflicting obligations under employment law. Sensitive data includes data relating to **racial origin**, **political opinions**, **religious beliefs**, **physical or mental health, sexual proclivities** and **trade union membership**.

(e) Data subjects have the right to a **copy of data** held about them and also the right to know **why** the data is being processed.

PART A   MAINTAINING EMPLOYEE RECORDS

> **Important!**
>
> As part of your evaluation, you are required to keep evidence in a personal file (portfolio). This includes photocopies or printouts of personal records. Does this breach the Data Protection Act 1998? Payroll is exempt from notification, providing the data is used purely for payroll processing and the Data Protection Principles are not breached. However, confidentiality is a big problem here.
>
> Therefore the AAT suggest that either the employee's name and personal details are Tippex-ed out or that key names and figures are omitted from the data to be printed out. Students should get witness testimony that the job was done correctly.

4.5 Asylum and Immigration Act 1996

The relevance of this Act to payroll arises from the restrictions on employment contained in s8.

Section 8 states that an employer can only employ **a person subject to immigration control** with the leave of the Secretary of State. This takes the form of a work permit signed by the Secretary of State, and is needed for everyone over the age of 16. Alternatively a passport with a work visa/permit is acceptable.

The only defence an employer can make is that such a document was produced, seemed to be genuine and that the employer either retained the document or kept a copy of it. The evidence must be kept during the whole of the employment period, plus up to six months after the employee left.

Failure to comply with this legislation will result in the employer being fined.

Activity 1.1

You run the payroll for a fruit farm in East Anglia and the farmer needs help for the harvest season. A family of refugees from Iraq offer to work for him in the harvesting. Should he accept their offer?

It is not always clear if an employee is covered by this Act, therefore an employer should obtain an NI number from all new employees (see Section 9). Note that it is not sufficient to be told an NI number, there must be **documentary evidence** (eg P45, P60, NI card). If no NI number is given, the employer must carry out the procedures in Section 9.

4.6 Information that must be kept

Having looked at the legislation, what information **must** be kept about each employee?

- Name and title (Mr, Mrs, etc)
- Address
- Date of birth
- Sex
- Tax code
- National Insurance number and category

- Starting date
- Leaving date
- Pensions status

Of these, name and address should be obvious. Date of birth is needed to show when state retirement age is reached, as this will affect NICs payable. Similarly sex is required, as state retirement age is different for men and women. Also most organisations need to show that they do not discriminate on grounds of sex.

The tax code tells you how much an employee can earn before tax has to be deducted. You need the National Insurance number as this has to be entered on period end documentation sent to the Inland Revenue. You also need to know the National Insurance category in order to be able to calculate the NICs to be deducted. These will be dealt with in detail later in this Text.

You also need to know the starting date, as no pay can be given to the employee until they have actually started to work for your organisation. Similarly, the leaving date is needed to ensure that no further payments are made to an ex-employee.

This may seem obvious, but some organisations make monthly round-sum expense payments to employees by standing order. If a record of the leaving date is not kept and acted upon, an ex-employee could continue to receive those expenses long after they have left employment.

Finally, you need a record of whether the employee is a member of the firm's pension scheme (if there is one). This record will enable you to make deductions from pay in respect of agreed pension contributions (see Chapter 10).

Activity 1.2

You are the payroll assistant for Dove Ltd. They have just employed Mrs Hawk part-time at a rate of £2,000 pa. You are aware that no tax needs to be deducted if the pay is less than the personal allowance for the year. This is £4,745 for 2004/05. Therefore do you need to keep a record of Mrs Hawk's employment?

5 Non-statutory data

Your organisation may well want to keep additional information about each employee.

Example: non-statutory data

Organisations that rely on public money, such as the BBC, have to show that they are non-discriminatory in their employment policies. What kind of additional data will they want to keep?

Solution

As well as the records of sex required by statute, these organisations may well ask their employees to complete forms detailing any (or all) of the following.

- Ethnic origin
- Disabilities
- Sexual inclination
- Languages (to translate for colleagues whose first language is not English)
- Religion or beliefs

5.1 Non-statutory data

For the purposes of your studies, you need to know about the following items of non-statutory data.

- Marital status
- Employee number
- Rates of variable elements of pay
- Details of fixed deductions
- Bank or building society details
- Pay frequency
- Eligibility for occupational sick or maternity pay
- Duration of contract

Marital status may come as a surprise. What business is it of your organisation whether you are single, married, separated, or divorced? However, many organisations offer benefits, such as private health insurance. It helps them budget for the cost of this insurance, if they have some prior indication whether an employee will want the single or married level of benefit. Also some married women can pay a lower rate of NICs. Divorcees may be subject to child support orders.

An employee may be allocated an employee number in a large organisation as an aid to accessing employee records. For example, an organisation with 10,000 employees could well have two or three John Smiths on the staff. However, if they each have a different employee number, it will be easy to access the correct employee record.

Rates of variable elements of pay include overtime rates. For example, hourly paid workers may be paid 1 ½ times the normal rate for weekday overtime and 2 times (double time) at weekends. Other workers may be entitled to special shift rates, eg night shifts, unsocial hours. The payroll records need to keep details of what rates each employee is entitled to receive.

Details of fixed deductions will include the following items:

- Pension contributions
- Trade union subscriptions
- Payroll giving to charities

Remember from Section 4.2, that an employee has a right not to suffer unauthorised deductions. In each case, you will need a **written authorisation signed by the employee** before making any of these deductions.

Many employers make payroll payments direct to an employee's bank or building society account. Therefore, the employee records will need details of this.

Pay frequency will depend on the employee's contract. Some employees will be paid weekly, others four-weekly or monthly. The employee records need to show this clearly.

If the employer offers **occupational** sick or maternity pay, then the records need to show which employees are entitled to these.

Finally, an employee may be on a fixed term contract, eg six months, two years. The records must show the start and expiry dates of the contract, to ensure that payments are not made outside the period of the contract.

5.2 Verifying changes and discrepancies

Any changes to employee records could have significant effects on the payroll and so any changes need to be **authorised** and **verified**.

Example: new employee

You are the payroll assistant for Eagle Ltd. Personnel tell you that Mr Golden will be starting employment on 01.01.X0, and that his salary will be £20,000 pa. Do you have sufficient evidence to include Mr Golden on the payroll?

Solution

Unfortunately fraud can not be ruled out. In large organisations, where there are a lack of controls, it has proved easy to add 'dummy' employees to the payroll. Therefore, you would want to verify that Mr Golden actually exists. You would need some documentary evidence before adding him to the payroll. Such evidence can include any or all of the following.

(a) Copy correspondence offering Mr Golden a job **and** Mr Golden's acceptance.

(b) Form P45 from his previous employer (see section 9). This form will show pay and tax deducted to date, tax code, National Insurance number and home address.

(c) Details of the building society or bank account that the salary will be paid into.

(d) Your organisation's starter form completed and signed by Mr Golden.

5.2.1 Changes

There are various sources of verification of changes, depending on which change has occurred. In most cases, employees should be asked to complete and sign a change of circumstances form, eg change of name, address, bank details.

If an employee says that they have changed their name by deed poll, a copy of the certificate will confirm this. You should ensure that you take a copy for your records.

PART A MAINTAINING EMPLOYEE RECORDS

If an employee has changed their name on marriage, a copy of the marriage certificate is needed. Always remember to take copies of any documents for the employee records.

An employee may tell you that you are using the wrong tax code. You check your records and find that you are using the code as notified by the Inland Revenue. However, the employee says that her code has changed and produces a copy of the Inland Revenue notification sent to her. This should be used as evidence to query the code with the Inland Revenue, but you should **not** change the code until you have received confirmation from them (see Chapter 2).

If an employee is promoted or demoted, this may well affect their pay or expenses. A change of status form should be sent to you by the personnel department setting out the new rates of pay and conditions.

In unusual circumstances, do not be afraid to ask your supervisor for guidance; particularly if you are unsure of your authority to act. Remember any changes to employee records must be **authorised**, either by internal notice (eg new starter form) or by the employee (eg voluntary deductions).

Activity 1.3

A gentleman, who you have never met before, tells you that he has been employed for six weeks but has received no salary. He tells you his name is Mr Biggs and that he is on a salary of £30,000 pa. He wants a cheque for back pay now. What do you do?

Activity 1.4

The paperwork for Mr Biggs joining the firm has now been passed to you. You are informed verbally by your boss that Mr Biggs' salary is £25,000 pa. However, when you check the evidence of appointment, the offer letter states £30,000 pa and this was what Mr Biggs had also told you. What do you do now?

6 Outline of payroll procedures for leavers

When an employee leaves, then all the amounts owing to and by that person must be settled.

The **personnel department** will send the **payroll department** a notification in writing, stating the date on which the leaver ceases to be an employee. This may not be the same date as the day of leaving, as the employee may be granted leave as part of the notice period.

The payroll department will deal with the following matters.

- Payment of the **final period's salary**, including any termination payment.
- Calculation and settling of any **holiday pay or leave**.
- Recovery of any **loans** which the employee has outstanding (eg season ticket loan).

The **payroll records** should be altered to ensure that there is no possibility of the employee's leaving being overlooked. You don't want to go on paying employees who have left!

However remember to ensure that you have **written confirmation** of who is leaving. If you have two John Smiths, you need to ensure the correct one is deleted. Do not rely on verbal instructions, these can be misunderstood.

If you hold a **reduced-rate NIC certificate** from a married woman or widow (forms CA4139, CF383, or CF380A) then you must return it to her, completed as explained on the form. Similarly **age exception cards** for these over state retirement age should be returned to the employee.

If a leaver has received Statutory Sick Pay (SSP) (see Chapter 5) in the eight weeks before they stop working for you, you may be asked to complete form SSP1(L). However you only need to complete this form **on request**.

If your employee is receiving statutory payments (SSP, SMP, SPP and SAP) or tax credits at the date of leaving, see Chapter 5 for what to do. You may still need to continue these payments **after the date of leaving**.

What about the **employee's PAYE and NIC position**? To ensure that employees who switch jobs during the year are not charged too much tax, or do not fall through the net completely, documents pass between the following.

- The Inland Revenue
- The employer
- The employee

In the rest of this chapter, we will be looking at these documents.

Important!

You must make sure that you know the most up to date format of the forms mentioned throughout this text.

The Inland Revenue website (www.inlandrevenue.gov.uk) is extremely useful for all kinds of PAYE information. In addition, you can access guidance leaflets, tax and NI tables, and the latest versions of PAYE stationery and forms. These can be downloaded and printed out by going to:

www.inlandrevenue.gov.uk/employers/emp-form.htm.

You do **not** need an employer's reference number to use this download facility.

Some forms, such as P45 and P38S, are only issued to employers. However, these can still be accessed and printed out, but they will have 'for information only' or 'specimen' printed across them to prevent unauthorised use.

Try accessing the website and seeing what form SSP1(L) looks like.

PART A   MAINTAINING EMPLOYEE RECORDS

7 Filling in a P45 for a leaver

7.1 The four parts of a P45

An example of a completed form P45 is shown on the next page.

- **Part 1** of the form is sent by the **old employer** to its **Tax Office**.
- **Parts 1A, 2 and 3** of the form are given to the **employee** on leaving.
- The **employee** keeps **Part 1A**, and gives Parts 2 and 3 to his new employer.
- The **new employer** keeps **Part 2**, and sends **Part 3** to its **Tax Office**.

Whenever an employee leaves, the employer **must complete Part 1** of form P45, using a ballpoint pen. The details copy through onto Parts 1A, 2 and 3.

However, a P45 is not completed if a deduction card (form P11) was not used or completed only to record NICs and/or tax credits. This will be explained later in this text.

If an employee joins after 6 April in one year, and leaves before 5 April in the next year, the P45 will include total pay to date and total tax to date, for the **whole tax year** from 6 April.

This includes pay and tax in the previous employment before joining the current employer. This information is obtainable **from Part 2 of the P45** that the employee received from his or her previous employer.

A separate entry for pay and tax in **this employment** is made in box 8.

If you were making student loan deductions (SLDs) and have not received a stop notification, enter Y in box 5. If you have received a stop notification, leave box 5 blank. See Chapter 2 for more details on SLDs and stop notifications.

1: STARTERS AND LEAVERS

Inland Revenue
Details of employee leaving work
Copy for Tax Office
P45 Part 1

1	PAYE Reference	District number: 135 / Reference number: B 3456
2	Employee's National Insurance number	BC 28 47 93 D
3	Surname (in capitals)	NEEDHAM (Mr Mrs Miss Ms): MR
	First name(s) (in capitals)	JOHN ANGUS
4	Leaving date (in figures)	Day 31 Month 05 Year 20 04
5	Continue Student Loan Deductions (Y)	
6	Tax Code at leaving date. *If week 1 or Month 1 basis applies, write 'X' in the box marked Week 1 or Month 1*	Code: 367 L / Week 1 or Month 1:
7	Last entries on Deductions Working Sheet (P11). **Complete only if Tax Code is cumulative.** Make no entry here if Week 1 or Month 1 basis applies. Go to item 8.	Week or month number: Month 2 / Total pay to date £ 3,000.00 p / Total tax to date £ 484.51 p
8	This employment pay and tax. ■ No entry needed if Tax Code is cumulative and amounts are same as item 7 entry.	Total pay in this employment £ / Total tax in this employment £
9	Works number/Payroll number	309
10	Department or branch if any	
11	Employee's private address and Postcode	17 MILL LANE, LINCESTER, AB2 3CD
12	I certify that the details entered above in items 1 to 10 are correct	
	Employer's name, address and Postcode	MIXUM METAL LTD, STEEL WORKS ROAD, LINCESTER AB2 3XL
	Date	31/5/04

To the employer — Please complete with care ★

For Tax Office use

- Complete this form following the 'Employee leaving' instructions in the *Employer's help book* (E13). **Make sure the details are clear on all four parts of this form.** Make sure your name and address is shown on Parts 1 and 1A.
- Detach Part 1 and send it to your Tax Office immediately.
- Hand Parts 1A, 2 and 3 (unseparated) to your employee when he or she leaves
- If the employee has died, write 'D' in this box and send all three parts of this form (unseparated) to your Tax Office immediately.

P45   BMSD9/99

PART A   MAINTAINING EMPLOYEE RECORDS

Activity 1.5

Job Less started working for Turnover Ltd in May 2004. He brought with him on his first day a P45 from his old employer stating that:

- his total pay to date on leaving was £720, and
- tax paid to date was £50.70.

This information was entered on his deduction card (P11) in May 2004. (To see form P11 turn to pages 199 and 200.)

Using this information and his deduction card (P11) below, write down the figures you will need to enter on his P45 in boxes 6, 7 and 8. He is leaving today. His P11 includes his final salary payment which will be given to him today.

	Tax code		Amended								
	461L		WK/mnth								
				K codes			K codes			K codes	
W e e k	Pay in the week	Total pay to date	Total free pay to date	Total additional pay to date	Total taxable pay to date	Total tax due to date	Tax due at end of current period	Regulatory limit	Tax deducted in the week	Tax not deducted owing to the regulatory limit	Tax Credits
	2	3	4a	4b	5	6	6a	6b	7	8	9
41	100.00	5,320.00	3,642.03		1,677.97	177.81			2.01		

7.2 What happens if a former employee loses his P45?

A former employee may ask for a **duplicate** P45, either because he or she has **lost** the original, or to rectify a **mistake** on it.

You must never provide another form P45, or amend it. Tell the employee to contact the Inland Revenue immediately.

If necessary, you may give the employee a letter stating the figures shown on the P45.

7.3 Employees who leave without notice

If an employee leaves your organisation suddenly and without giving notice, you should still complete a P45.

- Send Part 1 to the Tax Office
- Hold on to Parts 1A, 2 and 3 until the ex-employee eventually asks for it

You can post the P45 to his or her home address. However, you are not obliged to do this.

7.4 Payments to an ex-employee after the date of the P45

If you prepare a P45 for a departing employee, and subsequently find that an **additional payment** is due after the employee has left (eg sales commission, bonus, holiday pay), the procedure is as follows.

Step 1   **Do not make out a new P45**.

Step 2   **Deduct tax** from the gross payment at the **basic rate** (22%).

Step 3   **Amend the tax code on the ex-employee's P11** to **BR** (basic rate). If the payment is made in a new tax year, prepare a new P11 for the employee, but note that you still use basic rate (22%) and not starting rate (10%).

Step 4   Give the employee a letter detailing the date of payment, gross amount and amount of tax deducted.

Example: Payment after leaving

Ron Wilde was an employee of Suddsy Soaps Ltd. He left his job (as salesman) on 30 April 2004, when he was paid his monthly salary of £1,800, and he was given his P45 on that date. On 30 June he was paid a sales commission of £1,000 (gross) for the year up to the date he left. He was a monthly paid employee and his tax code was 410L. The free pay for a code of 410 in Month 1 is £342.42.

Solution

The P11 for Ron would appear as follows. Note the amended code.

Tax code		Amended		BR						
~~410L~~		WK/mnth		3						
				K codes			*K codes*		*K codes*	
Month	Pay in the month	Total pay to date	Total free pay to date	Total additional pay to date	Total taxable pay to date	Total tax due to date	Tax due at end of current period	Regulatory limit	Tax deducted in the week	Tax not deducted owing to the regulatory limit	Tax Credits
	2	3	4a	4b	5	6	6a	6b	7	8	9
1	1,800.00	1,800.00	342.42		1,457.58	300.33			300.33		
2											
3	1,000.00	2,800.00							220.00		

PART A   MAINTAINING EMPLOYEE RECORDS

Notes

(a) **The tax code is amended to BR for Month 3**. There is no free pay, as the new employer will be dealing with that. Just multiply the entry in column 2 by 22%.

(b) The gross pay of £1,000 has tax deducted at the basic rate of 22%. The Tax Office will be informed eventually (at the end of the tax year). In time it will then either claim more tax from Ron Wilde or refund tax to him, as an adjusting payment for the tax year.

(c) Do not worry if you do not understand the entries. Tax deductions will be dealt with in detail in Chapter 6. You may wish to return to this topic after you have studied Chapter 6, in order to check the entries.

Activity 1.6

It is a Friday morning in January 2005. You are the Payroll assistant at Turnover Ltd. Several people are waiting to see you. How do you deal with each of their queries?

(a) Hope Less left the company recently and was issued with a P45 in the normal way. She has come back to ask for another one as she has lost the original.

(b) Her brother, Job Less, is leaving today and has no work to go to. He says he wants his pay to date but won't bother waiting for a P45 as he is going on the dole (ie he is going to claim benefit from the DWP (Department of Work and Pensions)).

(c) Hope and Job tell you that their sister Grace has left the company too. You are not surprised to hear this as she has not been at work, or been in touch to explain her absence, for a fortnight. They ask you to give them her P45.

(d) Betty Latethannever has come down from the Sales Department to tell you that another member of the family, Whit Less, who left last month, should have received £200 under the firm's bonus scheme which he forgot to claim. It should be forwarded to him. She asks if he will need a new P45 to replace the one he received on leaving.

7.5 NICs and leavers

NICs are dealt with in detail in Chapters 8 and 9. As NICs are not shown on form P45, we will deal with the rules for calculating NICs for leavers in Chapter 9.

7.6 Death of employees

An employee might die while still working for your organisation. If this happens, you need to work out how much pay is due to the deceased employee.

Complete the deduction card and calculate net pay due to the deceased employee, making suitable deductions for income tax. **NICs are not due on payments after death**.

Complete a P45 for the employee

- If the final payment details are known, include the payment and tax due in the totals recorded at item 7 of the form.

- Write the name and address of the deceased employee's **personal representative** at **item 11 of the P45**. If you do not know the name of the person's next-of-kin or solicitor, leave this item blank.

- Enter D in the box at the bottom of the form.

- Send all four parts of the form to the Tax Office.

Make the payment. The payment after death should be made to a **personal representative** of the deceased employee. In the case of a widow or widower you can ask your supervisor to authorise the payment, in the reasonable expectation that you have paid the proper person. If in doubt, however, you should hold back any payment until you receive instructions from a suitable authority, such as the deceased employee's solicitor.

Example: Death

Thomas Andrew Noyes, an employee of DEF Ltd, died on 5 October 2004 (week 27 of the tax year). His next-of-kin and personal representative is his wife Mrs Sarah Noyes. His tax code is 490T. When he was last paid on 29 September (week 26), his total pay to date for the year was £4,400.00 and total tax deducted was £306.70. A further £160 was owing to him as at the time of his death, on which tax of £9.63 is payable.

A P45 would be made out as follows, and all four parts sent to DEF's Tax Office. Notice that total pay to date is £4,400 + £160, and total tax to date is £306.70 + £9.63.

PART A   MAINTAINING EMPLOYEE RECORDS

Inland Revenue

Details of employee leaving work
Copy for Tax Office

P45 Part 1

1. **PAYE Reference**
   District number: 224
   Reference number: M1234

2. **Employee's National Insurance number**: CD 12 34 56 D

3. **Surname (in capitals)**: Noyes   (Mr Mrs Miss Ms): Mr

   First name(s) (in capitals): Thomas Andrew

4. **Leaving date (in figures)**: Day 5 Month 10 Year 20 04

5. **Continue Student Loan Deductions (Y)**:

6. **Tax Code at leaving date.** *If week 1 or Month 1 basis applies, write 'X' in the box marked Week 1 or Month 1*
   Code: 490T   Week 1 or Month 1:

7. **Last entries on Deductions Working Sheet (P11) Complete only if Tax Code is cumulative.** *Make no entry here if Week 1 or Month 1 basis applies. Go to item 8.*
   Week or month number: Week 27
   Total pay to date: £ 4,560 00 p
   Total tax to date: £ 316 33 p

8. **This employment pay and tax.** ■ *No entry needed if Tax Code is cumulative and amounts are same as item 7 entry.*
   Total pay in this employment: £   p
   Total tax in this employment: £   p

9. **Works number/ Payroll number**: 123

10. **Department or branch if any**:

11. **Employee's private address and Postcode**:
    Mrs Sarah Noyes (Widow)
    18 High Towers, 200 Long Road
    Portsford, Bucks
    LU8 9ZH

12. I certify that the details entered above in items 1 to 10 are correct
    Employer's name, address and Postcode:
    DEF Ltd
    15 Station Green, Portsford
    LU1 9ZB
    Date: 6/10/04

For Tax Office use

To the employer   *Please complete with care* ★

- Complete this form following the 'Employee leaving' instructions in the *Employer's helpbook* (E13)). **Make sure the details are clear on all four parts of this form.** Make sure your name and address is shown on Parts 1 and 1A.
- Detach Part 1 and send it to your Tax Office immediately.
- Hand Parts 1A, 2 and 3 (unseparated) to your employee when he or she leaves
- If the employee has died, write 'D' in this box and send all three parts of this form (unseparated) to your Tax Office immediately.

D

P45

BMSD9/99

Activity 1.7

Later on Friday morning, you hear the sad news that the father of Hope, Job, Grace and Whit has dropped dead in the Packing Department. Lief Less was a monthly paid worker. The Managing Director gives written instructions to pay a full month's salary to Lief's personal representative. What steps should you take to complete the formalities in connection with this final salary payment?

8 Outline of payroll procedures for starters

No employee should be added to the payroll without proper authorisation.

Payroll must be informed **in advance in writing** about new employees. A special form can be used to notify the payroll department, such as the following.

ABC LTD

To: Accounts Office (Payroll)
From: Personnel Manager

NOTIFICATION OF START OF EMPLOYMENT

Full name of new employee ....
(underline surname or family name)

Sex: Male/Female

Position ....

Department ....

Date of commencement of employment:

Pay £............. per hour/day/week/month/year

Signed (Personnel Manager) .... Date ....

Other details about the new employee can be included on the form, or attached on a separate sheet of paper (for example, a copy contract of employment).

The payroll department should keep a list of **authorised signatories**. This list will consist of people, such as managers and the personnel department, authorised to hire and fire people. The list will also include a specimen signature. All new employee joining forms should be checked to this list, as should leaver's forms.

Once satisfied that the employee is genuine, payroll sets up a record file for the new employee.

PART A   MAINTAINING EMPLOYEE RECORDS

This record file needs to contain the **statutory and non-statutory data** from Sections 4 and 5.

On occasion, a new employee may request that his or her wages/payslip are sent to a third party (eg spouse or partner). Always obtain written authorisation from the employee before carrying out such instructions.

Any voluntary deductions, eg pension scheme contributions, also need to be authorised in writing by the employee.

The new employee should bring his or her form **P45** to work on the first day or, if the employee does not have a P45, a document showing his or her **National Insurance number** (eg NI card or P60).

The payroll office also needs to determine the National Insurance category letter applicable (see Chapter 8). Married women on reduced rate contributions and those exempt over state retirement age, should produce certificates to confirm their status.

A new employee may also have form SSP1(L) if they have received Statutory Sick Pay from their previous employer during the eight weeks prior to leaving.

9 Completing a P45 for a starter

A **starter** is a person who has never worked for the organisation before, or someone who used to work for you, left and is now coming back again.

9.1 Form P45

All starters should bring **Parts 2 and 3** of a **P45** with them if they have them. As payroll officer, you need the P45 to obtain details of the new employee's **pay and tax for the year to date, tax code and NI number.**

You should **only** be given Parts 2 and 3 of the P45.

- If for some reason you are given **Part 1** as well, you should detach this and send it to your Tax Office, with a letter explaining what has happened.
- If you are given **Part 1A**, give it back to the employee and tell him or her to keep it.

Part 2 of the P45 is for your own payroll records for the new employee. Detach it and keep it. It should be kept for **at least three years** after the end of the tax year to which it relates.

Check the details on **Part 2** in boxes 6 and 7 (tax code at date of leaving, week or month number of leaving, total pay to date and total tax to date). **These should be the same as the details in boxes 6 and 7 of Part 3** of the form. If they are not, something is seriously wrong and you should get in touch with your Tax Office about the matter immediately.

Part 3 of the P45 will have been partly completed before you receive it. The bottom half of Part 3 of the form should now be completed by you as the new employer and sent to the Tax Office as soon as possible.

9.2 Checking NI number and legality of employee

If the employee hands in a P45 with no **National Insurance number** on it, it is advisable to complete **form CA6855** and send it to the **National Insurance Contributions Office (NICO)** to obtain a National Insurance number.

Every employer is obliged to check that a new employee may legally work in this country under the Asylum and Immigration Act 1996. This applies to all new employees whatever their race, colour or sex. To comply, the employer must see **suitable documentation**. This includes a **form P45** or **P60** which contains what appears to be a valid National Insurance number. There are other documents which may be used (see Section 4.5).

A valid National Insurance number is in the format AB 12 34 56 A. The final letter can only be A, B, C or D.

If an employee does not have a tax form showing a National Insurance number, there should be a procedure to check eligibility to work here in accordance with **Home Office guidance**. An employer who fails to make this check may be **fined** £5,000 per employee.

Note that producing a form P45 or P60 with what appears to be a valid National Insurance number does not mean that the person may work in the UK, but it does mean that the employer will not be fined for failing to check.

9.3 Completing Part 3 of a starter's P45

Example: Starter's P45

Suppose that in the example of the leaver's P45 above, Mr John Needham starts work with a new employer, Staines Steel Ltd, on 3 June 2004. His new employer might complete Part 3 of his P45 as follows.

PART A MAINTAINING EMPLOYEE RECORDS

Inland Revenue

New employee details — For completion by new employer — **P45 Part 3**

1	Previous PAYE Reference — District number / Reference number	135 / B 3456
2	Employee's National Insurance number	BC 28 47 93 D
3	Surname (Mr Mrs Miss Ms)	NEEDHAM — MR
	First name(s)	JOHN ANGUS
4	Date left previous employment (Day/Month/Year)	31 / 05 / 20 04
5	Continue Student Loan Deductions (Y)	
6	Tax Code at leaving date. 'x' in the box means Week 1 or Month 1 basis applies — Code / Week 1 or Month 1	367 L
7	Last entries on Deductions Working Sheet (P11). If there is an 'X' at item 6, there will be no entries here	
	Week or Month number — Week / Month	2
	Total pay to date	£ 3,000 00 p
	Total tax to date	£ 484 51 p

To the new employer — Complete items 8 to 17 below and send this page of the form only to your Tax Office immediately.

8	New PAYE Reference	176/S 4529
9	Date employment started (in figures) Day/Month/Year	03 / 06 / 20 04
10	Tick here if you want these details to be shown on tax code notifications	✓
	Works/Payroll number Department or branch if any	102
11	Enter P if employee will not be paid by you between date employment began and next 5 April	
12	Enter code in use if different to code at item 6	
13	If the tax figure you are entering on P11 differs from item 7 above (see CWG (1999) card 4) please enter your figure here	£
14	Employee's private address	17 MILL LANE
		LINCESTER — Postcode AB2 3CD
15	Employee's date of birth (if known)	26 / 02 / 19 58
16	Employee's job title or description	SUPERVISOR
17	Declaration. I have prepared a Deductions Working Sheet (P11) in accordance with the details above.	
	Employer	STAINES STEEL LTD
	Address	16 IRONBRIDGE ESTATE
		LINCESTER — Postcode AB2 4DT — Date 3/6/04

P45

If you look at the details of items 8-17 on Part 3, some are more straightforward than others.

Item 8 This is the **new employer's tax reference number** (here, the reference number of Staines Steel Ltd, which you as payroll officer will already know).

Item 10 This is a **payroll or works or department number** for the employee. It is for the company's internal use, and so item 10 should only be completed if there is an employee number system in use. Tick the box if you want the Inland Revenue to quote this reference on tax codes, etc. This is useful if your files are in number order (see Section 12).

Item 11 This is an item that relates to a situation where an employee is taken on **near the end of the tax year** (5 April) but won't be paid for the first time until the new tax year (6 April onwards). This will happen with a monthly-paid employee who joins on 1 April, for example.

When this situation arises, enter P in the box.

Item 12 You may have to complete this if the employee left his or her old job in the **old tax year** and is starting work with you in the new tax year (see Section 9.6).

Item 13 **This is important. More about it later, in Section 9.5.**

Item 17 The declaration is not signed by an individual (the payroll officer). It simply shows the employer's name and address.

Notice too that when Part 3 of the P45 is prepared, the payroll officer should **already have prepared a P11** for the new employee. In practice, this should be prepared at the same time as Part 3 of the P45.

9.4 P11 and the P45

The P45 of a new employee should be used to prepare a **P11 deductions working sheet** (see Chapter 6).

Even if the employee is **re-joining** you, having worked for you earlier in the tax year and then left to work elsewhere, you should prepare a new deductions working sheet. (In other words, don't use the same working sheet for the employee as before he or she temporarily left.)

When you prepare a deductions working sheet for the new employee, **you must check that the figure on the P45 for total tax to date is correct given the total pay to date and the employee's tax code.**

Example: Starter's P11

Let's use our example of John Needham. He was paid monthly by his previous employer, and the P45 figures for Month 2 of 2004/05 are:

Total pay to date	£3,000.00
Total tax to date	£484.51
Code at date of leaving	367L

Is the amount of tax paid correct?

PART A   MAINTAINING EMPLOYEE RECORDS

Solution

The **date of leaving** (31 May) is in Month 2, and so the **month number** on the P45 is correct.

The Pay Adjustment tables (Tables A) for Month 2 and tax code 367L show an amount of £613.18.

	£
Total pay to date	3,000.00
Free pay	613.18
Taxable pay	2,386.82

The Taxable Pay Tables B show, for taxable pay of £2,386 in Month 2, that the tax should be:

	£
For £2,300	506.00
For £86	18.92
Less starting rate relief	(40.41)
	484.51

This shows that the tax figure in the P45 is correct, and can be entered in the P11.

Note. This is dealt with in detail in Chapter 6.

An extract from John Needham's P11 is shown below, as it should be completed by the payroll officer of Staines Steel Ltd.

Tax code	Amended	
367L	WK/mnth	

Month	Pay in the month 2	Total pay to date 3	Total free pay to date 4a	*K codes* Total additional pay to date 4b	Total taxable pay to date 5	Total tax due to date 6	*K codes* Tax due at end of current period 6a	Regulatory limit 6b	Tax deducted in the week 7	*K codes* Tax not deducted owing to the regulatory limit 8	Tax Credits 9
1											
2		3,000.00	613.18		2,386.82	484.51					

9.5 Errors in tax paid on the P45

In our previous example, the figure was correct. **But what happens if it is wrong?**

What to do		Consequence
Step 1	The **correct figure for tax** should be entered on the **P11**. This is the figure for tax that *should* have been paid.	Your organisation will deduct the 'correct' amount of tax when the employee gets paid for the first time, as if his or her tax payments had always been calculated properly. This will mean that if the previous employer hadn't deducted enough tax by, say £100, your organisation won't have to deduct this £100 from your new employee's first wage or salary payment.
Step 2	This correct figure should be notified to the **Tax Office**, by completing **item 13 on Part 3 of the P45**.	Any over-payment or under-payment of tax in the previous employment will be sorted out directly between the employee and the Tax Office.

The above steps refer to all tax codes, **except K codes**. However, to avoid confusion, the steps to be taken to check K codes are dealt with in Chapter 7.

9.6 P45 relating to an earlier tax year

Sometimes a new employee will bring a **P45 that relates to a previous tax year**. This situation will be quite common for new employees starting work in April.

If the employee starts work with you after 6 April 2004 and **before 24 May 2004**, the new employer can use the tax code shown on a P45 from 2003/04, after amending it, if necessary, in accordance with the general instructions about changes to codes issued by the Inland Revenue on form P9X. **Fill in box 12 in Part 3 of the P45 if you do this.**

If the code on the P45 is a **week 1 or month 1 basis** ignore this marking and operate it **cumulatively**.

The P11 should be filled in by copying this code from the P45. Enter nil total pay to date and nil total tax to date. (The figures on the P45 are not relevant to the new tax year.)

If the employee starts work with you **on or after 24 May 2004**, the tax code on a P45 from 2003/04 must be ignored. Instead, the employee should be given the **emergency code** operated on a Week 1/Month 1 basis.

For the 2004/05 tax year, the emergency code is 474L.

If the P45 is for a tax year before 2003/04 you should also use the **emergency code** (474L in 2004/05) on a **Week 1/Month 1 basis**.

These terms will be explained in more detail in Chapters 6 and 7. For the moment, you only need to know which code to record on the P11.

9.7 Deciding which rate of NIC to use

All employees aged 16 or over, and below state retirement age, have to pay NICs. The rate is determined by a category letter, which needs to be recorded on form P11. You will meet this in Chapter 8.

9.8 Student loan deductions

If there is a Y in box 5 of P45, you will need to make student loan deductions. These are dealt with in detail in Chapter 10. For the moment, all you need to do is make a note in the employee's record and on the P11 deduction card.

10 Starters without a P45

Sometimes, a new employee will not have a P45 when he or she starts work with you, and so the procedures to be followed by a payroll officer are different. A distinction is made between the following.

- Starters without a P45 who will be working for you for **more than one week**
- Starters without a P45 who will be working for you for just **one week or less (casual labour)**.

10.1 Starters who will be with you for more than one week: Form P46

If a new employee does not give you a P45, you should follow the **P46 procedure.**

Step 1   Ask the employee to read **Form P46**, and **tick** Statement A, Statement B, and/or Statement C. The employee must then sign and enter the date below Statement C.

Step 2   You should fill in Section 2 of the form. Ask your employee for details of their NI number, if available.

1: STARTERS AND LEAVERS

A copy of the P46 is shown below.

PAYE Employer's notice to Inland Revenue Office

Inland Revenue

Send in on the first pay day for employees who
- do not have a form P45, or
- were previously paid below the PAYE threshold.

Section 1 - to be completed by the EMPLOYEE

Read each statement carefully. Tick **each one** that applies to you. **If none of them apply, do not sign the statement.**

Statement A
This is my first regular job since leaving full-time education. I have not claimed Jobseeker's Allowance, or income support paid because of unemployment since then. ☐

Statement B
This is my only or main job. ☐

Statement C
I receive a pension as well as the income from this job. ☐

I confirm that I have ticked the statements that apply to me.

Signed _____   Date __/__/__

Section 2 - to be completed by the EMPLOYER

Your employer's Quick Guide to PAYE and NICs (CWG1, Card 5) tells you how to complete this form.

Employee's details

National Insurance number ☐☐ ☐☐ ☐☐ ☐

Surname including title Mr/Mrs/Miss/Ms/Other _____

First name(s) _____

Address _____
_____
_____ Postcode _____

Date of birth __/__/__

Male/Female (enter M/F) ☐

Works/payroll number, if any _____

Department/Branch, if any _____

Job title _____

Date employment started __/__/__

P46

Coding information

Existing employee now above PAYE threshold ☐
(enter X in box if this applies)
New employee who has signed statement (enter letter here) ☐
New employee who has not signed a statement ☐
Code operated for this employee ☐
Enter X in box if code operated on week1/month 1 basis ☐

Employer's details

Employer's PAYE reference _____
Name _____
Address _____
_____
_____
_____ Postcode _____

Date this form was completed __/__/__

PART A MAINTAINING EMPLOYEE RECORDS

The Statement(s) ticked on the P46 determine the **PAYE code** that you should operate until a revised tax code notice is received (remember for 2004/05 the emergency code is 474L).

Statement(s) ticked	Tax code
Statement A, or A and B	Emergency Code on a cumulative basis
Statement B only	Emergency Code on a week 1/month 1 basis
Statement C, or B and C, or A and C	Code BR
No statement ticked (or form not signed)	Code BR
All three statements ticked	Code BR

10.1.1 What to do with Form P46

There is a **top copy** of form P46 and a **carbon copy** of the information completed by the employer. Both copies of the P46 are normally sent to the employer's Tax Office. The top copy of the form is used by the **Inland Revenue**, the other by **NICO**. NICO uses its copy of the form to check or trace the employee's National Insurance number.

If the employee is paid **less than the PAYE threshold** (£91 per week; £395 per month).

Step 1   Form P46 should be kept by the employer and not forwarded to the Tax Office.

Step 2   Form CA6855 should be used to trace the employee's National Insurance number if he or she has not given you one.

Step 3   On the P11 record gross pay and NICs. Write 'NI' in the box for the tax code.

Step 4   If pay is **below the NIC Lower Earnings Limit** (£79 per week; £343 per month), no P11 is required but record name, address and pay amounts.

In practice, many employers will use a P11 for employees paid below the NIC Lower Earnings Limit. The reason being that only one set of records is maintained. Therefore in your skills test you may be asked to set up a P11 for an employee where no tax or NICs are due.

10.2 Casual labour

Casual labour - people who will be employees for just one week or less - must still have tax and National Insurance deducted, provided that they earn enough. However, you do not get such employees to complete Form P46.

The procedures to follow for casual labour can be shown in a flowchart.

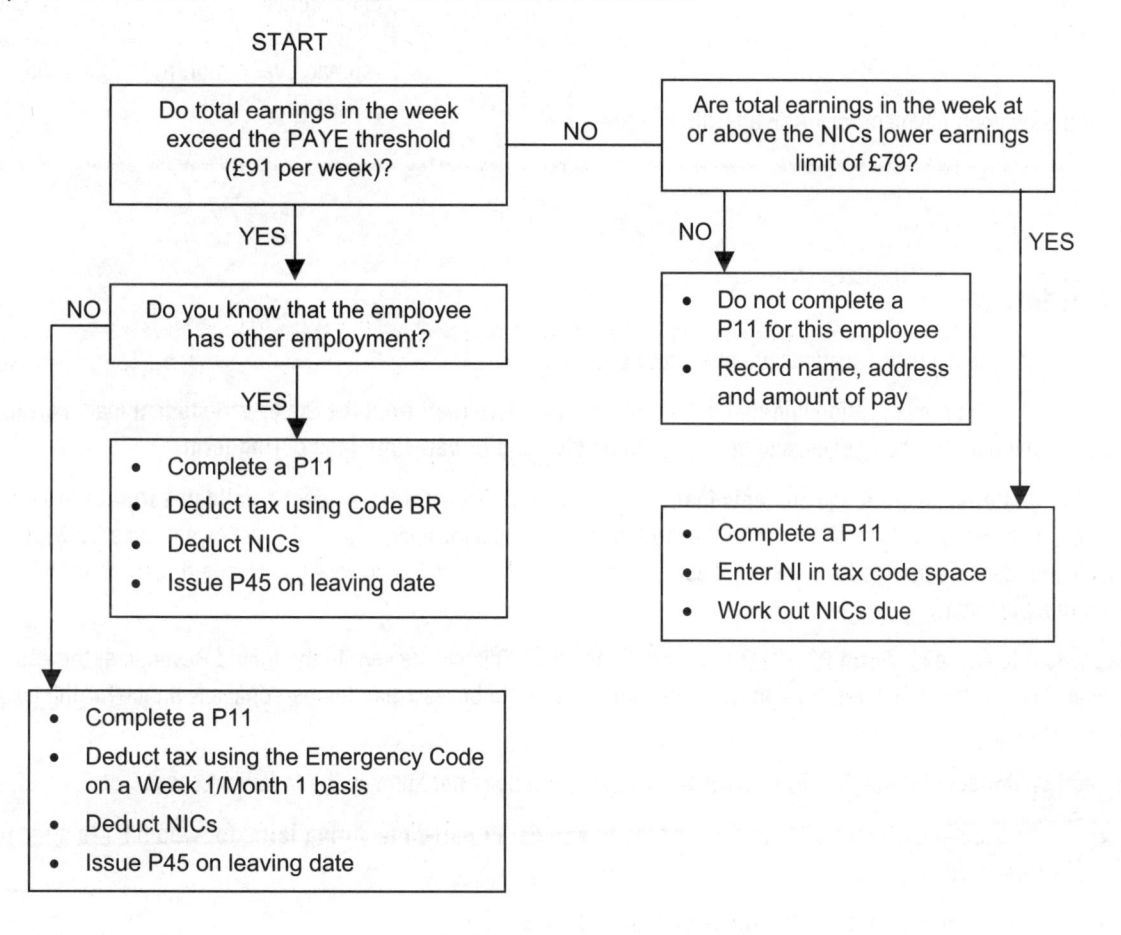

```
                            START
                              |
                              v
        +----------------------------+                +----------------------------+
        | Do total earnings in the   |      NO        | Are total earnings in the  |
        | week exceed the PAYE       |--------------->| week at or above the NICs  |
        | threshold (£91 per week)?  |                | lower earnings limit of £79?|
        +----------------------------+                +----------------------------+
                  | YES                                   NO |           | YES
                  v                                          v           v
        +----------------------------+            +-----------------------+
   NO   | Do you know that the       |            | • Do not complete a   |
 <------| employee has other         |            |   P11 for this employee|
        | employment?                |            | • Record name, address|
        +----------------------------+            |   and amount of pay   |
                  | YES                            +-----------------------+
                  v                                          
        +----------------------------+            +-----------------------+
        | • Complete a P11           |            | • Complete a P11      |
        | • Deduct tax using Code BR |            | • Enter NI in tax code|
        | • Deduct NICs              |            |   space               |
        | • Issue P45 on leaving date|            | • Work out NICs due   |
        +----------------------------+            +-----------------------+

        +----------------------------------+
        | • Complete a P11                 |
        | • Deduct tax using the Emergency |
        |   Code on a Week 1/Month 1 basis |
        | • Deduct NICs                    |
        | • Issue P45 on leaving date      |
        +----------------------------------+
```

Activity 1.8

It is Monday morning in the Payroll Office. Ruth Less has just joined the Packing Department to take over her father's job. List all the information you need for your **payroll record file. Note:** you aren't starting a personnel record file!

Activity 1.9

A sudden rush order has made it necessary to recruit some extra labour at Turnover Ltd. The Less family have returned in force, rising to the crisis. None of them provides you with a P45.

- Hope Less has a permanent part-time job at Desperate plc down the road.

PART A   MAINTAINING EMPLOYEE RECORDS

- Whit Less, Job Less and Grace Less appear to have no other work at the moment.
- They are paid as follows:

	Number of days employed	*Gross pay* £
Job	2 consecutive	95.00
Hope	3 consecutive	120.00
Grace	1	30.00
Whit	8 (spread over a month)	365.00

How do you treat each payment for PAYE and NIC purposes?

10.3 Students

Students working during their vacations are subject to special rules.

Many students in full time education find that the funding they receive (part from the State, part student loan, part from parents) is inadequate for their needs, and take on **holiday jobs** and/or **part-time jobs during term**.

The **student maintenance grant** and **students loans** are not taxable. Therefore, a student's **holiday earnings** are unlikely to be taxable as they are likely to be less than the student's personal allowance, although the normal rules for **NICs** still apply. (If the student's earnings for a week are equal to or above the employee's weekly earnings threshold for NICs, then NICs must be paid.)

Ask the student to complete **Form P38(S)** (see pages 38 and 39). This will be sent to the Inland Revenue at the end of the tax year. The student must declare that his or her earnings are to be less than the personal allowance for the tax year (£4,745 for 2004/05).

No tax need be deducted if the P38(S) is signed. This provision does **not** apply in the following cases.

- To students who work for you **during the evenings, or part-time during term**, for whom P11s must be prepared.
- To students who do **both holiday and term-time work** for you.
- To students who are **not on courses in the UK** (other rules apply to them).

There are some special procedures to note about the **P38(S)**.

- **It must be given by the employer to the student to sign**. If a student has a P38(S) from another source, then do not accept it.
- A P38(S) must be used for **each tax year**. Note that if the Easter holiday spans 6 April, two forms P38(S) will need to be completed – one for each tax year.
- Providing the P38(S) has been signed, **even when the student earns more than the PAYE emergency code threshold**, tax is not deductible.
- If the student earns an amount equal to or **more than the NICs lower earnings limit** (£79 a week or £343 a month) then write 'NI' in the tax code box at the top of the P11. You deduct NICs only if pay exceeds the employee earnings threshold (£91 a week or £395 a month).

- If a student earns **less than the NICs lower earnings limit** (£79 a week or £343 a month) no P11 is necessary, but you must record details of all payments made to the student, and these records must be kept for at least 3 years after the end of the tax year.

- No **P45** or **P46** is needed for a student for whom a P38(S) is held.

Activity 1.16

Billie, Pat and Lee are students working for your company.

- Billie is a full-time student at the local university. In term-time she works for your company on two evenings a week. She is currently working longer hours for you in the holidays.

- Pat is a student of an American university (although he is a UK citizen). He is working full-time for the company over the summer vacation.

- Lee is a part-time student at the local College of Further Education. She works for your company all year round, averaging 20 hours a week in term time and 35 in the holidays.

Can any of these students complete Form P38(S)? Give your reasons.

PART A   MAINTAINING EMPLOYEE RECORDS

Inland Revenue

For information only

Student employees

Income tax

You do not have to deduct tax from the pay of a student who works for you solely during a holiday if

- this form is filled in on the back, and
- the student's pay in your employment does not exceed £4,745.

Where the student's pay in your employment exceeds £4,745 you must

- deduct tax using code 'OT week 1/month 1' in accordance with paragraphs 110 and 111 of the booklet CWG2, *Employer's Further Guide to PAYE and NICs*.

If 5 April falls during the period of employment, the student must fill in two of these forms, one for the tax year up to 5 April, and one for the new tax year from 6 April.

National Insurance

If the student's pay is at, or above, the lower earnings limit for National Insurance contributions, you must

- use a form P11, *Deductions Working Sheet* (or your own equivalent pay record) to record the National Insurance contributions, and
- complete a form P14, *End of Year Summary* showing these contributions for submission with your form P35, *Employer's Annual Return*.

The present lower earnings limit is shown in the booklet E12, *PAYE and NICs rates and limits for 2004-2005*. Your Employer's Help Book E13, *Day-to-day payroll*, tells you how to fill in the P11, *Deductions Working Sheet*.

Please keep this form for at least three years after the end of the year to which it relates or longer if you are asked to do so.

Please turn over

P38(S)(2004)   BS1/04

1: STARTERS AND LEAVERS

Student's declaration

I, _____ **For information only**
Full name in CAPITALS

am a student attending _____
Name of school, college.

and shall continue to attend until after 5 April next. I have no employment except during holidays.

My total earnings **including Jobseekers Allowance paid because of unemployment** and other income from all sources, apart from scholarships and educational grants for the year ending 5 April next, will not be more than £4,745.

My National Insurance number is

My date of birth is __ / __ / __

My home address is

Postcode

Signature

Date __ / __ / __

Employer's statement

The declaration above has been completed and signed by the student.

The total pay from __ / __ / __ to __ / __ / __

was £ _____

Employer's name

Employer's address

Postcode

Employer's PAYE reference __ / __

Date __ / __ / __

PART A   MAINTAINING EMPLOYEE RECORDS

> **Important!**
>
> As forms P45 and P46 are included in Unit 71, we have to look at tax and NIC points before you study them in Unit 73! We recommend that you return to this chapter after studying Chapters 6, 7, 8 and 9.

11 Tax refunds for new employees

Sometimes a new employee will need a **refund of income tax** on his or her first pay day. This will occur when the new employee has been **unemployed** for some time and the entitlement to free pay is large enough to make a refund due.

Example: tax refund

Anna Davies joined ABC Ltd in Week 14 of tax year 2004/05. She had a P45 when she joined, showing that her tax code was 410L, and that she left her previous employment in Week 4 having earned total pay of £1,200 and having had tax deducted of £175.61. Table A shows free pay in week 4 of £316.08 for a code of 410L.

At the end of her first week (Week 14) her gross pay is £250. During the week, you receive a notice that her code is amended to 600L. The free pay in Week 14 for this code is £1,617.98.

Solution

Remember to check whether the entries on form P45 are correct.

Week 4 calculations

	£
Total pay to date	1,200.00
Free pay (code 410L)	316.08
Taxable pay	883.92

		£
Tax due	£800	176.00
	£83	18.26
Subtraction tables (week 4)		(18.65)
		175.61

The tax computations for her Week 14 pay are as follows.

	£
Total pay to date (£1,200 + £250)	1,450.00
Free pay (tax code 600L, Week 14)	1,617.98
Taxable pay	Nil

(Free pay exceeds pay to date by £167.98)

		£
Tax payable		0.00
Tax paid to date		175.61
Refund due		175.61

Anna should be paid £250, less NIC, plus £175.61. The income tax side of the P11 would be completed as follows, as at the end of Week 14.

Week	Pay in the week	Total pay to date	Total free pay to date	K codes — Total additional pay to date	Total taxable pay to date	Total tax due to date	Tax due at end of current period (K codes)	Regulatory limit (K codes)	Tax deducted in the week	Tax not deducted owing to the regulatory limit (K codes)	Tax Credits
	2	3	4a	4b	5	6	6a	6b	7	8	9
1											
2											
3											
4		1,200.00	316.08		883.92	175.61					
5											
6											
7											
8											
9											
10											
11											
12											
13											
14	250.00	1,450.00	1,617.98		NIL	NIL			(175.61)R		

12 Storage of data

Employee records will contain a lot of confidential information. Just imagine how upset you would feel if the whole office knew details of your salary, for example. Therefore it is essential that employee records are kept **secure** and that **confidentiality** is respected.

12.1 Access to records

An unauthorised person must not have access to employee records, or to information from those records, without permission.

PART A   MAINTAINING EMPLOYEE RECORDS

For example, a colleague asks for someone's change of address to send them a 'house warming' present. Employee information can **never** be given to **unauthorised** third parties without the employee's permission. Therefore, suggest that the present is given in the office instead.

Employee records may be kept manually and/or on a computer, but either way access must be restricted. Manual files should be kept locked in a cabinet and the key kept in your possession (not left in the lock!). Computer files should be protected, by restricted access to that part of the programme, by password or both.

Never leave employee files open (either manual or computer), when you are away from your desk.

It is a good ideal to have a standard format for keeping employee records to make it easier to locate data. If you are using a computer payroll module (such as SAGE payroll) there is usually a standard screen to complete for each employee. Whether the system is manual or computerised, a good standard format would include the following information.

Name:	John Smith	Salary:	£40,000 pa
Employee number:	15276	Starting date:	01.01.96
Address:	55 High Street Anytown Anywhere	Leaving date:	
		Job title:	Sales manager
		Voluntary deductions:	Pension 3%
Telephone number:	01234 567890		
Date of birth:	06.06.45		
Sex:	M	Tax code:	461L
Marital status:	Married	NI number	AB 22 23 24 D

As you can see in the above diagram, the employee record card has an employee number. This makes it easier to locate the record in a large organisation.

12.2 Filing system

Filing employee records is usually done either in alphabetical order or numerical order. Alphabetical order is usually followed in small organisations with only a few employees. However, large organisations usually find it easier to use a numerical system, as the latest employee can then be given the next number without have to slot it into the existing alphabetical section.

The usual way of filing under the alphabetical system is surname first, then forename. Where the surnames are identical, then the order is decided by the order of forenames, as follows.

Watson, Anne
Wilkins, James
Wilkins, Justin
Wilmot, Bryan
Wilson, Arthur

12.3 Timescales

All current employees' records should be easily accessible, so that any queries can be easily dealt with.

When an employee has left the organisation, you might be tempted to destroy the record after a year or so has elapsed. However, the Inland Revenue have the power to go back at least 6 years when investigating employees. The statutory minimum that PAYE records must be kept is **three years**. Therefore **all** PAYE data (including employee records) should be kept for at least 3 years. Your organisation's policy may be to keep records longer.

There is no need to keep old records with current records. It is perfectly permissible to weed out old files and put them in long term storage or to 'archive' them. The organisation should have a policy on storage of records, ie how long they are kept and how they are stored.

PART A MAINTAINING EMPLOYEE RECORDS

Key learning points

- It is essential to keep records of all employees. Therefore you need to be able to decide who is an employee, self-employed, or a single member limited company.

- Employees' records include **statutory** and **non-statutory** data.

- **Statutory data** is regulated by the Employment Rights Act 1996, the Employment Relations Act 1999, Data Protection Act 1998 and Asylum and Immigration Act 1996.

- **Statutory data** consists of:
    - Name and title
    - Address
    - Date of birth
    - Sex
    - Tax code
    - National Insurance number and category
    - Starting date
    - Leaving date
    - Pensions status

- **Non-statutory** data consists of any extra information that an organisation decides to keep.

- Employee records should not be changed without **verifying** the changes.

- For people who **leave an organisation**, the payroll officer must bring the deductions working sheet up to date and prepare a **P45**, sending Part 1 to the Tax Office and giving Parts 1A, 2 and 3 to the departing employee.

- People **joining an organisation** will normally bring **parts 2 and 3 of a P45** with them, and the payroll officer can use the details on this to prepare a **P11**.

- If long-term new employees don't come with a P45, they should sign a **P46**, which you will usually send to the Tax Office, and they will normally be taxed on **Emergency Code** (depending on their level of pay) until a coding comes through from the Tax Office.

- For **casual labour** (one week or less) who do not come with a P45, you do not need a P46, and the action to take will depend on the level of pay for the employee and whether he or she has other employment as well as the temporary job with you.

- **Students** are subject to special rules for vacation earnings (P38(S)).

- **Tax refunds** will occasionally be made to new employees who join during the tax year and have already paid some tax earlier in the year.

- It is important to obtain the **National Insurance number** of new employees, since this is their main identification tag for the Inland Revenue. Obtaining what appears to be a valid National Insurance number also ensures that the employer has fulfilled the obligation to check that a **new employee may legally work in this country**.

- All PAYE data should be **stored** for at least 3 years.

1: STARTERS AND LEAVERS

Quick quiz

1. Your supervisor asks you to obtain details of a new employee: name; address; telephone number and marital status. Which are statutory and which non-statutory?

2. What is the form to be sent to the Inland Revenue when an employee leaves?

3. How many parts does it have and what happens to each part?

4. If an employee dies whilst working for your firm, no NIC is due on payments of outstanding wages or salary made after death. True or false?

5. Why do you have to check the old employer's 'tax paid to date' figure?

6. You always use the tax code on the P45 to start off the new employee's P11. True or false?

7. When a new employee starts work for your organisation, what documentation do you have to submit to the Inland Revenue?

8. A new employee who also receives a pension and fills in a P46 will be given the emergency code. True or false?

9. When might a new employee be entitled to a tax refund on his or her first pay day?

10. When storing employee records, which is more important: security or confidentiality?

Answers to quick quiz

1. **Statutory:** name; address. **Non-statutory:** telephone number, marital status.

2. P45

3. 4 parts: Part 1 goes to the old employer's Tax Office; Parts 1A, 2 and 3 are given to the employee on leaving. The employee keeps part 1A. His or her new employer will ask for Parts 2 and 3 and will keep Part 2. Part 3 goes to the new employer's Tax Office. If the employee does not get a new job he or she needs to give Parts 2 and 3 to the DWP in order to claim jobseeker's allowance.

4. True (but income tax is deducted).

5. So that errors are picked up and the P11 is correct at the outset.

6. False. The P45 may relate to an earlier tax year, in which case you use the emergency code instead. If it is very soon after the end of the tax year you can use the old code (always on a cumulative basis), increased as directed by the Inland Revenue on Form P9X.

7. Part 3 of the P45; you check and file Part 2 and fill in the outstanding details on Part 3 before sending it off to the Inland Revenue. If the employee has no P45 and is going to be working for you for more than one week, he or she must read Form P46, tick the appropriate statement (A,B and/or C) and sign it. You then complete the form and send it to the Inland Revenue (top and carbon copy), unless the new employee will be below the tax threshold. In this case you keep the P46 on file. If the new employee has no NI number, you must use Form CA 6855 to trace the number through the NICO.

8. False. Code BR will apply.

PART A   MAINTAINING EMPLOYEE RECORDS

9   When he or she has been employed earlier in the tax year and then unemployed for some time before joining your organisation. The entitlement to free pay could be so large by then that it exceeds tax due to date.

10 They are both **equally** important.

Activity checklist

This checklist shows which performance criteria, range statement or knowledge and understanding point is covered by each activity in this chapter. Tick off each activity as you complete it.

Activity		
1.1		This activity covers knowledge and understanding point 4.
1.2		This activity covers performance criterion 71.1.B, concerning statutory input.
1.3		This activity covers performance criteria 71.1.A and 71.1.E, and knowledge and understanding point 8.
1.4		This activity covers performance criteria 71.1.A, 71.1.B and 71.1.E, and knowledge and understanding point 8.
1.5		This activity covers performance criterion 71.1.D.
1.6		This activity covers performance criteria 71.1.E and 71.1.H.
1.7		This activity covers performance criteria 71.1.A, 71.1.C and 71.1.D
1.8		This activity covers performance criterion 71.1.B and range statement 1: non-statutory data.
1.9		This activity covers performance criterion 71.1.B, range statement 2: source documentation and knowledge and understanding point 1 regarding starters and leavers.
1.10		This activity covers performance criterion 71.1.D and knowledge and understanding point 1 regarding starters and leavers.

chapter 2

Instructions from external agencies

Contents

1 The problem
2 The solution
3 Statutory deductions
4 Non-statutory deductions

Performance criteria

71.2.A Verify all payment and deduction instructions for accuracy, completeness and correct documentation

71.2.B Process instructions from **statutory agencies** or **non-statutory bodies** in accordance with statutory and organisational requirements and within the timescale specified

71.2.C Ensure all non-statutory deductions are authorised by the employee concerned

71.2.D Identify and resolve all discrepancies directly or by reference to the appropriate organisation or person

Range statement

1 Documentation: court orders; Inland Revenue documentation; Child Support Agency instructions; local authority attachment of earnings; individual mandates

2 Statutory agencies: Inland Revenue; Inland Revenue Contributions Office; Child Support Agency; courts; local authorities

3 Non-statutory bodies: pension funds; trades unions and associations; financial institutions; charities

PART A   MAINTAINING EMPLOYEE RECORDS

Knowledge and understanding

1. Tax and Social Security legislation affecting:
   Tax code changes (Element 71.2)
   Student Loan Deductions (Element 71.2)
   Tax Credits (Element 71.2)
   National Insurance category letters (Elements 71.1 & 71.2)
2. Employment Rights legislation (Elements 71.1, 71.2 & 71.3)
5. Legislation relating to attachments of earnings (Elements 71.1, 71.2 & 71.3)
6. Procedures for keeping data confidential and secure (Elements 71.1, 71.2 & 71.3)
7. Dealing with instructions from external agencies (71.2)
8. Who to refer discrepancies to (Elements 71.1, 71.2 & 71.3)
10. Types of information input from external agencies (Element 71.2)
11. Signatories and authorisations (Element 71.1, 71.2 and 71.3)
12. Timescales and schedules for updating, presenting and despatching data (Elements 71.1, 71.2 & 71.3)
13. Information flows within the organisation (Elements 71.1, 71.2 & 71.3)

1 The problem

From time to time, the payroll department receives requests and instructions from external agencies. How are these to be processed?

2 The solution

In all cases the key to whether a deduction should be made is **authorisation**.

External instructions include statutory and non-statutory deductions. All statutory deductions have to be made upon receipt of a valid order from the external authority (Section 3).

Non-statutory deductions from the payroll can only be made with the **written agreement of the employee** (Section 4).

> **Signpost**
>
> For this element, you are required to set up, alter and stop deductions. Detailed knowledge of the actual deductions and how they work will come later in your studies. The key to this element is **implementing** the orders, not **processing** them.

3 Statutory deductions

3.1 Tax and NIC

The following are the most obvious statutory deductions.

- Tax deducted under PAYE (Pay As You Earn)
- NICs

The deduction of tax and NICs is administered by the Inland Revenue and NICO. We will look at these deductions in detail in Chapters 6, 7, 8 and 9.

NICO is part of the Inland Revenue. Its full name is the Inland Revenue National Insurance Contributions Office. However in order to distinguish between tax and NICs, this Text will refer to the PAYE administrator as the Inland Revenue and the National Insurance administrator as NICO.

The Inland Revenue will send you instructions which must be carried out. For example, you may receive form P6(T) (notice of coding or change of coding) for an employee. This **must** be used **from the next payday**, even if the employee tells you that the code is wrong. It is up to the employee to get the Revenue to issue a further revised code.

Tax codes can also change following the annual Budget. In this case, the Inland Revenue will issue general instructions to employers selling them which codes to increase and by how much. The instruction forms include P9X and P7X.

Where an employee's tax code needs to be changed for the next tax year, and it is not covered by the general instruction forms P9X (or P7X), the Inland Revenue will issue a form P9T. This change of code will normally be issued in February, but **should not be used until the following 6 April**. For example a P9T issued in February 2005, for tax year 2005/06, will not apply until the first pay day on or after 6 April 2005.

We will look at these forms in more detail in Chapter 6.

When a new employee does not have a NI number, you usually need to complete either P46 or form CA6855. Once the number has been traced, NICO will send a form CA6856 confirming the number. This number should be entered in the payroll records.

Similarly an employee's NI category letter may change during the tax year. As an example, an employee may be NI category A, but reaches state retirement age during the year. At this point, the category letter will change to C. NI category letters can also change if the employee joins or leaves the firm's pension scheme. NI category letters are dealt with in detail in Chapter 8.

Both the Inland Revenue and NICO will send you letters from time to time, requesting details of employee's pay and deductions (eg if an ex-employee is claiming jobseeker's allowance). These letters must be answered promptly and usually within 28 days. Failure to do so will result in your organisation being fined.

Other deductions that **have** to be made from payroll, regardless of the employee's wishes, include the following.

- Student Loan Deductions (SLDs)
- Payments ordered by the Child Support Agency
- Payments under court order
- Payments under Council Tax order

Sometimes, statutory payments can be **added** to the payroll (called tax credits).

PART A   MAINTAINING EMPLOYEE RECORDS

3.2 Student Loan Deductions

The student loan legislation took effect from April 2000 and is only in respect of loans taken out after August 1998. The employer needs to take action only after a Start Notification is received from the Inland Revenue.

The Start Notification contains the following information.

- The name of the employee from whom SLDs need to be taken.
- When repayments are first due to begin.

When a Start Notification is received, tick box J on the deduction sheet (P11). The Inland Revenue provide deduction tables (SL3) to help the employer calculate the repayment. The deduction is a set amount depending on gross pay. All the employer has to do is look up the gross pay for the week or month in the tables and this will show the amount of SLD. This is entered into column 1j of the deduction sheet.

There is a box on the P45 (see Chapter 1) to indicate SLDs to a new employer. The new employer should continue making SLDs until a Stop Notification is received. A Stop Notification will be issued to tell the employer when to stop making SLDs, at least 42 days before cessation is to take effect.

The employer has to record the amount of SLDs on the following documents.

- The employee's payslip (see Chapter 10)
- The P11 deduction sheet (see Chapter 10)
- Year end documents (P60 and P35), dealt with at Level 3

Start and Stop Notifications are part of the payroll records and have to be kept for at least **three years** after the end of the tax year.

3.3 Tax credits

Tax credits have changed from 6 April 2003. Working Tax Credit (WTC) replaced Working Families Tax Credit and Disabled Person's Tax Credit.

WTC is normally paid through the payroll.

The Inland Revenue will send the employer a Start Notice (TC700), which includes the following details.

- Employee's details
- Starting date for WTC, at least 42 days after the date of the TC700
- Daily rate of WTC
- Daily rate table to enable the employer to calculate the amount to pay for each pay period.

Enter the details of tax credits in box M at the top of form P11 deduction sheet.

The employer has to pay WTC until a Stop Notice (TC702) is received. This usually gives 42 days' notice. In an emergency, less than 42 days' notice may be given, using Emergency Stop Notice (TC703).

WTC has to be recorded on the following documents.

- The employee's payslip (see chapter 10)
- The P11 deduction sheet (column 9) (see Chapter 5)
- Year end documents (NVQ Level 3)

Remember that the Start and Stop Notices form part of the payroll records and need to be kept for **at least three years** after the end of the tax year.

3.4 Child Support Agency

The Child Support Agency (CSA) administers the system of child maintenance. The CSA issues a leaflet called *Advice for Employers*, which can be downloaded from the CSA website (www.csa.gov.uk/newcsaweb/leaflets.asp).

The CSA gathers information about parents' income, in order to assess the amount an absent parent should pay towards the child's maintenance.

In some cases, the CSA will contact an employer direct.

(a) Payslips are not available.
(b) A parent asks the CSA to contact their employer for information.
(c) A parent does not co-operate in providing information.
(d) To get information in order to trace a parent.

Failure to provide information for child maintenance purposes is an offence under section 15 of the Child Support Act.

The CSA will issue a Deduction from Earnings Order (DEO) direct to an employer. The DEO will show the amount to be deducted and sent to the CSA. Failure to comply with a DEO is an offence under section 32(8) of the Child Support Act.

The order has to be noted in the payroll records and deductions made in accordance with the order. The mechanics of operating a DEO will form part of your Level 3 studies.

Remember to file the order with the payroll records.

3.5 Court orders

A court can make an Attachment of Earnings Order (AEO) in respect of an unpaid debt, eg maintenance debts.

Court issued AEOs can be priority or non-priority orders.

Priority

- Maintenance debts
- Court fines

Non-priority

- Judgement debts

A priority order will be deducted before a non-priority order. If there is insufficient pay to cover both types of orders, then it is usually the priority order that is deducted. The mechanics of dealing with an AEO form part of your Level 3 studies.

The employer is obliged to make the deductions under the AEO and to pay them to the court (or as directed in the order).

In the case of both DEOs and AEOs, it is essential that details are recorded accurately in the employee records. The orders must be kept with the employee records for future reference and any expiry date of the order(s) clearly noted.

PART A   MAINTAINING EMPLOYEE RECORDS

3.6 Council Tax orders

A council in England and Wales can recover arrears of Council Tax by applying to a Court for one of the following.

- Distraint of goods by a bailiff
- Distress warrant
- Attachment of earnings order (AEO)

In Scotland, the recovery is through the Sheriff's Courts. Procedure is for court orders, as in section 3.5 above.

For payroll purposes, you are interested in the AEO. Council Tax AEOs are issued by the charging authority in a set format which uses a set of percentage deduction tables.

Council Tax AEOs need to be carefully noted in the payroll records and the deduction tables correctly applied.

3.7 Discrepancies

In the case of any queries or discrepancies, the issuing authority must be contacted to clarify the matter.

4 Non-statutory deductions

All **non-statutory** deductions are **voluntary** and should only be made with the written agreement of the employee. Under the Employment Rights Act 1996, employees have the right not to suffer unauthorised deductions.

Common non-statutory deductions include the following.

- Pension contributions
- Trade Union subscriptions
- Charity contributions, eg GAYE (Give As You Earn)
- Financial institutions eg Sharesave, FSAVCs

In all cases, the employee's **written, signed consent** to the deduction(s) should be kept with the employee records. The record should clearly show the amount of the deduction and the expiry date of the agreement (if applicable).

4.1 Pension contributions

An **occupational pension scheme** is set up by an **employer** to provide **employees** with a **pension**.

Where a company has a pension scheme to which employees **contribute**, the payroll department will:

Step 1   Deduct pension contributions from the employees' pay

Step 2   Maintain records of those contributions

Step 3   Report them to the pension fund administrators

4.1.1 Occupational pension types

Occupational pension schemes come in two varieties.

(a) **Money purchase schemes.** These are **defined contribution schemes** (ie you contribute a set amount, and see what you can get for it).

(b) **Final salary schemes.** These guarantee to give a pension of a fraction of final salary for every year's service. It is common for this fraction to be 1/60th of final salary for every year of service, so that if you had served 20 years, your annual pension would be 20/60ths of final salary. A final salary scheme is a **defined benefit scheme** (the level of contributions is fixed by the benefits, which are defined in advance).

Most company pension schemes used to be final salary schemes. However, these are usually more expensive and complex for the employer and so money purchase schemes are increasingly common.

This difference is important for NIC purposes. We will look at this in detail in Chapter 9.

4.1.2 Types of contribution

As well as the employer's and employee's basic contributions laid down in the pension scheme, employees can make **extra contributions** to the funds for their retirement.

Pension contributions attract tax relief, but there are limits to the relief offered. An employee contributing to an occupational pension scheme is allowed to **contribute 15% of his or her earnings from employment** (salary and benefits) and get tax relief, subject to the earnings cap of £102,000 (in 2004/05). Therefore the maximum total of contributions for 2004/05 is £15,300 (15% × £102,000).

There are two types of **extra contributions**.

- Additional voluntary contributions (AVCs)
- Free-standing additional voluntary contributions (FSAVCs)

For the purposes of setting up the employee's payroll records, all you need to know is that there are three types of contribution (basic, AVC, FSAVC) and that separate records need to be kept of all three. Of course, no deductions can be made without the **written consent** of the employee, usually by means of a **signed mandate**. Basic contributions and AVCs will be paid to the pension fund, but FSAVCs are usually paid to an outside financial institution.

We will look at pension contributions in more detail in Chapter 10.

Activity 2.1

Brenda Thackeray has expressed interest in joining the company pension scheme. The head of Human Resources, Janet Dimmock, tells you that Brenda is eligible to join the scheme and will do so from next pay day. Janet follows this up with a memo signed by herself. Do you have sufficient authority to make the pension deductions?

Activity 2.2

Brenda gives you a signed letter authorising you to make 5% deductions from her pay. However, the usual contribution laid down by the pension scheme rules is 3%. What do you do?

Activity 2.3

The managing director wants to pay 15% of his salary into the pension scheme. How much can he get tax relief on, if his annual salary is:

(a) £100,000
(b) £110,000

Assume the rates for tax year 2004/05 apply.

4.2 Trade Union subscriptions

Trade Union contributions are often deducted from earnings. There are special requirements for **authorising** such deductions, as unions are no longer allowed to operate a 'closed shop' and so union membership must be **voluntary**.

The employee will need to sign a mandate authorising payroll to deduct the contributions from his or her pay.

This is known as the 'check off' system. Under this system, the employer may legally deduct trade union contributions provided the employee has given written consent and has not withdrawn his or her consent. If the contributions increase, the employer has to notify the employee in advance, but **does not need a revised consent form**. It is up to the employee to withdraw consent if he or she does not want to pay the new rate. This is an exception to the general rule that changes in deductions from pay need to be authorised by the employee.

The payroll department will need to keep records of all contributions and pay them to the appropriate trade union.

4.3 Give As You Earn

Also known as **GAYE**, this is sometimes referred to as **payroll giving**. It is entirely voluntary, so an employee can never be required to join a GAYE scheme.

In a GAYE scheme, an employee is allowed to set aside any amount without limit of his or her gross salary for charitable donations.

As the scheme is voluntary, no deductions can be made unless the employee signs a written instruction to do so. The detailed working of the scheme is covered in Chapter 10.

4.4 Sharesave

Some employers arrange Savings Schemes, which allow employees to buy shares in the employing company at a discounted price after a certain period.

Payments are made out of **net pay.** Records must be kept of the deductions made and paid over to the savings institution (eg a building society).

Activity 2.4

You are the payroll officer of Hope & Glory Ltd. One of your employees, John Taylor, has decided to leave the trade union and gives you a signed form telling you to stop making contributions with immediate effect. You comply with this order.

Two months later, the trade union contacts you querying the fact that it has received no payments on behalf of John Taylor. What do you do?

Activity 2.5

John Taylor comes to see you, saying that he never left the trade union and why haven't you paid his contributions. What do you do?

PART A   MAINTAINING EMPLOYEE RECORDS

Key learning points

- ☑ Statutory deductions have to be made regardless of the wishes of the employee.
  - PAYE tax
  - NICs
  - Student loan deductions
  - Child Support Agency orders
  - Court orders

- ☑ Communications from statutory authorities have to be replied to, regardless of normal confidentiality rules.

- ☑ Confidentiality applies by ensuring external agency enquiries are not common knowledge. Do not leave these enquiries lying around.

- ☑ Tax credits are additions to pay.

- ☑ Non statutory deductions can only be made with the written authority of the employee.
  - Pension contributions
  - Trade Union subscriptions
  - Charity contributions (GAYE)
  - Sharesave

Quick quiz

1. You receive a P6(T) from the Inland Revenue. When must the change of coding be used?
2. Does the Child Support Agency have the right to contact the employer direct for information?
3. What are the three steps to follow for pension contributions?
4. For 2004/05, what is the earnings cap?

Answers to quick quiz

1. From the next pay day after receipt, unless otherwise notified by the Inland Revenue (eg a second P6(T) is received before the first can be put into use).
2. Yes, even if the employee has not authorised this.
3. **Step 1** Deduct pension contributions from employee's pay
   Step 2 Maintain records of the contributions
   Step 3 Report the contributions to the pension fund administrators.
4. The earnings cap is £102,000 for 2004/05.

Activity checklist

This checklist shows which performance criteria, range statement or knowledge and understanding point is covered by each activity in this chapter. Tick off each activity as you complete it.

Activity

2.1	☐	This activity covers performance criteria 71.2.A and 71.2.C.
2.2	☐	This activity covers performance criteria 71.2.A, 71.2.C and 71.2.D.
2.3	☐	This activity covers performance criteria 71.2.A and 71.2.B (statutory requirements concerning tax relief on pension contributions).
2.4	☐	This activity covers performance criteria 71.2.A, 71.2.C and 71.2.D; also knowledge and understanding points 6 and 8.
2.5	☐	This activity covers performance criteria 71.2.A and 71.2.D; also knowledge and understanding points 8 and 11.

PART A MAINTAINING EMPLOYEE RECORDS

chapter 3

Recording permanent payroll variations

Contents

1 The problem
2 The solution
3 Payroll processing
4 Authorisation
5 Permanent variations
6 Filing and storage

Performance criteria

71.3.A Evaluate all data relating to permanent variations for accuracy and reasonableness
71.3.B Check all data and documentation received for proper authorisation
71.3.C Identify and resolve all discrepancies directly or by reference to the appropriate person
71.3.D Process permanent variations accurately and in a timely manner

Range statement

1 Permanent variations: changes of grade; changes of employment status; variation in voluntary deductions; changes to pay rates for fixed and variable pay; changes in personal details
2 Authorisation: authorised signatory list; authority from the employee; organisational instructions

Knowledge and understanding

2 Employment Rights legislation (Elements 71.1, 71.2 & 71.3)
6 Procedures for keeping data confidential and secure (Elements 71.1, 71.2 & 71.3)
8 Who to refer discrepancies to (Elements 71.1, 71.2 & 71.3)
9 How to record and store data (Element 71.1, 71.2 & 71.3)

PART A MAINTAINING EMPLOYEE RECORDS

Knowledge and understanding (continued)
11 Signatories and authorisations (Elements 71.1, 71.2 and 71.3)
12 Timescales and schedules for updating, presenting and despatching data (Elements 71.1, 71.2 & 71.3)
13 Information flows within the organisation (Elements 71.1, 71.2 & 71.3)

> **Signpost**
> In this element, the emphasis is on **processing** changes, not working out the pay (see Chapter 4) or managing the payroll (Level 3). Here the payroll clerk needs to check authorisation and put the change onto the system.

1 The problem

Payroll data is never constant. Some changes are temporary (eg overtime varies from week to week, some weeks there may be no overtime at all). Other changes are permanent (eg a promotion, a salary increase). How can the payroll clerk be sure that these changes are entered correctly in the records?

2 The solution

The key to dealing with all changes, but particularly permanent payroll changes, is that of **authorisation**. The payroll data is not altered until the change is properly authorised.

3 Payroll processing

The process of recording and calculating pay is known as **payroll processing** or **payroll accounting.** The main requirements of payroll processing are: **accuracy**, **timeliness** and **security**.

As a payroll officer, you probably do not consider yourself as part of the **government's tax collecting system**. However, as we shall see in more detail later, this is effectively what you are.

3.1 Employer's legal responsibilities to collect PAYE

If the Inland Revenue suspects an employer of any irregularities or deficiencies in processing, then Inland Revenue inspectors can arrange for a **PAYE Audit**, which is a detailed examination of an employer's payroll records. **Fines** can be severe.

The employer's duties are as follows.

- To **operate the PAYE system** for all who come within its scope.
- To **prepare** the necessary **records**.
- To pay the Income Tax and National Insurance collected from employees to the Inland Revenue **every month** (in most cases).
- To let the Inland Revenue **inspect the records**.

- To submit **end of year returns**.
- To give employees **payslips** detailing tax and NIC deducted and to give them an **annual statement (P60)**.
- To **keep for a minimum of three years** after the end of a tax year, the **records** relating to that year (as PAYE Audits can go back over six years, employers are wise to keep records for much longer than this minimum).

We will be looking at income tax and National Insurance in detail in later chapters of this Text.

3.2 Accuracy

One of the great problems in payroll work is the need for a high level of accuracy, particularly avoiding silly mistakes such as adding a number instead of subtracting it, using the wrong tables or making an arithmetical error. **This is equally a problem when sitting payroll assessments.**

These steps will increase the chances of your realising that a number is wrong.

Step 1   Perform **credibility checks**, such as using mental arithmetic on approximate numbers (see below).

Step 2   Never see payroll as a mechanical process of producing numbers. **Always understand what the numbers represent**.

3.2.1 Mental arithmetic

For all calculations, perform a **mental arithmetic check** to see approximately what you expect the number to be. If someone is paid £293.64 a month for seven months, the total pay to date is just below £2,100 (seven times £300). So if you get the answer £1,425.47 you have made a mistake. You may have pressed the wrong button on the calculator, or the calculator may still contain a number from an earlier calculation. When you get £2,055.48, you know the answer is reasonable.

This applies equally to fractions. If you are calculating 7/12 of an annual salary, you expect the answer to be a bit more than half the annual salary.

For **multiplication of two numbers**, another useful check is to multiply the last two digits of the numbers and check that the last digit of that answer is the last digit in the multiplication result. The calculation in the example above of 7 × £293.64 is probably beyond the mental arithmetic capability of most of us. But we can easily check that 7 × 4 = 28, so the last digit of the answer must be 8.

3.2.2 Consistency

The basis of the PAYE income tax system is that **allowances are spread evenly throughout the year**. This means that if the **gross pay** (see Part B) and **tax code** (see Chapter 6) do not change from month to month, **neither should the net pay**. There will be differences in pence because of **roundings** but if, when you are preparing a monthly payslip for the same gross pay and tax code, the figure is a few pounds different from previously, you have made a mistake.

PART A   MAINTAINING EMPLOYEE RECORDS

Activity 3.1

Try the following tests to see how well you can cope with performing credibility checks.

(a) You have calculated Biff's weekly wages as a counter assistant in a fast food shop as £1,089.67. Likely or unlikely?

(b) Kipper's gross pay for the year to date is £6,211.67 according to your working schedules. It is Month 3 (ie Kipper has received three months' salary). You know that Kipper's annual salary is in the region of £25,000. Is this gross pay to date a likely figure? (*Do not* use a calculator!)

(c) Molly's salary this month includes a large overtime payment because she has been working in the evenings and at weekends getting ready for the annual audit. If she has done 30 hours of overtime at £15 per hour, and her annual salary is £18,000, does it seem reasonable that her gross pay this month has been calculated as £1,545?

3.2.3 Variations

Accuracy and **reasonableness** must also be applied to variations. For example, if you receive a notification that Hugh, a storesman, has been promoted to stores foreman, this is reasonable. However, a promotion to chief accountant is not. You would need to double check the instruction.

Similarly if a change of salary form states that Hugh's salary was £18,000 and is now £19,000, you need to check that £18,000 was the old salary. If Hugh was receiving £18,500, you need to check whether his new salary is still £19,000 or should it be £19,500.

3.3 Timeliness

Payroll has to be prepared according to **strict deadlines**. If an employee is to be paid on the 30th of the month, the pay must be in her bank account on that date. Any changes to pay rates must be included on the first available payroll.

Tax deductions have to be paid over to the Inland Revenue by a due date. If payment is delayed, the employer may have to pay interest. This topic will be dealt with in detail at Level 3.

Similarly other deductions, such as pension contributions, need to be paid over to third parties regularly and on time. Otherwise the employee's entitlements could be affected.

3.4 Security

Payroll information must be kept secure and confidential. Unauthorised persons must not be able to access payroll information. **Security and confidentiality** are key elements of payroll processing and can not be overemphasised.

4 Authorisation

All variations to the payroll must be properly authorised. This applies not just to permanent variations, but also to temporary variations such as overtime.

Permanent variations, such as salary increases, will usually be authorised by senior managers and it is likely that you will be familiar with their signatures.

However, overtime is likely to be authorised by line managers. The employee's record or contract of employment will let you know if this employee is entitled to overtime payments. How do you know if the actual overtime figure has been correctly authorised?

Most large organisations will have a **list of authorised signatories** for each department. This is a list of people authorised to approve changes to the payroll, together with a specimen signature. The list should also indicate whether the person can authorise permanent and/or temporary changes, eg can they authorise promotions or only overtime.

As payroll officer, you should be given a copy of this list so that you can check that variations are correctly authorised.

If the promotion, for example, is not correctly authorised, you need to bring this to your supervisor's or manager's attention. Do not assume that there is a new line manager, the employee could be trying to obtain an increased salary fraudulently.

5 Permanent variations

You need to know about the following types of **permanent** variation.

(a) Changes of grade (promotion, demotion)
(b) Changes of employment status (temporary to/from permanent)
(c) Contract terms (hours, pay rate)
(d) Payment terms (payment method, payment frequency)
(e) Voluntary deductions (pension contributions, subscriptions, GAYE, SAYE)
(f) Changes to pay rates for fixed and variable pay (basic salary, shift allowance, overtime rates)
(g) Personal circumstances (marital status, name, address, bank/building society details)

In all cases you need to review the changes for **accuracy** and **reasonableness** and that they are properly **authorised**.

5.1 Changes of grade

Notification of changes in grade will normally be sent to payroll by the personnel or human resources department. Alternatively, for senior management, details could come direct from the Board or Chief Executive of the organisation. Other sources of authorisation are unlikely and should be treated with care

Promotions normally involve pay increases and may include better terms or conditions (eg more holiday entitlement, expense allowances, etc)

Demotions not only mean loss of status. There could be a salary decrease and loss of conditions (eg less holiday entitlement, no more expense allowances, etc).

A change of grade may involve promotion or demotion, however it could simply mean a 'sideways' movement within the organisation, eg moving from production to stores. This will mean a change in department and so a change in the authorised signatory for temporary variations, as well as a change in the department code.

All cases of change of grade mean that the payroll officer needs to make careful note of the changes needed in the payroll records.

5.2 Changes of employment status

Someone who has been employed on a temporary, casual basis (eg as a student or a weekend filing clerk) may become part of the permanent staff. When this happens, you should follow the rules for starters, as if the employee was a new employee.

The reason for this is to ensure that your records are completely up to date. The new permanent employee may have a form P45 from another employer, particularly if he or she had only worked casually for your organisation. In addition, the P46 procedures should be carried out if there is no P45, in order to satisfy employment law.

Similarly when an employee on the permanent staff becomes temporary, it is recommended that you check if the leaving procedures need to be applied and a P45 issued. For example, a manager is retiring, but will be coming back one day a month to ensure a smooth handover.

In these circumstances, you would treat the manager as leaving on his retirement. The casual, temporary work for one day a month would be treated as a new employment and form P46 completed accordingly, since he is likely to receive a pension.

5.3 Contract terms

Any changes to contract terms (eg working hours and new rates of pay) will mean an amended contract of employment.

A copy of the amended terms should be given to the employee by the personnel department and a further copy should be sent to payroll, once the employee has accepted the revised terms.

Any affect on payroll should be clearly noted on your employee records. For example, an employee may have a 40 hour week and a pay rate of £20 per hour. Under revised terms, the basic week may be 35 hours but the pay rate increases to £25 per hour. Under the original terms, basic pay was £800 pw (£20 × 40) and under the revised terms £875 pw (£25 × 35).

5.4 Payment terms

Your organisation may decide to stop paying wages by cheque and instead pay all employees by BACS. It will fall to the payroll department to obtain details of all employees' bank or building society accounts.

The problem here is to ensure confidentiality and that payments are made to the correct person. You may be asked to design a form to be sent to each employee requesting bank and building society details that is then signed by each employee.

Under no circumstances should a form be sent round asking all employees to fill in their details and then pass on to the next employee. Not only does this compromise employee confidentiality, but could lead to fraud if an employee's details are altered.

Activity 3.2

Design a form requesting an employee's bank/building society account details.

Payment frequency changes are less of a problem. For example, your organisation may decide to change from 4-weekly pay to monthly pay. Here you would only need to ensure that the correct pay was calculated, particularly on the first pay day after the changeover.

5.5 Voluntary deductions

We have already looked at these in some detail in Chapter 2. Be sure that you have authorisation **signed by the employee** for all voluntary deductions. Remember that employment rights legislation projects employees from unauthorised deductions.

5.6 Changes to pay rates

A shift allowance may become payable to an employee because he starts to work a different shift (eg transfers from day to night).

Any shift allowances must be properly authorised by the employee's superior or by personnel.

Basic salary changes usually come from personnel. However, salary changes for senior staff and directors may come from the Board.

Overtime rates may be changed. This could be an organisational change, so that overtime will be paid at 1.5 times basic pay instead of 1.25 times. Alternatively it could be change for a single employee only, perhaps related to a change of grade. Note that a promotion could lead to loss of overtime, as manager grades do not usually get overtime. As usual all changes need to be properly authorised, usually by personnel/human resources.

5.7 Personal circumstances

Any changes in personal circumstances must be verified. This is particularly true in a large organisation where you do not know the majority of employees by sight.

Your organisation should have a standard form for recording changes in personal circumstances. The employee should be asked to fill in one of these forms and to sign it.

If the change is of marital status, it is a good idea to ask to see the marriage certificate. This is particularly true if the marriage also causes a change of name (eg if the wife adopts her husband's surname).

PART A   MAINTAINING EMPLOYEE RECORDS

Any changes of name **must** be supported by evidence, eg marriage certificate, copy of change of name by deed poll.

5.8 Retention of documents

All documents supporting variations are part of the payroll records and need to be kept for a minimum of three years after the end of the tax year.

Activity 3.3

You are the payroll clerk of John Jones Ltd. You receive the following change of status form from an employee, Michael Jeffries. What changes do you make to the records.

CHANGE OF STATUS FORM

Name: Michael Jeffries

Address: 77 Main Road, Harper's Ferry, Oxon

Payroll number: 123456

Details of change: From 1 July 20X7, I will be moving to 81 Water Lane, Harper's Ferry, Oxon

Signature ....   Date ....

Activity 3.4

You receive a form from personnel stating that Michael Jeffries has been promoted and that his salary will increase from £20,500 to £24,000 with effect from 1 August 20X7. The form has been correctly authorised. However, when you check the payroll records, you find Michael Jeffries' current salary is £24,500 pa. What do you do?

6 Filing and storage

We looked at filing in Chapter 1, where we considered in what order employee records should be filed (usually alphabetically or in staff number order).

Some employee records will be quite bulky with copy contracts of employment, authorisations for payrises, expenses claims, etc.

Therefore you may want to divide up the information between **permanent** files and **temporary** files.

A **permanent** file will contain the employee record and contract of employment, details of pay increases and voluntary deductions. In short, all the information that you will want to keep referring to while the employee remains with your organisation.

The **temporary** file can be used to file information just needed for a tax year, eg copy payslips, deduction cards, expense information. At the end of the tax year (once the period end procedures have been completed), these files can go into **storage**. Remember that PAYE files have to be kept for at least three years after the end of the tax year and preferably longer.

PART A   MAINTAINING EMPLOYEE RECORDS

Key learning points

- ☑ Your employer has a legal responsibility to collect PAYE.
- ☑ Payroll processing must be accurate, timely and secure.
- ☑ All variations must be authorised and an authorised signatories list enables you to check that the authorisation is valid.
- ☑ Permanent variations include the following.
    - Status
    - Nature of employment
    - Contract terms
    - Payment terms
    - Voluntary deductions
    - Changes to pay rates
    - Personal circumstances
- ☑ Permanent variations need to be accurately recorded on the employee record.
- ☑ Filing can be split between permanent and temporary (or current) files. However, even temporary files need to be stored for at least three years after the end of the tax year.

Quick quiz

1. What are the employer's legal duties regarding PAYE?
2. How can you quickly check the accuracy of payroll calculations?
3. A payrise notification is received from a line manager. How do you check that this is correct?
4. An employee has decided to join the pension scheme. What information do you need before you deduct contributions from his salary?
5. Why is it advisable to keep PAYE records longer than the statutory period of three years after the end of the tax year?

Answers to quick quiz

1.
   - To operate the PAYE system for all who come within its scope
   - To prepare the necessary records
   - To send the tax and NICs collected from the employees to the Inland Revenue every month
   - To let the Inland Revenue inspect the records
   - To submit end of year returns
   - To give employees payslips and an annual statement (P60)
   - To keep records for at least three years after the end of the tax year.

2.
   - Perform checks for reasonableness (mental arithmetic)
   - Check on consistency from one pay period to another

3. A payrise notification should normally come from personnel or senior management. You should check that the line manager is on the list of authorised signatures. If not, then perhaps a fraud is being attempted. If he is on the list, it is likely that he can only authorise overtime. In either case, you should present the facts to your manager for his decision.

4. A form signed by the employee, authorising you to deduct pension contributions from his salary. The form should also state the contribution rate (eg 5%) and whether any AVC's (additional voluntary contributions - see Chapter 2) are to be paid.

5. PAYE audits can go back six years after the end of the current tax year. Therefore records should be kept for at least this length of time.

PART A MAINTAINING EMPLOYEE RECORDS

Activity checklist

This checklist shows which performance criteria, range statement or knowledge and understanding point is covered by each activity in this chapter. Tick off each activity as you complete it.

Activity

3.1	☐	This activity covers performance criterion 71.3.A.
3.2	☐	This activity covers performance criterion 71.3.B.
3.3	☐	This activity covers performance criterion 71.3.B and 71.3.C.
3.4	☐	This activity covers performance criterion 71.3.A, 71.3.B and 71.3.C.

PART B

Ascertaining gross pay

chapter 4

Calculation of gross pay

Contents

1. The problem
2. The solution
3. What is gross pay?
4. Calculating basic pay
5. Overtime and other allowances
6. Bonus payments, incentives and commissions
7. Holidays and holiday pay
8. Advances of pay
9. Backpay
10. Reimbursed expenses
11. Basic pay errors
12. Documentation and information flows
13. Computerised payroll processing
14. Computer bureaux

Performance criteria

72.1.A Evaluate all data relating to **temporary variations** for accuracy and reasonableness

72.1.B Ensure **documentation** relating to temporary variations is verified for authorisation

72.1.C Identify employees where input is required in order to ensure payment and ensure relevant details are correctly inserted

72.1.D Check rates for overtime payments against agreed scales for each type of employee affected

72.1.E Identify all payments in respect of their tax, National Insurance and pension liability

72.1.F Take appropriate action to apply the terms of statutory and organisational payment schemes, where variations arise as a result of sickness, maternity leave or holidays

72.1.G Identify and resolve all discrepancies directly or by reference to the appropriate person

72.1.H Process temporary payments and deductions accurately

72.1.I File source **documentation** in accordance with statutory and organisational requirements and in a logical and orderly manner

72.1.J Maintain security and confidentiality of sensitive information at all times

PART B   ASCERTAINING GROSS PAY

Range

1   Temporary variations: payments; deductions
2   Documentation: authorised time recording documentation; authorised instructions from management

Knowledge and understanding

1   Positive payrolls (those payrolls where employees will not get paid unless input is submitted such as hourly paid employees)
2   Negative payrolls (those payrolls where employees will be paid automatically unless action is taken to prevent payment such as salaried employees)
3   Employment Rights legislation (Elements 72.1 & 72.2)
10 The security and confidentiality of information (Elements 72.1 & 72.2)
12 The resolution of discrepancies (Elements 72.1 & 72.2)
13 How to record and store data (Elements 72.1 & 72.2)
15 Signatories and authorisations (Elements 72.1 & 72.2)
16 Timescales and schedules for updating, presenting and despatching data (Elements 72.1 & 72.2)
17 Information flows within the organisation (Elements 72.1 & 72.2)

Signpost

This chapter concentrates on processing temporary variations and the calculation of gross pay. However, statutory payments (tax credits, SSP, SMP, SAP, SPP) are subject to a separate element in the Standards and are dealt with in Chapter 5.

1 The problem

When calculating gross pay, what information is needed? Is the payroll positive or negative? How are temporary variations, eg overtime, dealt with?

2 The solution

As always, the key to calculating gross pay is **authorisation**. The payroll clerk has to enter authorised information in order to calculate gross pay. A key document is the **contract of employment**.

The payroll may be **positive**. This means that positive input has to be made or the employee will not get paid. An example of this is the hourly paid worker or one on piecework rates.

The payroll may also be **negative**. This means that the employee is automatically paid unless the payment is stopped. An example of this is the salaried employee, where a set amount is paid every month.

In **both types**, the payroll clerk needs to ensure that only the correct amounts are paid.

In this chapter, we will study the calculation of gross pay and how to deal with temporary variations.

3 What is gross pay?

At the end of every payroll period we have to work out the **gross pay** for each employee.

> **Important!**
>
> **Gross pay** is what an employee **earns**. It is not what the employee actually receives in cash or by transfer to the bank account (**net pay**). Here is an example which shows how the two can differ.
>
> | | £ | Chapter(s) in this text |
> |---|---:|---|
> | **Basic pay** etc: what your work has earned for you | 1,000 | 4 |
> | Other pay (includes statutory sick pay, statutory maternity pay, holiday pay, etc) | 200 | 4, 5 |
> | GROSS PAY | 1,200 | |
> | Less: deductions | | |
> | Income Tax | (140) | 6, 7 |
> | National Insurance | (100) | 8, 9 |
> | Other deductions (eg pension scheme) | (50) | 10 |
> | **Net pay**: what you take home or what goes into your bank account | 910 | 11 |

There are several ways to calculate an employee's **basic pay**.

- A **fixed rate** per week, month, etc
- On an **hourly rate**
- On a **performance basis** (eg per unit of output)

In addition there are other ways of remunerating employees.

- **Overtime** means that employees receive more for working extra hours.
- **Bonus schemes** are used so that employees can benefit from improvements in the overall performance of all or part of the employer's business.
- **Shift pay** and **unsocial hours** where employees work some of their basic hours during antisocial shifts, or very soon after a previous shift.
- **Commission** is calculated usually as a percentage of the sales achieved by an employee.

In each case, the contract of employment will show how the basic pay is calculated.

In addition, you need to identify whether a payment is taxable, subject to NICs or is pensionable. We will look at these in detail later in this text.

Activity 4.1

Think about the places you have worked. How were you paid there - did you get overtime, bonuses, commission or just a set rate for the job? What about your colleagues - and your classmates, friends, family? Ask some of them (tactfully) about how their basic pay is made up. This will help you start to get a 'feel' for real life payroll work (note the results in your payroll portfolio).

PART B   ASCERTAINING GROSS PAY

3.1 Contracts of employment

When you started work for your employer, you were probably given a piece of paper to sign which laid down the terms and conditions of your employment, eg that you work from Mondays to Fridays from 9.30 am to 5.30 pm, that you will have an hour for lunch, what your annual salary will be, and so on.

If you did, then you signed a **contract of employment**.

A **contract of employment** is a legally binding agreement between two parties that one will work for the other.

- The agreement can be oral or written.
- The agreement can be written in a single document.
- The agreement's terms can be contained in a number of documents.

The following **written particulars** have to be provided by the employer to the employee within eight weeks of starting work. This is required by the Employment Rights Act 1996.

- The **names** of the employer and employee.
- **Place of work** and address of employer
- The employee's **job title** (eg Payroll Assistant), or a **description of duties**.
- **When** the employee is to commence employment.
- **How much** the employee is to be paid (hourly rate, annual salary, overtime).
- **When** the employee is to be paid (eg weekly or monthly).
- **Normal working hours** (including requirement for **overtime**).
- **Holiday entitlement**, including any entitlement to accrued holiday pay.
- **Notice period** for leaving.
- **Pension scheme details**, if any.
- **Disciplinary and grievance procedures**.
- **Injury and sickness terms**.
- **Duration of contract** if for a fixed period (eg two years) or that the position is **permanent**.

Activity 4.2

Do you have a written contract of employment? Does it cover all the points listed above? What problems can you foresee might arise if an employer does not issue an employee with a contract of employment?

> **Important!**
>
> It would be useful for your studies if you assembled as many samples of payroll documentation as you can in a portfolio. You could start with your contract of employment!

3.2 The contract of employment and payroll processing

As far as a payroll officer is concerned, the part of the contract which is most important is that dealing with **payment of wages**. However other details need to be noted on the employee records, eg duration of contract.

Is a person entitled to be paid at all? There may be circumstances where this can be a matter of dispute. For example, if you stay on an hour or so after the working hours specified in the contract to finish off some task, are you legally entitled to overtime payment?

- Yes, if both you **and** your employer regarded it as paid work.
- No, if one of you didn't.

How much should a person be paid? The contract of employment should state the **basis** for the pay of employees, and can be used as evidence in an industrial tribunal. This does not mean that the exact amount an employee will receive is specified in advance.

The employment contract does not guarantee a **fair wage**: the court generally cannot rectify a bad bargain. The contract of employment does not have to mention **pay reviews**, or **pay increases**.

From 1 April 1999 all employees aged over 18 must be paid at least the **National Minimum Wage.** There is a very limited exception: some apprentices over 18 are excluded. **Agency** and **homeworkers** are included, even though some of these are not counted as employees for PAYE and National Insurance purposes.

The following hourly rates apply.

- **Development rate for workers aged 18 – 21 (inclusive)**

From 1 April 1999	£3.00
From 1 June 2000	£3.20
From 1 October 2001	£3.50
From 1 October 2002	£3.60
From 1 October 2003	£3.80
From 1 October 2004	£4.10

  This rate also applies to workers aged 22 and above during their first six months in a new job, with a new employer and who are receiving accredited training.

- **Adult rate for workers aged 22 and over**

From 1 April 1999	£3.60
From 1 October 2000	£3.70
From 1 October 2001	£4.10
From 1 October 2002	£4.20
From 1 October 2003	£4.50
From 1 October 2004	£4.85

- **Young workers' rate for 16 and 17 year olds**

From 1 October 2004	£3.00

  Note that apprentices aged 16 and 17 are exempt from this rate.

Employers must keep **adequate records** to show that they are paying all workers **at least** the relevant minimum wage. These records may be more than required for PAYE and National Insurance purposes. The **Inland Revenue** enforces the legislation, by inspection of the employer's records.

PART B   ASCERTAINING GROSS PAY

4 Calculating basic pay

Basic pay is usually the largest element in the gross pay calculation.

Basic pay is the rate for the job, and is what you expect to receive for a normal period's work, irrespective of overtime and any other additions (temporary variations).

4.1 Fixed salary

Your contract of employment states that you are paid, say, £9,000 per annum.

In order to calculate the salary for the pay period, you need to consult the contract of employment to see how this should be allocated. However, the following examples show the usual ways of calculating pay based on an annual salary.

Weekly pay is usually calculated by dividing the annual salary by 52 weeks. In our example of £9,000 pa, this is £173.08 per week (£9,000/52).

4-weekly pay is usually calculated by dividing the annual salary by 13 (52/4). In our example of £9,000 pa, this is £692.31 per four week period (£9,000/13).

Monthly pay is usually calculated by dividing the annual salary by 12. In our example of £9,000 pa this is £750.00 per month (£9,000/12).

Example: Fixed salary

Your contract of employment states that you are to receive an annual salary of £9,000. You join on 2 January 2004. You are told that the first three months of your employment are a probationary period, and that if it is satisfactory then from 1 April 2004 your annual salary will increase by 10%. You are informed on 20 May 2004 that on 1 July 2004 everyone in the company is to receive a pay rise: yours works out at £600 per year (in addition to the 10% rise you have already received).

Tasks

(a)   What will be your basic pay for:

    (i)   January 2004?
    (ii)   May 2004?
    (iii)   July 2004?

(b)   (i)   At 31 December 2004, how much basic pay would you have received since 2 January 2004?

       (ii)   Assuming no further rises, how much basic pay could you expect to receive in the 12 months to 31 March 2005?

Solution

(a) (i) January 2004: £9,000/12 = £750

(ii) £9,000 + (10% × £9,000) = £9,900, your new annual salary.

So, May 2004: £9,900/12 = £825

(iii) £9,900 + £600 is £10,500, your latest annual salary.

So, July 2004: £10,500/12 = £875

(b) (i) Remember that an annual salary is effectively a rate per month.

January to March	£750 per month for 3 months
April to June	£825 per month for 3 months
July to December	£875 per month for 6 months

You have therefore earned (3 × £750) + (3 × £825) + (6 × £875) which comes to a total of £9,975 in the 12 months to 31 December 2004.

(ii) In the 12 months to 31 March 2005:

2004

April to June	£825 per month for 3 months
July to December	£875 per month for 6 months

2005

January to March	£875 per month for 3 months

So, in total you will have received three months at £825, and nine months at £875, giving a total of £10,350.

4.1.1 Calculating payments for part of a period

Sometimes you will need to calculate basic salary for less than a complete pay period, for example for starters and leavers.

Example: Leaver

Assume that you are going to leave on 16 August 2004. Taking the salary details in the example above, what pay is due for the period 1 to 16 August 2004?

Solution

The calculation depends on the detail in your contract of employment. This usually calculates daily pay on one of three bases.

(a) A full year of 365 days
(b) Excluding weekends to give 261 working days (365 − (2 × 52))
(c) Excluding weekends and public holidays to give 253 working days (261 − 8)

PART B ASCERTAINING GROSS PAY

(In the UK, public holidays are 1 January, Good Friday, Easter Monday, May Day, Late Spring Bank Holiday, August Bank Holiday, Christmas Day and Boxing Day.)

However you must be aware that the contract could stipulate different ways (eg excluding annual holidays), and so you must use whatever basis is stated in the contract, or in your assessment.

Using the bases above, the pay for 1 to 16 August 2004 would be:

(a)   £10,500/365 × 16 = £460.27
(b)   £10,500/261 × 11 = £442.53
(c)   £10,500/253 × 11 = £456.52

In case (a), based on 365 days, the daily rate is multiplied by 16 (the number of days employed in August). In cases (b) and (c), based on working days, the daily rate is multiplied by 11 (the number of weekdays between 1 and 16 August 2004).

4.2 Hourly rate

Some workers get paid a **rate per hour**. If you work 40 hours per week at £5 per hour then your basic pay will be £200 per week. Remember that the National Minimum Wage legislation is in force (see Section 3.2).

The payroll system will need to **accurately record** the hours worked, eg clock cards, in order to be able to calculate gross pay.

Another point to note is that the law now requires most workers to work no more than 48 hours per week on average. See Section 5.1 of this chapter for more information about this.

4.3 Piecework

In a **piecework** scheme, wages are calculated by the formula:

Wages = Units produced × Rate of pay per unit

For example, an employee is paid £2 for each unit produced

Weekly production	Pay
Units	£
40	80
50	100
60	120
70	140

As output increases, the wage increases.

It is common for pieceworkers to be offered a **guaranteed minimum wage**, so that they do not suffer loss of earnings when production is low through no fault of their own. However, if this is too high, there isn't much incentive to increase **productivity**.

Example: Piecework

Penny Newman is 17 years old. She is paid 50p for each towel she weaves, but she is guaranteed a minimum wage of £60 for a 40 hour week. In a series of four weeks, ending 30 July 2004, she makes 100, 120, 140 and 160 towels. What was her pay each week?

Solution

Did you remember that Penny is too young to receive the National Minimum Wage? Remember that the young workers' rate only applies from 1 October 2004. We will be looking at how the NMW affects pieceworkers later in this section.

Week	Output Units	Calculated pay £	Actual pay £
1	100 × 50p	50	60 (minimum wage)
2	120 × 50p	60	60
3	140 × 50p	70	70
4	160 × 50p	80	80

There is no incentive to Penny to produce more output unless she can exceed 120 towels in a week.

4.3.1 Piecework hours

Sometimes an employee may make several different types of product, some of which take longer than others. In this case, it is not possible to add up the units for payment purposes; instead a **standard time allowance** is given for each unit to arrive at a total of **piecework hours** for payment.

Example: Piecework hours

An employee is paid £4 per piecework hour produced. In a 40 hour week the employee produces the following output:

	Piecework time allowed per unit Hours
15 units of product X	0.5
20 units of product Y	2.0

What is the employee's pay for the week?

Solution

Piecework hours produced:

		Hours
Product X	15 × 0.5 hours	7.5
Product Y	20 × 2.0 hours	40.0
Total piecework hours		47.5

Therefore the employee's pay = 47.5 × £4 = £190 for the week.

PART B ASCERTAINING GROSS PAY

4.3.2 Differential piecework

Differential piecework schemes offer an incentive to employees to increase their output by paying higher rates for increased levels of production.

Example: Differential piecework

A business may offer its pieceworkers the following pay structure.

Up to 80 units per week, rate of pay per unit = £1.00
80 to 90 units per week, rate of pay per unit = £1.20
Above 90 units per week, rate of pay per unit = £1.30

Employers must make it clear whether they intend to pay the increased rate on **all** units produced, or on the **extra output only**.

4.3.3 Piecework and the National Minimum Wage

Piecework rates (like all other pay rates) are also affected by **the National Minimum Wage (NMW)**. The complication is that the NMW is an hourly rate.

The regulations on the NMW require the employer first of all to distinguish between:

- Employees on piecework rate who have to work **hours fixed by the employer**; and
- Employees on piecework rate whose **hours are not set by the employer**.

Note. For the purposes of these examples, we will use a NMW rate of £4.85 per hour for adults and £4.10 for 18 – 21, the rates from 1 October 2004.

Example: Piecework and fixed hours

John is paid 50p for every satisfactory widget he produces. He must clock in at 9 o'clock and not clock off before 5 o'clock. He has an hour for lunch. This week he produced 250 widgets. What is his basic pay for the week? He worked a full 35 hour week. John is 52 years old.

Solution

The National Minimum Wage is £4.85 per hour for those over 21. John must therefore be paid at least 35 × £4.85 = £169.75. His piecework earnings are only 250 × 50p = £125, so he must be paid £169.75. Next week, if he makes 400 widgets in a 35 hour week, his piecework earnings will be 400 × 50p = £200, which is higher than the NMW and so his basic pay will be £200.

Example: Piecework and no fixed hours

Shanice receives £1 for every mug she paints which meets her employer's quality control criteria. She works from home and has no fixed hours. In one week she delivers 100 satisfactory mugs. How much should her basic pay be?

Solution

Shanice's piecework earnings are £100. However, the NMW regulations require the employer to identify the number of hours to be worked. This can be done in two ways.

- Pay the NMW for every hour worked.
- Come to a 'fair estimate' agreement of hours to be worked.

In order to pay the **NMW for every hour worked**, which is the simpler option, Shanice will have to keep a record of the hours she has worked. Her employer will have to pay her at least the NMW for every hour worked, regardless of output. So if, for example, she recorded that she spent 40 hours producing 100 mugs, then she should be paid 40 × £4.85 = £194, instead of the piecework rate of 100 × £1 = £100. However, if she only took 20 hours to produce 100 mugs then the piecework rate would be paid, as it exceeds the NMW (20 × £4.85 = £97.00).

You can see that **employers** are likely to prefer a system where they have some control over how many hours a worker takes. Very slow workers or workers who falsify their timesheets will earn much more on the NMW rate than on a low piecework rate.

The **'fair estimate' agreement of hours to be worked** is a written agreement with the worker.

- Sets out a **fair estimate** of the number of hours that the **employee** is likely to spend on doing the work in the pay period.

- Requires the employee to **keep a record of hours worked** in the pay period, which must be given to the employer as soon as possible after the pay period.

- Be supported by a **contract** giving the employee the right to be paid an agreed piecerate for each item produced in the pay period.

So Shanice and her employer may agree that 15 minutes is a reasonable time allowance for each mug. She is therefore expected to work 25 hours a week to produce 100 mugs. Her basic pay for producing 100 mugs should be £121.25 (25 × £4.85), as the piecerate of £100 is lower. Her record of actual hours worked may be used to review the fair estimate agreement as necessary.

This is a summary of the regulations on the 'fair estimate' agreement. The full provisions are more complex and if you have to deal with pieceworkers or other employees whose pay is not clearly above the NMW, you should get a copy of the detailed guidance on the NMW from the Department of Trade and Industry, website (www.dti.gov.uk/er).

PART B   ASCERTAINING GROSS PAY

Activity 4.3

Calculate the basic pay for each of the following employees.

(a) Tom is paid £10 for every motor claims form he fills out on behalf of clients. In week 1 he prepared 24 claims forms in 40 hours. He is 50 years old.

(b) Asif has a guaranteed minimum wage of £145 per 35 hour week. In week 1 he produced 200 processed films. He is paid 60p per film. He is 19 years old.

(c) Louise assembles umbrellas and bags. She is assumed to take 30 minutes to make one umbrella and 20 minutes to make a bag. In week 1 she produced 20 umbrellas and 60 bags. Her rate per piecework hour is £4.95.

(d) Patrick is on a differential piecework scheme. He gets £2 for each umbrella produced, up to 30 umbrellas. From 31 to 40 umbrellas, the rate is £2.50. Above 40 umbrellas, the rate is £3. In week 1 he produced 82 umbrellas. He is 70 years old and works a 40 hour week.

From a payroll point of view, piecework schemes can cause problems as hours and/or output have to be **recorded and authorised** before payment can be made.

5 Overtime and other allowances

5.1 Overtime

Overtime pay is payment for work done in excess of an employee's basic hours. Some overtime is contractual and some voluntary. Contractual overtime is usually a set number of hours and forms part of an employee's basic pay.

You must remember that **contractual overtime** hours form part of the contract of employment, whereas **variable overtime** needs to be **verified** (to timesheets, clock cards, etc) and **authorised** (check to authorised signatories list).

Generally speaking, overtime is paid at a **higher rate** per hour than basic hours. The employment contract of an hourly paid worker might specify that overtime is paid at time and a half. This means that the worker is paid half as much again for an hour of overtime as for an hour of at basic time.

For example, if a basic hour is paid at £4, how much is an hour of overtime at time and a half?

The payment per hour of overtime is £4 + (£4 × 50%) = £6 per hour, or £4 × 1.5 = £6.

Sometimes there are a **number of overtime rates** offered. For example, a contract may specify the following rates.

- 40 hours at a **basic rate** of £4 per hour.
- The first ten hours overtime at **time and a half** (ie £6) per hour.
- Overtime above ten hours at **double time** (basic rate times two, ie £8 per hour).

Example: Overtime

Marguerite Yourcenar works in a library. She is paid on an hourly basis. Her basic rate for the first 35 hours she normally works a week is £6 per hour. She has five hours contractual overtime at time and a quarter. Any more overtime hours worked are paid at time and a half.

In the week ended 3 August 20X2 she worked a total of 47 hours.

Task

For the week ended 3 August 20X2 calculate Marguerite Yourcenar's basic pay and the overtime payments she receives, showing how each is made up.

Solution

		£
Basic pay is	35 hours at £6 per hour	210.00
Contractual overtime	5 hours at [£6 × 1.25 =] £7.50 per hour	37.50
Variable overtime	7 hours at [£6 × 1.50 =] £9.00 per hour	63.00
Total	47 hours	310.50

Some miscellaneous points to note about overtime.

- **Compulsory overtime.** Some workers do not have to work overtime. For other workers, the requirement to work overtime may be included in the contract.

- There may be a **separate overtime rate** for working at **weekends** or **Bank Holidays**, or for **unsocial hours**, or for **working particular shifts**.

- In some cases, the overtime rate may be **less than for basic hours**, but the **National Minimum Wage should still apply**.

- In many cases, workers regard overtime as an **integral part of their weekly wage**. Cutting overtime hours means a drop in the standard of living.

- The law states that the maximum number of hours per week for most employees is **48 hours,** averaged over 17 weeks. However, the employee may **choose to agree** to work more than this. The **Working Time Regulations** are very complex and your employer should study them carefully if you have employees regularly working over 48 hours per week.

5.1.1 Overtime payments for employees on fixed annual salaries

Marguerite Yourcenar was an hourly-paid worker, and the calculation of her overtime payment was a fairly simple matter of assessing how many hours she worked at basic rate, and how many at each of the two overtime rates.

Overtime payments can also be paid to staff who receive a fixed annual salary divided into equal monthly instalments. The hourly rate for overtime would be set out in the **employment contract**.

PART B   ASCERTAINING GROSS PAY

It may, of course, be the employer's policy not to pay overtime at all. Staff might be expected to work extra hours as a matter of **professionalism** when the situation requires. This is particularly true of more senior employees and managers.

Activity 4.4

Nigel and Paula work in the accounts department of Chawley Ltd. Nigel is paid a monthly salary of £910. He is contracted to work for 35 hours each week and gets paid at time and a half for any hours worked over and above this. Work on Bank Holidays or at weekends is paid at double time.

Paula has an annual salary of £30,000 and is expected to work at least 35 hours per week. She often works more than this but is not usually entitled to overtime. However, in January and February she worked extremely long hours preparing the annual accounts and getting ready for the annual audit. In recognition of this extra work, she is to be given an extra one month's salary in addition to her normal salary for February. You have received a memo from personnel to this effect.

In February Nigel worked as follows.

Day	Date	Hours	Date	Hours	Date	Hours	Date	Hours
Monday	1	7	8	9	15	7	22	8
Tuesday	2	8	9	8	16	7	23	9
Wednesday	3	9	10	8	17	7	24	7
Thursday	4	7	11	8	18	8	25	7
Friday	5	7	12	9	19	8	26	7
Saturday	6	5	13	7	20	0	27	0
Sunday	7	0	14	3	21	0	28	0

His timesheet has been signed by his manager and so you are authorised to pay overtime based on this timesheet.

What is the overtime to be paid to Nigel and Paula in February? (There were no Bank Holidays in February.)

Tutorial note. You will need to calculate Nigel's hourly rate - assume his annual salary, although paid monthly, actually represents basic pay for 52 weeks × 35 hours.

5.2 Other allowances

The contract of employment may also allow additional payments.

- **Shift pay** – additional payments for night shifts, for example
- **Unsocial hours** – additional payments for long hours
- **Stand-by payments** – additional payments for staying at home but being available to work at short notice (also known as 'on-call')

In all cases, these amounts should only be paid if **authorised**, eg contract of employment, timesheet signed by authorised signatory.

Example: Authorisation

You have been asked to make unsocial hours payments to two employees: B Jones and M Smith. You check the contracts of employment and find that only B Jones should receive these payments. The payment to B Jones has been authorised by R Close, who is not on the authorised signatory list. The payment to M Smith has been signed by J Grant, who is an authorised signatory. Do you make any payments?

Solution

No payments should be made until the discrepancies have been resolved.

B Jones is entitled to unsocial hours, but the payment has not been correctly authorised. Return the paper work to his department to be properly authorised.

M Smith does not appear to be entitled to unsocial hours payments, but the payment has been correctly authorised. Have his terms and conditions changed? Refer the matter to your supervisor and, perhaps, personnel.

5.3 Temporary promotions

In some employments, particularly teaching, an employee may receive a temporary promotion, with increased salary, for covering for an absent colleague.

Written details of the temporary promotion should come from personnel/human resources. The dates of commencement and cessation need to be carefully noted. Payroll must ensure that the increased salary is only paid during the **authorised period**.

This is particularly important with **negative payrolls**, where the employee continues to be paid unless action is taken.

6 Bonus payments, incentives and commissions

6.1 Bonuses and incentives

Offering a **bonus** or an **incentive** is intended to motivate employees to work harder to reach or exceed some target (normally of sales or productivity). How it is calculated and to whom it is awarded tends to vary greatly from organisation to organisation.

Example: Bonus schemes

Carrot and Stick plc is a company which uses a variety of bonus and incentive schemes to motivate its employees.

- **Senior managers** get a bonus based on how well the company is doing as a whole. Their bonus is a **percentage of their salary**. For example if the company increases its annual profits by 1% then they get a bonus of 1% of their salary, paid on 30 June.

PART B ASCERTAINING GROSS PAY

- The **sales force**, which has 100 members, gets a bonus paid on the last day of the month, based on the **value of sales per month**. If the value of sales (excluding VAT) is over £35 million in a particular month, 1% of the excess is divided equally between the members of the sales force.

- **Factory workers** receive a bonus based on **productivity**. They normally produce 1,000 units an hour. If they produce more than this amount per hour, then they get a payment of 10p per worker for every extra unit produced.

- **All employees get a one-off bonus**, in addition to any others, of £30 if Carrot and Stick plc's **profits** in the year to 31 March exceed £127.5 million. This is paid on 30 June.

- **Weekly paid workers** are given an incentive of an extra one week's wages if their **performance at work** has merited them a Grade 1 assessment by their bosses for four consecutive weeks.

In the year ended 31 March 20X2, Carrot and Stick plc had made a profit of £130 million, a 3% increase over the year ended 31 March 20X1. This was £5 million more than expected. In the week ended 30 June 20X2 the factory staff produced 100 units per hour more than usual. In the month of June 20X2, the value of sales excluding VAT was £36 million.

Task

Calculate the bonuses which will be paid in the following cases.

(a) David Eadwood, Senior Manager Finance Department, earns £30,000 per year. What bonuses will he receive on 30 June 20X2 for the year?

(b) Bernadette Singh, Assistant Sales Executive, earns £18,000 per year. What bonuses does she receive on 30 June 20X2?

(c) Stan Takhanov is a factory worker with a Grade 1 assessment in the four weeks ended 30 June 20X2. He earns £150 per week. What bonuses will he receive in the four weeks ended 30 June 20X2?

Solution

(a) *David Eadwood*

	£
£30,000 × 3% profit increase is	900
One-off bonus	30
Total bonuses received on 30 June 20X2	930

(b) *Bernadette Singh*

	£
Sales bonus [£36m – £35m ×1%]/100 sales staff	100
One-off bonus	30
Total bonuses received on 30 June 20X2	130

(c) *Stan Takhanov*

	£
Grade 1 assessment bonus (ie one week's wage)	150
Extra production bonus 100 units at 10p each	10
One-off bonus	30
Total bonuses in the four weeks ended 30 June 20X2	190

Tutorial note. Remember that bonuses should only be paid when authorised. For a complex scheme, such as this one, each payment must be carefully checked to underlying records and authorised, eg notification from personnel, contract of employment, productions records signed by line manager.

6.2 Commission

Commission is a payment made on **percentage** for doing something - in the context of payroll, for selling a business's goods or services, for example.

Commission may form the bulk of an employee's earnings, especially if that employee works in a selling capacity (whereas bonus payments are often considered as 'extras' to basic salary).

Some jobs are advertised with a **low basic wage** to provide a bedrock of security, with promises of much more being earned as commission for increases in sales. An example of this type of job is one where employees sell advertising space in a newspaper.

Other jobs, for example as advertised by some life assurance companies, offer a basic salary for the first three months or so, to give the new recruit time to settle down and build up contacts. Then the basic salary is withdrawn and the recruit is paid on a **commission only basis**.

The **National Minimum Wage** is payable so employees' hours must be monitored.

Some examples of commission are given below.

- **Straight percentage of all sales** (eg 10% on sales of £1,000 and you get £100; for £100,000 you get £10,000).
- **Sliding scale**, so that more valuable contracts earn greater commission (eg on contracts up to £5,000, a 5% commission; on contracts over £5,000 a 7.5% commission).
- **Increase with the total volume of sales**. For example, total sales up to £100,000 earn 5% commission: if the target is exceeded, then 7.5% commission is paid on the excess.

The **timing of commission payments** is more than a matter of simple administrative convenience.

Sales often have to be approved by a **credit controller** whose job it is to ensure that customers are creditworthy and so will pay up.

Sometimes the sales commission is only paid to the salesperson **when the customer pays** for goods or services received.

For these reasons, commission is often paid **in arrears**. For example:

	Salary	*Commission*
January	Jan	Dec's sales
February	Feb	Jan's sales
March	Mar	Feb's sales

PART B   ASCERTAINING GROSS PAY

Example: Commission

The Bubbly Shampoo Company Ltd sells crates of Bubbly Shampoo for £100 each. The company employs two sales staff. Each is paid commission on a different basis.

(a) Michele Thuselah receives no commission on the first hundred crates of Bubbly Shampoo she sells a week, 10% commission on crates sold in excess of 100 up to 200, 15% on crates sold in excess of 200 up to 300 and 20% on crates sold in excess of 300. She receives her commission at the end of the month in which the sale is made. She receives a basic annual salary of £9,000 per year which is paid monthly.

(b) Jerry Bowen receives a basic salary of £4,500 per year (paid monthly) and a straight 7.5% commission on all he sells.

From 2 August 20X2, Michele sold 120 crates in the first week, 340 in the second week, 30 in the third week and 95 in the fourth week. She made no sales on 1 August, 30 August or 31 August. In the same month, Jerry sold 500 crates.

Task

What are Michele's and Jerry's earnings, both basic salary and commission, for August 20X2?

Solution

Michele

		£
Basic salary £9,000/12		750.00
Commission:		
Week 1	20 × £100 × 10%	200.00
Week 2	100 × £100 × 10%	1,000.00
	100 × £100 × 15%	1,500.00
	40 × £100 × 20%	800.00
Week 3	None, as fewer than 100 crates sold	
Week 4	None, as fewer than 100 crates sold	
Total earnings for August 20X2		4,250.00

Jerry

	£
Basic salary £4,500/12	375.00
Commission 500 × £100 × 7.5%	3,750.00
Total earnings for August 20X2	4,125.00

7 Holidays and holiday pay

Holiday pay is an amount which is owed to an employee in respect of the agreed number of days a year when he or she is not actually working.

The payroll department has to decide **if and when to pay** holiday pay, and **how to record** it. This is determined largely by **the way in which an employee is paid**.

7.1 Holiday entitlement

Holiday entitlement will usually be mentioned in the contract of employment. Holidays generally need to be approved in advance on a holiday request form signed by the employee's manager. A copy should be sent to payroll to confirm that the employee is entitled to be paid during holiday absence.

Under the ruling in the *BECTU case*, the European Court of Justice in 2001 confirmed that all employees are entitled to a **minimum** of four weeks paid leave annually and that there is no qualifying period. Previously employees in the UK had to have 13 qualifying weeks before becoming entitled to paid annual leave.

DTI guidelines state that, while there is no qualifying period, the four weeks paid annual leave can include Bank Holidays (if the employee is not otherwise paid for these) and accrues at the rate of one-twelfth of the annual entitlement per month worked.

A week's holiday is based on the employee's normal working week. So if an employee normally works 5 days per week, the annual leave is 20 days (4 × 5). While if the normal working week is 3 days, the annual leave is 12 days (4 × 3). So an employee with 12 days annual leave, accrues holiday at the rate of 1 day per month; while an employee with 20 days leave accrues 1.67 days per month. If the calculation results in part days, it is rounded up to the nearest half day.

In 2002, the Employment Appeal Tribunal ruled, in *Maconnachie v Leisure Leagues UK Ltd*, that accrued holiday pay should be calculated on a daily rate based on the number of **working days** in a year.

7.1.1 Jury service

Any employee on jury service should still receive full pay. However, you will need some sort of written confirmation, eg a copy of the letter calling the employee to jury service. In the case of long trials (eg a month or more), there may be a cut in pay. If in doubt, consult your supervisor.

7.1.2 Unpaid leave

An employee may take unpaid leave, eg parental leave or compassionate leave. In this case, you should receive a notice from personnel or the manager stating that the employee is taking unpaid leave. Some sick employees, or those on maternity leave, may be unpaid; but this is dealt with in Chapter 5.

7.2 Holiday pay for employees paid monthly

The **simplest way** of paying holiday pay is to **treat it as part of a normal monthly payment**. Such arrangements are so common that in most cases holiday pay is paid as monthly salary. It is often not even separately identified as holiday pay.

PART B ASCERTAINING GROSS PAY

Example: Monthly salary by direct credit to bank account

Sonny Tan earns an annual salary of £12,000 a year, and this is paid by direct transfer to his bank account at the end of every month. He has 20 days of annual leave a year. How should holiday pay be given to him?

Solution

Sonny Tan's basic monthly salary works out at £1,000, which includes any time taken on holiday. So, if he goes on holiday for the last week in July and the first week in August, he will receive five days' holiday pay in July and five in August. For each of those two months, he has five days' less basic pay, so he will continue to receive £1,000.

7.3 Holiday pay for employees paid weekly

It is usual for weekly paid employees to be paid one week in arrears, that is for the week they have just worked. If they are going on holiday, however, they may want some money for their holiday paid in advance. Weekly paid employees might therefore ask for an **advance of holiday pay**, in which case you will be paying them for the week just gone (which they have worked), and a week (or more) ahead (when they will be on holiday).

As far as **PAYE** goes, the total amount of holiday pay should be shown on the P11 on the line for the **last week** of holiday, so that the employee does not pay too much tax on his advance.

What about **National Insurance**? Holiday pay is part of gross pay for NIC purposes. There is no problem if the employee is paid **monthly** in arrears. There are problems if a worker is paid **weekly** and wants holiday pay **in advance**.

There are **two methods** of calculating the NICs payable.

Method A

If an employee is given 2 weeks holiday pay in advance on the same day that he or she is given the normal weekly wage in arrears, **calculate and record the NICs as if the holiday pay had been paid on the normal pay days**.

Method B

Step 1   Add together the earnings and holiday pay in one sum.
Step 2   Find the weekly average, and base the NICs on the weekly average.

Method B can be used for employees paid weekly, fortnightly or four-weekly but *not* monthly.

If there is a difference between the amounts calculated under Methods A and B, you may **choose the method that gives the lower NIC payable**.

7.3.1 What happens if holiday pay overlaps into the next tax year?

If the payment covers a period when **NIC rates** have changed (eg a new tax year) you can use either of the following methods.

- **Split the sum** into separate weekly amounts and do the calculation that way, using the appropriate table.
- Aggregate them together and use the **rate at the date of payment**.

4: CALCULATION OF GROSS PAY

For **PAYE purposes**, treat the payment as though all the earnings relate to the **old tax year** – ie as if paid in month 12, say, or week 52, but record on P11 when paid.

7.4 Accrued holiday pay for leavers

DTI guidelines state that, with regard to the minimum four weeks annual leave, any accrued leave must be paid when an employee leaves. In this case, the calculation is not rounded, so if an employee is entitled to 2.4 days he is paid for 2.4 days.

Example: Salaried leaver

Each employee of Timon Ltd gets 20 days annual leave a year, which must be taken in the calendar year to which it applies, from January to December inclusive. It is not possible to carry forward leave from one year to the next. Salaries are paid in equal monthly instalments.

William joins on 1 January 20X3, at an annual salary of £12,000, but leaves Timon Ltd's employment after six months. He has not taken any of his leave entitlement. He does not work on Bank Holidays or weekends.

Solution

William is entitled to 6/12 × 20 days leave = 10 days. As he has not taken any leave, he is entitled to 10 days holiday pay.

Holiday pay, as weekends and Bank Holidays are excluded:

10/253 × £12,000 = £474.31

This amount is added to his final salary payment. The PAYE implications are explained in Chapter 6.

Activity 4.5

Find out as much as you can about the arrangements for holiday pay in your organisation. You could usefully collect together specimen documents.

For example, are you allowed to carry unused holiday or annual leave into the next leave year? Or can you ask for it to be paid to you? Who keeps track of leave entitlements and leave taken? It could be the Payroll Department – or is it Personnel? How is holiday pay rate calculated: excluding weekends and Bank Holidays?

PART B   ASCERTAINING GROSS PAY

7.5 Holiday Pay Schemes in the Construction Industry

The construction industry has a holiday pay scheme, where a group of employers pay into an independent holiday pay fund.

The amount paid by the employer is allocated to all employees in the scheme, usually by credits or stamps.

When the employee goes on holiday, he receives a payment from the scheme.

If the scheme is **unapproved** by the Revenue, then the cost of the scheme is treated as gross pay for tax purposes at the time of **allocation**. Therefore, there is no PAYE due when the holiday pay is actually paid.

If the scheme is **approved**, the cost of scheme is tax free to the employee. However, when the holiday payment under an approved scheme is made to the employee, it is taxable. If paid by the employer, it goes on the deduction card. If paid by the fund, the fund will deduct basic rate tax and give the employee a certificate of tax deducted.

However, **for NIC purposes**, the cost of the scheme **and** the holiday pay (whether paid by the employer or direct by the fund) is **exempt from NICs**.

7.6 Other holiday pay schemes

Some schemes allow employees to voluntarily set aside amounts from their pay during the year to be paid at a certain time eg Christmas, or the annual holiday.

In this case, the amount set aside is included in gross pay for tax and NIC purposes **at the time it is set aside**. Therefore, the deduction is made from net pay.

Another alternative form of scheme is a **holiday credit scheme**. In this case money is set aside every pay day to be paid in a lump sum when the employees take their holidays.

For tax and NIC purposes, these amounts are included in gross pay **when deducted** if the employees can be paid the money at any time. In other words, the deduction is taken out of net pay.

If the employees can only be paid the money when they go on holiday, the deduction is excluded from gross pay. However the payment from the scheme is included in gross pay at the **date of payment**.

8 Advances of pay

8.1 Salary advances

Most employees are paid in arrears. Weekly paid employees are paid at the end of the week for the work done that week. Salaried employees work for a month without payment, and they get paid at the end of the month for the work they have done in the month.

An advance of salary is normally **an advance of net pay**. It is like a short term loan. The advance is 'repaid' by the employee on the next pay day, or whenever is stipulated in the arrangement. As it is an advance of net pay, there are no PAYE or NI effects when it is advanced, unless there are special circumstances (beyond the scope of NVQ/SVQ Level 2).

Example: Advances of pay

Philip Overty starts work for Softouch Ltd on 1 June 2004, at a gross salary of £600 per month. He is given an advance of £150 on his first day of work, which is to be deducted from the money he receives at the end of his first month.

So, the pay computation on his first pay day might look like this:

	£
Gross pay	600
Less: Tax – say	(38)
NI – say	(31)
Net pay	531
Less: advance already paid	(150)
Total paid on pay day	381

An employee may join his new firm too late in the month to be included in that period's payroll. In this case, he may receive a pay advance of a lump sum or the amount he would have received if he had been on the payroll.

Example: Joiner

Philip Overty joined Softouch Ltd on 26 May 2004, too late to be included on the May payroll. Normally the pay for the period from 26 to 31 May is included with the June salary. However, Philip needs a pay advance and his manager arranges for this to be equal to the gross pay due from 26 to 31 May. Philip's contract states that for part pay periods, a day's pay is 1/260 of annual salary and that only working days are taken into account. Philip's normal working week is Monday to Friday. His salary is £600 per month gross.

Solution

For the period from 26 to 31 May 2004, there are 3 working days. Therefore Philip will receive a pay advance of 3/260 × £600 × 12 = £83.07.

8.2 Repayment of loans

Sometimes employers will make a loan to an employee, for example to buy an annual season ticket.

A proper contract needs to be drawn up stating the amount of the loan, the period over which it is to be repaid and the repayment amount. In addition, it should contain a section authorising payroll to deduct the loan repayments from the employee's salary. This authority must be signed by the **employee**.

Once payroll receive the employee's authority, deductions are made from **net pay**.

Activity 4.6

Sean Masters borrows £3,000 from Browbeaten Ltd. He verbally agrees to make repayments of £250 over the course of the next 12 months. You are the payroll clerk of Browbeaten Ltd. Can you deduct the repayments from Sean's salary?

PART B ASCERTAINING GROSS PAY

Activity 4.7

Sean Masters has delivered the outstanding paperwork from activity 4.6. His gross salary for this month is £750. Tax and NIC total £200. What amount is paid to Sean?

Tutorial note. Refer to the illustration of gross and net pay of the beginning of Section 3 if you are not sure how to proceed.

9 Backpay

Backpay is an extra amount paid to an employee at a particular point in time to make up for the fact that, for a particular period, he or she has been underpaid.

If you receive a payrise in September 20X2, backdated to 1 April 20X2, then the amount of **backpay** is the increase due from 1 April. Where a pay increase is the result of long negotiations, then the pay rise for the year in question may only be agreed several months into the year. The backdated pay can be paid in **one lump sum**, or it might be **spread** over a number of instalments.

Example: Backpay

Ernest Sutton employs Robert Cratchitt at £14,000 basic per annum, payable in equal instalments at the end of each month. Cratchitt has been working for Sutton since 1 January 20X2. In November 20X2, Sutton gives Cratchitt a pay rise of 10% per year, backdated to be effective from 1 April. Cratchitt otherwise receives nothing but his basic salary.

Tasks

(a) How much will Cratchitt have earned in the 12 months to 31 December 20X2?

(b) Assuming that the backpay is to be paid to Cratchitt on 30 November 20X2 with his salary, calculate the gross pay which will appear on Cratchitt's salary slip on 30 November 20X2.

Solution

(a)
	£
Pay from 1 January – 31 March = £14,000 × 3/12	3,500
Pay from 1 April – 31 December = £14,000 + 10% = £15,400 × 9/12	11,550
Cratchitt's total earnings in the year ended 31 December 20X2	15,050

(b) Cratchitt's November gross pay comprises:

	£
Pay for November £15,400/12	1,283.33
Backpay for the seven months from April to October 20X2 is (£15,400 – £14,000) × 7/12	816.67
Total gross pay on 30 November 20X2	2,100.00

When calculating backpay remember:

Step 1   **Check that the employee was employed throughout the backpay period**. If Robert Cratchitt had started work on 1 June 20X2, he would only have been entitled to five months' backpay in his November payslip (£583.33).

Step 2   **Check which elements of gross pay the backpay affects**. Does a 10% pay rise apply to overtime rates?

Step 3   **Tax and National Insurance** on backpay is calculated at date of **payment**. Do not try to go back and recalculate the tax and National Insurance for previous periods. We shall look at this further in Chapters 6 and 8.

Activity 4.8

Big plc has an annual pay review date of 1 April. This year, however, union negotiations have taken a long time and the annual pay review for some workers was not finalised until November. The new rates will be backdated to 1 April.

Jemima Smith is one of these workers. She is currently on a basic salary of £1,200 per month. Her overtime claims in recent months have been as follows:

	Hours
June	18
July	15
August	16
September	25
October	10
November	21

Her overtime rate is £12 per hour. She started work at Big plc on 1 June. As a result of the pay review her new basic monthly salary will be £1,250 and her overtime rate will be £12.50 per hour. What is Jemima's gross pay in November?

10 Reimbursed expenses

10.1 Reimbursed expenses

An employee might incur **expenses** in the course of his or her duties as an employee.

- Professional subscriptions
- Entertaining a client
- Travel costs from the place of work to a client's location
- Reimbursement of hotel costs, if staying away overnight for business purposes

These expenses are often recorded on an **expense claim form**, which the employee should fill in at the end of every week or month, attaching invoices, receipts, etc wherever possible.

It is up to the employer to determine **which expenses are reimbursed** and which are not.

Payroll must keep accurate records of reimbursed expenses.

- If they are **legitimate business expenses**, then the employer may be able to recover the VAT on them.
- Some reimbursed expenses may be regarded as **taxable benefits** by the Inland Revenue, and may have **NICs** levied on them.

Expenses can be reimbursed in three ways.

- Through the **payroll system** on the payslip
- By a **separate cheque**
- By a **combination** of the above

The advantage of reimbursement through the payroll is that if **NICs** are payable, then these can be calculated along with NICs on pay.

10.2 What is an expense for tax and NICs?

When an employee has incurred expenses **wholly, exclusively and necessarily in the performance of his or her duties,** income tax does not have to be paid on the reimbursement. The law in this regard is strictly interpreted.

(a) Most reimbursed expenses have to be reported on a form called a **P11D** at the end of the tax year. Providing that they were incurred for business purposes, they can be **allowable** (the employee will not have to pay income tax). However, an employee might have to make a separate claim on his or her personal tax return, saying that the reimbursed expenses were incurred for business reasons only.

(b) Expense reimbursements do not generally appear on the deduction card. The Inland Revenue changes the employee's tax code to recover any amounts owing.

Forms P11D will form part of your NVQ/SVQ Level 3 studies.

For **NICs** the treatment is similar. **Reimbursed expenses do not count for NICs, providing the expenses were incurred for business purposes**. Expense reimbursements which relate to identifiable items of business expenditure are therefore not included in earnings, for NIC purposes.

10.3 Lump sums

Sometimes an employer may make lump sum payments each pay period, to cover an employee's expenses.

- To cover costs of using a personal vehicle for business purposes
- To provide accommodation
- For tools
- For protective clothing

In **most cases**, the Inland Revenue treats lump sum payments as additions to gross pay on which tax and NICs are payable. The reason being that lump sum payments are not directly related to an employee's actual expenses and so are not reimbursements.

4: CALCULATION OF GROSS PAY

11 Basic pay errors

We have seen that basic pay comprises various elements, such as basic salary, overtime, bonuses and commission. Any one can be a cause of **dispute**.

11.1 Salaried employees

Salaried employees normally receive a **pay review** once a year. An error in basic pay might be caused by an incorrect annual salary entered to the system, or confusion as to backpay. An employee might simply be confused as to what his pay should be.

Example: Error in basic salary

William Pitt is taken on as an employee at 1 October 20X2, on a salary of £20,000 pa initially, to rise to £24,000 from 1 January after he has successfully completed his probationary period. This is to last three months. You hear nothing from him or his boss until William contacts you on 31 January to enquire why his pay hasn't risen. There must be some mistake, he says, as his pay was to go up after three months. What do you do?

Solution

William might have a point. However, the payroll department should have received formal notification of the pay increase. There might have been a variety of reasons why you had heard nothing.

- His probationary period was being extended.
- His manager had forgotten all about it.
- The issue had got lost somewhere in personnel department.

In short, you should politely ask William:

- To talk to his manager about it; or
- To talk to personnel department about it.

You always have the option of paying the arrears next month.

11.2 Hourly paid employees

An hourly paid employee might question the following.

- The calculation of **hours worked**.
- The **rate** applied to his work.

As hourly paid workers are paid by the hour, it should be a relatively simple matter to go to the relevant **timesheet or clock card** to check the calculation. What could go wrong? Stop and think about this before reading on.

PART B ASCERTAINING GROSS PAY

Potential error	Comments
Illegibility	If it was completed by hand, there might have been a **simple clerical error** in reading the hours worked.
Number of hours worked	If the employee does not agree with the **total hours worked** he or she should be referred politely to the personnel department, and to his or her trade union officer, so that the matter can be resolved through the company's **disputes procedure.**
Rate applied	If the rate per hour is to be increased this should have been notified to you by the personnel department. • It may be that the employee was paid the wrong rate in error. In this case check with the **personnel department,** or the employee's file, for any changes. • There might be a misunderstanding as to what constitutes **overtime**. An employee might have taken a couple of hours off work to go, say, to a dental appointment. The absence is quite legitimate. If the employee made up the time, by working late, he or she might be expecting to be paid overtime rates. That expectation might be justified (if, for example, overtime rates are payable for day shift workers who work after 6pm, rather than for hours worked over a weekly minimum at standard rate). • The employee might have changed to a different **shift**, which commands a different rate and which no one has told you about.
Timing of overtime payments	The payroll department must receive **authorisation** before overtime can be paid - for instance, a supervisor or manager may have to countersign a timesheet.

Activity 4.9

On Friday afternoon two employees come to see you to complain that their weekly pay cheques are wrong.

(a) Natalie says that she worked 3 hours overtime on Tuesday evening and this was not included in her pay. You know that Natalie's supervisor was not at work this week. The company's rule is that all overtime must be authorised by supervisors by Wednesday lunchtime if it is to be included in gross pay for the current week.

(b) Percy complains that his supervisor told him that his hourly rate would be increased, but this has not happened. You check the information on Percy's payroll file and see that his last increase was nearly a year ago. No further changes have been notified to the payroll department.

What do you say to Natalie and Percy?

11.3 Recovery of overpayments

So far we have considered underpayments to employees. Suppose an employee is overpaid?

- An employee has gone part-time but the notice from personnel was not received by payroll.
- An error occurred in processing the pay, so too little tax and/or NIC has been deducted.

Employees have legal protection from unlawful deductions from wages. However, this protection does not extend to deductions to recover an earlier overpayment of wages. Therefore, the employer can recover overpayments of wages.

We will look at the question of underpayments of tax and NIC in detail in Chapter 10.

However, as a general rule, the employer is liable for any under deduction of tax, unless an order is made by the Inland Revenue to recover the under deduction direct from the employee.

For NIC, an employer can recover an underpayment of employee's NIC (subject to certain limits) within a tax year. However, once the end of a tax year is passed, the employer has to pay the underpayment.

12 Documentation and information flows

12.1 Personnel department

The following are the **main functions of the personnel department**.

- **Recruiting** and engaging employees.
- Setting up a **personnel file** with all necessary personal details for each new employee.
- **Updating** these personal files as required.
- **Passing information** to the payroll department as required (eg new employees' details, changes to pay rates, details of pay settlements, changes in pay policy such as when overtime will be paid).
- **Keeping records** of holidays taken, sickness records, progress of trainees and probationers, and so on.

12.2 Payroll department

The **payroll department** is concerned solely with payroll processing. Deciding the wage rate paid to employees, annual salary reviews and so forth, are not the payroll department's job. The payroll department usually has the following responsibilities.

- Calculation of gross pay.
- Calculation of tax, National Insurance and other deductions.
- Preparing payslips.
- Making appropriate returns to external agencies such as the Inland Revenue.
- Making up wages, or preparing data for Direct Credit (BACS).
- Distributing payslips.
- Preparing payroll statistics.

Note that **payroll documentation** is not necessarily the same as **personnel documentation**. The payroll department will obviously need information about employee hours, agreed salaries and so forth, but will not see documents relating to confidential personnel issues. If an employee is interviewed by his boss every year to discuss his performance, then the written record of the discussion will not reach the payroll department.

12.3 Accounts department

The **accounts department** and the **cashiers** are also involved in recording costs, drawing up cheques and bank transfers or making payments. The accounts department receives the payroll statistics prepared by payroll. In fact, because the payroll department is concerned with money, **it is likely to be controlled by the accounts department.**

12.4 Documentation for salaried employees

The personnel department has to tell the payroll department **how much** the employee is to be paid, and the **date** from which the rate of pay is effective. However a copy of the contract of employment can be useful for determining overtime rates and commission (where applicable).

The payroll department will subsequently receive instructions from the personnel department relating to **salary increases**, or other **alterations** to an employee's pay.

12.5 Hourly paid employees

There has to be a system in place for employees to record the hours they work. This system needs to be **easy to operate** and **easy to check**, so that errors are kept to a minimum. It should also be designed to make it very difficult for employees to record more hours than they have actually worked.

One common method is the **clock card**. Each employee has a card which is inserted into a **time recording clock** when they start and finish work (and when they **clock off** for lunch and **clock on** again after lunch).

At the end of each pay period, the records from the clock are used by the payroll department to calculate each employee's gross pay (including variable overtime). A specimen completed clock card is shown on the next page. (Note that only the unshaded areas would be completed by the clocking-on machine while the employee is in possession of the card. The lightly shaded areas would be completed in the payroll department.)

4: CALCULATION OF GROSS PAY

\multicolumn{6}{	c	}{CLOCK CARD}
Number: 07912				**Period:**	Week
Name: R Parsons				**Ending:**	29 June 20X1
Day	Time in	Time out	Total time Hrs mins	Basic time Hrs mins	Overtime Hrs mins
Mon 25	09.06	12.31	3.25		
	13.20	18.04	4.44		
			8.09	7.30	0.39
Tues 26	08.59	12.15	3.16		
	12.30	17.30	5.00		
			8.16	7.30	0.46
Wed 27	08.50	12.00	3.10		
	13.00	17.20	4.20		
			7.30	7.30	-
Thurs 28	09.02	12.30	3.28		
	12.45	18.30	5.45		
			9.13	7.30	1.43
Fri 29	09.00	12.00	3.00		
	12.42	17.50	5.08		
			8.08	7.30	0.38
TOTAL			41.16	37.30	3.46
Authorised					
PAID HOURS (round to nearest half hour)				37.50	4.00
RATES				£5.00	£7.50
AMOUNT				£187.50	£30.00
PAY FOR BREAKS					£25.00
TOTAL GROSS PAY					£242.50

Another common system uses **timesheets**, in conjunction with or separately from clock cards. Each employee fills in a timesheet (daily or weekly).

A timesheet is different from a clock card because as well as showing the total hours worked the employee has to record how much time was spent on each different job.

This information is used by the accounts department to build up **costing records** showing how much each job has cost to carry out. The **labour** element will be added to the other costs incurred, such as raw materials. The timesheet overleaf reflects the data from R Parsons' clock card.

PART B ASCERTAINING GROSS PAY

\multicolumn{7}{c	}{TIMESHEET}
\multicolumn{4}{l	}{Number: 07912 Name: R Parsons}			\multicolumn{2}{l	}{Period: Week Ending: 29 June 20X1}
Date	Job number/ Cost code	Start time Hrs mins	Breaks Hrs mins	Finish time Hrs mins	Total time exc. breaks Hrs mins	Standard rate £	Cost £
25/6	149/2/74	09.06	0.49	18.04	8.09	5.50*	107.25
26/6	"	08.59	0.15	17.30	8.16		
27/6	"	08.50	–	12.00	3.10		
					19.50**		
27/6	–	–	1.00	-			
27/6	149/3/07	13.00	–	17.20	4.20	5.50*	99.00
28/6	"	09.02	0.15	18.30	9.13		
29/6	"	09.00	0.42	14.00	4.18		
					18.00**		
"	150/2/91	14.00	-	17.50	3.50	5.50*	22.00
					4.00**		
Authorised by:			3.00		41.50		228.25

* The standard rate has been set by management accountants
** Hours are rounded to the nearest half an hour for costing as well

The timesheet will be filled in by the employee, for hours worked on each job (job code) or area of work (cost code). Idle time, lunch breaks etc, should also be recorded. The cost of the hours worked will be entered at a later stage in the accounting department (these have been filled in above).

12.6 Timesheets and salaried staff

You might think there is little point in salaried staff filling a detailed timesheet about what they do every hour of the day, as they are paid a flat rate every month. However, in many enterprises they are required to do so. There are several reasons for this.

- Payroll data are used to create **management information** about product costs, and hence profitability.
- The timesheet information may be needed to **generate the revenue** the enterprise receives (see below).
- Timesheets are used to record hours spent, and so support claims for **overtime** when this is paid to salaried staff.

This is also true of course for **hourly paid workers**. The only difference is that the hourly paid worker's basic pay is calculated from the timesheet, so it has an additional function to all those mentioned above.

4: CALCULATION OF GROSS PAY

Below is the type of timesheet which can be found in large firms in the **service sector** of the economy: examples include solicitors, accountants and management consultants. These are chiefly in the business of **selling the time and expertise of their employees to clients**. So if an employee spends an hour on work for a particular client, the client will be billed for one hour of the employee's time.

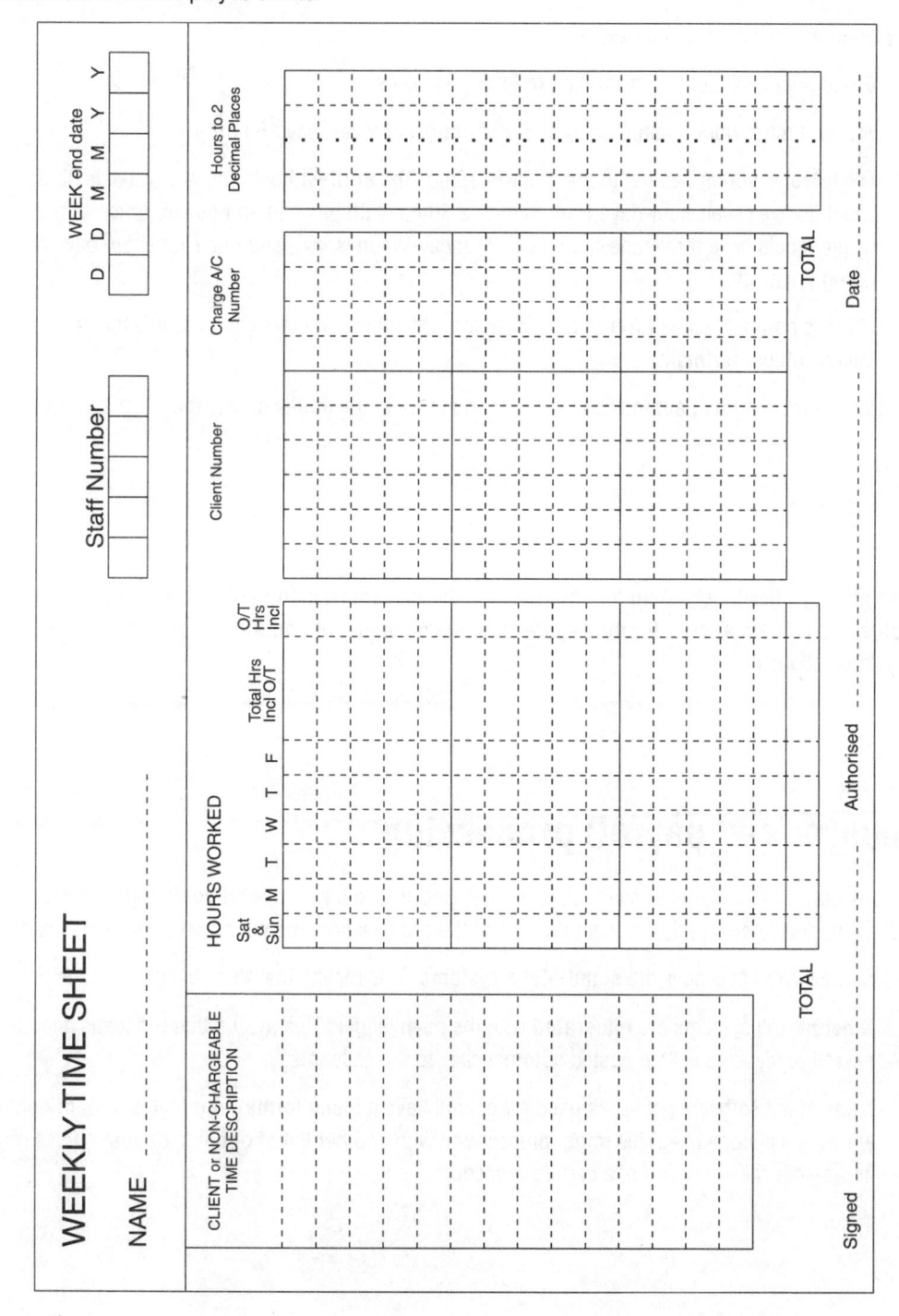

12.7 Flexitime

Flexitime is a system where employees must work a **set total number of hours** in a period, but have some **choice** as to when the hours are worked. For example, they might choose to work five hours on one day and ten hours the next.

The following could be a typical flexitime system.

- **Office hours** will be, say, from 8am to 6pm (ten hours).

- Workers must work a minimum number of hours per week: say 35 hours.

- The **latest** a worker can get to the office is 10am. The **earliest** he or she may leave is 3pm. Thus a worker could do five seven-hour days from 8am to 3.30pm, with just half an hour for lunch. Alternatively a worker could have three nine-hour days (Monday-Wednesday), and one eight-hour day (Thursday), taking Friday off.

- There is normally some **limit** to the discretion with which workers can organise their time (eg only one full day off per fortnight).

Flexitime is fairly common in **local authorities**, and is found more in the **public sector** than in the private sector.

Activity 4.10

Nice plc is introducing a flexitime system for employees in the accounts department. Think about how management can ensure that all employees are at work for the required minimum number of hours. List some methods of recording hours that could be adopted.

13 Computerised payroll processing

Since payroll processing is similar wherever you work, it is possible to buy a **payroll application package** to run on a computer. Which package you use depends on the size of the organisation and your own processing needs.

- Some payroll packages are **stand-alone systems**. This means that they just process the payroll.

- Other payroll systems are **integrated** with the main ledger. This means that the totals generated by the payroll processing will be posted automatically to the accounts.

- Many of the software packages used for payroll have a **menu format**. A menu is a list of options, from which you choose one. This might present you with another list of options, or your choice might commence the execution of a certain procedure.

4: CALCULATION OF GROSS PAY

13.1 Data

Whichever type of payroll package you use, a lot of **data** will be needed, just as with a manual system. Data is just another way of saying information.

- Some of that data will be data of a **permanent** or **long-term** nature. For example, an employee's name is unlikely to change. Other long-term data will be **cumulative** (eg total wages in the year to date).

- Some data will be of a **temporary** nature. For example hours worked in a particular week will only be of use in that week's processing. The data has to be kept, for auditors or for PAYE inspectors (for a minimum of three years), but you are unlikely to need it again once you have used it to update your cumulative records.

13.2 Records and master files

The long-term and cumulative data is collected in a **master file**. This also includes transactions to date.

Each employee has a **record**. This is because data must be kept about each employee, by law as you saw in Chapter 1.

An employee **master file record** will consist of the following permanent or cumulative items.

- Staff number unique to each employee (so that two employees called John Smith will not be confused with one another)
- Employee name
- Address
- National Insurance number
- Tax code (changes generally are infrequent, eg one or two per year)
- Date of birth
- NI Table letter applicable
- Department code
- Wage rate or salary
- Gross pay paid to date (as wages and taxes to date must appear on the pay slip)
- Tax and NICs paid to date
- SSP, SMP, SPP and SAP paid in the tax year (as this must appear on the P60)
- Pension scheme deduction
- Other voluntary deductions (eg GAYE, SAYE)
- Deductions under Court order, etc
- Date joined, if joined during tax year, or if the employer offers extra remuneration for length of service
- Date left (for P14, and P35)
- Pension scheme deduction

13.3 Payroll system input and processing

The main inputs into a **weekly-paid payroll package** are as follows.

- **Clock cards** or **time sheets** (sometimes both are used). Details of overtime worked will normally be shown on these documents. Remember to check that the overtime is authorised!

107

PART B ASCERTAINING GROSS PAY

- Amount of **bonus**, or appropriate details if the bonus is calculated by the computer.
- **SSP** or **SMP** or **SPP** or **SAP** details (see Chapter 5).
- With this information and the information on the master file the payroll package will then calculate the **gross pay**, the **PAYE and NI deductions** due and any **other deductions** that need to be made.

A **monthly-paid payroll package** is similar to that for wages, but it is usual for the monthly salary to be generated by the computer from details held on the master file and therefore there is little need for any transaction input. So the inputs for a salary system are just overtime, bonuses, SSP, SMP, etc (because the basic salary is already on the master file).

Notice that the weekly-paid package is an example of a positive payroll and the monthly-paid package is an example of a negative payroll.

13.4 Payroll system output

The payroll outputs include **payslips** and **information** both for **external use** (eg by the Inland Revenue) and for **internal use** (for management accounts).

Typical **inputs** to and **outputs** from a payroll system are given in the diagram on the next page. Note that nothing in the diagram relates to the computer. If you were to pick the diagram up without knowing where it came from, you would not be able to tell if it represented a computerised payroll system or a manual payroll system.

4: CALCULATION OF GROSS PAY

INPUTS

- Other amendments
- Joiners and leavers
- Salary details
- Timesheets, worksheets, clock cards etc

PROCESSING

- Payroll system
- Payroll file

OUTPUTS

- Payroll list
  - Wages cost by departments
  - Wages cost by job
- Year-end listings
  - Employee deductions
  - Note and coin analysis
- Credit transfer slips
  - Payroll action report
  - Cheque list
- Gross pay analysis
  - Audit trail control list
  - Payroll reconciliation
- Payslips
  - Payroll records
  - Employees records
- Direct Credit transmission data
- Data for input to other modules

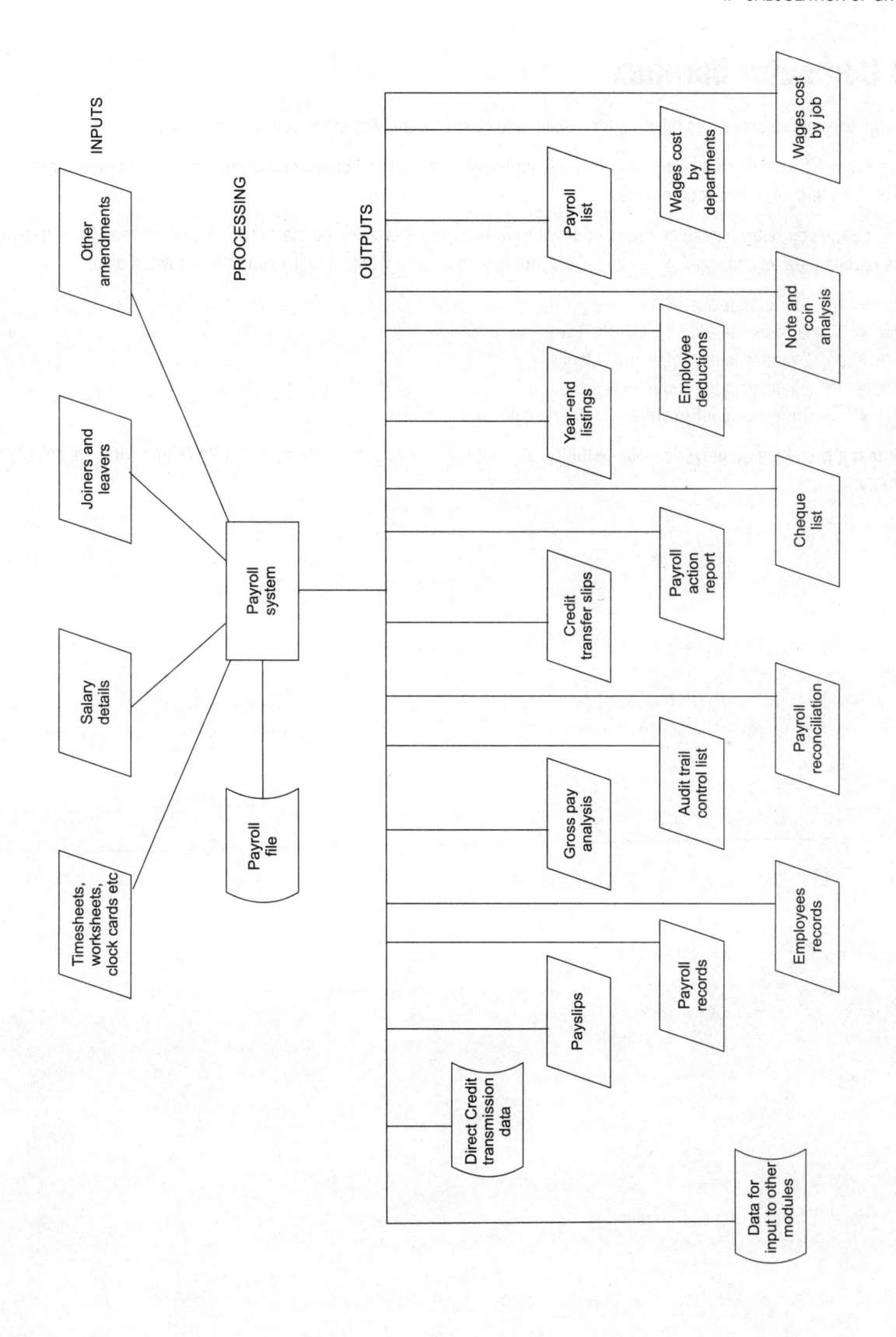

PART B   ASCERTAINING GROSS PAY

14 Computer bureaux

A **computer bureau** processes payrolls for clients, and offers a variety of other computing services.

As payroll is a relatively standard process, some employers send it to a **computer bureau** which may process the payroll for a large number of companies.

You send the computer bureau all the **permanent data** first, and it sets up the master file. You then send the bureau the **transactions data** as and when necessary. On a monthly basis, you would usually send the following data.

- Starters' details
- Leavers' details
- Changes in pay rates and salaries
- Changes in tax codes
- Timesheets for overtime, or hourly paid staff

Note that it is still the **employer's responsibility**, and not the bureau's, to make sure that PAYE and NICs are calculated properly.

4: CALCULATION OF GROSS PAY

Key learning points

- ☑ A person's wage packet or pay cheque is that person's **net pay** for a period. This is:
  - **gross pay**
  - less tax, National Insurance and other **deductions**

- ☑ A contract of employment, or written particulars of the employment, has to be given to a new employee within eight weeks of commencement.

- ☑ **Basic pay** is the pay for the employee's work done in a period. The most common elements are:
  - basic pay
  - overtime
  - commission, bonuses, and so forth

- ☑ The contract of employment will give details of an employee's pay entitlements.

- ☑ Basic pay may need to be increased to comply with the **National Minimum Wage**.

- ☑ There are a variety of ways of calculating basic pay.
  - **Piecework**, where the wage is calculated by the number of items produced (eg £1 per widget made).
  - **Hourly paid labour**, where basic pay is calculated by a rate per hour (so if you work 30 hours at a rate of £10 per hour you receive £300).
  - An **annual salary** basis, where an amount per year is divided into monthly or, occasionally, weekly periods.

- ☑ **Overtime** comprises hours worked over a standard working week. The overtime rate can be based on the hourly rate, or can be fixed by mutual agreement with hourly paid or salaried staff.

- ☑ **Commission** is often paid to employees who have succeeded in making a sale. It is normally a percentage of the value of the sale.

- ☑ **Bonuses** may be paid to employees if an agreed target is reached, or for any reason determined by management. Bonuses can take many forms.

- ☑ **Holiday pay:** every worker is entitled to four weeks paid annual leave

- ☑ **Holiday pay schemes** have special rules. Make sure you know these.

- ☑ **Advances of pay** are advances of net pay. There is no effect on PAYE or NI, as they will be correctly deducted at the pay day for which the payment was due.

- ☑ **Back pay** is pay due in respect of earlier periods, paid in the current period. It forms part of the gross pay for the current period.

- ☑ **Expenses** may be reimbursed through the payroll.

PART B ASCERTAINING GROSS PAY

> ☑ There are a number of **documents** associated with payroll preparation.
> - **Clock cards** and **timesheets** record the hours spent by each employee on each job, or doing the work of each client.
> - **Attendance records** are used by the personnel department to determine reasons for absence from work, and to administer the granting of annual leave.
> - Other personnel record documentation includes **cards** to record a person's career progress.
>
> ☑ Payroll can be prepared **manually,** by **in-house computer** programme or by an external **computer bureau.**

Quick quiz

1. Basic pay is what the employee receives in cash each week or month. True or false?

2. Differential piecework schemes offer an incentive to employees to increase their output. How?

3. Jennie is contracted to work 35 hours per week at £5 per hour. Overtime is paid at time and a half. If she works 12 hours overtime, what is her basic pay for the week?

4. Jo is a telesales operative. She earns 2% commission on sales of up to £1,000 per week, 5% commission on the next £9,000 of sales and 10% commission on sales above this level. If she makes £21,500 of sales in a week, what does she earn in commission?

5. What is a clock card?

6. What is flexitime?

Answers to quick quiz

1. False. Basic pay is what an employee earns before tax, National Insurance and other deductions.

2. Higher rates are paid for increased levels of production. For example, an employee might receive a basic rate of £5 per completed unit for the first 50 units in a week. The next 20 units might be worth £7.50 each and any above that £10 each.

3. (35 × £5) + (12 × £5 × 1.5) = £265. Her hourly rates are well above the NMW.

4.
Sales £	Commission £
1,000 at 2%	20
9,000 at 5%	450
11,500 at 10%	1,150
21,500	1,620

5. A clock card is a card which an employee inserts into a machine at the start and end of each shift, and at the start and end of meal breaks. The time recording clock stamps the card with the times when the employee was in the place of employment and therefore assumed to be working.

6. Flexitime is a system allowing employees to carry out at least some of their contracted work at times which suit them, rather than at times which are fixed by the employer.

PART B ASCERTAINING GROSS PAY

Activity checklist

This checklist shows which performance criteria, range statement or knowledge and understanding point is covered by each activity in this chapter. Tick off each activity as you complete it.

Activity

4.1	☐	This activity covers knowledge and understanding points 1, 2 and 3.
4.2	☐	This activity covers knowledge and understanding point 3.
4.3	☐	This activity covers performance criteria 72.1.A, 72.1.C and 72.1 H.
4.4	☐	This activity covers performance criteria 72.1.A, 72.1.B, 72.1.C, 72.1.D and 72.1.H.
4.5	☐	This activity covers performance criterion 72.1.F.
4.6	☐	This activity covers performance criteria 72.1.A, 72.1.B and 72.1.G.
4.7	☐	This activity covers performance criteria 72.1.B and 72.1.H.
4.8	☐	This activity covers performance criteria 72.1.A, 72.1.C and 72.1.H.
4.9	☐	This activity covers performance criteria 72.1.A, 72.1.B, 72.1.D and 72.1.G.
4.10	☐	This activity covers performance criteria 72.1.A and 72.1.B and range statement 2 on time recording.

chapter 5

Statutory pay entitlements

Contents

1 The problem
2 The solution
3 Statutory Sick Pay (SSP)
4 Statutory Maternity Pay (SMP)
5 Statutory Paternity Pay (SPP)
6 Statutory Adoption Pay (SAP)
7 Tax credits
8 Spreadsheets for the manual calculation of gross pay

Performance criteria

72.1.F Take appropriate action to apply the terms of statutory and organisational payment schemes, where variations arise as a result of sickness, maternity leave or holidays

72.2.A Determine entitlement to Statutory Sick Pay when entitlement to occupational sick pay expires or is not paid

72.2.B Process Statutory Sick Pay payments accurately on receipt of regulatory forms

72.2.C Determine entitlement to Ordinary and Additional Maternity Leave, Adoption Leave and Paternity Leave

72.2.D Determine entitlement to Statutory Maternity Pay, Statutory Adoption Pay, Statutory Paternity Pay, when entitlement to occupational payments are not made.

72.2.E Process Statutory Maternity Pay, Statutory Adoption Pay, Statutory Paternity Pay payments accurately on receipt of regulatory forms

72.2.F Process Tax Credit payments on receipt of regulatory forms

72.2.G Contribute to the resolution of individual employees' queries by checking statutory pay entitlements manually, using the appropriate tables

72.2.H Identify and resolve all discrepancies directly or by reference to the appropriate person

72.2.I Issue the correct **regulatory documentation** where entitlement to statutory payments does not arise or ceases

PART B ASCERTAINING GROSS PAY

Range statement

1   Regulatory documentation: SSP1; SMP1; stop notice and certificates of payment

Knowledge and understanding

3   Employment Rights legislation (Elements 72.1 & 72.2)
4   Statutory Maternity Pay – including the rules relating to entitlement, earnings, evidence of pregnancy, start date for payment, stopping payments (Element 72.2)
5   Statutory Sick Pay – including the rules relating to period of incapacity for work, qualifying days, waiting days, linking, earnings test, changeover to state responsibility, stopping payments (Element 72.2)
6   Statutory Adoption Pay – including the rules relating to entitlement, earnings, evidence of adoption, start date for payment, stopping payments (Element 72.2)
7   Statutory Paternity Pay including the rules relating to entitlement, earnings, evidence of parenthood, start date for payment, stopping payments (Element 72.2)
8   Parental Leave including the rules relating to entitlement, earnings, evidence of parental responsibility, payment (Element 72.2)
9   Time off for Dependents including the rules relating to entitlement, evidence of emergency, payment and their interaction with occupational schemes (Element 72.2)
10 The security and confidentiality of information (Elements 72.1 & 72.2)
11 Dealing with instructions from external agencies (Element 72.2)
12 The resolution of discrepancies (Elements 72.1 & 72.2)
14 Types of information input from external agencies (Element 72.2)
15 Signatories and authorisations (Elements 72.1 & 72.2)
16 Timescales and schedules for updating, presenting and despatching data (Elements 72.1 & 72.2)
18 How to use Statutory Sick Pay, Statutory Maternity Pay tables to perform manual calculations of statutory additions to gross pay
19 How to set up and use spreadsheets for the manual calculation of gross pay

> **Signpost**
>
> The emphasis of this element is **entitlement** and **documentation**. However the standards specifically state in pc 72.2.G that students must know how to calculate statutory payments **manually**. Note that statutory redundancy pay is dealt with at NVQ/SVQ Level 3.

Important!

Guidance to assessors, issued by the AAT, amplifies the documents that students need to know about.

- Self Certification form
- Medical certificate
- MAT B1
- Matching Certificate

- SSP1, SMP1, SAP1, SPP1
- Tax credit start and stop notices
- Tax credit certificates of payment

You also need to be able to do manual calculations of the following:

- Average earnings
- Entitlement to SSP, SMP, SAP, SPP

1 The problem

Employers are increasingly having to deal with payments to employees when they are ill or pregnant. These used to be dealt with by the government, but now the burden of deciding who is eligible for these payments falls on the employer.

In addition the employer is now expected to be able to deal with the payments due to fathers and adoptive parents, as well as payments due under the tax credit system.

2 The solution

Remember the **basic computation,** to see where everything fits in.

	£
Basic pay (what your work has earned you)	1,000
Other pay (includes SSP, SMP, SPP, SAP)	200
Gross pay	1,200
Less Income Tax (PAYE)	(140)
National Insurance (NI)	(100)
Other deductions	(50)
Net pay	910

SSP, SMP, SPP and SAP are all taxable and subject to NIC deductions. Therefore they form part of **gross pay**. Tax credits, however, are not subject to tax and NIC deductions and are **additions to net pay**.

The important thing to remember is that **statutory payments** are not covered by the contract of employment. So you must perform additional checks to ensure that the employee is **entitled** to these payments and that they have been correctly **authorised**.

- Determine entitlement
- Process the payments accurately
- Stop payments when no longer eligible
- Deal with regulatory forms for starting and stopping payments.

3 Statutory Sick Pay (SSP)

3.1 Eligibility

When an employee is unable to work due to sickness or disability, then employers must make payments for time off sick to **at least a minimum of the SSP amounts**. The employer may have an **occupational sick pay scheme**, which pays more than the statutory minimum.

Statutory sick pay is a flat rate benefit payable to employees aged 16 and over but under the age of 65, when they have been continuously sick for **four or more successive days**.

To be eligible for this benefit the employee must earn at least £79.00 per week (for 2004/05).

The employer will usually have rules for reporting sickness by telephone and requiring a medical certificate upon return to work.

PART B ASCERTAINING GROSS PAY

If the absence is for less than seven days, employees can complete a **self-certification certificate** (form SC2, reproduced on the following pages). This is usually available from their doctor's surgery or from the employer's payroll department. It includes details of the number of days off sick and the nature of the illness, and has to be signed by the employee.

Employers can not **demand** a medical certificate until the **eighth day** of sickness, regardless of what the occupational sick pay scheme rules might say. Therefore the employee will normally self-certificate sickness for time off up to seven days.

The employer will usually pay the employee in the same way and on the same day as when the employee would normally receive his or her wages.

Inland Revenue

Statutory Sick Pay

Employee's statement of sickness

1 About this form

Statutory Sick Pay (SSP) is money paid by employers to employees who are away from work because they are sick.

2 What to do now

Please:

- fill in part 6 of this form, **Your statement**, when you have been sick for 4 days or more in a row
- tear off **Your statement**, and give it to your employer, it will help them decide if you can get SSP
- keep this page for your own information.

3 What happens next

If you can get SSP, your employer will pay you in the same way they usually pay you your wages.

If you cannot get SSP, your employer will give you form **SSP1** to tell you why. You can use form **SSP1** to claim Incapacity Benefit.

If you disagree with your employer you can ask the Inland Revenue for a decision about your entitlement.

4 If you have changed jobs

If you have:

- changed jobs within the last 8 weeks, and
- received at least one weeks SSP from your old employer in the 8 weeks *(52 weeks if you are a Welfare to Work Beneficiary)* before this current spell of sickness (odd days of SSP may count), the SSP from your old employer can be counted towards your 28 weeks maximum SSP payment. This means you may be able to transfer to a higher rate of Incapacity Benefit earlier.

SC2   October 2003   1   ▶ *Please turn over*

PART B   ASCERTAINING GROSS PAY

4 If you have changed jobs (continued)

Ask your old employer to fill in form **SSP1(L)** *Leaver's statement of SSP*. Give form **SSP1(L)** to your new employer, it will help them to make sure that you get the right amount of SSP, and that you transfer to Incapacity Benefit at the right time.

5 Other help while you are sick

You can get more information about other help while you are sick in leaflet **SD1** *Sick and disabled?*

If you do not have much money coming in while you are sick, you may be able to get Income Support. Income Support is a Social Security benefit for people who do not have enough money to live on. You can find out more about Income Support from your nearest Jobcentre Plus or social security office, now part of the Department for Work and Pensions.

You can get leaflet **SD1** from:
- any Jobcentre Plus or social security office
- most advice centres like the Citizens Advice Bureau, or
- any Post Office, (except in Northern Ireland).

If you want to know more about benefit entitlement while you are sick, ring the Benefit Enquiry Line for people with disabilities.
The phone call is free. The number is 0800 882 200, or in Northern Ireland 0800 220 674.

If you have any problems with hearing or speaking and use a textphone, ring 0800 243 355 or in Northern Ireland 0800 243 787. The phone call is free.
If you do not have your own textphone system, they are available from the Citizens Advice Bureau and main libraries.

Working Tax Credit (WTC) was introduced on 7 April 2003 to replace Working Families Tax Credit (WFTC) and Disabled Persons Tax Credit (DPTC). The new tax credit helps people with an illness or disability to return to, or take up work by topping up earnings. It is a tax credit for people on low to middle incomes, who are working 16 hours or more a week and who have an illness or disability which puts them at a disadvantage in getting a job.

For further information on claiming WTC contact your nearest Jobcentre Plus or social security office

If you want to know more about SSP, contact your nearest Inland Revenue office. You can find the telephone number in The Phone Book under Inland Revenue

2   ▶ *Please see opposite page*

5: STATUTORY PAY ENTITLEMENTS

6 Your statement - *tear-off*

About you

Surname

Other names

Title Mr/Mrs//Miss/Ms

National Insurance number

Date of birth

Clock or payroll number

About your sickness

Please give brief details of your sickness

What date did your sickness begin?

What date did your sickness end?
If you do not know when your sickness will end, leave this box blank.

- The dates you put in these 2 boxes may be days you do not normally work.

- If you are sick for more than 7 days, your employer may ask you for a medical certificate from your doctor. Medical certificates are also called sick notes or Doctor's statements.

What date did you last work before your sickness began?

What time did you finish work on that date?   *am/pm

*Delete as appropriate.   3   ▶ *Please turn over*

PART B ASCERTAINING GROSS PAY

6 Your statement (continued) - *tear-off*

Was your sickness caused by
an accident at work or   Yes ☐   No ☐
an industrial disease?

If you answered 'Yes', you may be able to get Industrial Injuries
Disablement Benefit. If you want information about claiming
this benefit, ask at your nearest Jobcentre Plus or social security
office.

Your signature

Signature

Date   / /

Tear-off this page and give it to your employer.

3.2 Linking periods

SSP is limited to a maximum period of 28 weeks for each period of illness, but different periods of sickness may be linked for this purpose if they are less than eight weeks apart.

Example: Linking periods

An employee has been off sick for 20 weeks, she returns to work for 4 weeks and then has a relapse and is off for a further 10 weeks. Is SSP payable?

Solution

The two periods of sickness are less than 8 weeks apart and so are linked for SSP purposes. The maximum period that SSP can be paid is for 28 weeks. Therefore SSP is paid for the whole of the first period of sickness of 20 weeks. However, for the second period of sickness of 10 weeks, only 8 weeks' SSP is due. Nothing is paid for the final two weeks, and the employee must be given form SSP1.

The Inland Revenue booklet on SSP (E14) includes tables for working out linking periods.

Once the maximum period of 28 weeks' SSP is reached, the employer can pay no more SSP. The employer must give the employee form SSP1, which states that the employee is no longer eligible for SSP, to give the Department for Work and Pensions (DWP). The DWP will decide if other benefits, such as incapacity benefit, are due.

3.3 Earnings

SSP is only paid if the employee's earnings are at or above the Lower Earnings Limit for NIC purposes (£79 per week for 2004/05).

For employees on a set weekly or monthly salary, this is easily determined. However, some employees may work variable overtime and so their earnings vary from week to week.

For the purposes of SSP, you need to take the average earnings for the eight weeks prior to the illness. This includes bonuses, commission, SMP, SPP, SAP, SSP but excludes tax credits.

Example: Average earnings

An employee goes sick on 1 September. For the eight weeks prior to 1 September, she has earned the following amounts (gross pay): £70.00; £80.00; £87.50; £92.50; £60.00; £102.00; £72.00 and £70.00.

Is she entitled to SSP?

Solution

The total pay for the eight weeks prior to her illness is £634.00. The average week's pay during this period is £634.00/8 = £79.25 per week. As this exceeds £79.00 per week, she is entitled to receive SSP.

Tutorial note. If average earnings had been £75.25 per week, no SSP could be paid and the employer should issue form SSP1.

3.4 Daily rate

The rate of SSP is £66.15 per week for tax year 2004/05. The daily rate of SSP is the weekly rate divided by the number of qualifying days in the week.

3.5 Qualifying days

The **first three days** of any period of sickness are **waiting days** for which no SSP is paid. However, if two periods of sickness are less than eight weeks apart the linking rules treat them as the same period of sickness and so SSP is payable from the first day's illness of the second period.

Qualifying days are based on the number of days the employee **usually works** each week. So a full time employee may have five qualifying days a week; whereas a part time employee may have only two qualifying days a week.

In the case of the full-time employee, the daily rate is £66.15/5 which is £13.23 per day.

For the part-time employee, the daily rate is £66.15/2 which is £33.08 per day.

However, note that if the employees both have a week's sickness, they will both receive £66.15 a week.

Example: SSP rates

An employee has average weekly earnings of £100. He normally works five days a week and so the 'qualifying days' are 5. He is sick from Monday 5 July to Thursday 22 July 2004 (a total of 18 days). How much SSP is he entitled to receive?

Solution

Monday 5 July to Wednesday 7 July are waiting days, so no SSP is paid. Therefore in the first week, only Thursday 8 and Friday 9 July are days of sickness qualifying for SSP. The daily rate is £66.15/5 = £13.23 per day. So SSP for the first week is £26.46 (2 × £13.23). For the second week (Monday 12 July to Friday 16 July inclusive), a full five days' SSP is due, ie £66.15 (the weekly rate). In the third week, the employee is sick from Monday 19 July to Thursday 22 July and so is entitled to 4 days' SSP of £52.92 (4 × £13.23).

3.6 Recovery of SSP

Employers can recover part of the SSP if the total amount paid in a tax month exceeds 13% of their total Class 1 NICs (employee's plus employer's) for that month.

Example: SSP recovery

Your employer's total Class 1 NIC payment for July (after any rebates) totals £696.10. 13% of £696.10 is £90.49. From the above example, the total SSP paid during July was £145.53 (£26.46 + £66.15 + £52.92). How much SSP can your employer recover for July?

Solution

Your employer can recover £55.04 (£145.53 – £90.49).

Recovery is made by deducting the amount due from the payment made each month to the Inland Revenue. Any shortfall can be carried forward and deducted the following month.

3.7 Recording SSP

SSP forms part of an employee's gross pay and is taxable and subject to NICs. It is entered on the form P11 deduction card. The Inland Revenue also produce a record form SSP2, to enable employers to keep a separate record of each employee's SSP, if required.

SSP is the **minimum** payment that your employer has to pay a sick employee. Many employers will continue to pay full basic pay, at least for short-term illness. If this is the case, then SSP needs to be calculated and recorded separately on the deduction card.

Example: SSP on deduction card

An employee's basic pay is usually £125 per week. However this week, he is entitled to a full week's SSP of £66.15. What entries are made on the deduction card if the employer pays the full £125?

Solution

The figure for pay in the week is entered as £125 as this is the taxable amount. Tax and NICs are calculated as normal. However, there is a column on the deduction card (1f) for recording SSP and the figure of £66.15 would be entered here. This shows that, of £125.00 paid that week, £66.15 was SSP and £58.85 was occupational sick pay over and above SSP.

This enables the employer to keep a record of SSP paid, as required by law, and also for the purposes of calculating any recovery due. The employer *may* also wish to complete form SSP2 for the employee.

PART B   ASCERTAINING GROSS PAY

3.8 Exclusion

SSP is not payable in the following circumstances.

- If the employee is under 16
- If the employee is 65 or over
- If the employee's earnings are less than £79.00 per week
- If the employee has already received 28 weeks' SSP in this period of illness (including linked periods)

If an employee is excluded from SSP, the employer must give the employee form SSP1 stating the reason for exclusion.

The employee can then take form SSP1 to the DWP to see if he or she is eligible for other benefits.

Form SSP1 is reproduced on the following pages.

3.9 Leavers

All entitlement to SSP ceases on the date an employee leaves.

Due to the linking rules, an employee may ask for a certificate SSP1(L). This is also known as the leaver's statement of Statutory Sick Pay. An employer can only complete form SSP1(L) if the leaver was entitled to SSP during the 8 weeks prior to leaving. It is not issued automatically but only at the employee's request (see Chapter 1).

Activity 5.1

Sheree Jones has earned an average of £100.00 per week for the past eight weeks. She has been on sick leave from Thursday 1 July to Mon 5 July 2004. Sheree normally works Mondays to Fridays. How much SSP is she entitled to? She has completed a self certification certificate SC2.

Activity 5.2

Would your answer to activity 5.1 change if Sheree normally worked 4 days a week on Thursday, Friday, Saturday and Sunday?

5: STATUTORY PAY ENTITLEMENTS

SSP1 01/04

Claim form

19-07-2004 12:8:29 Page 1 of 11

Statutory Sick Pay (SSP) and Incapacity Benefit

About this form

Employers should complete this form when an employee is not entitled to Statutory Sick Pay (SSP), or when SSP has come to an end. **Once completed the form should be given to the employee, who will then make a claim to Incapacity Benefit.**

Employees – Please note this is not a claim form for benefit but it must be sent in with your claim form. See Section 2 How to claim.

Section 1
is for the employer to give information about Statutory Sick Pay (SSP). The information will help the Department for Work and Pensions decide your employee's Incapacity Benefit claim.

- **Part A** asks for information about the employee and SSP.
- **Part B** tells the employee why the employer cannot pay SSP.
- **Part C** asks for further information about sickness and SSP.
- **Part D** is a declaration by the employer that all information is correct and complete.

Parts A, B and **D** must be completed by the employer. **Part C** should only be completed when the employee in question has already received SSP from the employer.

Section 2
are notes for the employee explaining how and where to claim Incapacity Benefit.

Statutory Sick Pay is money paid by employers to employees who are away from work for 4 days or more in a row because they have an illness or disability.

Incapacity Benefit is a social security benefit employees may be able to get because of their illness or disability when their SSP ends or if they cannot get SSP.

Section 1

Part A

About SSP and your employee

About your employee

Please tell us about your employee

Surname	
Other names	
National Insurance (NI) number	Letters Numbers Letter
Clock or payroll number	
Tax reference number	
Address	
	Postcode

1

127

PART B ASCERTAINING GROSS PAY

Notes to the employer

When to fill in this form

If you cannot pay any SSP to this employee
fill in **Section 1** of this form as soon as they have been sick for 4 days in a row. Count weekends, holidays and other days that the employee would not normally work.

In these circumstances you must by law, give this form to your employee
- no later than 7 days after you knew that the employee was sick for 4 days in a row, or if this is not possible
- no later than the first payday in the tax month following your employee being sick for more than 4 days in a row

If you have been paying SSP to your employee but payments of SSP are about to stop even though your employee is still sick, or
If payment of SSP has not been made because you have decided to pay normal salary during the period of sickness, and this period is coming to an end, and the employee is still sick
fill in **Section 1** of this form **and you must then, by law, give this form to your employee**
- at the beginning of the 23rd week of SSP. This will let the employee know that their SSP will soon stop, or
- 2 weeks before you will stop paying SSP, if you know that this will be before they have had SSP for 23 weeks, or
- as soon as you can, if you have to stop paying SSP suddenly.

If you use a computer

Instead of filling in **this form** you can attach a computer print out of the information we need. But please make sure the print out
- is in a format which is easy to understand
- contains all the information we ask for
- contains all the details in the employer's declaration on **page 5**, and
- has been signed.

If you are not sure if your print out will be suitable, send a copy to your **Jobcentre Plus office, Jobcentre or social security office** and they will advise you. You can find their phone number and address on the advert in the business numbers section of the phone book. Look under **Jobcentre Plus** or **Social Security**.

If you want more information

For more information about SSP, please read
- E14 (2003) Employers' Help Book, *What to do if your employee is sick*, and
- from 6 April 2004 – E14 Supplement (2004), *What to do if your employee is sick – special cases*.

You can get these from any Inland Revenue office or visit Inland Revenue website **www.inlandrevenue.gov.uk/employers**

If you have any general enquiries about SSP, phone the Inland Revenue Call Centre
- for new employers (less than 3 years) – **0845 60 70 143**. Lines open Monday to Friday 8am to 8pm and Saturday and Sunday – 8am to 5pm
- for people who have been employers for more than 3 years – **08457 143 143**. Lines open Monday to Friday 8am to 8pm and Saturday and Sunday – 8am to 5pm
- for employers who have hearing or speech difficulties using a Textphone – **08456 021 380**.

Why you cannot get Statutory Sick Pay

Part B

I am filling in this form because

☐ I cannot pay you SSP

☐ I cannot pay you SSP after [/ /]

I have ticked a box to tell you why you cannot get SSP. The notes on **pages 6** and **7** explain the reasons in more detail.

I cannot pay you SSP because

A ☐ You claimed Incapacity Benefit or Severe Disablement Allowance during the last 8 weeks, or you are entitled to the 52 week benefit protection so you may be able to get Incapacity Benefit or Severe Disablement Allowance instead of SSP.

B ☐ Your contract of employment has expired.

C ☐ Your contract of employment has been brought to an end.

D ☐ You will soon have been getting SSP for 28 weeks or you have already had SSP for 28 weeks.

E ☐ You have not earned enough money to qualify for SSP.

F ☐ You are aged 65 or over.

G ☐ You are expecting a baby soon or you have just had a baby.

H ☐ You have already been sick on and off for 3 years.

I ☐ You were away from work because of a trade dispute on the first day you were sick.

J ☐ You were in legal custody or you were serving a term of imprisonment when you became sick.
Or you are now in legal custody or sentenced to a term of imprisonment.

K ☐ You were working outside the UK on the day you first became sick and I was not liable to pay employer's Class 1 NI contributions on your earnings on that day.

L ☐ You have not started working for me yet.

Notes on pages 6 and 7 explain the reasons in more detail

PART B ASCERTAINING GROSS PAY

More information we need

Part C

The employee's first day of sickness

To work out this date you will need to check
- your sick records for this employee, and
- any form **SSP1(L)** *Leaver's statement of SSP* from a previous employer.

If your employee has a form **SSP1(L)** from a previous employer and has been off work sick for 4 days or more within 8 weeks and one day of **date 2** on their **SSP1(L)**, the first day of sickness is **date 1** on form SSP1(L).

If your employee has had 2 or more spells of sickness of 4 days or more in a row which were 8 weeks or less apart, the first day of sickness is the first day they were off work sick at the beginning of these linked spells of sickness.

For all other employees who have been off work sick for 4 days or more in a row, the first day of sickness is the first day they were off work sick.

The first day of sickness or first day of linked spell. [/ /]

About the SSP that has been paid

How many weeks and days of SSP will have been paid to this employee when SSP ends?
Include all linked spells. Count from the first day you have paid SSP up to and including the date you have written on **page 3** of this form. If you are including any SSP paid by a previous employer, count from **date 1** on their form SSP1(L). [weeks] [days]

How many qualifying days are there in a week? [days]
Count the number of qualifying days in the full week, not just the number of days they can get SSP for. Remember, for most employees qualifying days are the days of the week that they normally work.

Please tick which days of the week the employee normally works?

☐ Monday ☐ Tuesday ☐ Wednesday ☐ Thursday ☐ Friday

☐ Saturday ☐ Sunday

Provide dates of all periods of sick absences from the first date of sickness, in the current Period of Incapacity for Work (PIW).
Use a separate sheet of paper if necessary.

From	To	From	To
/ /	/ /	/ /	/ /
/ /	/ /	/ /	/ /
/ /	/ /	/ /	/ /
/ /	/ /	/ /	/ /
/ /	/ /	/ /	/ /
/ /	/ /	/ /	/ /
/ /	/ /	/ /	/ /

5: STATUTORY PAY ENTITLEMENTS

Employer's declaration

Part D

I declare
that the information I have given is correct and complete.

I understand
that if this employee has been getting SSP, I must continue to pay SSP up to and including the date I have written on **page 3** of this form.

Employer's name	
Employer's Account Office reference number	
Signature	
Date	/ /
Position in firm	
Phone number and extension	extension
Fax number	
Address	
	Postcode
Business stamp	

What to do next

Please send this form to your employee with any medical certificates that cover a period you cannot pay SSP for.

Medical certificates are also called sick notes or doctor's statements.

Tick one of the following boxes

☐ I have enclosed Medical Certificates

☐ I have not enclosed Medical Certificates

PART B   ASCERTAINING GROSS PAY

Reasons why you cannot get SSP

A You cannot get SSP if you claimed Incapacity Benefit or Severe Disablement Allowance during the last 8 weeks, or if you are entitled to the 52 week benefit protection.

B You cannot normally get SSP after you stop working for your employer if your contract has ended.

C You cannot normally get SSP after your contract has been ended by your employer. However, your employer will have to pay you SSP if they ended your contract of employment solely or mainly to avoid paying SSP.

D You cannot get SSP after you have had SSP for 28 weeks in a row or for periods of sickness that are 8 weeks or less apart and that add up to 28 weeks. SSP paid by another employer may be counted.

E You cannot get SSP if your average weekly earnings are less than the Lower Earnings Limit for the 8 weeks before you went sick. All earnings before things like tax are taken off are counted.

Some employers have a special arrangement with the Inland Revenue to pay Class 1B NI contributions on some of your earnings. This could mean that your employer could not count all your earnings when working out your average earnings. Ask your employer if any of your earnings were included in such an arrangement and then ask them to recalculate your earnings as if you had been paying Class 1 NI contributions on them.

F You cannot get SSP if on the first day you became sick you are aged 65 or over.

G You cannot get SSP:
- during the 26 weeks you are entitled to Statutory Maternity Pay (SMP) from your employer, or
- during the 26 weeks you are entitled to Maternity Allowance(MA) from the Department for Work and Pensions.

Statutory Maternity Pay (SMP) is money paid by the employer to women who are away from work because they are pregnant. *Maternity Allowance (MA)* is a social security benefit you may be able to get if you are pregnant and cannot get SMP.

If you are not entitled to either SMP or MA you cannot get SSP for 18 weeks. The 18 week period starts:
- *If you are not already getting SSP* on the earlier of:
  - the Sunday of the week you are away from work because of your pregnancy, on or after the start of the 4th week before the expected week of childbirth, or
  - the Sunday of the week in which the baby is born.
- *If you are getting SSP*, on the earlier of:
  - the day after your baby is born, or
  - the day after the day you are first away from work because of your pregnancy if this is after the start of the 4th week before the week you expect your baby.

Reasons why you cannot get SSP – continued

H You cannot get SSP if during the last 3 years
- you have been sick on and off for 4 days or more in a row, and
- you have never been back at work for more than 8 weeks before going sick again.

I You cannot get SSP if you were away from work because of a trade dispute on the first day you were sick unless you had no direct interest in the dispute.
We use *trade dispute* to mean
- a strike
- a walkout
- a lockout
- another dispute about work.

J You cannot get SSP if you were
- in legal custody or sentenced to a term of imprisonment on the day you became sick, or
- SSP will stop if you are now in legal custody or sentenced to a term of imprisonment

K You cannot get SSP if are employed outside the United Kingdom (UK) on the day you first became sick unless your employer is liable to pay the employer's share of Class 1 National Insurance contributions for you, or would be if your earnings were high enough.

L You cannot get SSP until you start working for an employer.

4 Statutory Maternity Pay (SMP)

4.1 Eligibility

To be eligible to receive SMP, a woman must fulfil the following conditions.

- Supply medical evidence of pregnancy (MAT B1)
- Be employed for at least 9 months before the baby is due.
- Have average earnings of at least the National Insurance lower earnings limit
- Have stopped working
- Give 28 days notice of statutory maternity leave, unless it is impractical to do so (eg premature baby)

The Inland Revenue provide tables of the latest starting date to qualify for SMP in booklet E15.

4.2 Medical evidence

The employer needs medical evidence of the pregnancy. This is usually form MAT B1, signed by the doctor or midwife. Form MAT B1 is only available 20 weeks before the week the baby is due.

However, an employer can accept other medical evidence provided it is written, states the date the baby is due and is signed by a doctor or midwife.

The time limit for producing medical evidence for SMP is 21 days from the start of the SMP pay period. If the evidence is provided late, but there is a good reason, it must be accepted.

If a mother does not produce medical evidence, she is not entitled to SMP. However, she is entitled to ordinary maternity leave. This may be unpaid.

4.3 Maternity leave

4.3.1 Ordinary maternity leave

All mothers are entitled to ordinary maternity leave. This leave is up to 26 weeks around the time of the birth. If the mother also qualifies for SMP, it will be paid during this period. If the mother does not qualify for SMP, then the leave may be unpaid.

4.3.2 Additional maternity leave

Some mothers may be entitled to a further 26 weeks leave (ie 52 weeks in total). However, no SMP is paid during this period. To qualify for this leave, the mother must have worked for the employer for at least 9 months before the baby is due.

4.3.3 Other leave

All mothers are entitled to paid time off for ante-natal care.

4.4 Average earnings

To qualify for SMP, the mother has to have average earnings of at least the National Insurance level earnings limit. This is £79.00 per week for 2004/05. However, for babies due between 6 April and 17 July 2004, the limit is £77.00 per week. The increased limit of £79.00 per week applies for babies due between 18 July 2004 and 16 July 2005.

Earnings include holiday pay, bonuses, commission, overtime, backdated increases and SSP, SMP, SPP and SAP. However, tax credits are excluded from earnings. Average earnings are for the 8 weeks ending on the 15th week before the baby is due.

Example: Average earnings for monthly paid

Simbala Jones earns £320 and £380 in the two months prior to the 15th week before her baby is due. What is her average weekly earnings?

Solution

(a)   Add together the two payments: £320 + £380 = £700
(b)   Multiply this total by 6: 6 × £700 = £4,200 (equivalent to annual pay)
(c)   Divide this total by 52: £4,200 ÷ 52 = £80.77 per week

As this exceeds £79.00 per week, Simbala is entitled to SMP.

Activity 5.3

Suppose Simbala Jones had earned £350 and £345 in the two months prior to the 15th week before her baby is due. What are her average earnings now?

4.5 Notice for SMP and maternity leave

The mother should tell you when she expects to start maternity leave by the Saturday of the 15th week before the week the baby is due. Once again tables are provided in booklet E15 for calculating the 15th week.

The employer should confirm this in writing and also state the date the employee is expected back to work.

This notice also covers payment of SMP.

The employee cannot start maternity leave before the 11th week prior to the week the baby is due. If she chooses not to take her full entitlement of ordinary and/or additional maternity leave, she must give the employer 28 days notice of her return.

PART B   ASCERTAINING GROSS PAY

4.6 Rates of SMP

SMP payments start on the Sunday after the last day of work before maternity leave. SMP is paid for a maximum of 26 weeks.

For periods starting on or after 6 April 2004, the rates are as follows.

- First six weeks: 90% of average weekly earnings
- Remaining 20 weeks: 90% of average weekly earnings or £102.80, whichever is **lower**.

SMP is only paid while the mother has **stopped working**. If she decides to return to work early, then entitlement to the remainder of the SMP is lost. SMP is subject to tax and NIC deductions.

Activity 5.4

Given the information in Activity 5.3, what is Simbala Jones' SMP?

4.7 Recovery of SMP

An employer can always recover 92% of the SMP paid. However, if the employer's total NIC liability in a year is £45,000 or less, then 100% of the SMP can be recovered. In addition, compensation of 4.5% is also due.

Recovery is by deduction from the amounts paid to the Inland Revenue each month.

Activity 5.5

Telefon Ltd has an annual NIC liability of less than £45,000. During June 2004, it paid SMP of £1,000. How much can it recover?

4.8 Recording SMP

There is a column on the P11 deduction card for recording SMP, this is 1g. Remember SMP is taxable and NICable and so needs to be recorded as earnings in the week or month in column 2 of form P11. Tax and NIC is calculated in the normal way.

Employers may also have an occupational maternity pay scheme which pays more than the statutory minimum (SMP). In this case, the total pay is recorded in column 2, but the SMP element goes in column 1g.

The Inland Revenue also produce a SMP record sheet (SMP2), which employers can use. However, use of SMP2 is voluntary, as long as employers have sufficient detail recorded to enable completion of the year end forms (Level 3).

4.9 Exclusion

SMP can not be paid in the following circumstances.

- No medical evidence of the pregnancy is provided
- The employee has not been continuously employed for the nine months before the baby is due
- She does not earn enough
- She does not give 28 days notice of leave and has no good reason for being late.

In these circumstances, SMP can not be paid and the employee should be given form SMP1. The employer should keep a copy of MAT B1 but return the original to the employee.

A copy of form SMP1 is reproduced on the following pages.

PART B   ASCERTAINING GROSS PAY

27-07-2004 11:39:3 Page 1 of 3

Statutory Maternity Pay (SMP)

Employee's surname	
Other names	
Address	
	Postcode
National Insurance (NI) number	
Works or clock number	

Why I cannot pay you SMP

I have ticked the box that applies to you.

☐ I cannot pay you SMP.
I have ticked one of the boxes on the next page of this letter to tell you why.

☐ I cannot pay you any more SMP after the week which ends on   /   /   .
You are entitled to   weeks SMP from me until then.
I have ticked one of the boxes on the next page of this letter to tell you why I cannot carry on paying you after this date.

What to do if you disagree

If you disagree with this decision, please get in touch with me. My name, address and phone number are on page **3**. If you still disagree, you can ask Inland Revenue (NI Contributions) office for advice. You may be able to ask for an Inland Revenue officer's decision. You can contact them by phone, their phone number and address are in the phone book under **Inland Revenue**. You can get leaflet **NI17A** *A guide to Maternity Benefits* from your Jobcentre Plus office, Jobcentre or social security office for more information about SMP.

Maternity Allowance

You may be able to get Maternity Allowance if your earnings have been on average £30 a week or more. For more details contact your Jobcentre Plus office, Jobcentre or social security office. Ask your ante-natal clinic, Jobcentre Plus office, Jobcentre or social security office for a **MA1** *Maternity Allowance claim pack*. See page **3**.

Please turn over ▶

Why I cannot pay you SMP – continued

I have ticked one of the boxes to tell you why I cannot pay you Statutory Maternity Pay (SMP).

☐	**You were not employed by me for long enough**	To get SMP you must be employed by me for at least 26 weeks in a row into the 15th week before the week your baby is due, even if your baby is born early.
		You would not have been employed by me for long enough even if your baby had not been born early. This is because you still would not have worked for me 26 weeks in a row into the 15th week.
☐	**Your earnings were too low**	To get SMP your average weekly earnings must be at least equal to the Lower Earnings Limit. Some employers have a special arrangement with the Inland Revenue to pay Class 1B NI contributions on some of your earnings. This may mean that your employer may not count all your earnings when working out your average earnings. Ask your employer if any of your earnings were included in such an arrangement and then ask them to recalculate your earnings as if you had been paying Class 1 NI contributions on them.
☐	**You did not tell me soon enough that you would be away from work**	To get SMP you must give me at least 4 weeks notice that you will be away from work because you are pregnant.
		You did not have a good reason for giving me less notice than this.
☐	**You did not give me medical evidence soon enough**	To get SMP you must give me your *Maternity Certificate* **Mat B1**, or other acceptable evidence, within 3 weeks of the start of your Maternity Pay Period.
		If you had a good reason for taking longer than this, I could only allow you up to 13 weeks to give me this evidence.
☐	**You did not tell me soon enough that your baby had been born**	To get SMP you must tell me about your baby within 4 weeks of the date your baby is born.
		If you had a good reason for taking longer than this, I could only allow you up to 13 weeks to tell me.
☐	**You were in legal custody**	You cannot get SMP if you are in legal custody at the beginning of your Maternity Pay Period.
		If you have been getting SMP, you stop getting it when you go into legal custody.

Employer
Please fill in the information on the next page. It helps your employee to claim Maternity Allowance.

Work abroad

Remember, SMP can be paid anywhere in the world. If your employee is employed by a British employer but works outside the United Kingdom, they may still get SMP in certain circumstances.

For further information contact your local Inland Revenue office.

PART B   ASCERTAINING GROSS PAY

▮ Why I cannot pay you SMP – continued
27-07-2004 11:39:3 Page 3 of 3

■ Some important dates that affect your claim for SMP

- The week your baby is due — The first day of that week is   [/ /]
- The week that is 15 weeks before the week your baby is due — The first day of that week is   [/ /]
- Your Maternity Pay Period — Your Maternity Pay Period is the period during which you could get SMP.

  Your Maternity Pay Period starts or would have started on   [/ /]

■ How to claim Maternity Allowance

Fill in the claim form **MA1** which is in the pack and send it to your Jobcentre Plus office, Jobcentre or social security office with your *Maternity Certificate* **Mat B1** and this letter. If you gave me your **Mat B1**, I have sent it back to you with this letter. If you want to ask me anything about this letter, please get in touch with me.

If you claim Maternity Allowance more than 3 months after the date your Maternity Allowance is due to start, you will lose money.

Employer's signature	
Employer's name and address	
	Postcode
Phone number	
Date	/ /

Social Security Office
Part of the Jobcentre Plus network,
Department for Work and Pensions

4.10 SMP and leavers

If the employee is not returning to work, SMP must still be paid for the full 26 weeks.

However, if the employee leaves before the baby is born, but after the start of the 15th week before baby is due, she is still entitled to SMP **unless she starts working for a new employer**. The SMP pay period starts on the Sunday of the 11th week before baby is due, and ceases on the Saturday of the week she starts working (or returns to work) for the new employer **after the birth of the baby**.

If the employee does not request P45, use the tax code on the last day of employment and give her form P45 with the last payment of SMP. However, if she requests form P45 before the end of the SMP pay period, give her P45 and deduct tax at the basic rate after that date.

5 Statutory Paternity Pay (SPP)

Signpost

Note that, although the range statement does not include any SPP forms, you are expected to be able to complete form SPP1. The guidance to this Unit also expects you to be able to calculate SPP manually.

5.1 Eligibility

To be eligible for SPP, an employee must satisfy the following conditions.

- Be the biological father
- Be a partner/husband who is not the baby's biological father (eg IVF)
- Be a female partner in a same sex couple
- Provide evidence of family commitment
- Have worked continuously for 9 months prior to the week baby is due
- Continues to work right up to the actual birth.
- Have average weekly earnings of at least the National Insurance lower earnings limit.

The Inland Revenue booklet E15 includes a table of latest start dates to qualify for SPP, eg if the birth is due on 15 February 2005, then the employee must have started work by 15 May 2004.

5.2 Documentary evidence

The employer must give the employee form SC3 *Becoming a parent*. This includes a tear off slip, which the employee should complete and return to the employer.

This tear off slip includes a declaration covering family commitment. SPP can not be paid without this declaration. However, the employee will still be entitled to (unpaid) paternity leave.

Note that employers **cannot** ask for medical evidence of the pregnancy, the declaration must be accepted at face value.

The declaration must be produced 28 days before the start of payment. However, it can be produced late if there is a good reason.

PART B ASCERTAINING GROSS PAY

Inland Revenue

Statutory Paternity Pay/ Paternity Leave

Becoming a parent

If you want to take time off work to support the mother of a baby or look after the baby you may be entitled to

- Statutory Paternity Pay (SPP) - at least part of your wages will be paid for two weeks. You will get the weekly rate of SPP current at the time of your paternity leave, or 90% of your average weekly earnings, whichever is less
- Paternity Leave - up to two weeks time off.

Depending on your circumstances you may not qualify for SPP and/or paternity leave. Your employer will let you know. If this is the case you will get more advice and information at the time.

If you need help with this form please contact any Inland Revenue office. You will find the number in the phone book.

Please read through the terms and conditions on page 2 and if you think you might qualify, then

- fill in the statement on page 3
- give the completed statement to your employer.

Other help

The DTI publications *Maternity Rights - a guide for employers and employees*, and *Paternity Leave and Pay - a basic summary* gives information on these rights. The maternity publication also gives details of other booklets covering employment protection and related equal opportunities legislation. Available from

- DTI publications on **0870 1502 500**, or
- go to **www.dti.gov.uk/er**

A DWP publication *A guide to Maternity benefits*, leaflet *NI 17A*, has details of other booklets covering social security benefits and some brief information on paternity. Available from

- Jobcentre plus/social security office - see your phone book, or
- go to **www.dwp.gov.uk/advisers/index.asp#guides**

This also has details of other booklets covering social security benefits and some brief information on paternity.

You can also contact

- any Inland Revenue office
- any Arbitration and Conciliation Advisory Service (ACAS) office (see **www.acas.org.uk** for details)
- **www.tiger.gov.uk**

Information on all aspects of employment legislation is also usually available from any Citizens Advice Bureau, low pay units, Trade Unions and other bodies.

If you are not entitled to SPP you may be entitled to other government help. Contact your local Jobcentre plus/social security office.

SC3

BS11/03

5: STATUTORY PAY ENTITLEMENTS

Terms and conditions

On this form we haven't covered all of the law that relates to Statutory Paternity Pay (SPP) and leave. So if you are in any doubt about your entitlement talk to your employer or contact any Inland Revenue office.

SPP and paternity leave are available to

- a biological father
- a partner/husband that is not the baby's biological father
- a female partner in a same sex couple.

You must be able to declare that

- you are
  - the baby's biological father, or
  - married to the mother, or
  - living with the mother in an enduring family relationship, but are not an immediate relative, **and**
- you will be responsible for the child's upbringing, **and**
- you will take time off work to support the mother or care for the child.

You must be continuously employed during the pregnancy.

To get SPP you must also have average earnings over a set period above a set amount - your employer will work this out for you.

You can choose to take one or two whole weeks leave which must end by the 56th day after the date of birth. If the baby is born early you can choose to take your leave any time between the actual date of birth and the end of an 8 week period running from the Sunday of the week the baby was originally due. You cannot take odd days off work, but the weeks can start on any day, for example from Tuesday to Monday.

You must discuss your leave plans with your employer and tell them what time off you want by the 15th week before the week the baby is due. Your employer can tell you when this is if you're not sure. You can change your mind but you must give your employer 28 days notice of the dates. You and your employer may find it helpful if you filled in a new version of this form.

If you can't tell your employer what time off you want in time, or the baby is born sooner or later than expected, please discuss the situation with your employer. If you are unable to resolve any disagreement contact any Inland Revenue office for advice.

Disagreements

If your employer tells you that you are not entitled to SPP and/or paternity leave you can challenge that decision. If you need help with this, for

- SPP - contact your Inland Revenue office
- Paternity leave - contact ACAS, you will find the number in your phone book.

PART B   ASCERTAINING GROSS PAY

Your dates for pay and leave

The baby is due on   __/__/__

And, if the baby has been born, please enter the actual date of birth   __/__/__

I would like my SPP and/or paternity leave to start on   __/__/__

I want to be away from work for one/two* weeks   (*delete as appropriate)

Your declaration

Surname

First name(s)

National Insurance Number

You must be able to tick all three boxes below to get Statutory Paternity Pay and paternity leave.

I declare that

- I am   ✓
  - the baby's biological father, or
  - married to the mother, or
  - living with the mother in an enduring family relationship, but am not an immediate relative ☐
- I have responsiblity for the child's upbringing ☐
- I will take time off work to support the mother or care for the child. ☐

Signature

Date   __/__/__

Give this page to your employer, but keep the terms and conditions for your records.

5.3 Paternity leave

The employee can choose to have one or two whole weeks pay and leave. It must be taken as a single block, usually any time up to 8 weeks after the date of birth.

The employee may be entitled to paternity leave, but no SPP. However most employees will be entitled to both.

5.4 Average earnings

Average earnings are calculated in the same way as for SMP. For babies due between 6 April and 17 July 2004, average earnings must be at least £77.00 per week.

For babies due between 18 July 2004 and 16 July 2005, average earnings must be at least £79.00 per week.

5.5 Notice period

To qualify for SPP and paternity leave, an employee has to give notice of when 'he' expects to stop work by the Saturday of the 15th week before baby is due. Tables are given in booklet E15.

The employee has to confirm the date of birth and the employer can ask for this in writing. However, the employer **cannot** ask for evidence of the birth.

The employee has to give 28 days notice of leave, unless there is a good reason for short notice (eg baby born early).

If the notice is given late and there is no good reason for the delay, the employer can delay the start of leave and payment of SPP until 28 days after the date of notification.

5.6 Rate of SPP

SPP starts the day after the last day of work before starting paternity leave. SSP is paid at the **lower** of:

- 90% of average weekly earnings
- £102.80

It is paid for one or two weeks, as **chosen by the employee**. However, it can not be paid more than 8 weeks after the baby is due.

5.7 Recovery of SPP

The rules for recovery are exactly the same as those for SMP. Therefore all employers can recover 92% of SPP. Small employers (those whose annual NICs are £45,000 or less) can recover 100% of SPP, plus compensation of 4.5%.

PART B   ASCERTAINING GROSS PAY

5.8 Recording SPP

SPP is liable to tax and NIC, and so must be recorded on the P11 deduction card. There is a column (1h) for it. It should also be recorded in column 2 and tax and NIC calculated in the normal way. Remember SPP is the **minimum** payment due. Some employers may have occupational paternity pay schemes paying more than this. In this case, the full amount of occupational paternity pay is shown in column 2, with the SPP element in column 1h.

The Inland Revenue produce a record form SPP2. However, the employer does not have to use this, provided his own records include sufficient detail to prepare the end of year returns (see Level 3).

5.9 Exclusion

An employee is excluded from SPP in the following circumstances.

- Has not completed a declaration of family commitment
- Has not worked continuously for 9 months prior to the week baby is due
- Does not continue working right up to the actual birth
- Does not earn enough
- Does not give 28 days notice of leave and does not have a good reason for lateness.

In these cases, give the employee form SPP1. Keep a copy of the SC3 declaration and return the original to the employee.

Form SPP1 is reproduced on the following pages.

5.10 SPP and leavers

If the employee leaves before the baby is born, then he or she is not entitled to SPP, or paternity leave.

If the employee takes paternity leave, but is not returning to work, you still need to pay SPP for the full period. If the employee requests P45 before the end of the period, use the existing tax code to work out tax deductions to the date of the P45, then deduct tax at the basic rate thereafter. Otherwise use the tax code for the whole period and give the former employee P45 at the end of the SPP period.

5: STATUTORY PAY ENTITLEMENTS

Inland Revenue

Statutory Paternity Pay (SPP)

Why I cannot pay you SPP

Employee's surname

Other names

National Insurance number

Address

Postcode

Why I cannot pay you SPP

I have ticked the box that applies to you.

☐ I cannot pay you SPP. I have ticked one (or more) of the boxes overleaf to tell you why.

☐ I cannot pay you any more SPP after the week which ends on   /   /

    I have ticked one of the boxes on the next page of this letter to tell you why I cannot carry on paying you after this date.

What to do if you disagree

If you disagree with this decision, please let me know. My name, address and phone number are at the bottom of this page. If you still disagree, you can ask the Inland Revenue for a decision. You will find the number in your local phone book.

Other help

If you qualify for paternity leave but not SPP you may be able to get Income Support while you are on leave. For more details contact your local social security office or Jobcentre plus office, see the phone book.
Ask for claim form *A1*. Show this letter to confirm you are not entitled to SPP.

You may also want to claim Child Benefit or tax credits, see www.dwp.gov.uk or www.inlandrevenue.gov.uk for more information.

Employer's signature

Phone number

Date   /   /

Employer's name

Employer's address

Postcode

please turn over ▶

SPP1   BS11/02

PART B ASCERTAINING GROSS PAY

Why I cannot pay you SPP *continued*

I have ticked one (or more) of the boxes to tell you why I cannot pay you SPP.

☐ You were not employed by me for long enough	To get SPP
	• for a baby you must have worked for your employer continuously during the pregnancy
	• for a child that is being adopted you must have worked for your employer continuously
	  – for 26 weeks by the time the person adopting the child is notified by the adoption agency that they would be a suitable adoptive parent for the child
	  – from the time the person adopting the child is notified by the adoption agency that they would be a suitable adoptive parent for the child, until the child starts living with the adopter.

☐ Your earnings were too low	To get SPP your average earnings must be at least equal to the Lower Earnings Limit. Some employers have a special arrangement with the Inland Revenue to pay Class 1B National Insurance contributions on some of your earnings. This may mean that your employer may not count all your earnings when working out your average earnings. Ask your employer if any of your earnings were included in such an arrangement and then ask them to recalculate your earnings as if you had been paying Class 1 National Insurance contributions on them.
☐ You did not tell me soon enough that you would be away from work	To get SPP you must give your employer at least 4 weeks notice that you will be away from work. If you had a good reason for telling your employer late they may be able to accept late notice.
☐ You did not give me acceptable evidence of your entitlement soon enough	To get SPP you must give your employer acceptable evidence of your entitlement at least 4 weeks before you are away from work. If you had a good reason for giving the evidence to your employer late they may be able to accept it.
☐ You are entitled to Statutory Sick Pay	You cannot get SPP during any week when you are entitled to Statutory Sick Pay.
☐ You started work on / /	You cannot get SPP if you work for me or for a new employer.

2

5: STATUTORY PAY ENTITLEMENTS

6 Statutory Adoption Pay (SAP)

> **Signpost**
> Note that, although the range statement does not include any SAP forms, you are expected to be able to complete form SAP1. The guidance to this Unit indicates that you must be able to calculate SAP manually.

6.1 Eligibility

To be eligible for SAP, the employee must fulfil the following conditions.

- Adopting a child on their own
- Adopting a child with their partner
- Evidence of matching
- Be employed continuously for 26 weeks prior to the date of matching (see tables in booklet E16)
- Earn an average weekly amount at least equal to the National Insurance lower earnings limit
- Claim SAP at least 28 days before the pay period (or later with good reason) and within seven days of the date of matching.

Sometimes there is very little time between the adoption agency telling the employee that a child has been matched and placement. If this is the reason why evidence is late, the employer must accept it.

6.2 SAP/SPP

SPP and paternity leave are available to any employee (male or female) satisfying these conditions.

- The partner of someone adopting a child on their own
- Adopting a child with their partner

However, SAP and adoption leave and SPP and paternity leave are not available to foster or step parents that go on to adopt the child.

Where couples are adopting together, one partner can chose SAP and adoption leave, while the other has SPP and paternity leave. It is up to the couple to chose who gets what.

The employee who opts for SPP/paternity leave needs to complete form SC4, to be employed for 26 weeks prior to matching and during the period between matching and placement, otherwise all the rules are as for normal SPP.

Form SC4 is reproduced overleaf.

PART B ASCERTAINING GROSS PAY

Inland Revenue

Statutory Paternity Pay/ Paternity Leave

Becoming an adoptive parent

If you want to take time off work to support your partner who is adopting a child you may be entitled to

- Statutory Paternity Pay (SPP) - at least part of your wages will be paid for two weeks. You will get the weekly rate of SPP current at the time of your paternity leave, or 90% of your average weekly earnings, whichever is less.
- Paternity leave - up to two weeks time off.

Depending on your circumstances you may not qualify for SPP and/or paternity leave. Your employer will let you know. If this is the case you will get more advice and information at the time.

If you need help with this form please contact any Inland Revenue office. You will find the number in the phone book.

Please read through the terms and conditions on page 2 and if you think you might qualify, then

- fill in page 3
- give the completed statement to your employer.

Other help

The DTI publication *Adoptive Parents - rights to leave and pay - a guide for employers and employees* gives information on these rights, and details of other booklets covering employment protection and related equal opportunities legislation. Available from

- DTI publications on **0870 1502 500**, or
- go to **www.dti.gov.uk/er**

Go to **www.dwp.gov.uk** for details of social security benefits.

You can also contact

- any Inland Revenue office
- any Arbitration and Conciliation Advisory Service (ACAS) office (see **www.acas.org.uk** for details)
- **www.tiger.gov.uk**

Information on all aspects of employment legislation is also usually available from any Citizens Advice Bureau, low pay units, Trade Unions and other bodies.

If you are not entitled to SPP you should contact your adoption agency to find out if you can get any other help.

SC4　　　　　　　　　　1　　　　　　　　　　BS11/03

5: STATUTORY PAY ENTITLEMENTS

Terms and conditions

On this form we haven't covered all of the law that relates to Statutory Paternity Pay (SPP) and leave. So if you are in any doubt about your entitlement talk to your employer or contact any Inland Revenue office.

SPP and paternity leave are available to any employee (male or female) who is

- the partner of someone adopting a child on their own, or
- adopting a child with their partner.

It is not normally available to foster parents or step-parents who go on to adopt the child, or their partners.

You must be able to declare that

- you are
  - married to the person adopting the child, or
  - living with the person adopting the child in an enduring family relationship, but are not an immediate relative, **and**
- you will be responsible for the child's upbringing, **and**
- you will take time off work to support the person adopting the child or to care for the child.

If you and your partner are adopting a child together you must also declare that you have chosen not to receive Statutory Adoption Pay.

You must be continuously employed

- for 26 weeks up to and including the week the person adopting the child is told by the adoption agency that they have been matched with the child, **and**
- from the week the person adopting the child is told by the adoption agency that they have been matched with the child until the child is placed with them.

To get SPP you must also have average earnings over a set period above a set amount - your employer will work this out for you.

You can choose to take one or two whole weeks leave which must end by the 56th day after the date the child is placed with the person adopting them. You cannot take odd days off work, but the weeks can start on any day, for example from Tuesday to Monday.

You must discuss your leave plans with your employer and tell them what time off you want within seven days of the date the adoption agency told the person adopting the child that they have been matched with the child. You can change your mind, but you must give your employer 28 days notice of the new date. You and your employer may find it helpful if you fill in a new version of this form.

If you can't tell your employer what time off you want in time please discuss the situation with your employer. For example, sometimes a child is matched and placed very quickly. If you are unable to resolve any disagreement contact any Inland Revenue office for advice.

Disagreements

If your employer tells you that you are not entitled to SPP and/or paternity leave you can challenge that decision. If you need help with this, for

- SPP - contact your Inland Revenue office
- Paternity leave - contact ACAS, you will find the number in the phone book.

2

PART B ASCERTAINING GROSS PAY

Your dates for pay and leave

The adoption agency told the person adopting the child that they had been matched with the child on ☐☐ / ☐☐ / ☐☐

The child is expected to be placed on ☐☐ / ☐☐ / ☐☐

And, if the child has been placed, please enter the date they were placed ☐☐ / ☐☐ / ☐☐

I would like my SPP and/or paternity leave to start on ☐☐ / ☐☐ / ☐☐

I want to be away from work for one/two* weeks   (*delete as appropriate)

Your declaration

Surname

First name(s)

National Insurance number

You must tick this box if you are adopting a child with your partner.

I declare that I am adopting the child with my partner and I want to receive Statutory Paternity Pay and paternity leave not Statutory Adoption Pay and adoption leave. ✓ ☐

You must be able to tick all three boxes below to get Statutory Paternity Pay and paternity leave.

I declare that

- I am ✓
    - married to the person adopting the child, or
    - living with the person adopting the child in an enduring family relationship, but am not an immediate relative, and ☐
- I will have responsiblity for the child's upbringing ☐
- I will take time off work to support the person adopting the child or to care for the child. ☐

Signature

Date ☐☐ / ☐☐ / ☐☐

Give this page to your employer, but keep the terms and conditions for your records.

3

5: STATUTORY PAY ENTITLEMENTS

> **Important!**
> The rest of this section deals solely with SAP.

6.3 Notification

The employee **must** notify the employer of these dates

- Date the adoption agency tells them that they have been **matched** with a child
- Date the child is **placed** with the adopter.

Matching means the adoption agency has decided that the person is suitable to adopt that child.

Placing means the child starts living permanently with that person with a view to being formally adopted.

6.4 Evidence of matching

The employee must provide documentary evidence of matching. This may be a certificate or letter. However, it must include the following information.

- Name and address of adoption agency
- Name and address of employee
- Date the child is expected to be placed for adoption (or date child was placed)
- Date the employee was matched with child

The employer must not pay SAP if the evidence is not acceptable.

6.5 Adoption leave

Adoption leave is similar to maternity leave and can last for up to 52 weeks. SAP is only paid for up to 26 weeks. The employee can chose when they start adoption leave but it must be no later than the date of placement.

The employee can chose when they start adoption leave but it must be no later than the date of placement.

If the employee chooses to return to work early, they must give the employer 28 days notice of return to work.

If insufficient notice of taking leave is given, without good reason, then no SAP is payable. However, unpaid leave can be taken.

6.6 Average earnings

These are calculated in exactly the same way as for SMP and SPP. On the date of **matching**, average earnings for the previous 8 weeks must be at least £79.00 per week for 2004/05.

6.7 Rates of SAP

SAP is paid from the day after the last working day before taking adoption leave. SAP is taxable and subject to NICs.

SAP is paid at the lower of:

- £102.80
- 90% of average weekly earnings

SAP is usually paid for 26 weeks. However, if the child dies, or stops living with the adopter, payment ceases eight weeks later.

6.8 Recovery of SAP

Recovery of SAP is exactly the same as for SMP.

6.9 Recording SAP

Record SAP in column 1i of form P11. As SAP is taxable and NICable record the amount in column 2 as well and work out tax and NIC in the usual way.

If the employer has an organisational adoption pay scheme, then payments over the minimum (SAP) may be made. Record the full gross pay in column 2 and the SAP element in Column 1i.

The Inland Revenue produce a SAP record sheet (SAP2) but completion is voluntary. Employers can ignore it provided they have sufficient information to prepare the year end returns (see Level 3).

6.10 Exclusion

The employee is excluded from SAP in the following circumstances

- No evidence of matching or provided late without good reason
- Not employed continuously for 26 weeks prior to date of matching
- Earnings too low
- Insufficient notice of pay and leave

If the employee is excluded, give them form SAP1. Take a copy of the matching evidence and return the original to the employee.

Form SAP1 is reproduced on the following pages.

6.11 SAP and leavers

If the employee decides not to return to work, the employer still has to pay SAP for the full 26 weeks.

If the employee leaves during the period of adoption leave, you still have to make payments unless they are employed by someone else. If the employee does not request form P45, continue using the old tax code and complete P45 after the last payment of SAP. If the employer requests P45, make basic rate tax deductions for payments after the date of the P45.

6.12 Other types of leave

There are other types of time off for dependants, including flexible working. See Chapter 1 for full details.

5: STATUTORY PAY ENTITLEMENTS

Inland Revenue

Statutory Adoption Pay (SAP)

Why I cannot pay you SAP

Employee's surname

Other names

National Insurance number

Address

Postcode

Why I cannot pay you SAP

I have ticked the box that applies to you.

☐ I cannot pay you SAP. I have ticked one (or more) of the boxes overleaf to tell you why.

☐ I cannot pay you any more SAP after the week which ends on / /

I have ticked one of the boxes on the next page of this letter to tell you why I cannot carry on paying you after this date.

What to do if you disagree

If you disagree with this decision, please let me know. My name, address and phone number are at the bottom of this page. If you still disagree, you can ask the Inland Revenue for a decision. You will find the number in the phone book.

Other help

If you qualify for adoption leave but not SAP contact your adoption agency to find out if you can get any other help.

You may also want to claim Child Benefit or tax credits, see www.dwp.gov.uk or www.inlandrevenue.gov.uk for more information.

Employer's signature

Phone number

Date / /

Employer's name

Employer's address

Postcode

please turn over ▶

SAP1

BS12/02

PART B ASCERTAINING GROSS PAY

Why I cannot pay you SAP *continued*

I have ticked one (or more) of the boxes to tell you why I cannot pay you SAP.

☐	**You were not employed by me for long enough**	To get SAP you must have worked for me continuously, for 26 weeks by the time the adoption agency tell you that you have been matched with a child for adoption.
☐	**Your earnings were too low**	To get SAP your average earnings must be at least equal to the Lower Earnings Limit. Some employers have a special arrangement with the Inland Revenue to pay Class 1B National Insurance contributions on some of your earnings. This may mean that your employer may not count all your earnings when working out your average earnings. Ask your employer if any of your earnings were included in such an arrangement and then ask them to recalculate your earnings as if you had been paying Class 1 National Insurance contributions on them.
☐	**You did not tell me soon enough that you would be away from work**	To get SAP you must give your employer at least 4 weeks notice that you will be away from work. If you had a good reason for telling your employer late they may be able to accept late notice.
☐	**You did not give me acceptable evidence of your entitlement soon enough**	To get SAP you must give your employer acceptable evidence of your entitlement at least four weeks before you are away from work. If you had a good reason for giving the evidence to your employer late they may be able to accept it.
☐	**I paid you Statutory Sick Pay from** / /	You cannot get SAP during any week when you are entitled to Statutory Sick Pay.
☐	**You were in prison or detained in legal custody on** / /	You cannot get SAP from your employer if you are detained in legal custody on or after the first day of the SAP pay period. However you may be able to get SAP from the Inland Revenue after you are released. You will find the number in the phone book.
☐	**You worked from** / /	You cannot get SAP during any week when you work for your employer or if you start working for a new employer.

7 Tax credits

> **Signpost**
> The range for this element includes certificates of payment for tax credits. Under the 2004/05 tax rules, these are no longer relevant.

7.1 WTC

Working Tax Credit replaced the old Working Families Tax Credit and the Disabled Persons Tax Credit from 6 April 2003.

It is used to supplement the earnings of the low paid.

Payments are made by employers through the PAYE system.

7.1.1 Starting WTC payments

An employer does not pay tax credits until the Inland Revenue notifies them to do so.

A Start Notice (TC700) will be sent to the employer at least 42 days before payments are to start. Once payments are started, they continue until further notice from the Inland Revenue. The notice gives a daily rate of tax credit. To calculate the amount due, multiply the number of calender days in a pay period by the daily rate.

If the rate changes, the Inland Revenue will send an amendment notice (TC701).

7.1.2 Stopping WTC payments

Tax credit payments cease when one of the following occurs.

- A Stop Notice (TC702) is received, giving at least 42 days notice of cessation
- An Emergency Stop Notice (TC 703) is received
- The employee leaves
- The employee dies

There are no forms for the employer to complete in these circumstances.

7.1.3 Recovery of tax credits

As for SSP, SMP, SPP and SAP tax credits are recovered by deduction from the monthly payment made to the Inland Revenue. The employer recovers 100% but receives no compensation.

Advance funding is available from the Inland Revenue.

PART B   ASCERTAINING GROSS PAY

7.1.4 Recording tax credits

Tax credits are not taxable or NICable. They are added to net pay. Record tax credits in column 9 of the P11.

7.2 CTC

Child tax credit was introduced on 6 April 2003. It replaces Children's Tax Credit.

The employer does not need to take any action regarding CTC, as is paid direct to the main carer.

8 Spreadsheets for the manual calculation of gross pay

8.1 Spreadsheets

A spreadsheet is a computer's version of a handwritten schedule. It has advantages over a manual sheet, in that changes can be easily made and the computer can be programmed to do the calculations.

	A	B	C	D	E
1					
2					
3					
4					
5					
6					

A spreadsheet has columns designated by letters and rows designated by numbers. The squares formed are called **cells**. The shaded cell shown done is called cell E6.

8.2 Calculating gross pay

A spreadsheet can be used to calculate gross pay. Each column can be headed with a different element of pay. For example.

B = basic pay
C = overtime
D = Bonus, commission, etc
E = Backpay
F = SSP
G = SMP
H = SPP
I = SAP

Note that tax credits should **not** be included on this Schedule as they are additions to **net pay**.

The numbered rows can then be used for each employee, so that column A = employee name.

	A	B	C	D	E	F	G	H	I	J
1	B Jones	100	–	50	–	64.35	–	–	–	214.35
2										
3										
4										
5										
6										
7										

The different elements of pay are entered into each column. In the example above, column J = total gross pay. This is obtained by adding across columns B to I. Cell J1 can be set with the formula '= B1 + C1 + D1 + E1 + F1 + G1 + H1 + I1'. This can be done quickly by entering '=' in cell J1 and then highlighting cells B1 to I1.

When information is entered in any of the cells B1 to I1, the computer will carry out the addition and enter the total in J1.

As you grow more confident, you can program the computer to calculate individual pay elements, eg overtime, SSP, etc.

PART B ASCERTAINING GROSS PAY

Key learning points

- There are a number of items that may appear on an employee's payslip other than basic pay. **Some of these have a tax effect; some do not**.
- **SSP** is taxable and is paid at a rate of £66.15 per week.
- **SMP** and **SAP** are taxable and are paid at the higher rate of 90% of average weekly wage for the first 6 weeks, then at the lower of 90% of average weekly wage or £102.80 for the next 20 weeks.
- **SPP** is taxable and is paid at 90% of average weekly wage for one or two weeks.
- **Tax credits** are added to net pay.
- **Spreadsheets** can be used to calculate gross pay.

5: STATUTORY PAY ENTITLEMENTS

Quick quiz

1. Is SSP payable to all sick employees?
2. Is SMP payable to an employee who has worked for you only 20 weeks before the week the baby is due.
3. Is SPP payable to women?
4. What is the minimum notice period for SAP?
5. How much WTC is due to a weekly paid employee with a 5 day working week and a daily rate of £5.60?

Answers to quick quiz

1. No. SSP is only paid to sick employees who earn £79 per week or more. In addition, no SSP is paid for the first three days' illness.
2. No. SMP is only paid to employees who have worked continuously for the 9 months up to and including the week baby is due.
3. Yes. It can be paid to a woman in a same sex partnership, or to a woman in the case of an adoption where her partner receives SAP.
4. 28 days before the pay period or within 7 days of the date of matching.
5. £39.20 (7 × £5.60). WTC is paid for calendar days.

Activity checklist

This checklist shows which performance criteria, range statement or knowledge and understanding point is covered by each activity in this chapter. Tick off each activity as you complete it.

Activity

5.1	☐	This activity covers performance criterion 72.2.A and knowledge and understanding point 5.
5.2	☐	This activity covers performance criteria 72.2.A and 72.2.B and knowledge and understanding points 5 and 18.
5.3	☐	This activity covers performance criterion 72.2.D and knowledge and understanding point 4.
5.4	☐	This activity covers performance criteria 72.2.D and 72.2.E and knowledge and understanding points 4 and 18.
5.5	☐	This activity covers performance criterion 72.2.D and knowledge and understanding point 4.

PART B ASCERTAINING GROSS PAY

PART C

Determining net pay

chapter 6

Income tax: simple cases

Contents

1. The problem
2. The solution
3. PAYE system
4. 'Pay in the week or month'
5. Tax allowances and free pay
6. Tax codes
7. Taxable pay and tax rates
8. Tables A – pay adjustment tables
9. Tables SR, B, C and D: taxable pay tables
10. Using the tax tables: a summary
11. Form P11: deductions working sheet
12. Taxable pay tables: calculator tables

Performance criteria

72.1.E Identify all payments in respect of their tax, National Insurance and pension liability

73.1.E Contribute to the resolution of individual employees' queries by checking net pay calculations manually, using the appropriate tax and National Insurance tables

Knowledge and understanding

2 PAYE regulations in respect of the manual calculation of gross to net pay

13 How to use tax and NI tables to perform manual calculations of net pay

PART C   DETERMINING NET PAY

> **Signpost**
> The standards make it clear that students must know how to calculate tax deductions manually. This is not only useful in case of computer failure, but enables students to deal with queries. It is vital that students understand the different tax codes.

1 The problem

We have calculated gross pay, but now we need to make statutory and non-statutory deductions. Chief among the statutory deductions is tax.

How do we calculate an employee's tax liability?

2 The solution

Tax deductions are calculated on the basis of the following.

- Pay period
- Tax free pay (tax code)
- Taxable pay (after certain deductions)
- Tax tables

This chapter will deal with all of these points. In Chapter 7 we will look at the more complex issues which can arise.

Remember the main requirements for payroll processing.

- Accuracy (to the penny)
- Timeliness (employees paid when due, deductions paid when due)
- Security (all employee data is **confidential**)

3 PAYE system

3.1 Employees included in the PAYE system

PAYE stands for Pay As You Earn. It covers income tax and, by extension, NICs.

- PAYE applies to all the **employees** of an organisation, including **directors** and also **pensioners** who are being paid by the company out of a pension fund.

- PAYE does not cover **self-employed people**. If you are unsure about the difference, re-read Chapter 1.

166

Activity 6.1

You are the payroll officer at Clueless Ltd. How would you answer the following queries?

(a) Mr Dawson, the new Managing Director, has sent a memo to the Payroll Department stating that as a director of the company he should be paid gross and therefore instructing you to stop deducting income tax and National Insurance from his salary.

(b) Mrs Mone, the recently retired cleaner, is outraged that her company pension is subject to PAYE. She states that as she has worked all her life and paid all her taxes, her pension should be tax free.

(c) Ms Simmons is a self-employed graphic designer who has queried the fact that your company has not deducted any tax or National Insurance from her fees.

3.2 Tax offices and PAYE reference numbers

To operate the PAYE system, the **Inland Revenue** deals with **employers** through a network of **tax offices**. Each employer is allocated the following.

- A particular **Tax Office** to deal with
- A **PAYE reference number**

Employees have the same Tax Office as their (main) employer, and the Tax Office will attach this same employer's identity number to its records for each employee.

For example, if your employer has a PAYE reference code 836/B3629, your own PAYE reference code will be 836/B3629 too.

However, an employee also has an **individual reference number**, which is his or her **National Insurance number** (NINO), see Chapter 8.

3.3 The tax year

The **tax year** runs from **6 April** in one calendar year to **5 April** in the following calendar year. **The 2004/05 tax year runs from 6 April 2004 to 5 April 2005.**

Each tax year is divided up into pay periods.

- 53 weeks, for **weekly paid** staff.
- 12 months, for **monthly paid** staff.

The weeks and months of each tax year are given a number. These are shown below.

PART C DETERMINING NET PAY

Income tax calendar: monthly basis

Month No.	Period covered (dates inclusive)	Month No.	Period covered (dates inclusive)
1	April 6 - May 5	7	Oct 6 - Nov 5
2	May 6 - June 5	8	Nov 6 - Dec 5
3	June 6 - July 5	9	Dec 6 - Jan 5
4	July 6 - Aug 5	10	Jan 6 - Feb 5
5	Aug 6 - Sept 5	11	Feb 6 - Mar 5
6	Sept 6 - Oct 5	12	Mar 6 - April 5

Income tax calendar: weekly basis

Week No.	Period covered (dates inclusive)	Week No.	Period covered (dates inclusive)	Week No.	Period covered (dates inclusive)
1	April 6-12	22	Aug 31-Sept 6	43	Jan 25-31
2	April 13-19	23	Sept 7-13	44	Feb 1-7
3	April 20-26	24	Sept 14-20	45	Feb 8-14
4	April 27-May 3	25	Sept 21-27	46	Feb 15-21
5	May 4-10	26	Sept 28-Oct 4	47	Feb 22-28
6	May 11-17	27	Oct 5-11		
7	May 18-24	28	Oct 12-18		*Leap years*
8	May 25-31	29	Oct 19-25	48	Feb 29-Mar 6
9	June 1-7	30	Oct 26-Nov 1	49	Mar 7-13
10	June 8-14	31	Nov 2-8	50	Mar 14-20
11	June 15-21	32	Nov 9-15	51	Mar 21-27
12	June 22-28	33	Nov 16-22	52	Mar 28-Apr 3
13	June 29-July 5	34	Nov 23-29	53	April 4-5
14	July 6-12	35	Nov 30-Dec 6		
15	July 13-19	36	Dec 7-13		*Non-leap years*
16	July 20-26	37	Dec 14-20	48	Mar 1-7
17	July 27-Aug 2	38	Dec 21-27	49	Mar 8-14
18	Aug 3-9	39	Dec 28-Jan 3	50	Mar 15-21
19	Aug 10-16	40	Jan 4-10	51	Mar 22-28
20	Aug 17-23	41	Jan 11-17	52	Mar 29-Apr 4
21	Aug 24-30	42	Jan 18-24	53	April 5

The **pay day** for an employee will always fall within a particular week or month of the tax calendar.

- For example, if an employee is paid on 16 May, this is a payment in:
  - week 6, for weekly paid staff
  - month 2, for monthly paid staff.

- A payment of wages or salaries on 31 March is:
  - in week 52, for weekly paid staff
  - in month 12, for monthly paid staff.

Activity 6.2

Which tax month will the following pay days fall in?

(a) 24 June
(b) 8 November
(c) 19 December

In which tax weeks do the following pay days fall?

(d) 24 April
(e) 26 June
(f) 2 October
(g) 15 January

3.4 Weekly or monthly tax tables

The Inland Revenue produces two sets of tax tables.

- Tables for **weekly paid** employees
- Tables for **monthly paid** employees

This is because most employees are paid either weekly or monthly.

3.4.1 Tables for employees paid neither weekly nor monthly

However, sometimes the pay day is **every fortnight** or **every four weeks**, and occasionally employees are paid at **other regular intervals** or at **irregular intervals**.

Pay days occur	Guidance
Fortnightly	Use the tables for weeks 2, 4, 6 etc. up to week 52, even if pay days are actually in the odd-numbered weeks.
Four weekly	Use the tables for weeks 4, 8, 12 etc. up to week 52, even if the pay days are actually in other weeks.
Quarterly	Use the tables for months 3, 6, 9 and 12, regardless of when the pay days actually occur.
Half yearly	You can probably guess this one! Use the tables for months 6 and 12, even if the pay days are in different months.
Yearly	Use the tax tables for month 12, even if the payment is made in another month.

The frequency of pay days makes no difference at all to the total amount of tax paid.

PART C DETERMINING NET PAY

Income tax is usually calculated on a **cumulative basis**. Every pay day the amount earned so far in this tax year is used to calculate what should have been paid in tax so far.

That is why **backdated pay** is taxed in the period of payment and does not need to be spread back through the tax year.

> **Important!**
>
> You need to be able to deal with the following pay periods.
>
> - Weekly
> - Fortnightly
> - Four weekly
> - Monthly
> - Irregular

3.5 Calculating income tax

In this chapter we are **calculating the income tax to be deducted from employees at each pay day**. Before going into the detail, you may find the following overview useful – refer back to it as you work through this chapter.

Don't worry if you don't understand the **terms**. What *is* important is to grasp that calculating income tax is a methodical, logical procedure and that you have to work through the steps in the right order.

		£	Section(s) in this chapter
Step 1	Use gross pay calculation to calculate 'pay in the week or month'	X	4
Step 2	Add previous total pay to date	X	11
Step 3	Total pay to date	X	11
Step 4	Deduct total free pay to date (based on tax allowances, tax code and Tables A)	(X)	5, 6, 8
Step 5	Total taxable pay to date	X	7

Step 6	Calculate total tax due to date on taxable pay to date from:
	    Table SR (10% starting rate) or
	    Table B and subtraction tables (22% basic rate) *or*
	    Tables C and D (40% higher rate)
		X	9, 12

Step 7	Deduct total tax due at end of previous period	(X)	9, 11
Step 8	Tax deducted in this period	X	9, 11

The figures calculated above are recorded on the deduction card (Inland Revenue form P11 Deductions Working Sheet). We look at this in detail in Section 11 of this Chapter. You may find it helpful to have a quick look at this form now (it is reproduced on pages 195 and 196).

4 'Pay in the week or month'

4.1 Gross pay

We looked at calculating gross pay in Chapters 4 and 5. This figure is the **starting point** in calculating the **'pay in the week or month'**, also known as gross pay for tax purposes.

The more usual items of pay included in **pay in the week or month** are:

- **Salaries**, **wages**, **fees**, **overtime payments**, **bonuses**, **commissions**
- **Statutory sick pay**
- **Statutory maternity pay/statutory paternity pay/statutory adoption pay**
- **Holiday pay**
- **Lump sum payments** when an employee leaves (a '**golden handshake**') or when an employee joins (a '**golden hello**')

Holiday pay for leavers is included in gross pay for the final payday. Tax and NI is calculated on the total, including holiday pay, at the date of payment.

The gross pay paid to an employee may not be the same as his or her gross pay for income tax and/or National Insurance purposes. This is because some items of gross pay are tax-free, or NI-free, or free of both tax and NI (eg reimbursed expenses).

4.2 Expenses: not included

Payments for expenses claims, where the employee is repaid for **business** expenses that were initially paid out of his or her own pocket, **are not included in 'pay in the week or month'**. They are paid free of tax and NI deductions.

4.3 Benefits: not included

There are some other 'payments' to an employee that are not included by the employer in 'pay in the week or month'.

Often these are not payments in the cash sense at all, but are benefits which are deemed to have a certain value by the tax authorities. Examples include the following.

- The value of the employee's **company car and petrol**
- Payments for **private medical insurance** for the employee (and family)
- Other **assets given to the employee** by the organisation, such as television sets, furniture and private aeroplanes

You are not required to have detailed knowledge about benefits until NVQ/SVQ Level 3. The tax due on these benefits is collected by adjusting the employee's tax code, as explained later in this chapter and in more detail in Chapter 7.

PART C   DETERMINING NET PAY

4.4 Other items: not included

Certain other items do **not** count as 'pay in the week or month' for **income tax** purposes. They are deducted from gross pay in order to arrive at 'pay in the week or month'.

- Contributions made to **GAYE** (see Chapter 10).
- Contributions to an **occupational pension scheme** (see Chapter 10).

Example: Pension contributions

Ranjit Singh has gross pay for this month of £5,000. He is a member of the occupational pension scheme and will pay pension contributions of £250 this month. What is his 'pay in the week or month' for income tax purposes?

Solution

	£
Gross pay	5,000
Pension contributions	(250)
Pay in the week or month	4,750

Activity 6.3

Louise Halloran receives the following salary package when she joins your company. Which elements will you include in her 'pay in the week or month' for PAYE purposes?

- Annual salary of £50,000
- Annual bonus of 1% of the company's annual pre-tax profits if they exceed £1million
- Commission at varying rates on every sale she makes
- Private medical insurance
- Non-contributory occupational pension scheme (ie only the employer pays into the scheme)
- Company car
- Company credit card to cover business entertainment and travel expenses

5 Tax allowances and free pay

The **tax allowance** is the amount a person can earn without paying tax during a particular tax year. This **personal allowance** is deducted from 'pay in the week or month' to arrive at taxable pay.

5.1 Main tax allowances

Allowances are given to individuals for a number of different reasons. The most common allowance is:

A **personal allowance** (£4,745 for the 2004/05 tax year: ie the first £4,745 of income is tax-free).

This allowance is higher for people aged 65 or over, and higher again for those aged 75 or over. (Elderly couples will receive the married couple's allowance in 2004/05, which has been abolished for all other taxpayers.)

Tax allowances are usually altered each year in the **Budget**, when the next tax year's allowances are announced, ie the 2004 Budget announced the allowances for tax year 2004/05. However, some allowances, such as the personal allowance, can be announced earlier, eg Pre Budget Report in December 2003 for 2004/05 personal allowance.

There are **other allowances** that an individual might be able to claim from the Inland Revenue. This is a matter for the individual and his or her Tax Office.

5.2 Free pay

Free pay is the amount of pay which an employee may receive free of tax on any pay date.

The total of a person's tax allowances for the year is sometimes known as that person's **free pay** for the year (the amount they are paid *free of tax*).

Since most employees are paid weekly or monthly, it makes sense to **divide their allowances for the year into equal weekly or monthly portions**. This is what the PAYE system does.

At any time during a tax year, therefore, an individual will be entitled to a certain amount of **free pay to date**. This will be deducted from total pay to date, in order to give the **taxable pay** to date.

Example: Free pay

If a monthly-paid employee is entitled to allowances of £4,800 for the whole year, there will be tax-free pay in each month of £400, and his or her **total free pay to date** for the year so far would be:

- £400 in month 1.
- £800 in month 2.
- £1,200 in month 3.
- £2,800 in month 7.
- £4,800 in month 12.

Activity 6.4

It is Month 9 of the tax year. John Jones has tax allowances of £6,000 for the year. What is his free pay to date?

PART C   DETERMINING NET PAY

5.3 Changes in tax allowances/free pay

An employee's **entitlement to tax allowances** for the year can change during the course of a tax year (and often does).

When this happens, the employee's total free pay entitlement for the year to date is now based on the **new** amount of allowances. In the month the change occurs, there is a 'hiccup' in the tax free pay for the month as the free pay is adjusted to the new allowance.

Example: Change in free pay

A monthly-paid employee's tax allowances for the year are increased from £4,800 to £6,000 during Month 4. How this affects his free pay in Month 4 and subsequently is shown below.

Month	Tax allowances for the year £	Total free pay to date £	Free pay in the month £
1	4,800	400 (ie £4,800 × $1/_{12}$)	400
2	4,800	800	400 (£800 – £400)
3	4,800	1,200	400 (£1,200 – £800)
4	6,000	2,000 (ie £6,000 × $4/_{12}$)	800 (£2,000 – £1,200)
5	6,000	2,500	500 (£2,500 – £2,000)
6	6,000	3,000	500 (£3,000 – £2,500)
"	"	"	"
"	"	"	"
"	"	"	"
12	6,000	6,000	500 (£6,000 – £5,500)

So when allowances for the year go **up**, **less tax** is paid in the month when the change is made (there might even be a refund). If the allowances go **down**, **more tax** is paid. We will see exactly how this works later in this chapter.

6 Tax codes

> **Signpost**
> Guidance from the Chief Assessor states that students need to know how tax codes are derived and how they operate.

The **tax code** of an employee is used on every pay day to work out the employee's free pay.

The amount of **allowances** for each tax payer is converted by the Tax Office into a **tax code**. The tax code is notified in a coding notice by the Tax Office to:

- The taxpayer (**employee**), form P2T
- His or her **employer**, form P6T

Since you will not (on the whole) get involved in the details of an employee's tax allowances, your main concern is with **receiving and applying the tax code** that is given to you by the Tax Office for each employee.

6.1 Characteristics of tax codes

Except for special tax codes, every **tax code** consists of a **number** followed by a **letter**, such as 706L. These are called **suffix codes**.

The **number** is the individual's **tax allowances**, with the last figure removed.

- If an individual's tax allowances for the year are £4,745, the tax code will contain the number 474.
- If an individual's tax allowances are £4,821 the tax code will contain the number 482.

The **letter** is used by the Inland Revenue to save issuing individual coding notices in as many cases as possible following any changes announced in the Pre Budget or Budget. The amount of the change will vary from letter to letter. This is what the letters mean:

Letter	Estimated top rate of tax	MCA	Aged 65-74	Aged 75 and over
L	N/A	✗	✗	✗
P	N/A	✗	✓	✗
V	Basic	✓	✓	✗
Y	N/A	✗	✗	✓

MCA = Married couple's allowance.

The only other letter used in suffix codes is T. This is used in the following circumstances.

- A taxpayer asks the Tax Office not to use any of the other codes.
- The Tax Office needs to review other items in the code, eg a small underpayment of tax for a previous year which is being collected through the PAYE system by reducing free pay.

T codes are only changed by a coding notice, not in a general uplift.

Activity 6.5

Tyson Paul (who is single) comes to the Payroll Office with a query about his tax code. It was 474L at the start of the 2004/05 tax year. He has now received a coding notice telling him that his new code is 683P. He asks if this means he will be paying higher rate tax from now on. Explain to him what effect his new code will have on his net pay.

Note. Personal allowances for 2004/05

	£
Aged under 65	4,745
Aged 65 to 74	6,830
Aged 75 or over	6,950

6.2 Special tax codes

In some circumstances, you will be required to use an **emergency tax code** for an employee. This usually happens when the employee's tax position hasn't yet been worked out by the Tax Office, and there is no other code to use in the meantime. It will sometimes apply, for example, to people who have just joined your organisation without form P45.

An **emergency code** treats the employee as a single person with just a personal allowance, and so the emergency code for 2004/05 is 474L. It often operates on a **Week 1/Month 1** basis: the meaning of this will be explained in Chapter 7.

There are a few other **special tax codes**, which do not have numbers, or which have numbers that do not indicate the amount of a person's tax allowance. You might come across some of these codes in your job, and be asked what they mean. We shall look at most of them in Chapter 7.

Code	Meaning
BR	The individual has no tax allowance and all his or her income will be taxable at the **basic rate** (BR) of 22%. (Note that no pay will be taxed at the starting rate of 10% or the higher rate of 40%.)
0T	There are no personal allowances. However, tax will be deducted first at the starting rate, then at the basic rate, then at higher rate, depending on the amount of income earned.
D0	This indicates that all of the person's income is taxable at the higher rate of 40% (you might come across this if you are paying someone whose main employment is elsewhere).
NT	This stands for No Tax. No tax at all is to be deducted from the person's pay. (However, tax already deducted should not be refunded when a person is given this code, unless the Tax Office tells you to do so.) This code will be applied to individuals whose income in the year will be very low, where another arrangement has been made to collect any tax, or where duties are carried out overseas.
K (followed by a number)	This means that a person's benefits and other adjustments are more than his or her allowances. Therefore there is no free pay and an adjustment will have to be **added to** taxable pay.

Activity 6.6

Your company is a subsidiary of Big plc. One of Big plc's directors also sits on your company's board and so your company pays her a salary. Her tax code is D0. What does this mean? Why do you think she has this code?

6.3 Coding notices

When an employee's tax code changes during the year, an employer receives notification on a **Form P6(T)**. A similar form (P2T) is sent by the Tax Office to the employee, giving more details about the allowances and so how the tax code has been worked out. This is often called a **coding notice** or a Notice of Coding.

An example of a P6(T) sent to an employer is shown below.

Inland Revenue

Issued by
H.M. Inspector of Taxes

PAYE - Notice to employer of employee's tax code (or amended code) and previous pay and tax

Date

Employer's PAYE reference

Employee's name

National Insurance number
(To be entered on the Deductions Working Sheet and to be quoted in any communication)

Works/Payroll no., Branch etc.

Tax Code:
The code of this employee is amended to

for the year to 5 April 2005

Please use this Tax Code from the next pay day after you receive this form and follow the instructions in Part A overleaf.

Previous Pay and Tax
Where there is an entry here please follow the instructions in both Parts A and B overleaf.

Previous pay   Previous tax

P6 (T)

When a P6(T) arrives from the Tax Office, you **must amend the tax code** in the employee's payroll records. In a manual payroll system, these records are held on the **Form P11 (deductions working sheet)** which is described in Section 11.

The form P6(T) is used by the Tax Office in the following ways.

- To tell an employer about any amendment to an employee's tax code.
- To tell an employer about a new employee's tax code.
- To tell an employer about a **new employee's previous pay and tax to date.**

PART C   DETERMINING NET PAY

The last point may be necessary if the new employee does not have a form P45, eg because he or she has lost it, or because the P45 is incorrect.

In a **large organisation**, with a huge number of employees, sending individual P6(T) forms for each individual would be a waste of paper and effort. Instead of sending P6(T) forms for individuals, the Tax Office will do one of the following.

- Send a **list** of employees and their new tax codes through the post.
- Transmit these details electronically for computerised payroll systems.

You must never amend an employee's tax code unless the Tax Office tells you to do so.

If there are any **queries** about a P6(T), or items on a list, you should speak to or write to your Tax Office.

6.4 Budget changes to tax allowances and tax codes

The annual Budget in March each year contains the taxation proposals for the tax year starting the following April. The 2004 Budget, for example, was for the tax year starting on 6 April 2004 and ending on 5 April 2005.

If allowances are changed in the Budget, or by prior announcement, then everybody's tax code changes. So in February, the Inland Revenue send out coding notices **P9(T)** for the following tax year eg February 2005 P9(T) notices will be for tax year 2005/06.

Instead of sending out a P9(T) or list for every working person in the country, the Inland Revenue also issues general instructions to employers to change all codes by certain amounts (form P9X). The form P9X for 2004 instructed employers to add 13 to any tax code ending in L. So that, for example, a code of 461L becomes 474L.

Finally there is another general form, P7X. Changes in the Budget are usually effective in May or June of the tax year. Form P7X is issued just before this date to deal with any last minute changes. For example the 2004 form P7X is effective from 18 May 2004.

7 Taxable pay and tax rates

Taxable pay is the person's total pay to date minus free pay (allowances) to date. It is the figure used in the calculation of tax due. For example:

	£
Total pay for the year to date	18,420
Less allowances/free pay	3,129
Taxable pay for the year to date	15,291

In Section 11 of this chapter, we will see that the form P11 deduction card makes the calculations of these figures very easy to work out.

7.1 Tax rates

Taxable pay is taxed at rates set by Parliament each year. For the 2004/05 tax year, there are three **tax rates** on income, applying to different **bands of taxable pay** for the year.

	Tax rate %	Taxable pay band	Size of band (pa)
Starting	10	0 – £2,020	£2,020
Basic	22	£2,021 – £31,400	£29,380
Higher	40	Over £31,400	Balance of taxable pay

Remember that free pay is divided into equal portions over the tax year, so that the employee gets a bit of free pay on each pay day.

Similarly, **the starting rate and basic rate bands are spread over the whole tax year** so the employee doesn't pay all his starting rate tax in say, Month 1-3 and all his higher rate tax in Month 12. This will be clear if we look at an example.

Example: Tax rates and taxable pay

Jean Twigg earns £30,000 per annum and is paid monthly. Her allowances are £4,745 for 2004/05, so she is not a higher rate taxpayer – her taxable pay is £25,255 pa (£30,000 - £4,745).

	£
Per month	
Pay in the month (£30,000 ÷ 12)	2,500.00
Free pay (£4,745 ÷ 12)	395.42
Taxable pay	2,104.58

How much tax will Jean pay each month?

Solution

We allocate equal portions of each band against pay in each period.

	£	Rate %	£	£
Pay for month				2,500.00
Starting rate band (£2,020 ÷ 12)	168.33	10	16.83	
Basic rate band (balance)	1,936.25	22	425.97	
Taxable pay	2,104.58			
Tax due on taxable pay				(442.80)
Pay net of income tax each month				2,057.20

This evens out Jean's net pay over the 12 months of the year.

Further example: Tax rates and taxable pay

Julius Evans has **taxable pay** of £37,500 in a year. Tax will be deducted in each month as follows.

	Tax £
Starting rate band: £2,020 / 12 × 10%	16.83
Basic rate band: £29,380 / 12 × 22%	538.63
Higher rate band: (£37,500 − £31,400) × $\frac{1}{12}$ × 40%	203.33
Total tax payable each month	758.79

Activity 6.7

Gina James earns £35,000 per annum. If her tax allowances are £5,000, how much income tax will she pay in the tax year 2004/05?

7.2 The need for tax tables

You can see that a lot of repetitive calculations have been needed so far. You won't need to do these in practice. Note that the actual calculation will be carried out in one of two ways.

- By computer.
- Manually with the use of tax tables and forms supplied by the Inland Revenue.

Tax tables are used in a manual payroll system to work out how much tax to deduct from (or refund to) each employee on each pay day. They are designed for use with tax codes, and are supplied free of charge to an employer by the Tax Office. A set of tax tables consists of:

- Tables A - these are called Pay Adjustment Tables (see Section 8 below)
- Tables SR and B to D - these are called Taxable Pay Tables (see Section 9 below)

8 Tables A – Pay Adjustment Tables

There are 52 Tables A pay adjustment tables for **weekly paid employees**, with one table for each week of the tax year.

There are also 12 Tables A pay adjustment tables for **monthly paid employees**, with one table for each month of the tax year.

The tables for Week 3 and Month 3 are shown on the following pages. Have a look at them now.

Week 3
April 20 to April 26

Table A – PAY ADJUSTMENT

Code	Total pay adjustment to date £	Code	Total pay adjustment to date £	Code	Total pay adjustment to date £	Code	Total pay adjustment to date £	Code	Total pay adjustment to date £	Code	Total pay adjustment to date £	Code	Total pay adjustment to date £	Code	Total pay adjustment to date £	Code	Total pay adjustment to date £
0	NIL																
1	1.11	61	35.73	121	70.35	181	104.97	241	139.56	301	174.18	351	203.04	401	231.87	451	260.73
2	1.68	62	36.30	122	70.92	182	105.54	242	140.16	302	174.75	352	203.61	402	232.47	452	261.30
3	2.25	63	36.87	123	71.49	183	106.11	243	140.73	303	175.35	353	204.18	403	233.04	453	261.87
4	2.85	64	37.47	124	72.06	184	106.68	244	141.30	304	175.92	354	204.75	404	233.61	454	262.47
5	3.42	65	38.04	125	72.66	185	107.25	245	141.87	305	176.49	355	205.35	405	234.18	455	263.04
6	3.99	66	38.61	126	73.23	186	107.85	246	142.47	306	177.06	356	205.92	406	234.75	456	263.61
7	4.56	67	39.18	127	73.80	187	108.42	247	143.04	307	177.66	357	206.49	407	235.35	457	264.18
8	5.16	68	39.75	128	74.37	188	108.99	248	143.61	308	178.23	358	207.06	408	235.92	458	264.75
9	5.73	69	40.35	129	74.97	189	109.56	249	144.18	309	178.80	359	207.66	409	236.49	459	265.35
10	6.30	70	40.92	130	75.54	190	110.16	250	144.75	310	179.37	360	208.23	410	237.06	460	265.92
11	6.87	71	41.49	131	76.11	191	110.73	251	145.35	311	179.97	361	208.80	411	237.66	461	266.49
12	7.47	72	42.06	132	76.68	192	111.30	252	145.92	312	180.54	362	209.37	412	238.23	462	267.06
13	8.04	73	42.66	133	77.25	193	111.87	253	146.49	313	181.11	363	209.97	413	238.80	463	267.66
14	8.61	74	43.23	134	77.85	194	112.47	254	147.06	314	181.68	364	210.54	414	239.37	464	268.23
15	9.18	75	43.80	135	78.42	195	113.04	255	147.66	315	182.25	365	211.11	415	239.97	465	268.80
16	9.75	76	44.37	136	78.99	196	113.61	256	148.23	316	182.85	366	211.68	416	240.54	466	269.37
17	10.35	77	44.97	137	79.56	197	114.18	257	148.80	317	183.42	367	212.25	417	241.11	467	269.97
18	10.92	78	45.54	138	80.16	198	114.75	258	149.37	318	183.99	368	212.85	418	241.68	468	270.54
19	11.49	79	46.11	139	80.73	199	115.35	259	149.97	319	184.56	369	213.42	419	242.25	469	271.11
20	12.06	80	46.68	140	81.30	200	115.92	260	150.54	320	185.16	370	213.99	420	242.85	470	271.68
21	12.66	81	47.25	141	81.87	201	116.49	261	151.11	321	185.73	371	214.56	421	243.42	471	272.25
22	13.23	82	47.85	142	82.47	202	117.06	262	151.68	322	186.30	372	215.16	422	243.99	472	272.85
23	13.80	83	48.42	143	83.04	203	117.66	263	152.25	323	186.87	373	215.73	423	244.56	473	273.42
24	14.37	84	48.99	144	83.61	204	118.23	264	152.85	324	187.47	374	216.30	424	245.16	474	273.99
25	14.97	85	49.56	145	84.18	205	118.80	265	153.42	325	188.04	375	216.87	425	245.73	475	274.56
26	15.54	86	50.16	146	84.75	206	119.37	266	153.99	326	188.61	376	217.47	426	246.30	476	275.16
27	16.11	87	50.73	147	85.35	207	119.97	267	154.56	327	189.18	377	218.04	427	246.87	477	275.73
28	16.68	88	51.30	148	85.92	208	120.54	268	155.16	328	189.75	378	218.61	428	247.47	478	276.30
29	17.25	89	51.87	149	86.49	209	121.11	269	155.73	329	190.35	379	219.18	429	248.04	479	276.87
30	17.85	90	52.47	150	87.06	210	121.68	270	156.30	330	190.92	380	219.75	430	248.61	480	277.47
31	18.42	91	53.04	151	87.66	211	122.25	271	156.87	331	191.49	381	220.35	431	249.18	481	278.04
32	18.99	92	53.61	152	88.23	212	122.85	272	157.47	332	192.06	382	220.92	432	249.75	482	278.61
33	19.56	93	54.18	153	88.80	213	123.42	273	158.04	333	192.66	383	221.49	433	250.35	483	279.18
34	20.16	94	54.75	154	89.37	214	123.99	274	158.61	334	193.23	384	222.06	434	250.92	484	279.75
35	20.73	95	55.35	155	89.97	215	124.56	275	159.18	335	193.80	385	222.66	435	251.49	485	280.35
36	21.30	96	55.92	156	90.54	216	125.16	276	159.75	336	194.37	386	223.23	436	252.06	486	280.92
37	21.87	97	56.49	157	91.11	217	125.73	277	160.35	337	194.97	387	223.80	437	252.66	487	281.49
38	22.47	98	57.06	158	91.68	218	126.30	278	160.92	338	195.54	388	224.37	438	253.23	488	282.06
39	23.04	99	57.66	159	92.25	219	126.87	279	161.49	339	196.11	389	224.97	439	253.80	489	282.66
40	23.61	100	58.23	160	92.85	220	127.47	280	162.06	340	196.68	390	225.54	440	254.37	490	283.23
41	24.18	101	58.80	161	93.42	221	128.04	281	162.66	341	197.25	391	226.11	441	254.97	491	283.80
42	24.75	102	59.37	162	93.99	222	128.61	282	163.23	342	197.85	392	226.68	442	255.54	492	284.37
43	25.35	103	59.97	163	94.56	223	129.18	283	163.80	343	198.42	393	227.25	443	256.11	493	284.97
44	25.92	104	60.54	164	95.16	224	129.75	284	164.37	344	198.99	394	227.85	444	256.68	494	285.54
45	26.49	105	61.11	165	95.73	225	130.35	285	164.97	345	199.56	395	228.42	445	257.25	495	286.11
46	27.06	106	61.68	166	96.30	226	130.92	286	165.54	346	200.16	396	228.99	446	257.85	496	286.68
47	27.66	107	62.25	167	96.87	227	131.49	287	166.11	347	200.73	397	229.56	447	258.42	497	287.25
48	28.23	108	62.85	168	97.47	228	132.06	288	166.68	348	201.30	398	230.16	448	258.99	498	287.85
49	28.80	109	63.42	169	98.04	229	132.66	289	167.25	349	201.87	399	230.73	449	259.56	499	288.42
50	29.37	110	63.99	170	98.61	230	133.23	290	167.85	350	202.47	400	231.30	450	260.16	500	288.99
51	29.97	111	64.56	171	99.18	231	133.80	291	168.42								
52	30.54	112	65.16	172	99.75	232	134.37	292	168.99								
53	31.11	113	65.73	173	100.35	233	134.97	293	169.56								
54	31.68	114	66.30	174	100.92	234	135.54	294	170.16								
55	32.25	115	66.87	175	101.49	235	136.11	295	170.73								
56	32.85	116	67.47	176	102.06	236	136.68	296	171.30								
57	33.42	117	68.04	177	102.66	237	137.25	297	171.87								
58	33.99	118	68.61	178	103.23	238	137.85	298	172.47								
59	34.56	119	69.18	179	103.80	239	138.42	299	173.03								
60	35.16	120	69.75	180	104.37	240	138.99	300	173.61								

Pay adjustment where code exceeds 500

1. Where the code is in the range **501** to **1000** inclusive proceed as follows:
   a. Subtract **500** from the code and use the balance of the code to obtain a pay adjustment figure from the table above.
   b. Add this pay adjustment figure to the figure given in the box alongside to obtain the figure of total pay adjustment to date * **288.48**
2. Where the code **exceeds 1000** follow the instructions on **page 2**.

PART C DETERMINING NET PAY

Table A – PAY ADJUSTMENT

Month 3
June 6 to July 5

Code	Total pay adjustment to date £	Code	Total pay adjustment to date £	Code	Total pay adjustment to date £	Code	Total pay adjustment to date £	Code	Total pay adjustment to date £	Code	Total pay adjustment to date £	Code	Total pay adjustment to date £	Code	Total pay adjustment to date £	Code	Total pay adjustment to date £	Code	Total pay adjustment to date £
0	NIL																		
1	4.77	61	154.77	121	304.77	181	454.77	241	604.77	301	754.77	351	879.75	401	1004.76	451	1129.77
2	7.26	62	157.26	122	307.26	182	457.26	242	607.26	302	757.26	352	882.27	402	1007.25	452	1132.26
3	9.75	63	159.75	123	309.75	183	459.75	243	609.75	303	759.75	353	884.76	403	1009.77	453	1134.75
4	12.27	64	162.27	124	312.27	184	462.27	244	612.27	304	762.27	354	887.25	404	1012.26	454	1137.27
5	14.76	65	164.76	125	314.76	185	464.76	245	614.76	305	764.76	355	889.77	405	1014.75	455	1139.76
6	17.25	66	167.25	126	317.25	186	467.25	246	617.25	306	767.25	356	892.26	406	1017.27	456	1142.25
7	19.77	67	169.77	127	319.77	187	469.77	247	619.77	307	769.77	357	894.75	407	1019.76	457	1144.77
8	22.26	68	172.26	128	322.26	188	472.26	248	622.26	308	772.26	358	897.27	408	1022.25	458	1147.26
9	24.75	69	174.75	129	324.75	189	474.75	249	624.75	309	774.75	359	899.76	409	1024.77	459	1149.75
10	27.27	70	177.27	130	327.27	190	477.27	250	627.27	310	777.27	360	902.25	410	1027.26	460	1152.27
11	29.76	71	179.76	131	329.76	191	479.76	251	629.76	311	779.76	361	904.77	411	1029.75	461	1154.76
12	32.25	72	182.25	132	332.25	192	482.25	252	632.25	312	782.25	362	907.26	412	1032.27	462	1157.25
13	34.77	73	184.77	133	334.77	193	484.77	253	634.77	313	784.77	363	909.75	413	1034.76	463	1159.77
14	37.26	74	187.26	134	337.26	194	487.26	254	637.26	314	787.26	364	912.27	414	1037.25	464	1162.26
15	39.75	75	189.75	135	339.75	195	489.75	255	639.75	315	789.75	365	914.76	415	1039.77	465	1164.75
16	42.27	76	192.27	136	342.27	196	492.27	256	642.27	316	792.27	366	917.25	416	1042.26	466	1167.27
17	44.76	77	194.76	137	344.76	197	494.76	257	644.76	317	794.76	367	919.77	417	1044.75	467	1169.76
18	47.25	78	197.25	138	347.25	198	497.25	258	647.25	318	797.25	368	922.26	418	1047.27	468	1172.25
19	49.77	79	199.77	139	349.77	199	499.77	259	649.77	319	799.77	369	924.75	419	1049.76	469	1174.77
20	52.26	80	202.26	140	352.26	200	502.26	260	652.26	320	802.26	370	927.27	420	1052.25	470	1177.26
21	54.75	81	204.75	141	354.75	201	504.75	261	654.75	321	804.75	371	929.76	421	1054.77	471	1179.75
22	57.27	82	207.27	142	357.27	202	507.27	262	657.27	322	807.27	372	932.25	422	1057.26	472	1182.27
23	59.76	83	209.76	143	359.76	203	509.76	263	659.76	323	809.76	373	934.77	423	1059.75	473	1184.76
24	62.25	84	212.25	144	362.25	204	512.25	264	662.25	324	812.25	374	937.26	424	1062.27	474	1187.25
25	64.77	85	214.77	145	364.77	205	514.77	265	664.77	325	814.77	375	939.75	425	1064.76	475	1189.77
26	67.26	86	217.26	146	367.26	206	517.26	266	667.26	326	817.26	376	942.27	426	1067.25	476	1192.26
27	69.75	87	219.75	147	369.75	207	519.75	267	669.75	327	819.75	377	944.76	427	1069.77	477	1194.75
28	72.27	88	222.27	148	372.27	208	522.27	268	672.27	328	822.27	378	947.25	428	1072.26	478	1197.27
29	74.76	89	224.76	149	374.76	209	524.76	269	674.76	329	824.76	379	949.77	429	1074.75	479	1199.76
30	77.25	90	227.25	150	377.25	210	527.25	270	677.25	330	827.25	380	952.26	430	1077.27	480	1202.25
31	79.77	91	229.77	151	379.77	211	529.77	271	679.77	331	829.77	381	954.75	431	1079.76	481	1204.77
32	82.26	92	232.26	152	382.26	212	532.26	272	682.26	332	832.26	382	957.27	432	1082.25	482	1207.26
33	84.75	93	234.75	153	384.75	213	534.75	273	684.75	333	834.75	383	959.76	433	1084.77	483	1209.75
34	87.27	94	237.27	154	387.27	214	537.27	274	687.27	334	837.27	384	962.25	434	1087.26	484	1212.27
35	89.76	95	239.76	155	389.76	215	539.76	275	689.76	335	839.76	385	964.77	435	1089.75	485	1214.76
36	92.25	96	242.25	156	392.25	216	542.25	276	692.25	336	842.25	386	967.26	436	1092.27	486	1217.25
37	94.77	97	244.77	157	394.77	217	544.77	277	694.77	337	844.77	387	969.75	437	1094.76	487	1219.77
38	97.26	98	247.26	158	397.26	218	547.26	278	697.26	338	847.26	388	972.27	438	1097.25	488	1222.26
39	99.75	99	249.75	159	399.75	219	549.75	279	699.75	339	849.75	389	974.76	439	1099.77	489	1224.75
40	102.27	100	252.27	160	402.27	220	552.27	280	702.27	340	852.27	390	977.25	440	1102.26	490	1227.27
41	104.76	101	254.76	161	404.76	221	554.76	281	704.76	341	854.76	391	979.77	441	1104.75	491	1229.76
42	107.25	102	257.25	162	407.25	222	557.25	282	707.25	342	857.25	392	982.26	442	1107.27	492	1232.25
43	109.77	103	259.77	163	409.77	223	559.77	283	709.77	343	859.77	393	984.75	443	1109.76	493	1234.77
44	112.26	104	262.26	164	412.26	224	562.26	284	712.26	344	862.26	394	987.27	444	1112.25	494	1237.26
45	114.75	105	264.75	165	414.75	225	564.75	285	714.75	345	864.75	395	989.76	445	1114.77	495	1239.75
46	117.27	106	267.27	166	417.27	226	567.27	286	717.27	346	867.27	396	992.25	446	1117.26	496	1242.27
47	119.76	107	269.76	167	419.76	227	569.76	287	719.76	347	869.76	397	994.77	447	1119.75	497	1244.76
48	122.25	108	272.25	168	422.25	228	572.25	288	722.25	348	872.25	398	997.26	448	1122.27	498	1247.25
49	124.77	109	274.77	169	424.77	229	574.77	289	724.77	349	874.77	399	999.75	449	1124.76	499	1249.77
50	127.26	110	277.26	170	427.26	230	577.26	290	727.26	350	877.26	400	1002.27	450	1127.25	500	1252.26
51	129.75	111	279.75	171	429.75	231	579.75	291	729.75								
52	132.27	112	282.27	172	432.27	232	582.27	292	732.27								
53	134.76	113	284.76	173	434.76	233	584.76	293	734.76								
54	137.25	114	287.25	174	437.25	234	587.25	294	737.25								
55	139.77	115	289.77	175	439.77	235	589.77	295	739.77								
56	142.26	116	292.26	176	442.26	236	592.26	296	742.26								
57	144.75	117	294.75	177	444.75	237	594.75	297	744.75								
58	147.27	118	297.27	178	447.27	238	597.27	298	747.27								
59	149.76	119	299.76	179	449.76	239	599.76	299	749.76								
60	152.25	120	302.25	180	452.25	240	602.25	300	752.25								

Pay adjustment where code exceeds 500

1. Where the code is in the range **501** to **1000** inclusive proceed as follows:
   a. Subtract **500** from the code and use the balance of the code to obtain a pay adjustment figure from the table above.
   b. Add this pay adjustment figure to the figure given in the box alongside to obtain the figure of total pay adjustment to date * **1250.01**
2. Where the code **exceeds 1000** follow the instructions on **page 2**.

182

6: INCOME TAX: SIMPLE CASES

> **Activity alert**
>
> When examples and activities in this Tutorial Text, and activities in the Assessment Kit, require figures from Tables A, we will give you extracts from the tables.
>
> If you want a complete set of Tables A, these can be downloaded from the Inland Revenue website, (www.inlandrevenue.gov.uk/employers/emp-form.htm).

8.1 Points to note about Tables A

The **left hand column** of each Table A gives the **tax code**. Codes go from 0 to 500.

The **right hand column** shows for each tax code the total amount of **free pay** to date - as at the end of week 1, week 2, week 3 ... week 52 or as at the end of month 1, month 2, month 3 and so on.

'Pay adjustment' means free pay to date.

The current edition of the **Tables A** is the 1993 issue. **Other tax tables change each year**.

8.2 Tax codes of 500 and under

If you look at the pay adjustment for, say, code 200 in Week 3 you find the figure £115.92. This is the free pay figure.

To make sure that you understand how to find the pay adjustment, look up in the table for Week 3 the total adjustment to date for people with the following tax codes.

(a) 31L
(b) 343P
(c) 154T
(d) 461L

You should get the answers £18.42, £198.42, £89.37 and £266.49. There is no need to worry about the letter in the code at this stage.

8.3 Tax codes above 500

Tax codes only go up to 500 in the tables, but in practice codes might be much higher. What happens if a tax code is, say, 1697T?

Always take one figure from the main part of the table, then make up extra 500s using the figure in the box at the bottom of each page of the tables.

PART C   DETERMINING NET PAY

Example: Tax codes above 500

Taking a code of 1697T as an illustration and using the week 3 Table A, we can calculate that 1,697 = (3 × 500) + 197.

Step 1   The pay adjustment for the balance of the code (197) is looked up first.

Code	Pay adjustment
197	114.18

Step 2   Now look at the box at the bottom of the Table A for Week 3. Within this box is another box which in this case contains the figure 288.48. Multiply this figure by 3 in our example, giving £865.44.

Step 3   Now you simply add the looked-up figure and the calculated figure together.

	£
Amount for the balance of the code	114.18
Amount for 3 units of 500 (3 × 288.48)	865.44
Total free pay to date	979.62

8.3.1 What if there is no 'balance of the code'?

If the code is exactly divisible by 500, we do the following.

Step 1   Look at the figure for code 500 in the main table.

Step 2   Multiply the figure in the box by one less than the number of 'units' of 500 in the code.

A code of 2,000T (exactly four units) in Week 3 therefore has the following free pay.

	£
Looked-up amount for code 500	288.99
Calculated amount (3 × 288.48)	865.44
Total free pay	1,154.43

The rule to remember is that **if the code exceeds 500 there is always one looked-up code amount plus a calculated amount using the figure in the box.**

Example: Tables A

What is the total pay adjustment to date in *Month* 3 for employees with a tax code of:

(a)   397L
(b)   438L
(c)   556L
(d)   701V
(e)   1,004L?

Solution

(a)   Taken directly from Tables A: £994.77

(b)   Taken directly from Tables A: £1,097.25

(c) 556 = 56 + (1 × 500)

   Pay adjustment = £142.26 + (1 × £1,250.01)
                  = £1,392.27

(d) 701 = 201 + (1 × 500)

   Pay adjustment = £504.75 + (1 × £1,250.01)
                  = £1,754.76

(e) 1,004 = 4 + (2 × 500)

   Pay adjustment = £12.27 + (2 × £1,250.01)
                  = £2,512.29

Activity 6.8

Find the 'total pay adjustment to date' in Month 3 for the following tax codes.

(a) 541P
(b) 709T
(c) 3,904T

9 Tables SR, B, C and D: Taxable Pay Tables

Taxable pay to date is **total pay for the year to date** minus **free pay for the year to date** as shown in the pay adjustment tables.

The **Taxable Pay Tables** show how much tax should be paid for the year to date for any given amount of **taxable pay** (ie they do the tax rate calculation for you). They are normally used **cumulatively**, so you calculate the taxable pay to date and the tax due to date. They are revised each year and up-to-date copies are sent by the Tax Office to every employer.

- **Table SR** is for calculating tax payable at the starting rate (10%).

- **Table B** is for calculating tax payable at the basic rate (22%), together with **subtraction tables** to avoid the need to use Table SR. This is explained below.

- For higher rate taxpayers, **Table C** and **Table D** are used together.

   Step 1 First the tax due at the starting rate and the basic rate is found in Table C.

   Step 2 Table D is used to find the additional amount due at the higher rate (40%).

The tables are reproduced in Appendix 1 at the end of this text, starting on page 349. Have a look at them now, and put a marker or Post-it note at the appropriate place so that you can find Appendix 1 quickly.

PART C DETERMINING NET PAY

> **Important!**
>
> We always round taxable pay to the nearest pound *below*. £480.99 becomes £480.

9.1 How do you know which tables to use?

Always start by looking at the guide reproduced on pages 350 and 351 of this text. **Do this now**.

Examples: Which taxable pay table to use?

In Week 3 Donald Anderson has total taxable pay to date of £84. In Month 10 Claire Tolland has total taxable pay to date of £16,862. In Month 5 Guy Marchant has total taxable pay to date of £35,000. Which taxable pay tables should we use in each case?

Solution

Donald Anderson

Look first on page 351 of this text. Find Week 3. Donald's total taxable pay to date **does not exceed £117**, so now you know that you will use table SR to calculate the tax on his pay.

Claire Tolland

Look at page 350. Claire's total taxable pay to date does exceed £1,684 in month 10, so now you must look at Column 2. It **does not exceed £26,167**. So now you know that you need to use Table B.

Guy Marchant

Clearly this exceeds £842 as shown for Month 5 in Column 1 on page 350 and it also exceeds £13,084 as shown in Column 2. So you will need to use Tables C and D to calculate his tax.

Activity 6.9

Which taxable pay tables would you use in each of the following cases?

	Name	Total taxable pay to date £	Tax Week/Month
(a)	Robert Bruce	842	Week 8
(b)	Shelley Johnson	13,967	Month 4
(c)	Garth Wright	282	Week 12

9.2 Using tax tables

Since the taxable pay tables are normally used **cumulatively**, this is the procedure:

		£
Step 1	Calculate taxable pay to date	X
Step 2	Using tax tables, calculate tax due to date	X
Step 3	Deduct tax paid to the end of the previous period	(X)
Step 4	Tax due in this period	X

We will now concentrate on Step 2 – **using tax tables**.

9.2.1 Table SR

This is used to calculate the 10% tax rate, when the employee only has taxable pay of £2,020 or less, per annum.

Example: Table SR

It is the end of Week 4. Joe Blogg's **taxable** pay (after deducting free pay) is £25.50 per week, so he has taxable pay of £102 so far. Up to the end of Week 3 he had paid £7.60 in tax.

Step 1 If you look at column 1 on page 351 you will see the amount £156 against Week 4. As Joe's taxable pay is less than £156, use Table SR.

Step 2 Now go to Table SR and you will find a set of columns, detailing tax due on amounts between £1 and £99 (to the right of the page), and then tax due on amounts from £100 in steps of £100 up to £2,000 (to the left of the page). This table is simply a 10% ready reckoner.

Step 3 You will see that the table has a note telling you to add together two or more figures when the exact amount of taxable pay is not shown, as it isn't for 102.

	Taxable pay		Tax due to date
	£		£
Figures shown in table:	100.00		10.00
	2.00		0.20
Total taxable pay to date	102.00	Total tax due to date	10.20

Step 4 Deduct tax paid to the end of Week 3, to get his tax due for Week 4: £(10.20 – 7.60) = £2.60.

By the end of Week 8, having increased his hours considerably, Joe Bloggs has taxable pay to date of £700. What do you do now? Look at Week 8 on page 351 of this text; since by the end of Week 8 he has earned more than £311 but less than £4,831, you should go to **Table B**.

9.2.2 Table B

Table B is used for employees who are earning taxable pay over £2,020 per annum but not over £31,400 per annum.

PART C DETERMINING NET PAY

Table B comes in two parts.

- Total tax on taxable pay at 22%.
- Subtraction tables, so that the employee's starting rate of tax (10%) is accounted for.

Using Table B, then, usually involves two steps.

Step 1 Read off the tax from table B itself which gives the tax on taxable pay to date at 22%.

Step 2 Now subtract the amount specified in the subtraction tables for the week or month. This ensures that basic rate taxpayers get the benefit of the starting rate on the first £2,020 of taxable pay each year.

Look now at Table B in Appendix I. The **left hand side** of each column of Table B shows the **taxable pay to date**.

The **right hand side** of each column shows the **tax due to date** (at 22%) for each given amount of taxable pay.

The Table B figures for tax payable at 22% come in **two parts**.

- The first part shows tax on taxable pay from £100 to £31,400, in steps of £100.
- The second part shows tax on taxable pay from £1 to £99, in steps of £1.

Where the exact amount of an employee's taxable pay is not given in the Table, you should **add together** the figures for tax due as follows.

(a) Taxable pay to the nearest £100 *below* the amount you require, from the first part of Table B.
(b) Taxable pay from £1 to £99, as appropriate, from the second part of Table B.

Once you have worked out the tax due at 22% on taxable pay, **go to the subtraction tables for the week or month**. (The only exception is when an employee has a code BR, when the subtraction tables are **not** used.)

Example: Table B

(a) William Burroughs by Month 4 has received taxable pay of £6,100. Up to the end of Month 3 he had paid £1,003.50 in tax.

How much tax must he pay for Month 4?

(b) Thomas Pynchon has received a total of £17,160 in taxable pay up to the end of Month 10. Up to the end of Month 9, he had paid £3,405.87 in tax.

How much tax must he pay for Month 10?

(c) Jayne-Anne Phillips has received £21,783.62 in taxable pay by the end of Month 12. Up to the end of Month 11 she had paid £4,385.45 in tax.

How much tax must be paid for Month 12?

Solution

Use the following steps to workout the answers.

Step 1 Check which tax table to use (for all of them we need Table B).

Step 2 Calculate the tax due on the taxable pay from Table B.

Step 3 Take off, from the subtraction tables, the starting rate relief.

(a) **William Burroughs**

	Tax £
Tax on: £6,100	1,342.00
Less starting rate relief for Month 4	(80.81)
Total tax due to the end of Month 4	1,261.19
Less tax already paid	(1,003.50)
Tax payable at the end of Month 4	257.69

(b) **Thomas Pynchon**

	£	Tax £
Tax on:	17,100	3,762.00
	60	13.20
	17,160	3,775.20
Less starting rate relief for Month 10		(202.01)
Tax due to the end of Month 10		3,573.19
Less tax already paid		(3,405.87)
Tax payable at the end of Month 10		167.32

(c) **Jayne-Anne Phillips**

	£	£
Tax on:	21,700	4,774.00
	83	18.26
	21,783	4,792.26
Less starting rate relief (Month 12)		(242.40)
Total tax due to the end of Month 12		4,549.86
Less tax already paid		(4,385.45)
Tax payable at the end of Month 12		164.41

Activity 6.10

How much tax is payable this pay day in each of the following cases?

(a) Carol Scott has taxable pay to date of £2,350 at the end of Month 8. Her tax paid to the end of Month 7 is £329.13.

(b) John Devlin has taxable pay to date of £16,828 at the end of week 48. His tax paid to the end of week 47 is £3,513.45.

(c) Polly Grainger has taxable pay to date of £15,192 at the end of Month 7. Her tax paid to the end of Month 6 is £2,897.33.

PART C   DETERMINING NET PAY

9.2.3 Table C

Table C incorporates the starting rate relief already, so you need not do any extra calculations. No subtraction tables!

There is a Table C for **weekly paid employees** and a Table C for **monthly paid employees**, although both are shown on the same page.

- On the **left hand side** the week or month number is shown.
- **Column 1** indicates the amount of **taxable pay for the year to date** that will be taxed at the starting and basic rates.
- **Column 2** shows the amount of **tax payable at the starting and basic rates** (on the pay in Column 1).
- On the **right hand side** of the monthly pay and weekly pay Tables within Table C, there is an **instruction** for calculating the amount of taxable pay for which the **higher rate** of tax (40%) should be applied.

	£
Total taxable pay for the year to date	X
Less taxable pay in Column 1	Y
Equals taxable pay for which higher rate tax applies	X – Y

To obtain the tax payable at the higher rate, you should now use Table D.

9.2.4 Table D

Table D shows the amount of **tax payable at the higher rate** (40%) on given amounts of income from:

- £1 to £99, in steps of £1.
- £100 to £10,000, in steps of £100.
- £20,000 to £100,000, in steps of £10,000.
- £100,000 to £1,000,000 in steps of £100,000.

Where the amount of taxable pay is not shown exactly, you should **add together** the figures for two (or more) entries, to make up the total taxable pay amount.

Example: Tables C and D and weekly pay

Sunil Devjani has taxable pay for the year to date of £9,270 as at week 15. What is the amount of tax payable for the year to date?

Solution

If you look at the 'Finding out which Table to use' table you will see that the limit for tax at the basic and starting rate in week 15 is £9,058. Since Sunil has earned more than this amount, you are told to use Tables C and D.

6: INCOME TAX: SIMPLE CASES

	£
Total taxable pay, week 15	9,270
Basic rate tax limit (from Table C), week 15	9,058
Taxable at higher rate - use Table D	212

Tax payable for year to date

	£	£
On first £9,058, from Table C		1,922.89
From Table D		
On £200	80.00	
On £12	4.80	
On £212		84.80
Total tax payable		2,007.69

Example: Tables C and D and monthly pay

Kaz Randit has taxable pay for the year to date of £37,775 in month 10. What is the amount of tax payable for the year to date?

Solution

£37,775 exceeds the month 10 basic and starting rate limit of £26,167, and so you must use Tables C and D.

	£
Total taxable pay, month 10	37,775
Basic tax rate limit (from Table C)	26,167
Taxable at higher rate - use Table D	11,608

Tax payable for the year to date

	£	£
On first £26,167, from Table C		5,554.79
From Table D		
On £10,000	4,000.00	
On £1,600	640.00	
On £8	3.20	
On £11,608		4,643.20
Total tax payable		10,197.99

Activity 6.11

Pilar Gomez has taxable pay to the end of Month 5 of £20,000. How much tax is due to the end of Month 5?

PART C   DETERMINING NET PAY

10 Using the tax tables: A summary

You may be feeling a little bewildered by now!

The process of working out tax under the PAYE system can be summarised as follows:

Step 1   Calculate 'pay in the week or month' using PAYE rules to deduct or add items as necessary (section 4 of this chapter).

Step 2   Add 'pay in the week or month' to total pay to date brought forward from previous pay day, to give total pay to date.

Step 3   Use Tables A to make a pay adjustment according to the tax code. Deduct the pay adjustment from total pay to date – now you have taxable pay to date.

Step 4   Turn to the taxable pay tables. Look at the guidance on 'Finding out which tax table to use'. This will tell you whether you need:

- Table SR, for starting rate taxpayers.
- Table B and subtraction tables, for basic rate taxpayers.
- Tables C and D for higher rate taxpayers.

Step 5   Go to the appropriate Tax Table (weekly or monthly).

- Table SR (starting rate): simply read off the tax payable to date, if necessary adding two or more figures together.
- Table B (basic rate): read off the tax payable and then use the subtraction tables to give the employee his or her starting rate tax relief. Simply deduct the amount shown from the Table B figure.
- Tables C and D (higher rate): first turn to Table C and read off the figure in Column 1 for this tax week or month. Deduct this figure from total taxable pay to date. The remainder is taxable at the higher rate.

  To find the tax due to date, first read off the tax figure given in Table C. Then turn to Table D and read off the tax due on the higher rate taxable pay (if necessary add two or more entries together). Add the Table C and Table D tax figures together.

Step 6   Now you know the total tax due to date, deduct total tax due at the last pay day and the remainder is the tax due this pay day. If you have a negative remainder, then there is a tax refund this pay day.

Using this method, tackle the following activity.

Activity 6.12

You are required to calculate the tax due this month from three employees. Details are given below. Free pay in Month 3 can be found in Section 8 of this chapter.

Name	Tax Code at end of Month 3	Pay in Month 3 £	Total Pay at at end of Month 2 £	Tax paid at end of Month 2 £
Alice Adams	474L	1,250	3,750	605.31
Bob Brown	370T	615	615	NIL
Chris Cole	312T	3,750	19,565	6,704.79

11 Form P11: Deductions working sheet

Employers must keep a record of an employee's pay and statutory deductions (income tax and National Insurance contributions). This record is called a **deductions working sheet**. A deductions working sheet must be kept for each employee, and one sheet covers just a single tax year.

A **deductions working sheet** is a large form, supplied by the Tax Office. Its official form number is **P11**. A copy of the form for tax year 2004/05 is shown on pages 195 and 196.

- **The right half** of the form is used to calculate and record income tax (and tax credits).
- The **left half** of the form is used to record **National Insurance** (and also Statutory Sick Pay, Statutory Maternity Pay, Statutory Paternity Pay, Statutory Adoption Pay and Student Loan Deductions).
- There are also boxes at the top to be filled in for:
  - The employer's name and tax reference number.
  - The employee's name, NINO, payroll reference and date of birth.
  - Starting and leaving dates
  - Whether student deductions are to be made
  - Tax code and amendments
  - Details of tax credits

You must fill in the P11 whenever the employee is paid.

- For **weekly paid staff**, there will be an entry for each week, one per line, which you should fill in on each pay day as the year progresses.
- For **fortnightly paid staff**, enter the details on lines 2, 4, 6, etc, regardless of when payment is actually made.
- For **four weekly paid staff**, enter the details on lines 4, 8, 12, etc, regardless of the date of actual payment.
- For **monthly paid staff**, you only need one line per month. You can use any of the four or five lines available for that month.

For tax entries, look at the right hand side of the P11.

PART C DETERMINING NET PAY

You already know how to calculate all the figures that need to be entered on the tax side in straightforward cases. Columns 2, 3, 4a, 5, 6 and 7 should therefore be easy to fill in.

In Chapter 7 we shall be looking in detail at some of the complications that can arise in a PAYE system. These will include **K codes**, mentioned on the P11 at Columns 4b, 6a, 6b and 8, and you will learn how to fill in these columns then.

Column 9 is used to record tax credits (ie Working Tax Credit), as mentioned in Chapter 5.

Three final points:

- It occasionally happens that **free pay exceeds taxable pay**, in which case **no tax is due**. In this case **leave Column 5 blank**.

- **Columns 6 and 7** will always be the same in Week 1 or Month 1.

- If total tax due at the end of the current period is **less** than total tax due at the end of the previous period, then a **tax refund** is due. This can happen when an employee has a new, higher tax code, for example. In this case you mark the amount of the refund in **Column 7** with an R, and usually the amount is placed in brackets.

6: INCOME TAX: SIMPLE CASES

PART C DETERMINING NET PAY

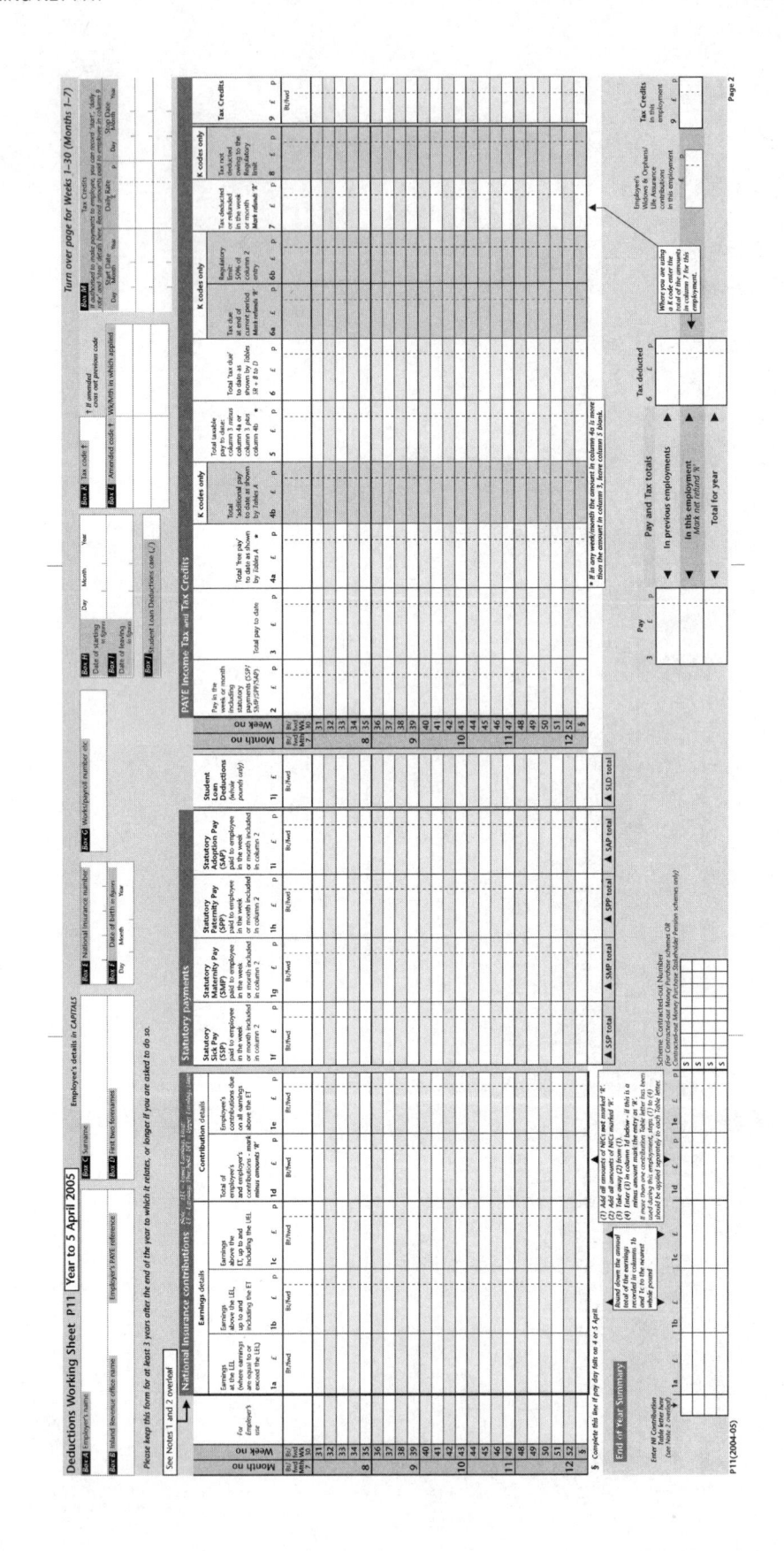

Example: P11

Let's now go through a simple example of filling in a P11 for a few weeks of the tax year.

One of the weekly paid employees of your company is Rachana Morjaria who has a tax code of 438L. Her weekly pay is £230. Her total pay to date (end of week 17) is £3,910 (17 × £230), the total tax paid is £465.25 and in week 17 she paid tax of £27.46. Tables A give the following figures for code 438.

Week	Free pay
16	1,350.56
17	1,434.97
18	1,519.38
19	1,603.79
20	1,688.20

Task

Fill in Rachana's P11 for weeks 18 to 20 assuming pay in each week is £230.

Solution

Week 18

The figures for columns 2, 3, 4a and 5 are obtained as follows.

	£
Pay for week 18 **(column 2)**	230.00
Total pay for week 17	3,910.00
Total pay to date **(column 3)**	4,140.00
Less free pay from Table A (week 18, code 438L) **(column 4a)**	(1,519.38)
Taxable pay for the year to date **(column 5)**	2,620.62

To calculate the tax due, since £2,620 in week 18 exceeds £700 but does not exceed £10,870, table B should be used in conjunction with the subtraction tables.

	£
Table B	
Tax on £2,600	572.00
Tax on £20	4.40
	576.40
Less lower rate relief (week 18)	(83.91)
Total tax due to date **(column 6)**	492.49

Now subtract the total tax paid to date at the end of the previous week.

	£
Total tax due to week 18	492.49
Total tax due to week 17	465.25
Tax to be deducted in week 18 **(column 7)**	27.24

PART C   DETERMINING NET PAY

The P11 (PAYE Income tax side) should be filled in as follows. (Weeks 1-16 are not shown.)

Week	Pay in the week	Total pay to date	Total free pay to date	K codes Total additional pay to date	Total taxable pay to date	Total tax due to date	K codes Tax due at end of current period	Regulatory limit	Tax deducted in the week	K codes Tax not deducted owing to the regulatory limit	Tax Credits
	2	3	4a	4b	5	6	6a	6b	7	8	9
17	230.00	3,910.00	1,434.97		2,475.03	465.25			27.46		
18	230.00	4,140.00	1,519.38		2,620.62	492.49			27.24		

Weeks 19 and 20

For subsequent weeks you follow exactly the same procedure.

The deductions working sheet follows as at the end of week 20. The tax deducted varies by a few pence from week to week, even though the employee receives the same gross pay. This is because of rounding in the tables.

Week	Pay in the week	Total pay to date	Total free pay to date	K codes Total additional pay to date	Total taxable pay to date	Total tax due to date	K codes Tax due at end of current period	Regulatory limit	Tax deducted in the week	K codes Tax not deducted owing to the regulatory limit	Tax Credits
	2	3	4a	4b	5	6	6a	6b	7	8	9
17	230.00	3,910.00	1,434.97		2,475.03	465.25			27.46		
18	230.00	4,140.00	1,519.38		2,620.62	492.49			27.24		
19	230.00	4,370.00	1,603.79		2,766.21	519.95			27.46		
20	230.00	4,600.00	1,688.20		2,911.80	547.18			27.23		

12 Taxable pay tables: Calculator tables

The 2004/05 issue of the taxable pay tables contains two tables designed to be used with a calculator, so that direct percentages of amounts are calculated. One is for **weekly paid employees** and the other is for **monthly paid employees**. The monthly table is reproduced in Appendix I at the end of this Text.

The principles are exactly the same as using the ordinary taxable pay tables (Tables SR, B, C and D).

- Find pay in the week or month as usual.
- Look at Tables A first to find the pay adjustment. Then you can calculate taxable pay to date.
- Finally, you look at the calculator table to find out what rate of tax to use, and then use that rate on taxable pay to get the figure for tax due to date.

For example, in Month 1, you are told:

- To calculate tax at 10% of taxable pay if taxable pay does not exceed £169.
- To calculate tax at 22% of taxable pay if taxable pay exceeds £169 but does not exceed £2,617, and then to *deduct* starting rate relief of £20.21.
- To calculate tax at 40% on the amount of taxable pay which exceeds £2,617, and then *add* to this the given Table C figure for tax at basic and starting rates (£555.59).

Example: Using the calculator tables

In Month 7:

- George had taxable pay to date of £800.
- Simone had taxable pay to date of £10,400.
- Rusty had taxable pay to date of £18,950.

Work out the tax due to date in each case, using the calculator tables.

Solution

You simply follow the instructions in the table.

George

Taxable pay does not exceed £1,179, so tax due to date is £800 × 10% = £80.

Simone

Taxable pay exceeds £1,179 but does not exceed £18,317, so tax due to date is:

	£
£10,400 × 22%	2,288.00
Less starting rate relief for Month 7	(141.41)
	2,146.59

Rusty

Taxable pay exceeds £18,317 so tax is:

	£
Table C figure (basic and starting rate tax on £18,317)	3,888.39
Balance of taxable pay (£18,950 − £18,317) × 40%	253.20
	4,141.59

You should be able to see that the calculator tables simply present the same information and rules as the other taxable pay tables but in a **different format**.

PART C DETERMINING NET PAY

Key learning points

- Nearly all paid employment is subject to **Income Tax**. The tax is collected through the PAYE (Pay As You Earn) system.

- The PAYE system divides the **tax year** into numbered months (12) and weeks (53), starting on April 6 and ending on April 5.

- Tax is normally collected on a **cumulative basis** over the year.

- Each individual is allowed certain **allowances**, that is income which is not taxed. Such income is known as **free pay**.

- The amount of free pay a person is entitled to is given by the **Tax Code** he or she has been given by the tax office. **Taxable pay** is gross pay for tax purposes less free pay.

- You work out the tax by using tables.
    - **Tables A** are for free pay.
    - **Table SR** is for employees taxed at the starting rate (10%).
    - **Table B** is for employees taxed at basic rate (22%).
    - **Tables C and D** tell you how to calculate tax at the higher rate (40%).

- The **P11 deductions working sheet** is used to record tax paid in each tax year.

Quick quiz

1. When does the tax year start and end?
2. How many weeks are there in a tax year?
3. If an employee is paid a 'golden hello', should this be recorded on the deductions working sheet?
4. What is a personal allowance?
5. Define 'free pay to date'.
6. What are the current tax rates on income?
7. What does it signify if an employee has the letters L, P, or V at the end of his or her tax code?
8. Which would you prefer to have as your own tax code, one starting with D or NT? Why?
9. When is the Budget speech delivered? What period does it relate to?
10. What is a P11?
11. Tables A change each year. True or false?
12. Tax codes go up to 500 in Tables A. What do you do if a code is higher then 500?
13. Which taxable pay table or tables would you use to calculate tax for someone paying tax at the higher rate on part of his or her earnings?
14. Which taxable pay table includes a subtraction table? Why?
15. What happens if total tax due to date in the previous month is higher than total tax due to date this month?

Answers to quick quiz

1. The tax year starts on 6 April and ends on 5 April in the next year.
2. 53
3. Yes
4. A personal allowance is the amount of income that each UK resident can earn each year without paying tax. In 2004/05 it is £4,745. It is usually increased in each annual Budget to allow for the effects of inflation.
5. Free pay to date is the proportion allowed so far from the total of a person's allowances for the year.
6. Starting rate: 10% on the first £2,020 of taxable pay
   Basic rate: 22% on the next £29,380
   Higher rate: 40% on the remainder over £31,400
7. L: the employee is entitled to the personal allowance only and is under 65 years of age.

   P: the employee or pensioner is aged between 65 and 74 years old and so receives a higher personal allowance.

   V: as P, but the married couple's allowance is also due; and is expected to be a basic rate tax payer.

PART C DETERMINING NET PAY

8 Probably NT. A tax code starting with D indicates that all of the person's income is taxable at 40% (so he or she is a high earner), whereas a code ending in NT indicates that no tax is to be deducted at all (usually because the employee carries out their duties overseas).

9 Usually in March, detailing proposals for the tax year starting on 6 April in the same year.

10 A deductions working sheet supplied by the Inland Revenue.

11 False. Pay adjustment tables are only revised periodically to correct errors. The **taxable pay tables** change annually to reflect Budget changes to tax rates and bands.

12 You take one figure from the main part of the table and then make up extra 500s using the figure in the box at the bottom of each table. For example, if a code is 521, you look up 21 in the tables and add the figure from the box. If the code is 1039, look up 39 and add the figure from the box multiplied by two (500 × 2).

13 Tables C and D.

14 Table B includes a subtraction table so basic rate taxpayers also get the benefit of the starting rate.

15 A tax refund is due.

Activity checklist

This checklist shows which performance criteria, range statement or knowledge and understanding point is covered by each activity in this chapter. Tick off each activity as you complete it.

Activity

6.1	☐	This activity covers performance criterion 72.1.E and knowledge and understanding point 2.
6.2	☐	This activity covers knowledge and understanding point 13.
6.3	☐	This activity covers knowledge and understanding point 13.
6.4	☐	This activity covers knowledge and understanding point 13.
6.5	☐	This activity covers knowledge and understanding point 13.
6.6	☐	This activity covers knowledge and understanding point 13.
6.7	☐	This activity covers performance criterion 73.1.E.
6.8	☐	This activity covers performance criterion 73.1.E and knowledge and understanding point 13.
6.9	☐	This activity covers performance criterion 73.1.E and knowledge and understanding point 13.
6.10	☐	This activity covers performance criterion 73.1.E.
6.11	☐	This activity covers performance criterion 73.1.E.
6.12	☐	This activity covers performance criterion 73.1.E.

PART C DETERMINING NET PAY

chapter 7

Income tax: more complex cases

Contents

1. The problem
2. The solution
3. Variations in pay and tax codes
4. Week 1/Month 1 basis
5. D codes, and Codes BR and NT
6. Week 53 payments
7. Trade disputes
8. K codes

Performance criterion

73.1.E Contribute to the resolution of individual employees' queries by checking net pay calculations manually, using the appropriate tax and National Insurance tables

Knowledge and understanding

2 PAYE regulations in respect of the manual calculation of gross to net pay
13 How to use tax and NI tables to perform manual calculations of net pay

PART C   DETERMINING NET PAY

1 The problem

In the previous Chapter, we looked at straightforward cases. What about the more complex topics mentioned?

2 The solution

In this chapter, we will look at variations in pay and tax codes during a tax year in Section 3.

Sections 4 and 5 will deal with coding difficulties, such as 'week1/month1' and BR, NT and D codes.

Section 6 looks at week 53 payments and how to use the tax tables in week 53.

Trade disputes lead to problems when strikers are not paid for some weeks. We look at this in Section 7.

Finally 'K' codes are dealt with in Section 8.

3 Variations in pay and tax codes

We will work through a more complicated example of filling in a P11. You will learn most if you do the calculations for yourself and look up the figures in the tables in Appendix I. If you have the basics sorted out the rest will be much easier to cope with.

> **Important!**
>
> Use this example as a way of checking that you really understand the material covered so far. This type of assignment is the basis of payroll work – if you can't do this quickly and easily you will struggle with the other topics in this chapter.

Example: Income tax deductions

One of the monthly paid employees of your company is Mohammed Ali, who starts the tax year 2004/05 with a tax code of 300T. The free pay shown in Table A for this code is £250.75 in Month 1. We need to build up his P11 over three months.

Solution (month 1)

His pay for the month is £2,166.67.

	£
Pay for the month and for the year to date	2,166.67
Less free pay to date from Table A (month 1, code 300)	250.75
Taxable pay for the year to date	1,915.92

£1,915 is over the starting rate limit but not over the limit for tax at basic rate, and so Table B should be used, with the subtraction table to give relief for the starting rate tax.

Table B

	£
Tax on £1,900	418.00
Tax on £15	3.30
	421.30
Less starting rate relief (Month 1)	(20.21)
Tax on £1,915	401.09

The P11 (PAYE Income Tax side) should be filled in as follows.

Tax code	Amended									
300T	WK/mnth									

Month	Pay in the week 2	Total pay to date 3	Total free pay to date 4a	K codes Total additional pay to date 4b	Total taxable pay to date 5	Total tax due to date 6	K codes Tax due at end of current period 6a	Regulatory limit 6b	Tax deducted in the week 7	K codes Tax not deducted owing to the regulatory limit 8	Tax Credits 9
1	2,166.67	2,166.67	250.75		1,915.92	401.09			401.09		

Solution (month 2)

In Month 2, Mohammed Ali's pay is £5,214.67, since a bonus of £3,048 becomes payable to him at the end of May 2004. You have also received a notification from the Tax Office on a P6(T) which tells you that Mr Ali's tax code is now 315T. The Table A free pay figure for this code in Month 2 is £526.50.

		£
1	Pay for the year to date £(2,166.67 + 5,214.67)	7,381.34
	Free pay to date from Table A (Month 2, code 315)	(526.50)
	Taxable pay for the year to date	6,854.84

2   For month 2 £6,854 is above the basic rate limit of £5,234, and so some income is taxable at the higher rate of 40%.

	£
Total taxable pay	6,854
Limit on taxable pay at basic rate, for Month 2 (Table C)	5,234
Taxable at higher rate	1,620

PART C DETERMINING NET PAY

3 Tax payable for the year to date (Month 2)

	£	£
On first £5,234 (from Table C)		1,111.19
From Table D: on £1,600	640.00	
on £20	8.00	
		648.00
Total tax payable for the year to date		1,759.19

4 Tax payable by Mohammed Ali in Month 2 is therefore as follows:

	£
Tax payable for the year to date	1,759.19
Less tax paid in the year so far (Month 1)	(401.09)
Tax payable in Month 2	1,358.10

The P11 should be filled in for Month 2 as follows. Note how the old code, 300T, has been crossed out and the new code entered.

Tax code	Amended	315T
~~300T~~	WK/mnth	2

Month	Pay in the week (2)	Total pay to date (3)	Total free pay to date (4a)	K codes Total additional pay to date (4b)	Total taxable pay to date (5)	Total tax due to date (6)	K codes Tax due at end of current period (6a)	Regulatory limit (6b)	Tax deducted in the week (7)	K codes Tax not deducted owing to the regulatory limit (8)	Tax Credits (9)
1	2,166.67	2,166.67	250.75		1,915.92	401.09			401.09		
2	5,214.67	7,381.34	526.50		6,854.84	1,759.19			1,358.10		

Solution (month 3)

In Month 3, you receive another P6(T) from the Tax Office showing that Mohammed Ali's tax code has been changed to 515T. Use Table A for Month 3 (page 187).

Mohammed Ali has also begun working part time, and his pay in Month 3 is only £1,166.67.

1 As the tax code exceeds 500, we need to calculate free pay following the instructions on monthly Table A Month 3.

	£
Pay adjustment figure for 15 (515 – 500)	39.75
Figure from Tables A box	1,250.01
	1,289.76

	£
2 Pay for the year to date £(7,381.34 + 1,166.67)	8,548.01
Free pay to date from Tables A (Month 3, code 515)	(1,289.76)
Taxable pay for the year to date	7,258.25

7: INCOME TAX: MORE COMPLEX CASES

3   £7,258 is below the basic rate tax limit for Month 3 of £7,850, and so Tables B and the subtraction tables must be used.

4   Tax payable for the year to date (Month 3)

		£
Table B	£7,200	1,584.00
	£ 58	12.76
	£7,258	1,596.76
Less: starting rate (month 3)		(60.60)
Total tax payable for year to date		1,536.16
Total tax paid up to Month 2		(1,759.19)
Tax payable in Month 3		(223.03)

Since tax payable is **negative**, a refund of £223.03 is due to Mr Ali for over-payment of tax. This is because of the increase in his tax code in Month 3, and his reduction in earnings.

The P11 should look like this at the end of Month 3 (again, the code box has been amended).

Tax code	Amended	~~315T~~	515T
~~300T~~	WK/mnth	2	3

Month	Pay in the week 2	Total pay to date 3	Total free pay to date 4a	K codes Total additional pay to date 4b	Total taxable pay to date 5	Total tax due to date 6	K codes Tax due at end of current period 6a	Regulatory limit 6b	Tax deducted in the week 7	K codes Tax not deducted owing to the regulatory limit 8	Tax Credits 9
1	2,166.67	2,166.67	250.75		1,915.92	401.09			401.09		
2	5,214.67	7,381.34	526.50		6,854.84	1,759.19			1,358.10		
3	1,166.67	8,548.01	1,289.76		7,258.25	1,536.16			(223.03)R		

Notice the refund, identified by an R.

If you are not sure what the refund entails, note that Mohammed Ali will receive in pay at the end of Month 3:

	£
Pay for the month	1,166.67
Plus refund of tax	223.03
	1,389.70
Less other deductions, such as NIC (say)	(400.00)
Amount received	989.70

PART C   DETERMINING NET PAY

Activity 7.1

In Month 4 Mohammed Ali's tax code and new part-time salary level are the same as in Month 3. Complete the P11 below and fill in the entries for Month 4. In Month 4 the free pay for code 15 is £53.00 and the figure in the box is £1,666.68.

Month		Tax code		Amended WK/mnth								
									K codes		K codes	
	Pay in the week	Total pay to date	Total free pay to date	Total additional pay to date (K codes)	Total taxable pay to date	Total tax due to date	Tax due at end of current period	Regulatory limit	Tax deducted in the week	Tax not deducted owing to the regulatory limit	Tax Credits
	2	3	4a	4b	5	6	6a	6b	7	8	9
1											
2											
3											
4											

4 Week 1/month 1 basis

Tax codes can be used in either of two ways.

- **Cumulative**
- **Non-cumulative**

The usual method is cumulative, and this is the method we have applied so far in illustrating the Tax Tables.

4.1 Cumulative tax codes

You have seen the advantage of the cumulative system in the example used in Section 3 of this chapter.

Mohammed Ali paid a lot of tax in Month 2 because of his large bonus. In Month 3 he had a lower salary payment and a much higher tax code.

Since he had a **cumulative basis tax code**, his tax for Month 3 was calculated by first looking at what he owed for the year to date as a whole. Then this was compared with what he had paid so far. The refund due was the **balancing figure**.

If Mohammed Ali's tax had been worked out just for Month 3 without reference to earlier tax payments, he would not have got his refund until he filled in a tax return **after the end of the tax year**. This is not just unfair to him, but also creates extra work for the Inland Revenue.

4.2 Non-cumulative tax codes

However, sometimes employees have **non-cumulative tax codes** given to them by the Inland Revenue, usually in order to avoid one of the following.

- A very large deduction of tax in one month or week where a code has been reduced significantly.
- An under-deduction of tax where an employee's tax allowances for the year are currently unclear, such as when a new employee starts and the payroll office does not have a correct tax code for him or her (see Chapter 1).

When the **non-cumulative basis** is used, the employee is taxed on what is called **a week 1 or month 1 basis**. The P6(T) notice of coding will indicate this, for example by showing an individual's tax code as 440T **WEEK 1/MONTH 1**.

When a week 1 or a month 1 basis is applied, **the only tax tables (pay adjustment and taxable pay tables) you should use are for Week 1 or Month 1** (depending on whether the employee is weekly or monthly paid).

Instead of taking the employee's total pay for the year to date, you should take **his or her pay for just the week or the month concerned**, and then calculate the tax payable **as if it were Week 1 or Month 1 of the tax year**.

If the employee is paid two-weekly, use Week 2, and for four-weekly payments, use Week 4.

The Tax Office decides which way a code should be used. They will notify you when the cumulative basis should start to be used instead of the non-cumulative (week 1/month 1) basis by issuing a new P6(T).

The only exception is when a new tax year starts. In this case you must not carry over the week 1/month 1 basis into the new year, but start using the cumulative basis instead.

Example: Week 1/month 1 basis

An employee's tax code is 520L WEEK 1/ MONTH 1. His pay in Month 7 is £3,060.44.

The tax payable by the employee is calculated as follows.

Step 1 Work out the free pay for code 520L from Table A for **Month 1**. The free pay for code 20 is £17.42 in Month 1, and this must be added to the figure of £416.67 in the box at the foot of the table to give £416.67 + £17.42 = £434.09.

Step 2 Calculate the taxable pay for the month.

	£
Total pay for Month 7	3,060.44
Free pay Month 1	(434.09)
Taxable pay for Month 7	2,626.35

Step 3 Since taxable pay for the month (£2,626.35) exceeds the **Month 1** limit of £2,617 on the use of Table B, Tables C and D should be used.

Step 4 Taxable pay at the higher rate is £2,626 – £2,617 = £9. So tax payable in Month 7:

	£
On £2,617 (from Table C, Month 1)	555.59
On £9 (from Table D)	3.60
Tax payable on £2,626 in Month 7	559.19

Activity 7.2

How much tax would Mohammed Ali have paid in Month 3 if his new tax code 515T had been on a Week 1/Month 1 basis? (Free pay would have been £429.92 in Month 1.)

4.3 Filling in the P11 for a Week 1/Month 1 basis

When a **Week 1/Month 1** basis applies, the P11 should be filled in differently.

Step 1	Column 2	Enter total pay for the week or month.
Step 2	Column 3	Do not fill in.
Step 3	Column 4a	Enter the amount of free pay for the week or month, as obtained from the free pay tables (Table A week 1 or Table A month 1).
Step 4	Column 5	Subtract the figure in Column 4a from the figure in Column 2. This gives taxable pay for the week or month. Enter this in Column 5.
Step 5	Column 6	Do not fill in.
Step 6	Column 7	Enter the amount of tax payable for the week or month, as obtained by applying the Taxable Pay Tables for Month 1 or Week 1 to the taxable pay in Column 5.

4.4 Going from Week 1/Month 1 to cumulative

When the Tax Office notifies you that you should start using the **cumulative basis** again:

Step 1 Add up Columns 2 and 7.

Step 2 Enter the total of Column 2 as the total pay to date in Column 3 against the last date when a payment was made, and the total of Column 7 as the total tax due to date in Column 6 on the same line.

Step 3 Carry on as for the normal cumulative basis (very often there will be a refund due in the first period in which the cumulative basis is applied).

Example: Week 1/month 1 to cumulative

Dan Kimar starts work with you in Month 3, earning £1,200 gross pay per month. His tax code is 320T Week 1/Month 1, which you use from the first pay day at the end of Month 3. In Month 7 you get a P6(T) from the Tax Office, advising you that his code is now 438L.

Task

Prepare a P11 for Dan to the end of Month 9, assuming his gross pay remains at £1,200 per month.

			£
Table A figures:	Month 1	Code 320	267.42
	Month 7	Code 438	2,560.25
	Month 8	Code 438	2,926.00
	Month 9	Code 438	3,291.75

Solution

Tax code	Amended	438L
~~320T M1~~	WK/mnth	7

Month	Pay in the week (2)	Total pay to date (3)	Total free pay to date (4a)	Total additional pay to date (K codes) (4b)	Total taxable pay to date (5)	Total tax due to date (6)	Tax due at end of current period (K codes) (6a)	Regulatory limit (6b)	Tax deducted in the week (7)	Tax not deducted owing to the regulatory limit (K codes) (8)	Tax Credits (9)
1											
2											
3	1,200		267.42		932.58				184.83		
4	1,200		267.42		932.58				184.83		
5	1,200		267.42		932.58				184.83		
6	1,200	4,800	267.42		932.58	739.32			184.83		
7	1,200	6,000	2,560.25		3,439.75	615.17			(124.15)R		
8	1,200	7,200	2,926.00		4,274.00	778.67			163.50		
9	1,200	8,400	3,291.75		5,108.25	941.96			163.29		

PART C DETERMINING NET PAY

Activity 7.3

(a) Jim Juniper's tax code from Month 1 is 433L Week 1/Month 1. In Month 2 he earns £3,115. Fill in his P11 for Month 2.

	Tax code		Amended								
	433L W1/M1		WK/mnth								
				K codes				K codes		K codes	
Month	Pay in the week	Total pay to date	Total free pay to date	Total additional pay to date	Total taxable pay to date	Total tax due to date	Tax due at end of current period	Regulatory limit	Tax deducted in the week	Tax not deducted owing to the regulatory limit	Tax Credits
	2	3	4a	4b	5	6	6a	6b	7	8	9
1	3,000		361.59		2,638.41				563.99		
2											
3											
4											

(b) In Month 3 he earns £3,675. His tax code is changed to 465T. Free pay for this code in Month 3 is £1,164.75. Now complete his P11 for Month 3.

5 D Codes, and codes BR and NT

5.1 D Codes: always Week 1/Month 1

You may remember from the last chapter that **D Codes** are codes which instruct the employer to deduct tax at the **higher rate only**.

This is usually because the employee has a main job with a different employer. He or she has an ordinary suffix code used by that employer, so all the available allowances are being set against the earnings from that employer.

D Codes are always used on a Week 1/Month 1 basis so the Inland Revenue will not notify you that an employee's code is 'D0 Week 1/Month 1'; the coding notice will just say 'D0'.

Calculating tax for someone with a D code is easy – there is **no free pay** and you can turn **straight to Table D**. You fill in the P11 as follows:

Step 1 Fill in pay for the month in Column 2 as usual

Step 2 Leave Column 3 blank

Step 3 Write Nil in Column 4a

Step 4 Copy the figure from Column 2 into Column 5

Step 5 Leave Column 6 blank

Step 6 Enter into Column 7 the amount of tax shown in Table D for this amount of pay

Example: D Codes

Charlotte Ray earns £2,000 per month from your employer. Her code is D0. Her P11 for Months 1 to 3 is completed as follows:

	Tax code		Amended									
	D0		WK/mnth									
				K codes			K codes			K codes		
Month	Pay in the week	Total pay to date	Total free pay to date	Total additional pay to date	Total taxable pay to date	Total tax due to date	Tax due at end of current period	Regulatory limit	Tax deducted in the week	Tax not deducted owing to the regulatory limit	Tax Credits
	2	3	4a	4b	5	6	6a	6b	7	8	9
1	2,000		NIL		2,000				800		
2	2,000		NIL		2,000				800		
3	2,000		NIL		2,000				800		

5.2 Code BR: cumulative or Week 1/Month 1

Code BR instructs the employer to deduct tax at the **basic rate** (22% for 2004/05).

When you are calculating tax for an employee on code BR:

- **You only use Table B and you do not use the subtraction tables**
- There is no free pay, **so you do not need Tables A**

Code BR can be used cumulatively *or* on a Week/Month 1 basis. We will now look at each case in an example.

Example: Code BR cumulative and week 1/month 1

Brendan Brown is on Code BR, cumulative basis, in Month 1. He earns £250 per month. In Month 3, his code changes to Code BR, Month 1. Fill in his P11 for Months 1, 2 and 3.

PART C   DETERMINING NET PAY

Solution

	Tax code		Amended		BR Mnth 1						
	~~BR~~		WK/mnth		3						

				K codes				K codes			K codes	
M o n t h	Pay in the week	Total pay to date	Total free pay to date	Total additional pay to date	Total taxable pay to date	Total tax due to date	Tax due at end of current period	Regulatory limit	Tax deducted in the week	Tax not deducted owing to the regulatory limit	Tax Credits
	2	3	4a	4b	5	6	6a	6b	7	8	9
1	250	250	NIL		250	55.00			55.00		
2	250	500	NIL		500	110.00			55.00		
3	250		NIL		250				55.00		

Important!

The Chief Assessor regularly comments that students do not know the difference between a BR code and a OT code.

Remember that a OT code works like any other suffix code, except that free pay is NIL. The tax due to date is calculated using the appropriate tables SR, B or C and D as appropriate.

For a BR code, again there is no free pay but tax is calculated on **all pay** at 22% only (no subtraction tables).

5.3 Code NT

Code NT instructs the employer **not to deduct any tax at all**. Filling in the P11 is therefore *very* simple:

Step 1   Fill in Columns 2 and 3 in the normal way

Step 2   Leave Columns 4a and 5 blank

Step 3   Enter 'NIL' in Columns 6 and 7

Activity 7.4

How much tax is due from each of the following employees in Month 1?

(a)   Dickie Dawson, Code D0, monthly pay £400.
(b)   Bryonie Branson, Code BR, monthly pay £100.
(c)   Naomi Taylor, Code NT, monthly pay £500.
(d)   Mary Wong, Code OT, monthly pay £100.

Use the tax tables, for practice, but you should be able to do this in your head!

5.4 Section summary

This summary will help you to remember what columns of the P11 to fill in and how, and what tax tables to use, for the codes and bases covered so far.

Code	Basis	P11 columns					Pay adjustment Tables A	Taxable pay tables		
		2	3	4a	5	6	7		SR	B	C & D
All except D, BR and NT	Cumulative	✓	✓	✓	✓	✓	✓	✓ for Week/ Month of pay day	✓	✓ for Week/Month of pay	✓
	Week 1/ Month 1	✓	✗	✓	✓ for week or month	✗	✓	✓ only for Week 1 or Month 1	✓	✓ for Week 1 or Month 1	✓
D	Week 1/ Month 1	✓	✗	NIL	✓ for week or month	✗	✓	✗	✗	✗	✓ for Week 1 or Month 1
BR	Cumulative	✓	✓	NIL	✓	✓	✓	✗	✗	✓ no subtraction tables	✗
	Week 1/ Month 1	✓	✗	NIL	✓ for week or month	✗	✓	✗	✗	✓ no subtraction tables	✗
NT	Cumulative or Week 1/ Month 1	✓	✓	✗	✗	NIL	NIL	✗	✗	✗	✗

6 Week 53 payments

Week 53 payments: when employees are paid weekly, in some years they will actually be paid in Week 53 (on 5 April in non-leap years, and on 4 or 5 April in leap years).

Week 53 payments are dealt with slightly differently to other pay days.

- Tax is calculated as if the payment were in Week 1 of a new tax year, but using this year's tax tables.
- Free pay for the week is therefore obtained from Table A Week 1.
- Taxable pay is pay for the week minus free pay for the week.
- Tax payable is calculated accordingly.

There is a **special line** (denoted by a squiggle) at the bottom of the P11 for a Week 53 payment. The week number (53) can be entered in the column in place of the squiggle.

The entries in the P11 for Week 53 will be as follows.

- **Column 3**: total pay to date is the cumulative total pay for the 53 weeks.
- **Column 4a**: total free pay is free pay up to Week 52 **plus** free pay on a Week 1 basis for Week 53.

PART C DETERMINING NET PAY

- **Column 5**: total taxable pay to date is the taxable pay up to Week 52, plus the taxable pay for Week 53 (gross pay for Week 53 less free pay for Week 1).

- **Column 6**: similarly, total tax due to date is the tax due up to Week 52, **plus** the tax due for Week 53 (see Column 7 notes below).

- **Column 7**: this shows the tax due for Week 53. Fill this in before you calculate Column 6, to make life easier for yourself. Tax is calculated as if the additional taxable pay was in week 1 of a new tax year.

If the employee is paid **fortnightly** the extra week is called **Week 54** and free pay is taken from Tables A for Week 2.

If the employee is paid **four-weekly** the extra week is called **'Week 56'** and the free pay is taken from Tables A for Week 4.

Activity 7.5

Julia Blaydon is paid £100 per week. Her tax code is 453L. On 5 April 2005 she receives her weekly pay. Complete her P11 for Week 53. Free pay for this code in Week 1 is £87.29.

	Tax code	Amended									
	453L	WK/mnth									
				K codes			K codes			K codes	
W e e k	Pay in the week	Total pay to date	Total free pay to date	Total additional pay to date	Total taxable pay to date	Total tax due to date	Tax due at end of current period	Regulatory limit	Tax deducted in the week	Tax not deducted owing to the regulatory limit	Tax Credits
	2	3	4a	4b	5	6	6a	6b	7	8	9
51	100.00	5,100.00	4,451.79		648.21	64.80			1.20		
52	100.00	5,200.00	4,539.08		660.92	66.00			1.20		
53											

7 Trade disputes

Organisations occasionally suffer from **trade disputes** that result in a **strike** or a **lock-out**. You will be informed by your supervisor which employees are involved in a trade dispute, and if any employee denies that he or she is involved, the matter should be referred to your supervisor.

When an employee is on strike or laid off because of a trade dispute, he or she **might not receive any pay**. (They won't get any pay if they are on strike, but they might get paid something if they are laid off.) This means that the employee will build up an entitlement to a **tax refund**, since **free pay** for the year increases as the tax year progresses, whilst their taxable pay is not increasing at all.

However, in the case of any employee involved in a trade dispute, **you must not make any refund of tax to the employee** (unless given special authorisation to do so by the Tax Office) until the dispute is over.

If you are not paying the employee anything during the dispute, you can put off calculating any PAYE for him or her until one of four things happens.

- The tax year ends.
- The employee leaves your employment.
- The trade dispute ends.
- The employee dies.

If you are paying the employee some money during the trade dispute, you should make PAYE calculations in the normal way and fill in the deductions working sheet. However, if the employee is entitled to a **refund of tax**, you should not make any such payment as long as the dispute lasts.

If an employee **leaves your employment** during a trade dispute, **you must then pay any refund of tax due to him or her**.

When the trade dispute ends, you can make any refund of tax due for the **current tax year** on the first **'normal' pay day** that follows.

If the trade dispute started in one tax year and ends in the next tax year, there are special **end-of-tax-year procedures** that are followed, which will be dealt with at NVQ/SVQ Level 3.

Activity 7.6

You are the Payroll Officer in a company where some employees are on strike.

- George Lo has been on strike but now writes to inform the company that he has taken another job.
- Adelaide Grant has been on strike but has now returned to work.
- Jez Nielsen remains on strike.

All three employees are owed tax refunds. Can you pay any of them these refunds now?

8 K Codes

You may have noticed that at several points we said that certain things should happen **except when the tax code is a K Code**. By now you are probably very curious to know what a K Code is.

8.1 What is a K Code?

K Codes take account of the fact that some people receive **taxable benefits which add up to more than the allowances** they are entitled to.

Ordinarily if someone has, say, a company car, then the benefit of having a company car is given a value and that value is **deducted** from the person's allowances by the Inland Revenue. If, for example, you had allowances of £4,745 and your employer supplied you with a company car for which the taxable benefit was £3,000, your allowance would be reduced accordingly.

	£
Personal allowance	4,745
Less car benefit	(3,000)
Allowance	1,745

You would therefore be given a code of 174 by the Inland Revenue.

Suppose, however, that your employer gave you lots of other perks, like a cheap mortgage, a free TV, a huge Christmas hamper and so on. Most of these things are taxable even though you don't receive any actual cash. It could be that you would end up in the following position.

	£
Personal allowance	4,745
Total taxable benefits	5,000
Shortfall	(255)

Here taxable benefits exceed allowances by £255. **We deal with this by pretending that the employee receives additional pay** of £255 a year (spread over the year), and working out tax accordingly. The employee's tax code would be **K24** (note the K is a prefix - it precedes the number). This adds an extra £249 to taxable pay per annum. Note that a code of K25 would add £259, which exceeds £255. Therefore the K code is always **rounded down**.

Additional pay is the opposite of free pay. It is calculated, as you might expect, by consulting the Pay Adjustment tables (Tables A). So in Month 3 a person with a tax code of K11 would have additional pay to date of £29.76.

Example: Working out additional pay

Sid Perks has a K code of K112. How much additional pay will he have in week 3? Look up code 112 in Tables A for week 3. He will have additional pay of £65.16.

8.2 The regulatory limit

There is a **regulatory limit** in the use of K codes which means that **no-one has to pay in tax more than 50% of their gross pay for the week or month**.

Example: The regulatory limit

An employee has gross pay in Month 1 of £500 and (because he has been given a K code) 'additional pay' of £1,000. The total taxable pay to date is therefore £1,500, and the tax due on this would be £309.79 (check this if you like).

If this much tax were deducted from his pay of £500 he would only receive £190.21 after tax for his month's work. (Remember the 'additional pay' is not money actually paid to him; it is taken in the form of other benefits.)

To prevent such a large proportion of salary being deducted **the regulatory limit of 50% is applied**. This means that the employer is only allowed to deduct £250 in tax (£500 × 50%). The remaining tax due (£309.79 – £250 = £59.79) will be carried forward to the next pay day and collected then (if the regulatory limit does not prevent).

> **Important!**
>
> Make sure that you understand this example and can do the activity below. The entries on the P11 will seem very complicated if you do not get this right.

Activity 7.7

Which of the following employees will benefit from the regulatory limit for K Codes? (Assume that they had received no pay in previous weeks/months.)

Name	K Code	Period	Gross pay £	Additional pay £	Taxable pay £	Tax due £	Tax deducted £
Bob Melon	K49	Mnth 3	1,200				
Ann Apple	K150	Wk 3	800				
Sam Pear	K920	Wk 3	1,000				
Jasmin Grape	K2400	Mnth 3	1,000				

PART C   DETERMINING NET PAY

8.3 K Codes and the P11 (cumulative basis)

Most employees will not have K codes. In all such cases the 'K codes' columns on the P11 can be ignored and left **blank**.

When you encounter an employee who has a K code on a cumulative basis you fill in the P11 as follows:

	Tax code		Amended								
			WK/mnth								
				K codes			K codes		K codes		
M o n t h	Pay in the week	Total pay to date	Total free pay to date	Total additional pay to date	Total taxable pay to date	Total tax due to date	Tax due at end of current period	Regulatory limit	Tax deducted in the week	Tax not deducted owing to the regulatory limit	Tax Credits
	2	3	4a	4b	5	6	6a	6b	7	8	9
1	✓	✓	✗	✓	✓	✓	✓	✓	✓	✓	
2											
3											
4											

Step 1   Make entries in Columns 2 and 3 as usual.

Step 2   No entry is made in Column 4a. There is no free pay.

Step 3   Column 4b: Total 'additional pay' to date is obtained from Tables A: just look up the number in the appropriate week or month.

Step 4   The entry in Column 5 is the total of the entries in Columns 3 plus 4b. The entry in Column 6 is calculated in the normal way.

Step 5   The entry in **Column 6a** is calculated as in the following proforma. You are now calculating the tax due this month. **This may not be the amount deducted because of the regulatory limit**.

	£
Figure in Column 6 this pay day	X
Figure in Column 6 last pay day	(X)
Increase/(decrease) in tax due to date	X/(X)
Add figure in Column 8 last pay day (ie tax due last period but uncollected because of the regulatory limit)	X
Figure to be entered in Column 6a, ie 'tax due at end of current period' (this could be a refund)	X/(X)

With K Codes, the payment of some tax may sometimes be deferred until a later pay day. The calculation above is made to ensure that the amount deferred is eventually paid.

Step 6   Column 6b is much easier. Look at the figure in Column 2 (Pay in the week or month) and multiply by 50%.

Step 7 In Column 7 you enter the lower of the figures in Columns 6a and 6b so that the employee does not lose more than half of his gross pay in one month. If the figure in Column 6a is a refund, this figure should automatically be entered in Column 7 marked R.

Step 8 If the Column 6b figure has been entered in Column 7 because it is lower than the Column 6a figure, then more tax is due than has been deducted, as explained above. An entry is now made in Column 8 as follows.

	£
Column 6a figure	X
Less Column 6b figure	(X)
Column 8 figure – ie amount deferred to a later period	X

In the following month this Column 8 figure will be taken into account as explained in Step 5 above.

Example: K codes and the P11

Bipin Kotecha, a director of a company, normally receives a salary of £75,000 per annum plus a substantial benefits package. However, due to unforeseen circumstances, he took unpaid leave in Month 2. The Inland Revenue have notified you that his tax code is K2500. From Month 4 his salary is raised to £120,000 per annum.

Tables A give the following figures for Months 1 to 4.

	Month 1	2	3	4
Code				
500	417.42	834.84	1,252.26	1,669.68
Boxed 500	416.67	833.34	1,250.01	1,666.68

Task

Complete Mr Kotecha's P11 for Months 1 to 4.

You will learn more if you try yourself, so here is a blank P11. Work through all steps for each month completely before proceeding to the next month.

	Tax code		Amended								
			WK/mnth								
				K codes			K codes			*K codes*	
Month	*Pay in the week* 2	*Total pay to date* 3	*Total free pay to date* 4a	*Total additional pay to date* 4b	*Total taxable pay to date* 5	*Total tax due to date* 6	*Tax due at end of current period* 6a	*Regulatory limit* 6b	*Tax deducted in the week* 7	*Tax not deducted owing to the regulatory limit* 8	*Tax Credits* 9
1											
2											
3											
4											

PART C   DETERMINING NET PAY

Solution

Month	Step 1 Pay in the week 2	Step 1 Total pay to date 3	Step 2 Total free pay to date 4a	Step 3 K codes Total additional pay to date 4b	Step 4 Total taxable pay to date 5	Step 4 Total tax due to date 6	Step 5 K codes Tax due at end of current period 6a	Step 6 Regulatory limit 6b	Step 7 Tax deducted in the week 7	Step 8 K codes Tax not deducted owing to the regulatory limit 8	Tax Credits 9
1	6,250.00	6,250.00		2,084.10	8,334.10	2,842.39	2,842.39	3,125.00	2,842.39		
2		6,250.00		4,168.20	10,418.20	3,184.79	342.40	0	0	342.40	
3	6,250.00	12,500		6,252.30	18,752.30	6,027.20	3,184.81	3,125.00	3,125.00	59.81	
4	10,000.00	22,500		8,336.40	30,836.40	10,369.59	4,402.20	5,000.00	4,402.20		

Step 1   Columns 2 and 3 are simple:

    Column 2   This is the current annual salary divided by 12:

        Month 1:   £75,000 ÷ 12 = £6,250
        Month 2:   no pay
        Month 3:   as month 1 = £6,250
        Month 4:   £120,000 ÷ 12 = £10,000

    Column 3   This is the cumulative total of the figures in Column 2:

        Month 1:   £6,250
        Month 2:   £6,250 + 0 = £6,250
        Month 3:   £6,250 + £6,250 = £12,500
        Month 4:   £12,500 + £10,000 = £22,500

Step 2   Column 4a   This column is blank for K codes, as there is no free pay.

Step 3   Column 4b   This addition to gross pay is calculated by adding the Tables A figure for code 500 plus four times the figure for boxed 500, to give the adjustment for a code of 2500:

        Month 1:   £417.42 + (4 × £416.67) = £2,084.10
        Month 2:   £834.84 + (4 × £833.34) = £4,168.20
        Month 3:   £1,252.26 + (4 × £1,250.01) = £6,252.30
        Month 4:   £1,669.68 + (4 × £1,666.68) = £8,336.40

Step 4   Column 5   This column is the addition of Columns 3 and 4b for each month:

        Month 1:   £6,250.00 + £2,084.10 = £8,334.10
        Month 2:   £6,250.00 + £4,168.20 = £10,418.20
        Month 3:   £12,500.00 + £6,252.30 = £18,752.30
        Month 4:   £22,500.00 + £8,336.40 = £30,836.40

7: INCOME TAX: MORE COMPLEX CASES

Column 6   This is calculated as usual using Tables C and D.

		£		£
Month 1:		2,617	(tax per Table C)	555.59
		5,717	(per Table D)	2,286.80
		8,334		2,842.39
Month 2:		5,234	(tax per Table C)	1,111.19
		5,184	(per Table D)	2,073.60
		10,418		3,184.79
Month 3:		7,850	(tax per Table C)	1,666.40
		10,902	(per Table D)	4,360.80
		18,752		6,027.20
Month 4:		10,467	(tax per Table C)	2,221.99
		20,369	(per Table D)	8,147.60
		30,836		10,369.59

Step 5 Column 6a   This is tax due for the month if there were no 50% limit for tax under K codes. It is calculated as Column 6 for the current month, less Column 6 for the previous month, plus Column 8 for the previous month.

Month 1:   £2,842.39 – 0 + 0 = £2,842.39
Month 2:   £3,184.79 – £2,842.39 + 0 = £342.40
Month 3:   £6,027.20 – £3,184.79 + £342.40 = £3,184.81
Month 4:   £10,369.59 – £6,027.20 + £59.81 = £4,402.20

Step 6 Column 6b   This column is simply half Column 2 – the 50% regulatory limit which applies for a K code (so the employee does not have to pay more than half his gross pay on tax).

Month 1:   £6,250 × 50% = £3,125
Month 2:   £0 × 50% = 0
Month 3:   £6,250 × 50% = £3,125
Month 4:   £10,000 × 50% = £5,000

Step 7 Column 7   This is the amount of tax deducted for the month. It is the lower of Columns 6a and 6b.

	Column 6a	Column 6b	Column 7 (lower)
	£	£	£
Month 1:	2,842.39	3,125	2,842.39
Month 2:	342.40	0	0
Month 3:	3,184.81	3,125	3,125.00
Month 4:	4,402.20	5,000	4,402.20

PART C DETERMINING NET PAY

Step 8   Column 8   This is the amount of tax due in the month which cannot be deducted because of the 50% regulatory limit. This is the excess of Column 6a over Column 6b.

			Excess
			£
Month 1:	£2,842.39 – £3,125	=	0
Month 2:	£342.40 – 0	=	342.40
Month 3:	£3,184.81 – £3,125.00	=	59.81
Month 4:	£4,402.20 – £5,000	=	0

If you managed to get all the answers correct, congratulate yourself! This was an extremely difficult example.

If you did not, do not despair. Instead, check your workings carefully with the detailed workings above, line by line, to see where you went wrong. Remember to work through each month separately, box by box. And always bear in mind that the object of the K Code regulatory limit is to prevent an employee from paying more than half his Column 2 figure as tax. Appreciating the overall point of the rules makes it much easier to apply them!

A situation such as the one above is **not that implausible**. A code of K2500 indicates that the employee (who may be a director) has taxable benefits of £25,000 above his personal allowances. This could easily be met by a luxury car and a house purchase loan.

K codes can also be applied on a week 1/month 1 basis. In this case the column 8 is **not** completed or carried forward, as each pay period is treated separately.

Activity 7.8

Jaswinder Kaur Grewal has a tax code K1200. Her salary in Month 1 is £250.00. Fill in her P11.

Tables A – Pay Adjustment Month 1

Code	£
200	167.42
500	417.42

Boxed figure £416.67

7: INCOME TAX: MORE COMPLEX CASES

M o n t h	Tax code		Amended WK/mnth									
				K codes			K codes			K codes		
	Pay in the week	Total pay to date	Total free pay to date	Total additional pay to date	Total taxable pay to date	Total tax due to date	Tax due at end of current period	Regulatory limit	Tax deducted in the week	Tax not deducted owing to the regulatory limit	Tax Credits
	2	3	4a	4b	5	6	6a	6b	7	8	9
1											
2											

Activity 7.9

For Month 2, Jaswinder Kaur Grewal's code changes to K1200 MI. Assuming her salary remains the same, complete the P11 for month 2.

8.4 P45 figures for starters

As you should now appreciate, sometimes the total tax deducted on a K code will be less than the tax due because of the regulatory limit.

Therefore, when checking a starter's P45 that shows a K code, use the **lower** figure of your check calculation and that shown on the P45.

PART C   DETERMINING NET PAY

Key learning points

- Due to **variations in pay levels** and **tax codes**, employees do not pay the same amount of tax on every pay day. The PAYE system, P11 and the tax tables are designed to cope with such changes.

- PAYE is normally operated on a **cumulative basis**, but sometimes every pay day is treated as if it were the first in the tax year, that is a **non-cumulative (Week 1/Month 1) basis** is used. The basis to use is decided by the Inland Revenue.

- When there are **53 weekly pay days** in the year (or 27 fortnightly ones or 14 four-weekly ones) tax is calculated as if the last payday were Week 1 of a new tax year (or Week 2 or Week 4) but using this year's tax tables.

- While an employee is involved in a **trade dispute** you should not normally make any refunds of tax.

- **K codes** make people pay the tax due on the benefits they receive. The P11 is specially designed to make the tax due easy to calculate.

7: INCOME TAX: MORE COMPLEX CASES

Quick quiz

1 When a Week 1 or Month 1 basis is applied, which tax tables do you use?
2 The normal basis for PAYE is that most codes are non-cumulative. True or false?
3 D codes are always used on a cumulative basis. True or false?
4 Outline how you would use the tax tables to calculate tax in code BR cases.
5 What entries would you make on the P11 for an employee with an NT code?
6 Some of your employees are on strike and are consequently not receiving any pay. What is likely to be the effect on their tax position when the dispute is resolved and they go back to work?
7 When does an employee get a K code?
8 If an employee has a K code, what is the maximum amount of tax they have to pay each week or month?
9 In a K code case, which column on the P11 is **always** left blank?
10 When an employee has a K code used on a cumulative basis, what is the difference between the figures in Column 6 and Column 6a on the P11?

Answers to quick quiz

1 The only tables (both for pay adjustment and for taxable pay) needed are those for Week 1 or Month 1, as appropriate.
2 False. Most codes are cumulative.
3 False. D codes are always used on a Week 1/Month 1 basis (ie on a non-cumulative basis).
4 Tables A are not required in code BR cases as there is no free pay. Table SR and the subtraction tables are also not required as tax is only to be deducted at 22%. Table B is the only tax table required and it is used without the subtraction tables.
5 Columns 2 and 3 (pay this period and to date) are filled in as normal. Columns 4a and 5 are left blank (as, of course, are all the K code Columns – 4b, 6a, 6b and 8). In Columns 6 and 7 you write 'NIL' (ie in the columns recording tax due to date and this period you record that none is due).
6 They will accumulate free pay during the dispute but when they are next entitled to be paid their total pay to date will be much lower than it would have been if they had worked continuously throughout the tax year. It is likely, therefore, that tax due to date will be less than on the last pay day before the strike began and so a tax refund will be due. This cannot be paid while the strike is in progress.
7 K Codes are allocated by the Inland Revenue to employees who receive so many benefits that their personal allowances are less than the total benefits. The K Code signals that they should be taxed as if they received extra pay.
8 The maximum amount of tax to be deducted is half the gross pay (ie cash, ignoring benefits). So, for example, if an employee with a K code has gross pay of £2,000 per month, the maximum deduction for income tax is £1,000.

PART C DETERMINING NET PAY

9   Column 4a, as there is **no** free pay.

10 In Month 1 or Week 1, Columns 6 and 6a should contain the same figure (tax due to date). In subsequent pay periods, Column 6a will have a different figure as it will be used to record the difference between tax due to date last period and this period (including any tax deferred because of the regulatory limit, shown in Column 8 last pay period).

Activity checklist

This checklist shows which performance criteria, range statement or knowledge and understanding point is covered by each activity in this chapter. Tick off each activity as you complete it.

Activity

7.1	☐	This activity covers performance criterion 73.1.E.
7.2	☐	This activity covers performance criterion 73.1.E.
7.3	☐	This activity covers performance criterion 73.1.E.
7.4	☐	This activity covers performance criterion 73.1.E.
7.5	☐	This activity covers performance criterion 73.1.E.
7.6	☐	This activity covers performance criterion 73.1.E.
7.7	☐	This activity covers knowledge and understanding point 2.
7.8	☐	This activity covers performance criterion 73.1.E.
7.9	☐	This activity covers performance criterion 73.1.E.

chapter 8

National Insurance: basic NICs

Contents

1. The problem
2. The solution
3. What is National Insurance?
4. Classes of National Insurance
5. The National Insurance number
6. Calculating NICs
7. Completing form P11

Performance criteria

72.1.E Identify all payments in respect of their tax, National Insurance and pension liability

73.1.E Contribute to the resolution of individual employees' queries by checking net pay calculations manually, using the appropriate tax and National Insurance tables

Knowledge and understanding

4   Social Security regulations governing contributions in particular the manual calculation of gross to net pay (Element 73.1)

13 How to use tax and National Insurance tables to perform manual calculations of net pay

PART C   DETERMINING NET PAY

> **Signpost**
> The more complex NI topics, such as directors' NI, are dealt with at Level 3. Note that the guidance issued confirms that students will not be expected to deal with changes of NI letter within the same pay period.

1 The problem

We have seen how to calculate tax deductions. How are National Insurance Contributions (NICs) calculated?

Is the gross pay for NI purposes the same as for tax purposes?

2 The solution

In some ways NICs are easier to calculate than tax. However, complications arise as you have to decide which contributions table to use (the NI letter).

As you should have appreciated from Chapter 6, gross pay for NI purposes is **not** always the same as for tax. Section 6 of this chapter will look at this in detail.

3 What is National Insurance?

National Insurance (NI) is a system of **compulsory contributions** for each employee, borne in part by the employee and in part by the employer, to fund social security payments. National Insurance payments are known as **National Insurance Contributions (NICs)**.

3.1 The basics

The National Insurance scheme is controlled by the Inland Revenue (National Insurance Contributions Office).

Employees' NICs are one of the statutory deductions from salary in arriving at net pay. Just to recap on the basic computation:

	£
Basic pay etc (what your work has earned you)	1,000
Other (includes statutory sick pay, statutory maternity pay, holiday pay etc)	200
Gross pay	1,200
Less: Income Tax (PAYE – see Chapters 6 and 7)	(140)
Employees' National Insurance (NI) – Chapters 8 and 9	(100)
Other non-statutory deductions (such as pension contributions) – see Chapter 10	(50)
Net pay (amount paid to the employee)	910

In addition, employers have to pay **employer's NICs**. This is a **charge on the business**, not the employee.

3.2 Sources of NI information

Various publications are issued by the Inland Revenue to help you work out NICs. These publications are reissued every year after the Budget.

The **Employer's Help Books** (E10 to E13)

Employer's Further Guide to PAYE and NICs, ref CWG2 (2004/05).

Sets of Tables to calculate National Insurance

- All employers need the basic one, **CA38 National Insurance contributions** Tables A and J
- Employers that have female employees paying the lower rate, or pensioners as employees, will also need CA41 National Insurance Contributions Tables B and C
- Some employers may need CA40 Employee only contributions
- If you have a **contracted-out company pension scheme**, you will need **CA39** or **CA43** as well.

See section 7 for an explanation of these different tables.

Further information can be obtained from the **local Inland Revenue National Insurance Contributions Office** (NICO).

We reproduce **selected pages** from CA38, CA41, CA39 and CA43 in **Appendix II** at the end of this Text. Have a brief look at them now, and keep the CA38 page marked with a Post-it.

If you want to have a complete set of these tables, they can be downloaded from the Inland Revenue website: www.inlandrevenue.gov.uk/employers/emp-form.htm. You do not need an employer's reference number to do this.

4 Classes of National Insurance

National Insurance is divided into **six classes**, based on the type of person paying them. These are as follows.

NICs	Type of person/calculation method
Class 1	Paid by **employers** and **employees** in respect of employment - **percentage of earnings**.
Class 1A	Paid by **employers only** – based on all **taxable** P11D benefits employees receive, such as **cars** provided by their employers for private use, but **not** the provision of childcare.
Class 1B	Paid by **employers only** in respect of PAYE settlement agreements (PSAs).
Class 2	Paid by the **self-employed - fixed contributions**.
Class 3	These are **voluntary contributions**. Why would anyone volunteer to pay NI? If a person has not paid enough into the scheme, then he or she is only entitled to reduced benefits. Class 3 contributions enable a person to **'top up'** contributions to the scheme.
Class 4	Paid by the **self-employed - based on profits**.

This chapter concentrates on Class 1 NICs.

Class 1A and Class 1B contributions will be dealt with in detail at Level 3.

PART C   DETERMINING NET PAY

5 The National Insurance number

The **National Insurance number** is a unique code identifying each individual in the NI scheme. The number is also used by the Inland Revenue as an employee's individual **PAYE reference** (as we saw in Chapter 6).

The NI number is given to you at the age of 16, although you can get one later in life (eg if you are an immigrant to the UK). It takes the following form.

XY 12 34 56 A (ie two letters, six numerals, one letter).

Any **new employee** should give you his or her NI number (NINO). Amongst other places, it can be found in the following ways.

- On the employee's P45 or P60 from his or her previous employment (see Chapter 1).
- On the employee's NINO card.
- By using a special number-tracing form.

The procedures for new employees who cannot give you their NINO were discussed in Chapter 1.

The NINO is important. NICs must be paid - number or no number - but the employee will have difficulty claiming **social security benefits based on contributions** if these contributions are not recorded against his or her number.

6 Calculating NICs

6.1 Form P11

By now you should be familiar with the P11 for PAYE, but we have only looked at one side of the document. Turn to page 195 and 196 for the P11 form. The left hand side is for recording NICs.

You will see that columns 1a, 1b and 1c are used to record earnings. Columns 1d and 1e record contributions. We will look at these in detail.

As previously indicated in Chapter 5, columns 1f, 1g, 1h and 1i are used to record statutory payments (SSP, SMP, SPP and SAP respectively). The **gross amount**, before deductions of tax and NICs, are recorded in these columns.

Finally column 1j is used to record student loan deductions, which will be dealt with in Chapter 10.

Exactly the same **calendar** is used to administer the PAYE system and the NI system.

6.2 NIC age limits

Class 1 NIC is affected by the employee's **age**.

Employees pay Class 1 NICs when they are **16 years of age and over** (on the first payment after the employee's 16th birthday, even if the pay covers a period before the employee is 16). **Employers also pay no NICs for employees under 16.**

8: NATIONAL INSURANCE: BASIC NICs

Employees pay Class 1 NICs on earnings until state pension age (currently 60 if female, and 65 if male). An employee ceases to be liable for NICs after he or she reaches this age. But the employer **continues to be liable** for employer's NICs.

For earnings in respect of periods spanning the state pension age, employees' NICs are not due on payments made after that date. However there is anti-avoidance legislation to catch payments delayed until after state pension age.

Employee's age	Employees' Class 1 NICs	When payable	Employer's Class 1 NICs	When payable
Under 16	None	n/a	None	n/a
16th birthday	Yes, on full amount of pay since last pay day	On first pay day after 16th birthday	Yes, on full amount of pay since last pay day	On first pay day after 16th birthday
16 and over	"	Every pay day	"	Every pay day
60th birthday (female) 65th birthday (male)	No, on full amount of pay since last pay day	Affects first pay day after birthday	"	"
Over 60 (female) Over 65 (male)	None	n/a	"	"

6.3 NIC earnings limits and threshold

Both employees' NICs and employer's NICs have starting points depending on the employee's **earnings**.

	Employees' contribution on earnings from the ET and above				Employer's contribution due on all earnings from the ET and above
	Table A	Table B	Table C	Table J	Tables A, B, C and J
Earnings below LEL	Nil	Nil	Nil	Nil	Nil
Earnings at LEL, up to and including ET	0%	0%	Nil	0%	0%
Earnings above ET, up to and including UEL	11%	4.85%	Nil	1%	12.8%
Earnings above UEL	1%	1%	Nil	1%	12.8%

Rates for 2004/05

LEL = Lower earnings limit (£79.00 per week, £343.00 per month, £4,108.00 per annum)
ET = Earnings threshold (£91.00 per week, £395.00 per month, £4,745 per annum)
UEL = Upper earnings limit (£610.00 per week, £2,644 per month, £31,720 per annum)

PART C DETERMINING NET PAY

The easiest way to follow all this is with a flowchart.

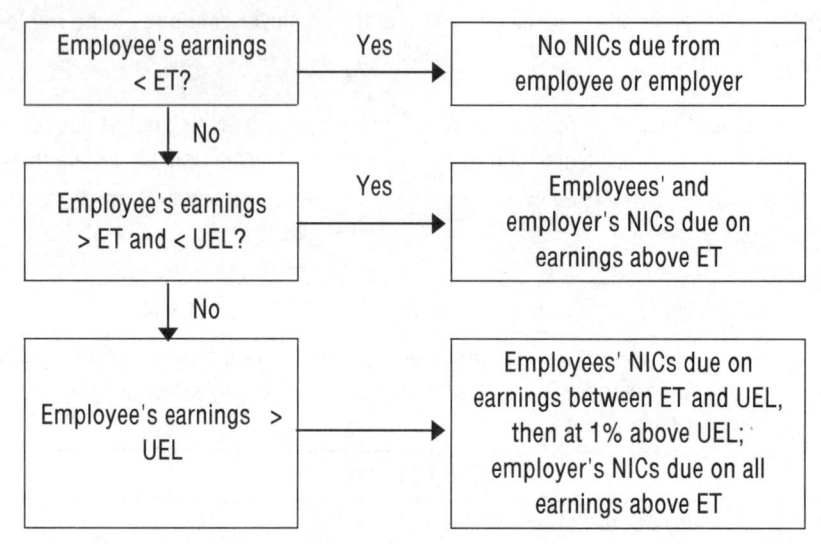

```
Employee's earnings < ET?  --Yes-->  No NICs due from employee or employer
        |
        No
        v
Employee's earnings > ET and < UEL?  --Yes-->  Employees' and employer's NICs due on earnings above ET
        |
        No
        v
Employee's earnings > UEL  ------>  Employees' NICs due on earnings between ET and UEL, then at 1% above UEL; employer's NICs due on all earnings above ET
```

Example: NIC limits (1)

Cliff was born on 15 August 1988 and started work on 1 July 2004. He is paid at the end of every calendar month. His earnings every month amount to £450.

(a) When is the first pay day on which he is liable to pay Class 1 NICs?
(b) How much of his earnings will be assessable to Class 1 NICs in the first payment after he becomes liable?

Solution

(a) Cliff becomes liable on the first pay day after his 16th birthday, ie 31 August 2004.

(b) He will be assessed on £55 (£450 – £395), even though some of this was earned before he reached the age of 16.

Example: NIC limits (2)

Kermit was born on 21 July 1988 and started work on 1 July 2004. He earns £250 per month, which is paid on the 15th of every month.

(a) When is the first pay day on which he is liable to pay Class 1 NICs?
(b) What proportion of his earnings will be liable to assessment?

Solution

(a) 15 August 2004. On 15 July 2004, he is still not 16.
(b) None, as his monthly earnings are less than £395.

8: NATIONAL INSURANCE: BASIC NICs

Example: NIC limits (3)

Methuselah is 65 on 16 June 2004. He receives earnings of £600 a month, paid at the end of the month. How much of his pay, at 30 June 2004, is assessable to Class 1 NICs payable by:

(a) Methuselah?
(b) His employer?

Solution

(a) Methuselah will pay no NIC's.
(b) His employer will pay contributions based on Methuselah's total earnings of £600.

Activity 8.1

You are the Payroll officer at Young & Olde Ltd. The following employees are on the payroll on 30 April 2004, a pay day for both weekly and monthly paid employees

	Date of birth	Weekly pay £	Monthly pay £
Gary Lennox	12.12.88	25.75	
Trevor Owen	14.5.44	52.50	
Petra Brown	26.4.75	80.00	
Marsha Lewis	28.4.44		1,666.66
Dilip Patel	4.5.81		1,250.00
Sandra Bell	31.8.64		2,883.33

(a) Which of these employees is liable for Class 1 NICs and on how much of their pay on 30 April 2004? Give your reasons.

(b) Will Young & Olde Ltd be liable for employer's NICs in respect of any of these employees? If so, which ones? Give your reasons.

6.4 What are earnings for Class 1 NICs purposes?

The NI system is not cumulative, unlike the tax system. NICs are deducted from a payment made now, with little reference to what has occurred earlier in the tax year.

Earnings for NI computations are not necessarily the same as earnings for Income Tax calculations.

This means that you cannot, and must not, assume that the pay in the week or month figure on the Tax side of the P11 is the same as earnings for the NIC side. On most occasions the amounts are the same, but you should always remember that, although detailed on the same form, the **PAYE and NI systems work on different bases**.

PART C   DETERMINING NET PAY

Earnings for NIC purposes comprise:

- Basic pay, overtime and so on
- Company pension scheme payments (tax exempt, but not exempt from NICs)
- Earnings donated under Give As You Earn schemes (tax-exempt but not exempt from NICs)
- Arrears, advances and backpay
- Bonus payments
- Personal bills (eg phone, credit card) reimbursed by the employer
- Vouchers which can be cashed
- Tips in certain circumstances
- Non-cash vouchers (eg Marks & Spencer tokens, Air Miles)
- Statutory Sick Pay, Statutory Maternity Pay, Statutory Paternity Pay, Statutory Adoption Pay
- Certain other items, detailed in the Employer's Further Guide to PAYE and NICs (CWG2)

Notice that **some items which are not taxed are subject to NICs**. Contributions you make to a **company pension scheme** or to **GAYE** can be deducted from your gross pay for income tax purposes (a 'net pay' scheme).

If you earn £1,000 but pay £50 to GAYE and £100 to a company pension scheme, then your 'pay in the week or month' will be £850 for tax purposes, but your earnings for NI purposes will be £1,000.

The only voluntary deductions that can be used to reduce pay for NIC purposes are contributions to an approved **Share Incentive Plan (SIP)**.

An employee does **not** usually pay National Insurance on:

- A **benefit**, such as a company car, interest free loan or free medical insurance
- **Business expenses** which the employer reimburses to the employee.

However these may be subject to a charge on the employer (Class 1A NIC). This will be dealt with at Level 3.

These general rules are subject to many exceptions. If you are in doubt, you should consult the Employer's Guide CWG2. Over 100 categories of expense are covered by the Guide.

6.4.1 NIC on backpay

Note that the backpay is treated as one lump sum for the pay period in which it is paid. It is not related back to prior periods.

Activity 8.2

Gabrielle Hyde has the following salary package from Jekyll Ltd.

- Annual salary of £20,000 in return for a 35 hour week.
- Overtime is paid at time and a half.
- Four weeks paid holiday each year.

- Membership of the company pension scheme: her contributions are fixed as 5% of her salary and the company pays contributions on her behalf of 6% of her salary.
- Company bonus scheme, paying an annual bonus of 1% of salary when conditions of scheme are met.
- Interest-free season ticket loan.
- Use of subsidised staff restaurant.
- Private health insurance.
- Company car.

Which elements of the package will be treated as earnings for NI purposes? Are there any items on which Gabrielle will pay NI but not Hyde Ltd, or vice versa?

7 Completing form P11

7.1 Total NICs and employees' NICs (P11 columns 1d and 1e)

Column 1d of the P11 shows the total amount of NICs payable by the **employer and the employee together**.

Column 1e shows the amount of contributions payable by the **employee only**.

There is no column on the P11 that shows the amount of employer's contributions separately.

7.2 NIC tables

The figures to be entered in Columns 1d and 1e can be read from **NIC tables** produced by NICO (see Appendix II).

Each table runs from the **lower earnings limit** to the **upper earnings limit**.

There are tables for **weekly pay** running from £79 to £610 in steps of £1 and tables for **monthly pay** running from £343 to £2,644 in steps of £4.

For each entry in the first (unnumbered) column between the lower and upper earnings limits the tables show the entries to be made in **columns 1a to 1e**, and also give a figure for **employer's contributions** which does not go on the P11 (it is for information only).

Remember that there is an extra 1% payable by employees on pay over the UEL and **no upper limit for employer's NICs**. Therefore, the tables also include a **calculator** for working out employees' and employer's NICs on amounts over £610 a week or £2,644 a month (this is also in Appendix II).

7.3 The NIC table booklets

There are five booklets containing National Insurance tables:

- Booklet **CA38** contains Tables **A** and **J**

PART C   DETERMINING NET PAY

- Booklet **CA41** contains Tables **B** and **C**
- Booklet **CA40** contains Tables **A** and **B** for employee contributions only
- Booklet **CA39** contains Tables **D, E, L**
- Booklet **CA43** contains Tables **F, G, S**

(There is a special sixth booklet for mariners (CA42) which we are ignoring.)

New sets of tables are published each year. Booklet CA40 is for employees who are authorised to pay their own contributions and is outside the scope of this Text.

Tables A and J (CA38) and **Tables B and C (CA41) are used for employees who are *not* in a contracted-out pension scheme run by the employer**.

Not all employer pension schemes are contracted-out – you must check for your scheme.

Even if you have a contracted-out pension scheme, not all employees may be members of it. For those who are not, you use Tables A, J, B and C.

It is possible for an employee to 'contract out' using a personal pension scheme. You must use Table A for such an employee.

For employees who are members of a **contracted-out pension scheme run by the employer**, you must find out whether the scheme is:

- A contracted-out salary related scheme (COSRS) - use Tables D, E or L (CA39)
- A contracted-out money purchase scheme (COMPS) - use Tables F, G or S (CA43)

The differences between the schemes will be explained in Chapter 10. In practice, and in assessment, you will be told what type of scheme your employer has.

7.4 Which table?

An employee may have a number of employments, or be employed **and** self employed (eg doctors in the NHS with a private practice). In this case, they can **defer** employees' contribution. They have to provide you with a valid **certificate of deferment (CA2700)**. For those employees, you only deduct 1% NICs on all earnings over the ET.

	Neither reduced rate nor non-liable	Reduced rate	Non-liable Through age	CA2700
Not contracted out	A	B	C	J
Contracted out into a COSRS	D	E	C	L
Contracted out into a COMPS	F	G	C	S
Contracted out into a personal pension	A	n/a	n/a	n/a

The flowchart on the next page should help to clarify this.

These **contribution letters** are very important and need to be entered on the P11 (in the summary box after month 12).

8: NATIONAL INSURANCE: BASIC NICs

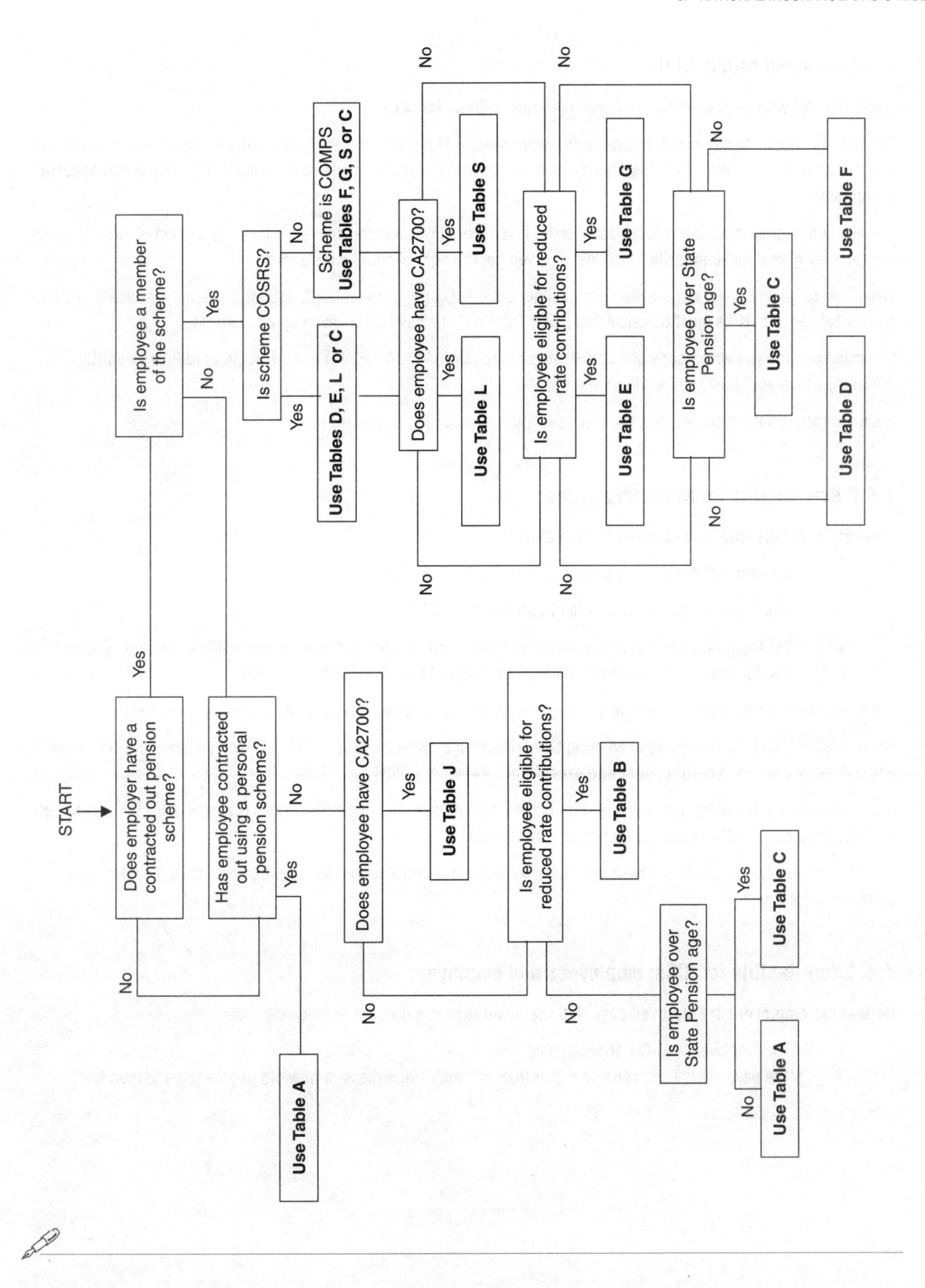

PART C   DETERMINING NET PAY

7.4.1 Reduced rate liability

Some married women and widows have **reduced rate liability for NICs**.

The right to choose to pay at reduced rates was withdrawn in May 1977, but those women who had made the choice may continue with it, even when they change jobs. Those who pay this reduced rate are entitled to **less social security protection**.

The election to contribute at a reduced rate can be **lost** in certain circumstances (such as if the woman divorces), or the woman may **give it up voluntarily**. Once lost or given up, the right cannot be reclaimed.

When lost or given up, the woman changes to either table A, D or F, or to tables C, J, L or S. Remember that if she has a personal pension, NICs must be calculated using Table A if she has lost or given up reduced rate.

She must provide you with a copy of a **certificate of election** (CA4139, CF383) or **certificate of reduced liability** (CF380A) which you must keep while paying reduced rate.

If a certificate is **not** produced, then the employer must deduct NICs at the **full rate.**

7.4.2 Non-liability for NICs: employees

Non-liability for the employee can arise in several ways.

- **Age exemption:** the employee has reached the State Pension age.
- The employee has a **certificate of deferment (CA2700)**.
- For **legal reasons**, the employee is not liable to pay UK NICs. A common example is an employee from another state in the European Union who does not pay UK NICs for one year.

If the employee is not liable, you will be given a certificate which you must keep while operating non-liability.

For non-liability because of **age** you can accept any reasonable evidence of age, eg a birth certificate, but NICO prefers employees to apply for a **certificate of age exception** (CA4140 or CF384 or CF381).

If an employee comes within the scope of non-liability through age, you use table C. This gives rates for the **employer's contributions only**, as the employee makes no contributions.

For CA2700, use tables J, L or S. These give the employees' 1% contribution, for earnings over the ET, and the employer's contribution.

7.4.3 Non-liability for NICs: employees and employers

Neither the employer nor employee pays National Insurance in either of the following cases.

- The employee is **under 16** when paid.
- The payment is for a **pension** rather than earnings (regardless of how old or young the person is).

Activity 8.3

Complex plc has two contracted-out occupational pension schemes. Employees are only eligible to join scheme A after two years' employment. Scheme A is a contracted-out money purchase scheme. Scheme B is a contracted-out salary related scheme, and only the longest standing employees still belong to it.

Date of birth	Name	Scheme A	Scheme B	Not in either scheme	Table to use
15.11.70	Jerome Johnstone			✓	
3.6.40	Finlay Mackay		✓		
14.2.48	Meredith Anderson (R)	✓			
20.1.36	Joan Waters	✓			
4.4.65	Paul Ingle			✓	
28.6.53	Sylvia Chalmers (R)		✓		
4.7.52	Ursula Wilson-Jones (R)			✓	
1.8.31	Oliver Barnett		✓		
17.8.74	Oonagh O'Shaughnessy	✓			

- The women marked (R) have reduced rate liability.
- Paul Ingle has another job and has given you a certificate of non-liability for NIC (CA2700).
- Jerome Johnstone has a private pension plan.

Which table will you use to calculate NICs for each of these employees on 31 July 2004?

7.5 Samples of NIC tables

Samples of **some** of the pages of the tables (those you need for activities) are given in Appendix II at the end of this Text. If you want complete sets, these can be downloaded from the Inland Revenue website.

Table	Weekly/Monthly	For	Complete?
A, J	Both	Not contracted out exact percentage calculations	Yes
A	Weekly	Not contracted-out, standard rate.	Yes
A	Monthly	Not contracted-out, standard rate	No
J	Monthly	Not contracted-out, 1% rate	Yes
All	Both	Additional gross pay table for earnings over UEL	Yes
B, C	Both	Not contracted-out exact percentage calculations	Yes
B	Monthly	Not contracted-out, reduced rate	No
C	Monthly	Employer only contributions	No
D, E, L	Both	COSRS contracted-out exact percentage calculations	Yes
D	Weekly	COSRS, standard rate	No
D	Monthly	COSRS, standard rate	No

PART C   DETERMINING NET PAY

Table	Weekly/Monthly	For	Complete?
E	Monthly	COSRS, reduced rate	No
L	Monthly	COSRS, employer only contributions	No
F, G, S	Both	COMPS contracted-out exact percentage calculations	Yes
F	Monthly	COMPS, standard rate	No

7.6 Filling in the P11 using tables: earnings below UEL

If the exact gross pay is not shown in the table, the **nearest lower figure is used**. This means that pennies are ignored in the **weekly tables**, and that the nearest £4 step **below** the gross pay is taken in the **monthly tables**.

Filling in the P11 is quite simple.

Step 1   Decide which table needs to be used

Step 2   Look up the earnings figure in the relevant table

Step 3   Read off the figures for columns 1a, 1b, 1c, 1d and 1e and enter on the P11

Example: National Insurance and the P11

Suppose you were calculating the NICs for a female employee aged 34 who was not contracted out and who was not entitled to reduced rate liability. Her weekly pay is £100.54. What entries should be made on the NIC side of the P11?

Solution

Table A applies to this employee and so the letter A should be written in the summary box. The Weekly Table A shows the following entries to be made for weekly pay of £100. Remember that you don't write in the employer's contributions figure.

	Earnings details			Contribution details		Statutory payments				Student Loan Deductions Whole pounds only
W e e k	Earnings at the LEL (where earnings reach or exceed the LEL)	Earnings above the LEL, up to and including the Earnings Threshold	Earnings above the Earnings Threshold, up to and including the UEL	Total of employees' and employer's contributions payable	Total of employees' contributions payable on earnings above the ET	SSP	SMP	SPP	SAP	
	1a	1b	1c	1d	1e	1f	1g	1h	1i	1j
1	79	12	9	2.26	1.04					

244

7.7 Filling in the P11 using tables: earnings over UEL

Where there are earnings above the upper limit, the procedure is as follows.

Step 1 Decide which table needs to be used.

Step 2 Look up the UEL in the relevant table (ie the last entry).

Step 3 Read off the figures for columns 1a, 1b and 1c and enter on the P11.

Step 4 Deduct UEL from actual earnings. Calculate the employees' and employer's contributions due on the excess by reference to the additional gross pay table.

Step 5 Add contributions due on the excess to the total contributions payable for the UEL shown in columns 1d and 1e in the table. Enter in columns 1d and 1e on the P11.

	£
Total employees' and employer's contributions on UEL from table	X
Employees' and Employer's contributions due on excess	X
Column 1d figure	X

	£
Total employees' contributions on UEL from table	X
Employees' contribution due on excess	X
Column 1e figure	X

Example: Earnings above the upper limit

Suppose the same employee as in the above example earns £652 the following week.

Step 1 Table A is still used.

Step 2 The weekly table only goes up to £610, which is the Upper Earnings Limit.

Step 3 Fill in columns 1a, 1b and 1c as shown in the table (see below).

Step 4 Further NICs are due on earnings above the UEL: £652 – £610 = £42.

The NICs due on the additional gross pay of £42 are found by consulting the 'additional gross pay table' (see Appendix II). The amount must be built up from the fewest possible number of entries in the table: in this case £42.

Additional gross pay £	Total of employees' and employer's contributions £	Employees' contributions £	Employer's contributions £
42	5.80	0.42	5.38

Step 5 Total employees' and employer's contributions are therefore £5.80 + £123.52 = £129.32 and the employees' contribution totals £0.42 + £57.09 = £57.51. (The employer's contribution is £5.38 + £66.43 = £71.81. To check your arithmetic: £57.51 + £71.81 should equal £129.32.)

PART C DETERMINING NET PAY

Week	Earnings details			Contribution details		Statutory payments				Student Loan Deductions
	Earnings at the LEL (where earnings reach or exceed the LEL)	Earnings above the LEL, up to and including the Earnings Threshold	Earnings above the Earnings Threshold, up to and including the UEL	Total of employees' and employer's contributions payable	Total of employees' contributions payable on earnings above the ET	SSP	SMP	SPP	SAP	Whole pounds only
	1a	1b	1c	1d	1e	1f	1g	1h	1i	1j
1	79	12	9	2.26	1.04					
2	79	12	519	129.32	57.51					

7.8 Other pay periods

Some employees are paid two-weekly or four-weekly, others are paid at irregular intervals. This poses no problems if you use the exact percentage method (see Chapter 9). Just multiply the LEL, ET and UEL by the number of weeks or months in the pay period. If using tables, use the following methods.

Pay interval	To work out NICs
Weekly	Use weekly NIC tables
Two-weekly	• Divide earnings by 2 • Look up NIC in weekly tables • Multiply result by 2
Four-weekly	• Divide earnings by 4 • Look up NIC in weekly tables • Multiply result by 4
Monthly	Use monthly NIC tables
Quarterly	• Divide earnings by 3 • Look up NIC in monthly tables • Multiply result by 3
Half yearly	• Divide earnings by 6 • Look up NIC in monthly tables • Multiply result by 6
Annually	• Divide earnings by 12 • Look up NIC in monthly tables • Multiply result by 12

Activity 8.4

Using the extracts from NI Table A in Appendix II fill in P11 columns for each of the employees below.

	Age	Monthly salary £
Thomas Taylor	57	380.00
Stephanie Cheung	29	1,517.25
Lorna Campbell	43	602.21
Piers Smith	41	2,750.00

None of them are contracted-out or paying reduced rates of NIC.

Employee	Earnings at the LEL (where earnings reach or exceed the LEL) 1a	Earnings above the LEL, up to and including the Earnings Threshold 1b	Earnings above the Earnings Threshold, up to and including the UEL 1c	Total of employees' and employer's contributions payable 1d	Total of employees' contributions payable 1e

PART C   DETERMINING NET PAY

Key learning points

- ☑ National Insurance (NICs) contributions are used to fund social security benefits.
- ☑ Most employees pay **Class 1 contributions**:
    - some pay at standard rate
    - some pay at a reduced rate
    - some are contracted out, if they pay contributions to an approved pension scheme run by the employer, which may be salary-related or money purchase.
- ☑ NICs are paid by the employee and the employer on **earnings**. Earnings for NIC purposes are not necessarily the same as earnings for income tax purposes.
- ☑ If an employee's earnings are below the **lower earnings limit**, no NICs are paid by the employee or employer.
- ☑ Employees pay only 1% NICs on earnings above the **upper earnings limit**.
- ☑ Employers do not pay NICs on earnings below the **employer's earnings threshold** but there is no upper earnings limit on employer's NICs.
- ☑ NIC calculations are not cumulative. For most employees, NICs payable can be found in **NIC tables**. You need to be careful to use the correct table. This means checking each employee's age and pension arrangements.

Quick quiz

1. There are six classes of National Insurance Contributions. Which ones concern you most?
2. Where can you find an employee's NI number?
3. The NIC system is cumulative. True or false?
4. X Ltd employs only pensioners, to save NIC. Will they?
5. There is an upper earnings limit on all NICs. True or false?
6. GAYE donations are exempt from NIC. True or false?

Answers to quick quiz

1. Class 1 contributions, paid by employer and employee.
2. On a P45 or P60; on an NI card; or ask NICO to trace it.
3. False. PAYE is cumulative. NICs are calculated on this period's earnings, with no reference to previous periods.
4. No. Men over 65 and women over 60 are no longer required to pay NICs, but their employers are, so **X Ltd** will save nothing.
5. False. There *is* an upper earnings limit for employees' NICs at the main 11% rate, but not for employer's NICs.
6. False. They are exempt from PAYE but not from NIC.

Activity checklist

This checklist shows which performance criteria, range statement or knowledge and understanding point is covered by each activity in this chapter. Tick off each activity as you complete it.

Activity

8.1	☐	This activity covers knowledge and understanding points 4 and 13.
8.2	☐	This activity covers performance criterion 72.1.E.
8.3	☐	This activity covers knowledge and understanding points 4 and 13.
8.4	☐	This activity covers performance criterion 73.1.E and knowledge and understanding point 13.

PART C DETERMINING NET PAY

chapter 9

National Insurance: advanced NICs

Contents

1 The problem
2 The solution
3 The exact percentage method
4 Contracted out earnings and contributions
5 Changes during the tax year

Performance criterion

73.1.E Contribute to the resolution of individual employees' queries by checking net pay calculations manually, using the appropriate tax and National Insurance tables

Knowledge and understanding

4 Social Security regulations governing contributions in particular the manual calculation of gross to net pay (Element 73.1)

13 How to use tax and National Insurance tables to perform manual calculations of net pay

PART C   DETERMINING NET PAY

> **Signpost**
>
> Other complex NIC topics, such as calculation of NICs using two NI letters for the same pay period, aggregation of earnings and share options are outside the scope of Level 2.

1 The problem

NICs may have seemed fairly straightforward but, of course, there are problem areas.

In real life, as well as the assessment, you may find yourself without tables. How do you cope without NI tables?

In the last Chapter, we mentioned contracted-out contributions. What are these and how do you calculate them?

What happens if the contribution letter changes during the year (eg an employee passes their State Pension age)? What about leavers?

2 The solution

Section 3 shows you how to calculate NIC by the exact percentage method.

Employees who are part of the firm's pension scheme may be contracted out. Section 4 deals with the calculation and recording of contracted out contributions.

Section 5 deals with the special circumstance of changes of contribution letter during the tax year, and also NIC for leavers.

3 The exact percentage method

It is possible to calculate NICs payable by using the **exact percentage method**.

The advantage of learning how to do this is that it teaches you how the NIC payments are actually calculated. Also you can calculate NICs if you do not have access to the relevant tables.

In your assessment, you are likely to be given the percentages and have to calculate NI using this method.

You must still indicate on the P11 (in the boxes in the left hand bottom of the page) **which Table rates apply**.

Have a look at Appendix II. The first table shows the rates of NICs payable by those who are **not contracted out**.

Table A employees pay the following rates of NICs.

- **No** NICs on earnings up to the ET
- 11% on earnings between the ET and the UEL
- 1% on earnings above the UEL

The only difference for **Table B employees** is that they pay 4.85% instead of 11% on earnings between the ET and the UEL. **Table C employees**, of course, pay no NICs at all.

Employers pay no NICs on employees' earnings below the ET and a flat rate of 12.8% on all earnings above the ET, including those of Table B and Table C employees. There is **no upper limit** for employers.

The exact percentage method calculations are therefore very simple. You simply need to know the UEL, ET and LEL and the appropriate percentages.

You must round each calculation to the nearest 1p. Amounts of 0.5p should be rounded down. In columns 1b and 1c record any pence and round down to the nearest pound only at the end of the tax year when calculating the totals.

Example: Exact percentage method

Say a Table A employ**ee** earns £108 per week. The employee will pay NIC at 11% on (£108 – £91) = £17, so the employees' NIC is £1.87.

However, the employ**er** will pay NIC at 12.8% on (£108 – 91) = £17, so the employer's NIC is £2.18.

The total of the employer's and employees' contributions is £4.05 (£1.87 + £2.18).

Activity 9.1

Calculate the NICs due this week for the following employees. None of them is in an occupational pension scheme. Use the exact percentage method.

	Age	Reduced rate?	Weekly pay £
Arthur Adams	66	N	125
Beatrice Blair	15	N	90
Catherine Cross	49	Y	181
Dilys Dunn	38	N	37
Eric Edwards	26	N	202
Frederick Fellowes	48	N	625

4 Contracted out earnings and contributions

The NIC is meant to fund two different types of benefit: **pensions** and **social security** (eg the jobseeker's allowance).

However, there are a number of ways of saving up for a pension.

- Through the NI system (the **basic retirement pension** and the **State Second Pension (S2P)**).
- Through an **occupational pension scheme** run by your employer, in which case the employee need not participate in S2P.
- Through a **personal pension** scheme run by a financial services company, where the employee may contract out of S2P.

PART C   DETERMINING NET PAY

The point to note here is that by making alternative pension provision, the employee (and in the case of an occupational pension scheme, the employer too) earns the right to pay less NI as less help should be needed from the State.

4.1 Occupational pension schemes

If the employer runs a **pension scheme** (an 'occupational pension scheme'), it may be used to contract the employees out of the state scheme, S2P. This means that **both employer and employee pay less National Insurance**.

The amount of the reduction in National Insurance depends on whether the scheme is **COSRS (salary-related)** or **COMPS (money purchase)**. These terms are explained in Chapter 10.

Earnings	Employees						Employers					
	COSRS			COMPS			COSRS			COMPS		
	D	E	L	F	G	S	D	E	L	F	G	S
	%	%	%	%	%	%	%	%	%	%	%	%
< LEL	NIL	NIL	NIL	NIL	NIL	NIL	NIL	NIL	NIL	NIL	NIL	NIL
LEL to ET	0	0	0	0	0	0	0	0	0	0	0	0
> ET to UEL	9.4	4.85	1	9.4	4.85	1	9.3	9.3	9.3	11.8	11.8	11.8
> UEL	1	1	1	1	1	1	12.8	12.8	12.8	12.8	12.8	12.8

NIC rebate for **employees** on earnings between LEL and ET is 1.6% for tables D, L, F and S. No NIC rebate is due for tables E or G.

NIC rebate for **employers** on earnings between LEL and ET is 3.5% for all COSR tables D, E and F; but only 1% for COMP tables F, G and S.

Employer's NICs on earnings above the UEL are calculated at 12.8%, just as for non-contracted out employees. Similarly, employees still pay 1% on earnings above the UEL.

4.2 Rebates

		Employee £	Employer £
COSRS:	1.6% × (91 − 79)	0.19	
	3.5% × (91 − 79)		0.42
COMPS:	1.6% × (91 − 79)	0.19	
	1.0% × (91 − 79)		0.12

This may seem a small amount, but over a year and with a large workforce, it can mount up. For example, with a workforce of 1,000 in a COMPS, the employer's rebate over a year is £6,240 (1,000 × 0.12 × 52).

Example: Calculating NICs for a contracted-out employee

Lewis Corbin is 25 and earns £120 per week. His employer runs a salary-related pension scheme (COSRS), and Lewis contributes to it. He is contracted out. Therefore you need to use table D.

Using the exact percentage method of calculation, Lewis's contributions are (£120 – £91) × 9.4% = £2.73 less rebate £0.19 = £2.54.

Look at the extract from the weekly table D in Appendix II. You'll see the table figure is £2.58, because of rounding used in the table.

In practice you would put down £2.54 or £2.58, according to whether you had been told to use the exact percentage method or tables.

The employer pays (£120 – £91) × 9.3% = £2.70. The rebate is £0.42 as calculated above, giving a net figure of £2.28. The figure in Table D is £2.32.

Tutorial note. Notice that tables D, and all the other contracted-out tables, show the contributions **net of the rebate**.

Activity 9.2

Calculate the NICs due for Month 1 for each of the following employees. Extracts from the relevant tables are given in Appendix II (or you can use the exact percentage method if you preper).

	Monthly salary £	Member of pension scheme COSRS	COMPS
Bella Thomas	1,209.88	✓	
Muriel Thorne	1,447.15		✓
Peter Abrams	893.00	✓	
Darcus Groves	2,685.30		✓

Bella Thomas pays reduced-rate contributions. Peter Abrams has given you a valid CA2700.

	Table	Earnings at the LEL (where earnings reach or exceed the LEL) 1a	Earnings above the LEL, up to and including the Earnings Threshold 1b	Earnings above the Earnings Threshold, up to and including the UEL 1c	Total of employees' and employer's contributions payable 1d	Total of employees' contributions payable on earnings above ET 1e
Bella Thomas						
Muriel Thorne						
Peter Abrams						
Darcus Groves						

PART C   DETERMINING NET PAY

5 Changes during the tax year

There are a number of alterations which may need to be made during the tax year. Some examples are given below.

- An employee becomes **16 years old**. NI becomes payable by both employer and employee.
- An employee receives a pay rise which brings his or her pay to more than the LEL or ET. NI is now payable.
- An employee reaches **retirement age**, but **continues working**.
- An employee who was in the company's **contracted-out occupational pension scheme** decides to withdraw from it, or vice versa.
- An employee **starts employment**.
- An employee **retires or leaves** to go to another job.

All of these require some adjustment to your P11.

5.1 Changes to NI letter

If, for example, you change to a different Table or a different contribution rate, as you will to Table C in the third example above, or in the fourth example above where you will change from Table D to Table A or vice versa, then you will need to note this fact down on the P11 and **identify separately the contributions made under different contribution rates**.

If you start to use another Table during the year, you should:

Step 1   Enter the total NI paid at the previous rate at the bottom of the sheet, next to the box in which you have noted down the Table letter

Step 2   Write the new NI letter, which you are now using, below the old letter

Step 3   If you wish, note the change in the column 'for employer's use' alongside the week or month in which it is instituted

9: NATIONAL INSURANCE: ADVANCED NICs

Example: Change during the year

An employee paid £505 per month has reached retirement age at the beginning of Month 11. You should recall that from the date an employee reaches pensionable age, only the employer should pay NICs, and so Table C should be used.

Month	For employer's use	Earnings at the LEL (where earnings reach or exceed the LEL) 1a	Earnings above the LEL, up to and including the Earnings Threshold 1b	Earnings above the Earnings Threshold, up to and including the UEL 1c	Total of employees' and employer's contributions payable 1d	Total of employees' contributions payable on earnings in 1c 1e
1		343	52	108	26.18	12.10
2		343	52	108	26.18	12.10
3		343	52	108	26.18	12.10
4		343	52	108	26.18	12.10
5		343	52	108	26.18	12.10
6		343	52	108	26.18	12.10
7		343	52	108	26.18	12.10
8		343	52	108	26.18	12.10
9		343	52	108	26.18	12.10
10		343	52	108	26.18	12.10
11	Table C	343	52	108	14.08	–
12		343	52	108	14.08	–

Enter NICs here ↓   End of Year Summary

	1a	1b	1c	1d	1e
A	3,430	520	1,080	261.80	121.00
C	686	104	216	28.16	–

Activity 9.3

You are preparing the monthly payroll. A number of changes have occurred since last month.

(a) Selina Harcourt, a part-time employee earning £350 per month, has had her sixteenth birthday. She will not be joining the company pension scheme.

(b) Brian Ellis has had a pay rise, from £290 per month to £360. He belongs to the company pension scheme (COSRS) and is 62 years old.

(c) David Deighton (aged 40 and earning £1,200 per month) has joined the company's COSR pension scheme.

(d) Louise Wallis (aged 52 and earning £800 per month) has left the COSR pension scheme. She has been paying contributions at reduced rate.

Which NI table would you have used for each employee last month? Which will you use this month?

PART C DETERMINING NET PAY

5.2 NICs and leavers

If a person is normally **monthly paid**, but leaves, say, at the end of the first week after the beginning of a tax month, still use the monthly tables to calculate NICs.

If final salary payments after the date of leaving attract NICs, use the same table letter and earnings period (month or week) **as when the employee left**. However, the contribution rates are those at the **date of payment**.

For **irregular payments**, such as bonuses or backdated pay increases, paid after the employee has left, use the same table letter but at the **weekly rate** at the date of payment (it makes no difference if the employee had been monthly paid).

If the payment is made **more than six weeks after the employee leaves, Table A rates will apply to the final payment** even if the employee was contracted out.

> **Signpost**
>
> Now that you know how to deduct tax and NICs, go back to Chapter 1 and revise the sections on form P45. It should all make sense now. Check the tax deduction figures shown on the forms P45, for both starters and leavers.

Key learning points

- Most employees pay **Class 1 contributions**:
  - some pay at standard rate
  - some pay at a reduced rate
  - some are **contracted out**, if they pay contributions to an approved pension scheme run by the employer, which may be salary-related or money purchase.
- NICs are paid by the employee and the employer on **earnings**. Earnings for NIC purposes are not necessarily the same as earnings for income tax purposes.
- If an employee's earnings are below the **lower earnings limit**, no NICs are paid by the employee or employer.
- Employees do not pay NICs on earnings below the **earnings threshold**. They pay at only 1% on earnings above the **upper earnings limit**.
- Employers do not pay NICs on earnings below the **earnings threshold** but there is **no upper earnings limit** on employer's NICs.
- NIC calculations are not cumulative. For most employees, NICs payable can be found in **NIC tables**. You need to be careful to use the correct table. This means checking each employee's age and pension arrangements.

PART C DETERMINING NET PAY

Quick quiz

1. Why do you need to know about your employees' pension arrangements?

2. Employers and employees pay less NICs if the organisation's occupational pension scheme is COSRS than if it is COMPS. True or false?

Answers to quick quiz

1. Members of an occupational pension scheme are likely to be contracted-out and so pay lower NICs. Employees belonging to a non-contracted out scheme or a personal pension plan or with no pension provision at all pay higher rates of NICs. You use different NI tables depending on the type of scheme each employee belongs to.

2. COSRS = Contracted-Out Salary Related Scheme.
   COMPS = Contracted-Out Money Purchase Scheme.

Reduction in rate of NICs	COSRS	COMPS
Employer	3.5%	1.00%
Employee	1.6%	1.6%

   Partially true. Employees get the same reductions but employers get a higher reduction if they have a COSRS.

Activity checklist

This checklist shows which performance criteria, range statement or knowledge and understanding point is covered by each activity in this chapter. Tick off each activity as you complete it.

Activity

9.1	☐	This activity covers performance criterion 73.1.E.
9.2	☐	This activity covers performance criterion 73.1.E.
9.3	☐	This activity covers performance criterion 73.1.E.

chapter 10

Other deductions

Contents

1. The problem
2. The solution
3. Court orders and other compulsory deductions
4. Student loan deductions
5. Pension contributions
6. Give as you earn (GAYE)
7. Sharesave (SAYE)
8. Employee loans and advances
9. Trade Union and social clubs contributions
10. Errors in PAYE and NIC
11. Miscellaneous deductions
12. Payslips

Performance criteria

- 72.1.E Identify all payments in respect of their tax, National Insurance and pension liability
- 73.1.A Check the payroll status of all employees for validity for the pay period
- 73.1.B Input any applicable pre-tax deductions
- 73.1.C Input all relevant statutory and non-statutory deductions
- 73.1.D Produce and distribute accurate and legible payslips in accordance with statutory and organisational requirements
- 73.1.E Contribute to the resolution of individual employees' queries by checking net pay calculations manually, using the appropriate tax and National Insurance tables
- 73.1.F Check net pay totals to ensure that the full range of applicable allowances and deductions has been made
- 73.1.G Check net pay figures against the parameters for the payroll concerned and resolve any discrepancies or refer them to the appropriate person for resolution

Range statement

1. **Pre-tax deductions**: contributions to occupational pension schemes; charitable giving
2. **Statutory deductions**: attachment of earnings; student loans
3. **Non-statutory deductions**: pensions contributions; recovery of overpayments; repayment of loans and advances; voluntary deductions

PART C   DETERMINING NET PAY

Knowledge and understanding

1   Data Protection legislation (Elements 73.1 & 73.2)
3   PAYE regulations in respect of charitable giving (Element 73.1)
5   Pension legislation in respect of tax relief (Element 73.1)
6   Checking validity of all employees (Element 73.1)
7   Timescales and schedules for despatching payslips (Element 73.1)
9   Procedures for the security and confidentiality of information (Element 73.1 & 73.2)
10 Procedures for initiating and monitoring payments (Element 73.1)
12 Information and timescale requirements of systems for transmission of disbursements to employees (Element 73.1)

> **Signpost**
>
> The guidelines again emphasise that Court and Attachment of earnings orders are dealt with in detail at Level 3. For the purposes of this element, you just need to know that these are collected by deduction from pay.

1 The problem

We have looked at **two statutory deductions**: tax and NIC. However, we have a lot of other deductions to make. Are these deductions before tax or after tax?

What about the authority for these deductions? Do we even have to pay the employee this pay period?

2 The solution

Look at performance criteria 73.1.A.: Check the payroll status of all employees for validity for the pay period. What does this mean?

It is the most important question to ask: 'Is the employee still with us?' If they are, they need paying. If they are not, they need removing from the current payroll.

There may be other points to consider eg 'Is the employee on unpaid leave?' In this case, no pay is due but you need to keep the employee on the current payroll.

Let's just have another look at our **basic computation** to see where everything fits in.

	£
Basic pay (what your work has earned you)	1,000
Other pay (includes SSP, SMP, SPP, SAP, holiday pay etc)	200
Gross pay	1,200
Less Income Tax (PAYE)	(140)
National Insurance (NI)	(100)
Other deductions	(50)
Net pay	910

Remember that **statutory deductions are compulsory**. However, you will need the right documents before making the deductions (correct tax code, correct NIC table, Court Order).

Non-statutory deductions are voluntary. They might be part of the contract of employment (contractual, eg membership of the pension scheme) or they might be completely voluntary (eg Social Club membership). For either type of non-statutory deduction, the payroll department needs the **written signed authority** of the employee before any deductions can be made.

Don't skimp on this chapter. These are more straightforward topics than tax and NICs, but none the less **they are important**.

3 Court orders and other compulsory deductions

3.1 Child Support Agency

The CSA administers the system of child maintenance.

The CSA issues a Deduction from Earnings Order (DEO) direct to an employer.

The DEO will show the amount to be deducted and sent to the CSA each pay period. The amount of the DEO is **deducted from net pay**, ie after tax and NICs have been deducted.

The DEO will also show the **protected earnings rate**. This is the amount of net pay that the employee should receive and payments under the order must not take net pay below the protected earnings rate.

If earnings fall below the protected earnings rate, no deductions are made. Instead, the shortfall of protected earnings is carried forward and recovered in future earnings periods before any more deductions can be made.

We will deal with this in full detail at Level 3.

The employer can take £1 towards administrative costs each pay period. This can reduce income below the protected earnings rate.

Activity 10.1

You are the payroll assistant for Dove Ltd. You have received a DEO for Mr Hawk. The DEO shows a normal deduction rate of £30 per week and a protected earnings rate of £120 per week. Dove Ltd will take the £1 per week administrative fee from Mr Hawk's pay. What is Mr Hawk's net pay for weeks 1-4, if his pay after tax and NICs is as follows?

(a) Week 1 £150
(b) Week 2 £175
(c) Week 3 £120
(d) Week 4 £250

PART C   DETERMINING NET PAY

3.2 Court orders

The court can make an Attachment of Earnings Order (AEO) in order to collect unpaid debts, eg judgement debts. In Scotland, this is called an Arrestment. Orders can be priority or non-priority.

A priority AEO works in a similar way to the CSA's DEO, with a normal deduction rate and protected earnings rate. Any shortfall of protected earnings rates and deductions are carried forward.

However, with a non-priority AEO any shortfall of the deductions and protected earnings are **not** carried forward. Instead the employer continues to make deductions until the debt is cleared.

Payments are forwarded to the court or as directed in the order. Employers can deduct an admin charge of £1 per pay period (Scotland 50p).

Once again, we will deal with court orders in detail at Level 3.

> **Remember**
>
> Payments can only be made in accordance with a **current** statutory order (DEO or AEO).

3.3 Attachable earnings

Earnings that can be 'attached' (ie have orders deducted from them) are as follows in England and Wales.

- Wages
- Salary
- SSP (but **not** SMP, SPP or SAP)

Orders are deducted after tax and NIC.

3.4 Arrestable earnings

In Scotland, arrestable earnings are the same as attachable earnings in England and Wales. Orders are deducted after tax and NIC.

4 Student loan deductions

Student loan deductions should only be made on receipt of a start notification from the Inland Revenue, or if box 5 is marked with a 'Y' on the P45 of a new employee, see Chapter 2.

Gross pay for SLDs is the **same as gross pay for NICs**. Therefore, if a student has pension and GAYE contributions, those are ignored for SLD purposes.

The amount of the SLD has to be recorded on the P11. Looking back at pages 195 and 196, you will see that on the NIC side of the P11, there is a column **1j** for student loan deductions.

The amount of the SLD depends on pay and the Inland Revenue issue Student Loan Deduction Tables SL3 (also available on the download area of the Inland Revenue website).

For each pay period, either weekly or monthly, just look up the **gross earnings** in the tables and read off the SLD.

If employees are paid 2 weekly, 4 weekly or at irregular intervals, calculate the SLD in the same way as for NICs.

For example, with two weekly pay of £1,000, divide the pay by 2 (£500). Look up £500 in the weekly tables.

Extract from tables

£482 – £492 = £26
£493 – £503 = £27
£504 – £514 = £28

£500 falls in the £493 – £503 range and so the SLD is £27. Multiply this by 2 (£54). So you deduct £54 for the 2 weekly pay period.

Each pay period make a note of the student loan deduction in column **1j** and **remember to deduct the amount from the employee's net pay**.

Student loan deductions are paid over to the Inland Revenue with other deductions each month.

5 Pension contributions

> **Important!**
>
> The Pensions Bill issued in 2004 aims for simplification of pension scheme tax rules. However this is not due to take effect until 6 April 2006. Therefore its provisions are ignored in this section.

5.1 Types of occupational pension scheme

From Chapter 2, you should remember that an occupational pension scheme can be one of two types:

- Money purchase scheme
- Final salary scheme

The scheme may be contracted-out for NIC purposes (see later in this section). In this case you use COMPS tables for the first (contracted out money purchase scheme) and COSRS tables for the second (contracted out salary related scheme).

5.2 Company pension schemes

Pension contributions by members of a firm's **occupational pension scheme** can be of the following types.

- Basic
- Additional Voluntary Contributions (AVCs)
- Free Standing Additional Voluntary Contributions (FSAVCs)

PART C   DETERMINING NET PAY

5.2.1 Pensionable earnings and basic contributions

Contributions to company pension schemes can be of two types.

- The employer only (a non-contributory pension scheme)
- The employer and the employee (called a contributory pension scheme)

Contributions are based on the employee's **pensionable earnings**. In a typical contributory scheme, the employee contributes say 6% of his or her pensionable earnings. The employer then contributes a further sum of, say, 10% of the employee's pensionable earnings. These are **basic contributions**.

Pensionable earnings are often different from gross pay for the following reasons.

- **Pensionable earnings for the year** may be earnings defined at a particular date (eg 1 January each year). Pension contributions would not increase until 1 January the following year, even if there had been a pay rise in June.

- **Pensionable earnings may exclude bonuses and commission**. If included, these might be averaged over a number of years.

- There is an **earnings cap** for contributions. In 2004/05 this cap is £102,000. For employees earning more than this amount, it may not be worth their while paying contributions on the excess through the company scheme.

Activity 10.2

Authentic Instruments Ltd runs a company pension scheme for its employees, contributing a sum equal to 10% of each employee's gross salary into the scheme. Each employee who joins has to contribute 5% of his or her gross salary to the scheme.

- Horatio Arpsichord earns £15,000 per annum and belongs to the company pension scheme.
- Letitia Ute earns £21,000 per annum and belongs to the company pension scheme.

In a typical month how much will:

(a) Horatio and Letitia earn gross?
(b) Horatio and Letitia hand over in cash to the pension scheme?
(c) Authentic Instruments Ltd contribute to the pension scheme on Horatio's and Letitia's behalf?

Note: Calculate a month's pay as $1/_{12}$ of annual salary.

5.2.2 Tax and NIC effects of company schemes

In most company-run schemes:

- The employee's contribution is deducted from **gross** pay, so that tax relief is given on pay day.
- The employee **contracts out**, so that a lower level of NICs is paid.

However, remember that the pension contribution is ignored for the purpose of calculating NICs.

5.2.3 Additional voluntary contributions (AVCs)

Additional voluntary contributions (AVCs) are extra contributions an employee makes, on top of what is deducted contractually from his or her salary every month, either as a regular payment or as a one-off contribution.

Remember, from Chapter 2, that an employee can get tax relief on pension contributions of up to 15% of their earnings from employment (salary and benefits). This is subject to the earnings cap (£102,000 for 2004/05). So the maximum contributions eligible for tax relief for 2004/05 are £15,300 (15% of £102,000).

AVCs have the following characteristics.

- Like basic employee's contributions they are deducted from pay **before tax**.
- Employers **must** offer the facility to make AVCs if they run a pension scheme.
- **Employers may not contribute AVCs.**

AVCs count as part of the employee's contributions to the company scheme, and so are 'frozen' with them if the employee **leaves** the company (for reasons other than retirement).

5.2.4 Free-standing additional voluntary contributions (FSAVCs)

Free standing additional voluntary contributions (FSAVCs) are AVCs which do not go to the company pension scheme. Instead they go to an **external pension provider**. FSAVCs are paid on retirement in pension form, not as a lump sum.

The employer might have an arrangement with an external provider (eg a bank, or investment company, building society, or whatever) to accept FSAVCs. However, the employee is free to go to **any pension provider**.

FSAVCs do not count as part of an employee's contribution record to the company's pension scheme. They are **portable**, ie go with the employee, giving some of the advantages of a personal pension scheme.

Note that FSAVCs are made out of **net pay**: basic rate tax relief is claimed on the employee's behalf by the financial institution operating the scheme. A higher rate taxpayer has to claim the balance of the tax relief from the Inland Revenue.

So if an employee pays £78 to a FSAVC, the institution will claim £22 from the Inland Revenue and credit the employee with £100. If the employee is a higher rate taxpayer, she will claim the balance of relief of 18% (40%-22%) from the Inland Revenue, ie £18. The employee will then have paid £60 (£78 - £18) net of tax relief and the pension fund will have received the gross amount of £100.

All the employer needs is an instruction to pay £78 per month to the institution, signed by the employee, and then deduct this from net pay.

The employer does **not** have to make any special arrangements for the FSAVC, so this need not involve the payroll at all (eg the employee sets up a direct debit from his or her personal bank account).

The employer may be required to give certain **information** to the external provider.

- Whether the employee's details have also been sent to another external provider.
- What percentage of salary the employee is currently paying to the occupational pension scheme.
- Occupational pension scheme benefits.

PART C DETERMINING NET PAY

This is because of the **limit** on the amount an employee can set aside for a pension and still benefit from tax relief. The external institution needs to know the relevant facts.

However, remember confidentiality. You can only reply with the employee's permission.

Activity 10.3

Max Fraction comes to the Payroll Office with a request. He is 50 years old and no longer has any dependent children so his disposable income has gone up considerably. He feels he would like to increase his pension provision and asks how to increase his contributions to the company scheme each month from 5% of his gross salary to 10%. He also asks if it is possible to contribute lump sums to the scheme from time to time.

Obviously, the exact details of your answer will depend on the scheme regulations. But in general terms what can you say to Max in answer to his requests? (The pension scheme is salary related.)

5.3 Maintaining contribution records

Why do we need to keep a record of payments made to the company pension scheme?

Company pension schemes are set up as a **trust**, which is a separate legal entity from the employing organisation. Usually the fund is administered by an entirely separate organisation, and amounts transferred to the fund must therefore be **recorded**.

The company is funding the scheme and so declares the amount it pays in its **published financial statements.** Records are also therefore needed for this purpose.

So that retired employees receive their dues from the scheme, adequate records must be maintained of **their contributions** and their **entitlement**.

Different schemes will have different records of contributions. Some will be recorded manually; some will be computerised. A **contribution record** might look like the record set out on the following two pages.

10: OTHER DEDUCTIONS

NAME:	ISAAC NEWTON			ACCOUNT:	NEW 01
RECORD OF CONTRIBUTIONS					
SEX:	M			NI NO:	AB 123456 C
DATE OF BIRTH:	1/5/61	DATE JOINED COMPANY:	1/9/96	CNTRCTD OUT?	Y (N)
DATE JOINED SCHEME:	1/3/99	DATE LEFT SCHEME:		AVCs?	(Y) N
ESTIMATED DATE OF RETIREMENT:	1/5/2024	AGE AT RETIREMENT:	63	RATES:	5% & 10% of employee's pay at 1 September
YRS IN SCHEME:		1,2,3,4,5,6,7,8,9,10,11,12,13,14,15,16,17,18,19,20,21,22,23,24,25,26,27,28,29,30,31,32,33,34,35,36,37,38,39,40				

DATE	NARRATIVE	SALARY	EMPLOYEE'S CONTRIBUTIONS PERCENTAGES	EMPLOYER'S	EMPLOYEE'S CONTRIBUTIONS PER MONTH	EMPLOYER'S	TOTAL MONTHLY CONTRI- BUTIONS
		£			£	£	£
1/3/99	JOINED SCHEME	15,000	5%	10%	62.50	125.00	187.50
1/9/99	PAY RISE	18,000			75.00	150.00	225.00
1/9/00	PAY RISE	21,000			87.50	175.00	262.50
1/9/01	PAY RISE	22,800			95.00	190.00	285.00
1/9/02	PAY RISE	23,500			97.90	195.80	293.70
1/9/03	PAY RISE	25,000			104.17	208.33	312.50

NAME:	ISAAC NEWTON		ACCOUNT:	NEW 01	
RECORD OF ADDITIONAL VOLUNTARY CONTRIBUTIONS					
DATE	COMMENTS	AMOUNT £	DATE	COMMENTS	AMOUNT £
31/3/00	TO MONEY PURCHASE	500	31/3/04	TO MONEY PURCHASE	1,500
31/3/01	TO MONEY PURCHASE	1,000			
31/3/02	TO MONEY PURCHASE	1,000			
31/3/03	TO MONEY PURCHASE	1,500			

PART C DETERMINING NET PAY

NAME: ISAAC NEWTON					ACCOUNT NO: NEW 01				
DATE PAY DATE	TAX MONTH	CONTRIBUTIONS IN MONTH			CONTRIBUTIONS IN YEAR			TOTAL EMPLOYEES & AVCS	ALL CONTRIB
		EMPLOYEE	EMPLOYER	AVCS	EMPLOYEE	EMPLOYER	AVCS		
		£ p	£ p	£ p	£ p	£ p	£ p	£ p	£ p
31/3/99	12	62.50	125.00		62.50	125.00		62.50	187.50
30/4/99	1	62.50	125.00						
31/5/99	2	62.50	125.00						
30/6/99	3	62.50	125.00						
31/7/99	4	62.50	125.00						
31/8/99	5	62.50	125.00						
30/9/99	6	75.00	150.00						
31/10/99	7	75.00	150.00						
30/11/99	8	75.00	150.00						
31/12/99	9	75.00	150.00						
31/1/00	10	75.00	150.00						
28/2/00	11	75.00	150.00						
31/3/00	12	75.00	150.00	500.00	837.50	1,675.00	500.00	1,337.50	3,012.50
30/4/00	1	75.00	150.00						
31/5/00	2	75.00	150.00						
30/6/00	3	75.00	150.00						
31/7/00	4	75.00	150.00						
31/8/00	5	75.00	150.00						
30/9/00	6	87.50	175.00						
31/10/00	7	87.50	175.00						
30/11/00	8	87.50	175.00						
31/12/00	9	87.50	175.00						
31/1/01	10	87.50	175.00						
28/2/01	11	87.50	175.00						
31/3/01	12	87.50	175.00	1,000.00	987.50	1,975.00	1,000.00	1,987.50	3,962.50
30/4/01	1	87.50	175.00						
31/5/01	2	87.50	175.00						
30/6/01	3	87.50	175.00						
31/7/01	4	87.50	175.00						
31/8/01	5	87.50	175.00						
30/9/01	6	95.00	190.00						
31/10/01 CONT'D	7	95.00	190.00						

Activity 10.4

(a) Why is there no column for FSAVCs?
(b) Why do we need to keep separate records of employees' contributions, employer's contributions and AVCs?

5.4 Stakeholder pensions

Stakeholder pensions were introduced on 6 April 2001. They are treated as personal pension schemes. The legal changes for stakeholder also apply to occupational pension schemes under the money purchase system that have opted to be treated as personal pension schemes.

All employers with five or more employees are required to offer their employees a stakeholder scheme by 8 October 2001, or within three months of acquiring a fifth employee. However employers do not have to contribute to the scheme.

An employer does not have to provide stakeholder schemes for the following employees.

(a) Those under 18 or within five years of normal retirement date
(b) Those paid below the NI LEL within the last three months
(c) Those employed for a continuous period of less than three months
(d) Non resident employees
(e) Those offered membership of an occupational scheme
(f) These offered access to a personal pension scheme available to all employees (with certain additional requirements as to administration and employer's contributions)

5.4.1 Contributions

A member of an occupational pension scheme can also contribute to a stakeholder pension, provided she earns less than £30,000 pa (or has earned less than £30,000 in 2003/04) and is not a controlling director (and was not in 2003/04).

Contributions of up to £3,600 pa gross can be paid without reference to earnings. So children and the unemployed can have pension plans.

Contributions over £3,600 pa gross can be made but can not exceed a percentage of taxable non-pensionable remuneration (salary, benefits, commission, etc). The maximum percentage for 2004/05 are as follows.

PART C   DETERMINING NET PAY

Age at 6 April in year of assessment	Maximum percentage of taxable remuneration
	%
35 or less	17.5
36 – 45	20.0
46 – 50	25.0
51 – 55	30.0
56 – 60	35.0
61 or over	40.0

The earning cap (£102,000 for 2004/05) applies.

5.4.2 Benefits

Retirement can be between the ages of 50 and 75. The fund is used to purchase an annuity to pay a regular sum during retirement.

Up to 25% of the fund can be taken as a tax free lump sum.

5.4.3 Tax treatment

All premiums are paid net of basic rate tax to the provider. Higher rate tax relief is given by adjustment to the employee's tax code.

Therefore, treatment for payroll purposes is the same as for FSAVCs, ie deducted from **net pay**.

Activity 10.5

An employee already makes the maximum 15% contribution to the firm's pension scheme. Can he also contribute to a stakeholder pension?

5.5 Tax and NIC considerations of personal pensions

If any of the employees on the payroll you administer contributes to a **personal pension scheme**, then your job is very simple. You simply ignore it!

This is because the pension is a private arrangement between the employee, the Government and the investment institution receiving the employee's contributions.

- **NICs**

    Most personal pension schemes are **COMPS (Contracted Out Money Purchase Schemes).** The employee is not part of S2P, being **contracted out**. That is an arrangement between the DWP and the pension provider, **so has nothing to do with you in the payroll department**. You just carry on paying NICs at the **not-contracted out rate, Table A**

- **Income tax**

    Again, the way in which the employee is given **tax relief** does not involve the payroll department at all. This is because the basic rate tax relief is given **direct** by the Government to the pension provider. Any higher rate tax relief is given in the tax code.

Example: Tax relief on personal pensions

Paul Rudent has asked the Natlays Bank to transfer £78 every month to the Shark Pension Fund Company Ltd, who run an approved personal pension scheme. Paul pays tax at 22%.

The £78 a month that Paul pays comes from his **net salary**. As his pension contributions are **eligible for tax relief**, the Government hands back £22 to the pension fund provider so that Paul's fund is credited with a gross sum every month of £100.

If Paul paid **higher rate tax**, the Inland Revenue would make any adjustment, probably by changing his **tax code**. Again, this would not affect your work (except that you would apply the new code issued).

5.6 Joining a company scheme

It is **illegal** to **require** an employee to join a company scheme as a condition of his or her employment.

An employee also has the **right to leave** a company scheme if he or she so wishes, and take up some other pension arrangement.

For those hoping for long-term employment with one employer, joining a company scheme offers a **secure pension**, often with added extra benefits (eg free life assurance, death-in-service benefits and so on). The value of the employer's contributions, a non-taxable benefit, can be considerable.

For those who value **job mobility**, a personal pension scheme (particularly under the stakeholder rules) might be a better idea, particularly if they are young (say under 40). A long series of frozen company pensions will not be worth much in the long run.

5.6.1 Administration for joiners

In terms of **administration**, what should be done when someone joins the company scheme?

Like most voluntary deductions from pay, the **deduction for payments** to the company pension fund must be **authorised** by the employee.

You will be told the amount of **pensionable earnings** on which to base the deductions, either by the Scheme Administrators or personnel.

In some schemes an employee may only be permitted to join the pension scheme after he or she has completed a **specified period of service** (eg six months).

PART C DETERMINING NET PAY

The **contracted-out rate of NICs** (whether COSRS or COMPS) only applies if the employer has received a contracting-out certificate from the Contracted-Out Employments Group. This means that an employee participating in the scheme has been **contracted out of S2P**.

Every pay day, or as soon as possible afterwards, the **pension fund** should be credited with the employees' and employer's contributions for the period. You should ensure that the right amounts of contributions are credited to the right accounts. These can involve:

- In a **manual system**, sending a detailed contribution schedule with the funds (see Section 5.3).
- Ensuring, in a **computer-based system**, that the program automatically analyses the total contribution by employee.

Pensionable earnings for a company scheme usually includes the following items.

- Basic pay (usually at a set date for each year, eg 1 January, so payrises are ignored until the following year)
- Contractual overtime
- Earnings deducted under GAYE (tax-exempt but earnings for pension purposes)
- Bonus and commission (depends on the Scheme, usually an average of the last 3 or 4 years)
- Benefits

Of course, pensionable earnings are **before** any deductions for payments to the company pension scheme.

5.7 Leaving a company scheme

An employee ceases contributions to a company scheme in the following ways.

- On death
- On retirement
- On leaving the employment
- On changing over to a personal pension plan

5.7.1 Employees leaving within two years

An employee who leaves **within two years** is entitled to a **refund** of his or her own contributions, **but not the employer's contributions**.

- The employer does not have to pay **interest** on the refund.
- **20%** of the contributions must be deducted as **tax**.

Example: Early leavers

Fred Lighty has contributed to the pension scheme run on behalf of Buggins and Terne for 18 months. His pensionable earnings were £10,000 for the first year and £10,800 thereafter. Fred contributes 5% of his pensionable earnings. Buggins and Terne contribute a further 10% of Fred's pensionable earnings.

Fred leaves Buggins and Terne. What will be the amount of his refund from the pension fund?

Solution

	£
(5% × £10,000) + (5% × £10,800 × 6/12)	770
Less tax of 20% × £770	(154)
Net refund	616

The scheme might offer alternatives to a refund. The employee might be offered a **deferred pension** for the contributions, or might be able to **transfer** the amount to another scheme.

5.7.2 Employees leaving after two years

Leavers with more than two years' pensionable service have two options.

- The contributions can be **transferred** to another scheme, such as another company scheme or a personal pension scheme, at a determined **transfer value**.
- They may **freeze** the pension.

Freezing the pension involves keeping the contributions (including any AVCs) made so far in the fund. A pension will be given to an employee on the basis of those frozen contributions when that employee reaches State retirement age.

Example: Later leavers

Phil Aupered contributes four years' worth of contributions to a pension scheme whose benefits are based on 1/60 of final salary for each year's service (up to 40 years). His salary on leaving was £2,100 per annum. Had he stayed, his final salary in 36 years time would have been, say, £30,000.

- If the contributions are frozen, Phil will receive from that employment:

    £2,100 × 4/60 = £140 per annum. Since 1988, such a 'deferred' pension must be increased by either 5% a year or the rate of inflation (if lower) between the date of leaving and the date of retirement.

- He has lost the chance to base his final salary on his last years of employment, in which case the pension based on those four years' contributions would have been:

    £30,000 × 4/60 = £2,000 per annum (out of a total annual pension of £30,000 × 40/60 = £20,000 per annum).

PART C   DETERMINING NET PAY

This detail is given so that you understand why, in some cases, you will need to maintain contribution records for **former employees** who no longer contribute to the scheme.

- They will eventually be paid a **small pension** from the fund.
- This will be based on the **salary** and **contribution records** that you have maintained.

Activity 10.6

How would you answer the following queries about your company pension scheme?

(a) The scheme rules require employees to pay contributions of 6% of annual salary. The employer pays 8%. Charlotte Bax tells you that she would like to pay more as a way of regular saving. How much more can she pay? She earns £24,000 per year.

(b) Richard Pierce has left the company. He joined the scheme 12 months ago and paid contributions of £1,200 in that time. The company paid £1,600. He asks for a refund of contributions. How much will the cheque be?

(c) Marlene Drayton has left the company after 20 years service. She joined the pension scheme 18 years ago. She is going to work for another company which has no occupational pension scheme. She asks what her options are in respect of her contributions to your scheme.

6 Give as you earn (GAYE)

GAYE stands for **Give As You Earn**. This is sometimes referred to as **payroll giving**. It is entirely voluntary, so an employee can never be required to join a GAYE scheme.

An employee is allowed to set aside any amount a year of his or her gross salary for charitable donations.

This portion of gross salary is not taxed, although both **employer's and employees' NICs are still payable on this amount**.

The employer pays the amounts collected to **'an approved agency charity'** such as the **Charities Aid Foundation** which acts as a clearing house. The agency will, according to the employee's instructions, either:

- **Pay the charity** which the employee wishes to support; or
- **Pay the money into an account**. The employee is issued with a book of vouchers which can be sent to any charity as and when desired. The charity sends the voucher to the agency, which then transfers the funds.

Apart from paying the money to the agency charity, all the **payroll office** has to do is ensure that the correct deductions from gross pay are made **according to the employee's instructions**, and that the correct entries are made on the P11.

At the end of every month the employer sends the agency a form listing GAYE donations. This includes the following details.

- Employee name and payroll number

10: OTHER DEDUCTIONS

- Employee NINO
- Amount of donations

Example: GAYE

Gene Rowse earns a gross salary of £12,600 a year, payable in equal monthly instalments. The company which employs him, Tea and Sympathy Ltd, operates a payroll giving scheme. Gene contributes £50 per month from his gross pay.

Tasks

(a) What is his gross monthly pay?

(b) What will be entered in column 2 of the P11 for month 1?

(c) Fill in columns 2, 3, 4a, 5, 6, and 7. For the purposes of this question assume that his total free pay in month 1 is £275.00.

(d) Assuming that Gene Rowse is liable for Class 1 Not contracted out NICs, fill in columns 1a to 1e. Use the monthly table A in Appendix II.

Try completing the following extracts from the P11 for yourself before looking at our solution.

Month	Pay in the week 2	Total pay to date 3	Total free pay to date 4a	Total additional pay to date (K codes) 4b	Total taxable pay to date 5	Total tax due to date 6	Tax due at end of current period (K codes) 6a	Regulatory limit 6b	Tax deducted in the week 7	Tax not deducted owing to the regulatory limit (K codes) 8	Tax Credits 9
1											

Month	Earnings details			Contribution details		Statutory payments				Student Loan Deductions Whole pounds only
	Earnings at the LEL (where earnings reach or exceed the LEL) 1a	Earnings above the LEL, up to and including the Earnings Threshold 1b	Earnings above the Earnings Threshold, up to and including the UEL 1c	Total of employees' and employer's contributions payable 1d	Total of employees' contributions payable on earnings above the ET 1e	SSP 1f	SMP 1g	SPP 1h	SAP 1i	1j
1										

PART C   DETERMINING NET PAY

Solution

Month	Pay in the week	Total pay to date	Total free pay to date	K codes Total additional pay to date	Total taxable pay to date	Total tax due to date	K codes Tax due at end of current period	Regulatory limit	Tax deducted in the week	K codes Tax not deducted owing to the regulatory limit	Tax Credits
	2	3	4a	4b	5	6	6a	6b	7	8	9
1	1,000.00	1,000.00	275.00		725.00	139.29			139.29		

Month	Earnings details			Contribution details		Statutory payments				Student Loan Deductions
	Earnings at the LEL (where earnings reach or exceed the LEL)	Earnings above the LEL, up to and including the Earnings Threshold	Earnings above the Earnings Threshold, up to and including the UEL	Total of employees' and employer's contributions payable	Total of employees' contributions payable on earnings in 1c	SSP	SMP	SPP	SAP	Whole pounds only
	1a	1b	1c	1d	1e	1f	1g	1h	1i	1j
1	343	52	652	155.65	71.94					

Workings

1   His gross pay is £12,600 pa divided into twelve months or £1,050 per month.

2   His pay in the week or month will be only £1,000 for the purposes of income tax.

	£
Gross pay	1,050
Less GAYE	50
Per P11 Column 2	1,000

3   Free pay has been given in the question, so taxable pay is pay to date less free pay to date. This works out at £725. Tax on £725 is per Table B and the subtraction tables.

4   GAYE is irrelevant as far as NICs are concerned, so there is no deduction. Using NIC monthly Table A for £1,050 gives us the figures shown.

The effect on Gene's net pay is as follows:

	GAYE		NO GAYE	
	£	£	£	£
Gross pay		1,050.00		1,050.00
Less: TAX	139.29		150.29	
NIC	71.94		71.94	
GAYE	50.00	261.23	–	222.23
Net pay		788.77		827.77

278

So by giving £50 of gross pay per month, Gene's net pay has reduced by only £39 (£827.77 – £788.77). He is saving £11 in tax by making a GAYE donation. However the charity gets the full £50. If Gene was a higher rate tax payer, he would save tax of £20 (£50 × 40%). So he would pay a net contribution of £30, but the charity still gets £50.

Activity 10.7

Julie Nicholls earns £30,000 per annum and makes GAYE donations of £100 per month. What is 'pay in the month' (P11 box 2) and 'Employee's earnings up to and including the UEL' as shown in the NIC tables?

7 Sharesave (SAYE)

Sharesave payments are deductions from *net pay* linked to **share options**. They do not affect PAYE and NIC calculations. Sharesave is also called **Save As You Earn (SAYE)**.

Sharesave schemes are run by the **employer** with the co-operation of a **building society** or **bank**. The employer deducts an **agreed sum** from the net pay of the employee and deposits it in a building society or bank, perhaps via BACS (dealt with in Chapter 11).

Remember that you need a written agreement to the deduction, signed by the employee.

Participants must save money for a **minimum of three years**, which can sometimes be extended to five or seven years. Therefore careful records need to be kept of any extensions and the employee's agreement to these extensions.

Interest is free of tax, providing the scheme is allowed to run for **three years**.

The following items are included on the **monthly return**.

- The scheme **code number**
- The **building society account number**
- The **monthly amount**, or weekly equivalent
- The **number of shares allocated**, if the scheme is to purchase shares

8 Employee loans and advances

Some organisations **lend their employees money** to cover the following costs.

- Season tickets for travel to work
- House purchase (especially for employees in the financial services industry)

Loans may also be made for other purposes but there are certain **restrictions** on lending (eg it is generally forbidden for a company to lend a person money to buy shares in the company).

You should note what type of loan it is, what it is used for, and the interest rate if any, as there are implications for the employee's tax bill. (The difference between the interest on the loan and what interest would be at a market rate *might* be a **benefit for tax purposes**.)

PART C   DETERMINING NET PAY

If the employer decides to **waive** the loan, and tells the employee that it does not have to be repaid, this is both **taxable** (benefit dealt with at the end of the tax year) and **assessable for NICs** (payable at the date of the waiver).

You are not expected to know the details of the tax and NI treatment at this level, but you should realise that it is important that **records are kept of company loans** to employees.

8.1 Season ticket loan

A **season ticket loan** is used to help employees find the large sum needed to buy an annual ticket for public transport to and from work, which works out much cheaper than buying tickets weekly or monthly.

This loan is repaid over the life of the ticket from **net pay**, in a similar way to the **repayment of advances from salary** (see Chapter 4).

Some organisations grant an employee a season ticket loan only after that employee has been in service for a **specified period**.

If an **employee leaves before the season ticket expires**, the employee should be required to pay back the rest of the loan before leaving. This may mean that he or she has to cash the season ticket in.

Although a loan is not an advance of pay, **repayments** do come out of pay in the same way as an advance of pay. That is, they are deducted from the net amount after tax and NICs.

	£
Net pay	1,500
Less loan repayment	(25)
Amount paid	1,475

Remember, for both recovery of advances and repayment of loans, that you need the employee's **written consent** to deduct the repayments. Usually the employee will **sign a form** acknowledging receipt of the advance and/or loan and **authorising deductions from pay** to cover the amount of the advance and/or loan.

Activity 10.8

Gilbert is a salaried employee paid monthly in arrears.

- He makes GAYE donations of £60 per month.
- His annual salary is £27,000.
- In Month 1 2004/05 he repaid an advance of salary of £1,000 made in January 2004 to help with removal expenses.
- He makes SAYE payments of £50 per month.
- He has a season ticket loan of £600, advanced on 1 January 2004 and repayable in 12 equal monthly instalments.
- His tax code is 424T. He pays NIC under Table A. Free pay for code 424 is £354.09 in Month 1.

What is Gilbert's net pay in Month 1? Assume that you have all the relevant authorisations for the various deductions.

9 Trade union and social club contributions

Trade Union contributions are often deducted from earnings after tax and NIC in arriving at net pay. There are special requirements for **authorising** such deductions, as no one can be forced to join a union.

Strike pay received from the Trade Union is not taxable as it is regarded as a refund of union contributions, so the payroll department need not be concerned with this.

The business may have a Social Club. Subscriptions can also be deducted from net pay. However, as usual, the employee must give written authorisation.

10 Errors in PAYE and NIC

10.1 Tax

Avoid errors as far as possible! But if you have deducted **too much tax** in a period, this will usually be recovered in the next period automatically.

This is the beauty of the cumulative basis: it means that every time you do a PAYE calculation you are making allowance for everything, including mistakes, that has been done to date.

Tax deducted in the week or month will be the difference between this week or month's correct cumulative figure and the erroneous cumulative figure calculated last month.

However, you can not recover under deductions for an earlier tax year.

10.2 NIC

If you have deducted **too much NIC**:

- Refund overpayments since the beginning of the tax year to the employee.
- Adjust the P11 by putting a mark beside the wrong figures – do not change any of the original figures.
- Adjust the next monthly payment.

If the overdeduction goes back **further than the start of the tax year**, consult NICO.

If you have **not deducted enough NIC**, make more deductions from later pay. However you can only recover for each pay period an amount equivalent to the employee's payment of NI for earnings in the current period. Also you can not recover under deductions made in an earlier tax year.

For example, if you have under deducted £30 and the current month's NIC is £20, you can only deduct £40 (2 × £20) this months. You will have to carry forward the remaining £10 (£30 – £20).

10.3 General

It is generally the employer's responsibility to ensure that income tax and NICs are correctly deducted. It is quite possible, then, that the employer will **not be able to recover any underpayment from the employee**, especially if the mistake is not found until a later tax year.

PART C   DETERMINING NET PAY

11 Miscellaneous deductions

Other deductions may have to be made from pay.

- Deductions for a incomplete work period
- Recovery of overpayments
- Contributions to benefits

Deductions for an incomplete work period may arise if an employee has taken unauthorised leave or just not shown up for work. This is usually accounted for by adjusting basic or additional pay. However you should only make these deductions if authorised by personnel or another **authorised signatory.**

Recovery of overpayments, not arising from PAYE or NIC errors (see section 10 above for these), can happen if an employee's allowances are changed, but payroll is not notified until after the first pay day following the change.

Once again, the overpayments can only be recovered if properly **authorised**. If the contract of employment does not mention overpayments, then the employee's **written permission** must be given.

Contributions to benefits (eg cars) may be made by the employee to cover private use and so avoid a taxable benefit. Benefits are dealt with in detail at Level 3. However you can only make a deduction for this, if authorised by the **employee**, as with all voluntary deductions.

12 Payslips

An employee has a **legal right** to receive a payslip under the Employment Rights Act 1996.

A **payslip** must by law show the following.

- An employee's gross pay
- Deductions from gross pay and what they are
- Net pay
- Payment method

It is not always necessary to **itemise** deductions. **Fixed deductions** (ie those which do not change from month to month) can be shown as one deduction provided an employee has been informed of them beforehand. Such a statement must be reissued every 12 months. Broadly speaking, however, a payslip should state the following.

Compulsory disclosures (unless aggregated fixed deductions)	Not compulsory but usually disclosed
The employer's name	The employee's tax code/basis
The employee's name	Total pay to date
Gross pay, showing how made up	Tax paid to date (ie in the current tax year)
Additions to and deductions from pay	NICs to date (ie in the current tax year)
Employee's pension contributions, if any	Pension contributions to date
Student Loan deductions, if any	The employee's payroll number
Statutory Sick Pay, if any	The employee's National Insurance number
SMP, SPP, SAP, if any	The method of payment
Redundancy pay, if any	Distribution address
WTC, if any	Employer's tax reference

10: OTHER DEDUCTIONS

Compulsory disclosures (unless aggregated fixed deductions)	Not compulsory but usually disclosed
Tax in the period NICs for the period Date Net pay The method of payment for each segment of net pay, if they are paid in different ways	

There is **no standard format for a payslip**, but you might find that yours looks something like the example below.

120 MR A.N. OTHER				EXAMPLE LTD		
NI No: WE123456C Tax Code: 433L Pay By: EFT				Date: 21/02/X0		Tax Period: Mt 11
DESCRIPTION					AMOUNT	THIS YEAR
01 BASIC SALARY 02 OVERTIME					1,350.00 10.00	
		TOTAL	PAY >>>		1,360.00	14,960.00
INCOME TAX - PAYE EMPLOYEE'S NI (EMPLOYER 121.88) TABLE A SEASON TICKET LOAN					213.29 107.40 40.00	2,347.11 1,181.40
(HOL PAY ACCRUED	0.00)	TOTAL	NET PAY >>>		999.31	

The payslip can be produced in either of the following ways.

- Manually
- By computer (in some payroll systems, the payslip is merely one of several computer generated reports)

However they are produced, payslips need to be:

- Accurate
- Legible
- Comprehensible (ie easily understood)
- Mathematically correct (ie they add up correctly)
- Comply with statutory requirements
- Contain such additional information as is laid down by your organisation

You will need to check that everyone has a payslip by comparing the total number of payslips to the total number of employees on the payroll.

A reconciliation may be necessary if an employee on the payroll has not been paid for some reason. For example, with weekly paid employees, an employee may not be paid if he or she is on holiday and has received holiday pay in advance.

Once you are sure that you have the correct number of payslips, these need to be distributed to the employees. You should have a note of the method on the employee records.

You should keep a copy of each payslip in case of queries and for inspection by the Inland Revenue.

PART C DETERMINING NET PAY

Copy payslips, together with supporting documents (eg timesheets, piecework details, gross pay calculations), should be placed on the employee's file.

This will usually be the current tax year's working file, rather than the permanent file. However, follow your organisation's rules (if there are any).

Remember that copy payslips and supporting documents form part of the PAYE records and so need to be kept for at least three years.

We will look payment procedures in Chapter 11.

Key learning points

- ☑ There are a number of items that may appear on an employee's payslip other than gross pay, tax and NICs. **Some of these have a tax effect; some do not**.

- ☑ There are various ways in which people can save up for their **retirement**.

- ☑ It is possible, but not compulsory, to **contract out** if you:
  - Take out a **personal pension plan**; or
  - Join an approved **company pension scheme** run by your employer.

- ☑ **Payments** to the approved **company pension scheme**, by both the employee and by the company, are made:
  - **Every pay day.**
  - **Gross** of tax (ie your tax is calculated *after* the pension contributions are deducted).

- ☑ Employees can make **AVCs (additional voluntary contributions)** to the company pension scheme. These are also gross of tax.

- ☑ Employees can make **FSAVCs (free standing additional voluntary contributions)** but these have nothing to do with the company pension scheme. If made by payroll, then they are deducted from pay after tax and NICs.

- ☑ There are **limits to the contributions** (including AVCs and FSAVCs) an employee can make if those contributions are to be eligible for tax relief.

- ☑ Those who leave the scheme are entitled to a **refund (less 20% tax)** if they leave before two years. Otherwise, their contributions can be **transferred to a new scheme**, or **frozen** in the company scheme.

- ☑ **Give As You Earn** allows certain payments to charities to be deducted from a person's gross pay before income tax is calculated. However, GAYE payments are not deducted from gross pay in NIC calculations.

- ☑ **Sharesave** payments are deductions from net pay which are paid to a building society or bank.

- ☑ **Company loans** are sometimes repaid as deductions from net pay, through the payroll system.

- ☑ The **payslip** shows the employee exactly what he or she is being paid and how this figure is calculated.

PART C   DETERMINING NET PAY

Quick quiz

1. GAYE has another common name. What is it?
2. In a GAYE scheme how much can an employee give tax-free each year out of gross salary?
3. For how long must Sharesave scheme participants save to get interest on their savings free of tax?
4. Why do you need to record the rate of interest, if any, charged on loans made to an employee by an employer?
5. If you find that you have deducted too little NI from an employee's pay, how much NI can you deduct from the current period's pay to correct the mistake?
6. If an employee leaves a company pension scheme within two years of joining, what happens?
7. An employer is legally obliged to provide payslips to all employees'. True or false?

Answers to quick quiz

1. Payroll giving.
2. No limit for 2004/05.
3. 3 years minimum.
4. If the loan is interest-free, or at a rate of interest lower than the market rate, then there could be a taxable benefit to the employee. This has to be recorded on the P11D at the year end, as you will see at Level 3.
5. Up to the amount that would double the employee's payment of NI in the current period, provided that the current period is not in a new tax year.
6. Refund employee's contributions less 20% tax.
7. True.

10: OTHER DEDUCTIONS

Activity checklist

This checklist shows which performance criteria, range statement or knowledge and understanding point is covered by each activity in this chapter. Tick off each activity as you complete it.

Activity

10.1	☐	This activity covers performance criterion 73.1.C and range 2: attachment of earnings.
10.2	☐	This activity covers performance criteria 72.1.E and 73.1.B.
10.3	☐	This activity covers range 3: pension contributions.
10.4	☐	This activity covers range 3: pension contributions.
10.5	☐	This activity covers range 3: pension contributions.
10.6	☐	This activity covers range 3: pension contributions.
10.7	☐	This activity covers performance criteria 72.1.E, 73.1.B and 73.1.C.
10.8	☐	This activity covers performance criteria 72.1.E, 73.1.B, 73.1.C and 73.1.E.

PART C DETERMINING NET PAY

chapter 11

Net pay and aggregate payroll totals

Contents

1. The problem
2. The solution
3. Net pay
4. Aggregate payroll totals
5. Methods of payment
6. Spreadsheets

Performance criteria

73.2.A Reconcile actual payroll totals against authorised totals for all pay periods
73.2.B Reconcile the number of no pays and actual pays promptly with the number of employees on the payroll
73.2.C Ensure that aggregate **statutory payments** and non-statutory deductions are correctly calculated and reconciled against control totals.
73.2.D Check aggregate **statutory payments** against control totals
73.2.E Calculate sums recoverable from the National Insurance Contributions Office in respect of **statutory payments** and net them off against payments due
73.2.F Calculate and reconcile aggregate amounts payable to **statutory and non-statutory bodies**, in respect of **statutory and non-statutory deductions** against control totals
73.2.G Resolve discrepancies and where they cannot be resolved, refer them to the appropriate supervisor(s)
73.2.H Meet all organisational and statutory timescales

PART C   DETERMINING NET PAY

Range statement

1   **Statutory payments:** Statutory Sick Pay; Statutory Maternity Pay; Statutory Adoption Pay; Statutory Paternity Pay
2   **Non-statutory deductions:** employee and employer pension contributions; charitable giving; recovery of overpayments; repayment of loans and advances; voluntary deductions
3   **Statutory bodies:** Inland Revenue; courts; Child Support Agency; local authorities
4   **Non-statutory bodies:** pension provider; bodies responsible for miscellaneous deductions; trade unions; social clubs
5   **Statutory deductions:** tax; Employee and Employer National Insurance contributions; student loan deductions; earnings attachments; Scottish arrestments of earnings; child support orders and attachment of earnings orders

Knowledge and understanding

1   Data Protection legislation (Elements 73.1 & 73.2)
8   Information flows within the organisation (Element 73.2)
9   Procedures for the security and confidentiality of information (Elements 73.1 & 73.2)
11 Methods of disbursement (Element 73.2)
14 How to set up and use spreadsheets for reconciliations and the manual calculation of net pay

> **Signpost**
>
> The main emphasis of this element is being able to prepare the **wages control account**.

1 The problem

You have prepared the payroll and distributed all the payslips.

How do you know you have paid every employee?

How do you know that you are paying the correct amounts to statutory bodies (eg Inland Revenue, Courts) and other external bodies (eg pension fund)?

2 The solution

In Chapter 10 we have already mentioned using the payslips to ensure everyone is paid.

Total number of employees on payroll = Number of payslips + Number of no pays

Remember that weekly paid employees on holiday may have received their holiday pay in advance and so are 'no pays' this week.

In order to check that you have accounted for everything, you need to prepare a **wages control account**.

3 Net pay

In the preceding chapters we have discussed the following.

- How **gross pay** is calculated.
- How **statutory and non-statutory deductions** are calculated.
- Some **unusual items**.

But none of this is of any use if the employees do not get paid!

Net pay is the amount to be actually paid to the employee. Net pay consists of basic pay plus additional pay and allowances, less statutory and voluntary deductions.

In a **small firm**, with say only ten or fifteen employees, the preparation of the payroll will probably be done every week or month by one of the firm's own clerks. Alternatively, if the expertise is lacking, they might employ an **accountant** or a **computer bureau** to do the payroll.

In either case, the exercise is likely to be fairly simple. The pay is worked out, the necessary documentation is filled in, and arrangements are made for payment.

Paying people who work for a **large organisation**, on the other hand, can be a **costly** and **time consuming** exercise. No matter how few or how many people an organisation employs, the same requirements for payroll processing apply. It must be:

- **Accurate** (to the penny)
- **On time** (to the day)
- **Secure**, both in terms of the data it contains and the cash

Basic pay and additional pay must agree to the underlying contract and records, and any non contractual additions authorised. Remember that an employee may be entitled to statutory additions (SSP, SMP, SPP, SAP, tax credits).

All gross pay must be accurately calculated and employee records checked to ensure that only genuine employees are paid.

In the case of statutory deductions, tax and NICs must be calculated in accordance with the tax and NI regulations, the correct tax and NIC rates and using the correct taxable and NIC incomes (see Chapters 6, 7, 8 and 9).

In the case of pension contributions, deductions must be in accordance with the following.

- The pension scheme rules
- The correct rate (whether basic, AVC or FSAVC)
- The correct pensionable income
- The employee's authorisation

See Chapter 10 for further details.

All other deductions should be checked to the employee records (eg court orders, voluntary deduction authorisations), see Chapters 2 and 10.

PART C DETERMINING NET PAY

Remember that net pay is calculated as follows.

	£	£
Basic pay		X
Additional pay and allowances		X
Gross pay		X
Less: statutory deductions		
Tax	X	
NIC	X	
Court orders, CSA orders, etc	X	X
		X
Less: voluntary deductions		
Pension	X	
GAYE	X	
Sharesave, etc	X	X
Net pay		X

Payment must be made in accordance with the organisation's procedures (eg weekly, monthly, cash, cheque, BACs). Employee records need to be checked to ensure that an employee's pay and payslip are correctly delivered (eg correct bank or building society details are used).

4 Aggregate payroll totals

4.1 Record keeping

Even when the employees have been paid, that is not the end of the payroll process. **A record of each payment has to be maintained on a cumulative basis.**

Here are a few examples.

- You have recorded the tax and NICs on the **P11** deductions sheet. As you have learnt, income tax is worked out on a cumulative basis, so finding out the correct amount of income tax for a period in part depends on what has been paid to date. Moreover, the P11 is source material for some of the **end of tax-year returns** which have to be sent to the Inland Revenue. (We look at these at Level 3.)

- Records should be kept of **reimbursed expenses** for the annual **P11D** returns (to be dealt with at Level 3).

- Records of **gross pay** and **employer's NICs** are needed to analyse an organisation's labour costs. Keeping records for individual employees is necessary so that their costs can be correctly allocated to the right departments.

- If your employer operates an **occupational pension scheme** (ie a company pension), then **records of contributions** have to be maintained, as the employee's benefits may depend on them. Bad record keeping now can adversely affect employees not just in the present but in future decades.

- In the case of **loans to employees**, the **repayments** should be noted down so that it is clear when the loan has been repaid.

Employee records should, therefore, be updated with the same data that is found on the payslip.

You will also want to ensure that there is a **reconciliation** between gross pay as calculated and net pay as paid.

- Column 2 of the **P11** is **gross pay for tax purposes** (ie gross –pension contributions – GAYE)
- The **P11** does not include all those items that make up net pay, as they are not relevant (eg voluntary deductions).
- A reconciliation is important to ensure that **all the money is accounted for**.

The document sometimes used for this, in manual systems, is a **wages analysis book**. An example is shown on the next page. Note that the totals of columns 2 to 8 should equal the total of column 1. (check: 232.51 + 111.85 + 18.00 + 35.00 + 1,517.64 = 1,915.00).

The other records that must be updated are the **accounting records**, as we shall see below.

4.2 Accounting records

Entering payroll data into the correct **ledger account** is normally quite straightforward.

- Payroll is normally only done **weekly** or **monthly**
- **Same types of entry** take place every period
- The **wages control account** makes it easy to ensure that the entries are being made correctly.

The wages control account summarises all the payroll transactions. After all the entries have been made for each pay day, the balance on the account should be NIL.

PART C DETERMINING NET PAY

WAGES ANALYSIS BOOK - WEEKLY PAYROLL — PAGE 13

PAYMENT DATE: 12/7/20X3

PAYE WEEK 14

	Employee	No	1 Gross Pay £	2 Tax £ p	3 Employees' NICs £ p	4 Trade Union contributions £ p	5 Sharesave £ p	6 Other	7 Other	8 Net pay £ p	9 cheque no.
1	Brown F	010	250 -	34 20	16 15	2 00				197 65	100783
2	Holmes S	011	210 -	25 22	12 15	2 00	10 00			160 63	100784
3	Maigret G	012	230 -	29 82	14 15	2 00				184 03	100785
4	Marlowe P	013	210 -	25 22	12 15	2 00				170 63	100786
5	Marple M	014	150 -	11 42	6 15	2 00	20 00			110 43	100787
6	Poirot H	015	275 -	40 17	18 65	2 00				214 18	cash
7	Smiley G	016	140 -	9 12	5 15	2 00				123 73	100788
8	Watson J	017	230 -	29 82	14 15	2 00	5 00			179 03	100789
9	Wimsey P	018	220 -	27 52	13 15	2 00				177 33	100790
10											
11	TOTAL		1,915 -	232 51	111 85	18 00	35 00			1,517 64	
12											

294

4.3 Double entry bookkeeping

Although bookkeeping is outside the scope of your syllabus, you are expected to be able to post the entries to the main ledger.

An **asset** is something used by a business to earn profits. It is either cash or something that can be turned into cash.

A **liability** is something that a business owes to a third party. It will eventually have to be paid in cash.

In terms of payroll, the bank account is an asset. The amount of tax and NIC deducted from the payroll is a liability until actually paid.

Bookkeeping records income, expenses, assets and liabilities by means of **debit** and **credit** entries. For every debit, there has to be an equal credit (double entry bookkeeping).

A **debit** records an increase in expenses, an increase in an asset, a decrease in income and a decrease in a liability.

A **credit** records an increase in income, an increase in liability, a decrease in an expense and a decrease in an asset.

Example: Double entry bookkeeping

Payroll for month 1 totals £20,000 net pay, paid by direct credit (BACS). Tax and NIC deductions total £5,000 owed to the Inland Revenue (a liability). Show the bookkeeping entries.

Solution

We can write the entries out, so that for each entry, there is a debit and a credit (called a **journal entry**).

		Debit £	Credit £
1	Net pay to wages control	20,000	
	Bank account		20,000
	Net payments for month 1		
2	Tax and NIC deductions to wages control	5,000	
	Inland Revenue account		5,000
	Deductions for month 1		

PART C DETERMINING NET PAY

4.4 Wages control account

Example: Payroll ledger accounts

Comecon Ltd pays its workers every month. In Month 1, the payroll details are as follows.

	£
Gross wages	31,200
Employer's NICs	2,000
Net wages paid to workers via Direct Credit (BACS)	25,000
Deductions for PAYE made from workers' wages	4,000
Deductions for employees' National Insurance	1,000
Employees' contributions to the pension fund	1,200
Employer's contributions to the pension fund	1,500

Assume there was £50,000 in the bank at the beginning of Month 1 (an asset of £50,000).

Solution

Let's post the entries to the accounts below, doing one entry at a time. The individual accounts are shown later. For convenience here we shall show the entries in **journal** form.

Step 1 Entry for **gross pay**

	Debit £	Credit £
Staff costs (gross wages)	31,200	
Wages control		31,200

Step 2 Wages costs do not only include gross wages, so some more entries are necessary for other **employer's costs**.

	Debit £	Credit £
Staff costs (employer's NICs)	2,000	
Staff costs (employer's pension contributions)	1,500	
Wages control		3,500

Step 3 Net wages paid to employees out of cash must be entered.

	Debit £	Credit £
Wages control	25,000	
Cash (net paid)		25,000

Step 4 The **Inland Revenue** must be paid soon after the month end. However, they do not have to be paid at the same time as the workers, so let us enter that into a liability account. This is because we will pay the Inland Revenue at a future date.

11: NET PAY AND AGGREGATE PAYROLL TOTALS

	Debit £	Credit £
Wages control	4,000	
PAYE account: Inland Revenue for PAYE		4,000

Step 5 We also have to set up a creditor for NICs, as we have collected money as **employees' NICs** which must be paid to the Inland Revenue.

	Debit £	Credit £
Wages control	1,000	
PAYE account: Inland Revenue for NICs		1,000

Step 6 Do the same again for **employer's NIC**

	Debit £	Credit £
Wages control	2,000	
PAYE account: Inland Revenue for NICs		2,000

Step 7 Then there are **deductions from employees' wages for pension fund contributions**. The amount owed to the pension fund is a liability, as it is owed money. Pension funds are separate legal entities from the companies for whom they operate.

	Debit £	Credit £
Wages control	1,200	
Pension fund		1,200

Step 8 Finally there are the **employer's contributions to the pension fund**.

	Debit £	Credit £
Wages control	1,500	
Pension fund		1,500

By making these entries:

(a) all the amounts owing to **external agencies** have been collected in their own **liability accounts** for them to be dealt with later.

(b) the employees' **gross pay** together with the other payroll related costs of **employer's NICs and pension contributions**, have been collected in a **staff costs expense account.**

We had better look at the individual accounts (called T accounts) now to see which accounts have a balance. Don't forget that we had £50,000 cash to start with.

STAFF COSTS ACCOUNT

	£		£
Gross wages	31,200		
Employer's NICs	2,000		
Employer's pension contributions	1,500	Balance c/d	34,700
	34,700		34,700
Balance b/d	34,700		

297

PART C DETERMINING NET PAY

WAGES CONTROL ACCOUNT

	£		£
Cash – net pay	25,000	Gross wages	31,200
PAYE liability	4,000	Employer's NICs and pension	
NICs liability – employees'	1,000	Contributions	3,500
NICs liability – employer's	2,000		
Pension fund liability – employees'	1,200		
Pension fund liability – employer's	1,500		
	34,700		34,700

(Note that both sides have the same total, and so there is no balance to carry forward.)

CASH ACCOUNT

	£		£
Balance b/d	50,000	Wages control – net pay	25,000
		Balance c/d	25,000
	50,000		50,000
Balance b/d	25,000		

PAYE LIABILITY

	£		£
Balance c/d	4,000	Wages control – PAYE	4,000
		Balance b/d	4,000

NICs LIABILITY

	£		£
		Wages control – employees' NICs	1,000
Balance c/d	3,000	Wages control – employer's NICs	2,000
	3,000		3,000
		Balance b/d	3,000

PENSION FUND LIABILITY

	£		£
		Wages control – employees' contributions	1,200
Balance c/d	2,700	Wages control – employer's contributions	1,500
	2,700		2,700
		Balance b/d	2,700

Study the T accounts carefully and make sure that you can find both entries for each transaction: number them according to steps 1 to 8.

In fact, it would have been possible to bypass the wages control account altogether, and simply produce the following **posting summary**.

11: NET PAY AND AGGREGATE PAYROLL TOTALS

POSTING SUMMARY: PAYROLL	Month: 1	
Account	Dr £	Cr £
Staff costs – gross wages	31,200	
– employer's NICs	2,000	
– employer's pension contributions	1,500	
Cash – net pay		25,000
Inland Revenue – PAYE		4,000
– employees' NICs		1,000
– employer's NICs		2,000
Pension fund – employees' contributions		1,200
– employer's contributions		1,500
	34,700	34,700

This summary helps to show how the total expenses that Comecon incurred in employing staff are settled - most to the employees, but also to the Inland Revenue and the company pension fund.

The end result is that we have balances of £34,700 on the staff costs account (representing the total staff costs for the month), £25,000 in cash, liabilities of £4,000 and £3,000 to the Inland Revenue for PAYE and NIC respectively, and another liability of £2,700 to the pension fund.

The liabilities will be settled by payment over the next week or two, clearing the various account balances to NIL.

	Debit £	Credit £
PAYE liability	4,000	
NICs liability	3,000	
Pension fund liability	2,700	
Cash account		9,700

The balance on the **staff costs account** stays there - this is the record in the ledger accounts of the payroll expenses for the month. Next month, Month 2's staff costs will be added to it.

4.5 Proforma wages control account

The wages control account contains entries as in the proforma shown below.

WAGES CONTROL ACCOUNT

	£		£
Cash - net wages	X	Staff costs	
PAYE liability	X	- gross wages	X
NIC liability - employees'	X	- employer's NICs	X
NIC liability - employer's	X	- employer's pension contributions	X
Pension fund liability - employees'	X	- other staff costs	X
Pension fund liability - employer's	X		
Other deductions liability accounts	X		
	X		X

PART C DETERMINING NET PAY

Provided all the postings are carried out correctly, the balance carried forward on the wages control account should be NIL.

The wages control account should be prepared once a month to ensure that payments to external bodies (particularly the Inland Revenue) are correct.

Activity 11.1

Popeye plc has the following payroll details in Month 1. Write out the journal entries to post all these transactions and show the wages control account at the end of all the transactions.

		£
Gross wages and salaries:	Administrative staff	102,531
	Sales and marketing staff	226,704
	Production staff	1,067,895
Employer's NICs		104,782
Employees' NICs		83,829
PAYE deductions		351,826
Pension deductions:	Employer's	41,728
	Employees'	37,860
Net wages and salaries		903,893
GAYE donations		10,180
Season ticket loan repayments		9,542

If SSP, SMP, SPP and SAP have been paid, these will need to be separately recorded, so that any SSP and SMP/SPP/SAP recoveries can be calculated (see Chapter 5). The recovery is then posted to the **debit** of the Inland Revenue NIC account to **reduce** the payment to be made to the Inland Revenue and **credited** to the wages control account.

Remember liability accounts will have to be set up to cover all deductions and so could include any or all of the following.

- Inland Revenue (tax and NICs)
- Child Support Agency (DEOs)
- Courts (for court orders)
- Local authorities (community charge, poll tax)
- Trade Union (subscriptions)
- Pension fund administrators (basic contributions and AVCs)
- Charity agency (eg CAF for GAYE)
- Financial institutions (eg building society for SAYE)
- Medical insurers (eg BUPA for company medical insurance scheme)

Activity 11.2

Olive Co has the following payroll details in month 1. Prepare the wages control account on the basis that Olive Co is not a small employer for SMP rebate purposes.

	£
Gross salaries (excluding SSP and SMP)	50,000
SSP	1,000
SMP	4,200
Tax	2,500
NIC – employer's	1,500
– employees'	1,000
Pension fund – employer's	1,800
– employees'	1,800
GAYE	600
Medical insurance – employer's contributions only	500
SAYE	1,200
Net pay	48,100

5 Methods of payment

The main methods of paying wages are cash, cheque and BACS.

Cash has been the traditional method of paying hourly or weekly paid employees. However, due to the security risks of handling large amounts of cash, most employers prefer to use other payment methods.

Cheques are popular as a way of paying monthly paid or salaried employees. However, there are still security problems with theft and fraud.

More organisations are turning to BACS as a way of paying their employees.

5.1 Payment in cash

Employees taken on **since 1 January 1987** do not have the right to demand payment in cash. Employees engaged before that date may require to be paid in cash if this is stipulated in their contract. Cash payment is still quite common in the cases of **part-time employees, temporary staff and casual labour**. Employers are slowly abandoning cash payment for the following reasons.

- **Counting notes and coins is a time consuming exercise**, and requires more payroll staff than would otherwise be the case.
- **Employees have to count their pay** when they receive it, and **sign for the amount.**
- The notes and coins required to make up an employee's pay have to be **worked out in detail,** before they are ordered from the bank.
- The handling and transport of large amounts of cash pose **security problems**.

PART C   DETERMINING NET PAY

Activity 11.3

Although employers prefer not to pay wages in cash, can you think of any reason why employees might prefer it? List as many as you can.

5.1.1 Ordering money

The cash needed to pay an employee has to be **worked out in detail** before the bank can be told what to send. To do so, a **coinage analysis** might be prepared for each employee. An example is given below.

MONARCH BUILDERS LTD

NAME	NET WAGE £	NET WAGE p	£50	£20	£10	£5	£2	£1	50p	20p	10p	5p	2p	1p
L Bourbon	178	41	3	1		1	1	1		2				1
C Windsor	99	63	1	2		1	2		1		1		1	1
N Romanov	121	15	2	1				1			1	1		
F Habsberg	156	21	3			1		1		1				1
A Osman	174	51	3	1			2		1					1
R Rajah	180	62	3	1	1				1		1		1	
M Incah	79	90	1	1		1	2		1	2				
VALUE	990	43	£800	£140	£10	£20	£14	£3	£2	£1	30p	5p	4p	4p
NUMBER	—	—	16	7	1	4	7	3	4	5	3	1	2	4

Remember some employees may not want a note larger than £20.

Where employees are paid in cash, it is quite common for a breakdown of the notes and coins to be added to the documentation. Sometimes it will be **printed on the payslip** next to, or after, the figure for net pay.

A very simple example, for an employee who received £156.88 net pay for a week, follows.

Notes/Coins		£
£50 × 2		100.00
£20 × 2		40.00
£10 × 1		10.00
£5 × 1		5.00
£1 × 1		1.00
50p × 1		0.50
20p × 1		0.20
10p × 1		0.10
5p × 1		0.05
2p × 1		0.02
1p × 1		0.01
Net pay		156.88

Activity 11.4

Prepare a note and coin analysis for the following employees.

Name	Net wage due
	£
Bigg	120.12
Little	36.05
Large	129.71
Small	87.04
Stout	276.94
Thynne	110.25
Fatt	89.71
Skinnie	122.43
	972.25

The employees do not want to receive £50 notes, preferring lower denominations.

5.1.2 Handing cash over

Each employee should be required to **count** the money and then **sign** for it. There are pay packets available which allow this to be done without opening the packet.

- What happens if an employee is **unable to collect** his or her wage packet (eg because of illness)? The **unclaimed wages packet** would be held in a **safe** until it is collected.

- What happens if the employee sends someone else to collect the wages? The employee should send **written authority** naming the person collecting the wages, and that person should provide **proof of identity**.

PART C   DETERMINING NET PAY

5.1.3 Payment out of petty cash

Part-time or **casual** workers are sometimes paid out of **petty cash.** This is not usually a good practice because it can lead to problems with the **Inland Revenue**.

It is the duty of the employer to ensure that PAYE and NICs are paid. Failure to record all payments to employees can result in **penalties** for the employer, and can mean that the employer is liable to pay the PAYE and NICs which should have been deducted.

Petty cash is sometimes used to make **informal advances** to employees. If this is the case, the borrower should sign an IOU. Money cannot be deducted from pay unless there is a specific agreement to do so; so if an IOU is to be repaid in this way, the employee should also sign a form expressly authorising payroll to reclaim the loan from pay. Alternatively, the amount of the IOU should be repaid directly by the employee.

Activity 11.5

Your company made the following payments out of petty cash this month. What should you, as Payroll Officer, do about each one?

- Gina Chatterjee received £50 for looking after the plants in the reception area and meetings room. She receives this sum every month. She works for several other local businesses providing the same service. She does not provide an invoice.

- Jo Kent received £100 as an advance of salary. She signed a petty cash voucher. A copy of this has been passed to you.

No. 291	
Petty Cash Voucher	
	Date: 10.3.X0
	AMOUNT £ p
Advance of salary for March	100 00
Signature: Jo Kent	
Authorised by: Alison Brown	

- Lewis Taylor received £30 for helping out in the post room on several occasions recently, when a member of staff was off sick. Lewis is a full-time student with various part-time jobs. He signed no receipt.

5.2 Cheque payments

A **cheque** is the simplest form of **cashless pay**. The cheque will display the **name** of the employee, and the **amount** to be paid which will agree exactly to net pay shown on the payslip.

The cheque will normally require **signature** or some other form of **authorisation** like a rubber stamp. If a rubber stamp is used, the person who looks after it has the same sort of power as a cheque signatory.

Most organisations have a list of **authorised cheque signatories**. Two or more may be required for cheques exceeding a certain amount. Moreover, it is possible that directors' pay cheques may be signed by more senior personnel.

The problem with cheque payments is that so much **time** is spent preparing them. Also, while the **security problems** with cheques are less than with cash, there is still the possibility of **theft** or **fraud**. Obviously, any organisation must keep a chequebook, but it can be a problem when it comes to be treated as just another part of the stationery.

Some of the effort of writing out a cheque can be spared if they are **printed** beforehand, so that only the signature or stamp is necessary. Printing the cheque can be the final run of the normal payroll processing. In fact, some organisations have an arrangement whereby the **cheque** is the second half of a perforated sheet of paper which has the **pay slip** on top. The employee receives both, tears off the cheque and takes it to the bank. An example is given on the following page.

The cheques must be **numbered in sequence**, and must be kept under **strict control**.

Even though cheques, particularly for monthly paid staff, are used less as **automated payment systems** take over, they will still be used for **exceptional circumstances.**

- An **employee leaving** part way through the month
- A **new employee** joining during the month
- **Advances of salary**

In the case of starters and leavers, you should check the exact date of starting or leaving to the notification sent to you by the personnel department.

PART C   DETERMINING NET PAY

EMPLOYEE	NAME	CODE	MONTH	BLOGGS AND CO
0152	A. WORKER	461L	11	21/2/X3

Narrative	Amount	Year To Date
	£ p	£ p
BASIC PAY	1,000 00	11,000 00
GROSS PAY	1,000 00	11,000 00
INCOME TAX NICs	116 10 61 40	1,277.10 675.40
NET PAY	822 50	

Any Bank
449 SOMEWHERE ROAD, LONDON W5 2LF

21 2 20 X3

20-27-48
SOUTHERN BANK PLC

Pay   A. WORKER   or order

EIGHT HUNDRED AND TWENTY-TWO POUNDS AND FIFTY PENCE

£ 822-50

ACCOUNT PAYEE

Authorised signature   *Any Body*
Authorised signature   *Some Body*

Bloggs and Co

Cheque No.   Branch No.   Account No.
⑃101129⑃   20⑃2748⑃   30595713⑃

5.3 Direct credit (BACS)

Most companies now use some form of **automated payment system**. This means that instead of filling up pay packets with cash, or signing large numbers of cheques which the employees take to their various banks, the whole operation is done speedily and automatically through the banking system.

Direct Credit is a system which enables you to make payments by electronic transfer directly into bank or building society accounts. It is operated by **BACS**, the UK's automated payments clearing service, which is owned by the major banks and building societies.

An organisation can use Direct Credit in one of two ways.

- **Indirect access:** the organisation uses a **bureau service** provided by its bank or by a computer bureau. You provide the information by fax, telephone, post or PC input, and in return for a charge, the bureau transmits the data to BACS. The bureau may also provide payslips or a full payroll service.

- **Direct access:** the organisation has a direct telecommunications link to BACS, called **BACSTEL**. You need a PC, appropriate modem and the required software. Your transmission is secured using **passwords** and a confirmation receipt comes back down from BACS so that you know your transmission was successful. This may be faster and cheaper than indirect access but you incur the initial costs of the software etc.

Whichever method your organisation adopts, when you have completed the payroll calculations in the normal way, you follow this procedure.

Day 1   Send off a list of payees with the amount of net pay, sort code of their bank or building society and their account numbers.

Day 2   Your payment instructions are processed overnight for distribution by the banks and building societies on Day 3.

Day 3   Payment day. The organisation's bank account is debited with a single entry covering the value of all the payments made, and simultaneously the accounts of all individual payees are credited.

Benefits to employers	Benefits to employees
Greater security	Having their money in their accounts on pay day as **cleared funds** (guaranteed to be available for withdrawal straight away, unlike cheques)
Reduced costs of cheque stationery or cash handling	**Increased security**
Less administration	**No time wasted** checking pay packet or paying a cheque in
Increased control of cash flows, as the date of the payment is known exactly and it is on pay day, not before (as with cash payments)	**No difficulty in collecting pay** whilst on holiday or off sick

The **disadvantage to employees** could be that they have to open a bank or building society account to get paid. However, 80% of the UK population now have a current account at a bank or building society, and over 70% of all salary and wage payments are now made directly to personal accounts.

Some **smaller employers** may not consider it worthwhile to use Direct Credit if they only have a small workforce. Others, especially if they have computerised all other aspects of their accounting systems, may see this as a logical next step.

It is essential, under this system, to keep details of the employee's bank or building society account in the employee records. Employees should be asked to complete forms giving these details when they join the organisation and to sign new forms if the account details are changed.

You may also need to make a note of the payslip destination. Under cash and cheque payments, the payslip goes with the payments. However, with cashless pay, the payslip is given or sent to the employee separately and the employee records will need to show where it should go.

PART C   DETERMINING NET PAY

Activity 11.6

You have just started work with a brand new software company which has taken on 20 staff in all. They are all going to be paid monthly. The company's accounting systems will all be computerised (including payroll). What method of payment would you recommend the company adopts for payroll? List the advantages and disadvantages of the following.

(a) Cash
(b) Cheque
(c) Direct Credit

Example: Direct credit

Arnold Bax is an employee of yours. His gross pay was £2,000 in June. Tax and NICs for the month came to £620. Arnold Bax banks at Natlays Bank. The sort code of his branch is 17-31-98, and his bank account number is 12345678.

Of the information above, what would you transmit to BACS?

Solution

Arnold Bax. £1,380 [ie £2,000 – £620]. 17 - 31 - 98. 12345678

5.4 Payment of payroll creditors

Payroll creditors (eg the Inland Revenue, pension fund) will normally be paid by cheque or BACS. Remember that there may be **deadlines** to be met.

For Inland Revenue payments, the deadline is 14 days after the end of the PAYE month. So for month 2 (ending 5 May 2004), payment must be made by **19 May 2004**. Interest and penalties may be charged on late payment.

6 Spreadsheets

Remember, for the purposes of your assessment, you must be able to process deductions manually. Therefore, spreadsheets should be used as simple summaries of gross pay and deduction, similar to the wages analysis book, for totals to feed into the wages control account.

Spreadsheets can also be used to replace the P11, as addition and subtraction can be done automatically.

Key learning points

- **Net pay** shows the amount actually due to the employee.
- One way of ensuring that every payroll expense is properly analysed is to use a **wages control account**.
- Payment can be made by cash, cheque or direct credit.

PART C   DETERMINING NET PAY

Quick quiz

1   What is a wages analysis book?
2   What is the double entry to account for the employer's pension contributions of (say) £500?
3   When all the entries relating to the payroll have been made, what does the balance on the wages control account represent?

Answers to quick quiz

1   A wages analysis book is an accounts book used in a manual accounting system to record, for each employee, details of gross pay and all deductions. The totals for each item can then be used to make the correct postings to the nominal ledger and to reconcile gross pay with net pay as paid out. This ensures that proper security is maintained over the organisation's cash.

2
		Debit £	Credit £
1	Staff costs	500	
	Wages control account		500
2	Wages control account	500	
	Pension scheme trustees account		500

3   An error! The wages control account should balance exactly. If it doesn't, then a mistake has been made somewhere.

Activity checklist

This checklist shows which performance criteria, range statement or knowledge and understanding point is covered by each activity in this chapter. Tick off each activity as you complete it.

Activity

11.1	☐	This activity covers performance criteria 73.2.A, 73.2.C and 73.2.F.
11.2	☐	This activity covers performance criteria 73.2.C, 73.2.D, 73.2.E and 73.2.F.
11.3	☐	This activity covers knowledge and understanding point 11.
11.4	☐	This activity covers knowledge and understanding point 11.
11.5	☐	This activity covers performance criterion 73.2.G.
11.6	☐	This activity covers knowledge and understanding point 11.

Answers to Activities

Answers to activities

Chapter 1

Answer 1.1

You will need to ask the family whether they have permission to work in the UK. If they each produce a work permit, then they can work on the farm. However, you should ensure that you keep a copy of the documents for future reference.

Answer 1.2

The answer is yes, yet it is surprising how many small employers get this wrong. Under the law, you are obliged to keep all details listed in section 4.6, even though Mrs Hawk will probably not be having any tax deducted from her pay. One of the reasons for doing this is that Mrs Hawk may have another part-time job or be in receipt of state pension (so that her earnings with Dove Ltd are taxable). She may not tell you this, but by keeping a record, you will be able to make a return to the Inland Revenue of her earnings at the end of the tax year. Then if it turns out that tax should have been deducted, your firm will not be penalised; as the Inland Revenue can collect the tax from Mrs Hawk. However, if you had not kept records, your firm could be penalised when the Inland Revenue make a PAYE inspection.

Answer 1.3

The first thing to do is to check your employee records for any evidence that Mr Biggs is a new employee. Do not forget to check your in-tray, as it could be that paperwork has been delayed and so you have not set up a formal file yet. If you can find no record, you must tell your boss and ask him for instructions. At all times, be polite to Mr Biggs and explain that you cannot pay him until you have received authorisation. **Never** give in to pressure and make a payment without authority.

Answer 1.4

The written evidence shows a salary of £30,000 pa and this is what the employee is obviously expecting. However, you cannot assume that your boss is wrong. It may be that circumstances have changed since the offer letter was made. Perhaps Mr Biggs is working reduced hours or has reduced responsibilities. You need to query the matter with your supervisor and show him the offer letter. Ask if he has any evidence to support the lower figure. You will only cause problems in employee relationships if you pay Mr Biggs too much and then your organisation has to recover it; or too little and then have to make additional payments.

ANSWERS TO ACTIVITIES

Answer 1.5

P45, Box 6	461L
P45, Box 7 (figures from P11)	£
Total pay to date	5,320.00
Total tax to date	177.81

The P11 figures already include pay brought forward from Job's previous employer.

P45, Box 8	£
Total pay in this employment (5,320 – 720)	4,600.00
Total tax in this employment (177.81 – 50.70)	127.11

Answer 1.6

(a) Hope Less cannot be issued with a new P45. She can, however, be given a letter stating the figures on the original P45.

(b) Job Less should be advised to wait for his P45 as he will need to give parts 2 and 3 to the DWP when he claims jobseeker's allowance. The DWP will then arrange for a tax refund to be made to him, if applicable.

(c) Grace Less has not given notice, it would seem. However you can not take the word of Hope and Job for this. When the company gets direct confirmation from Grace that she has left, then you should prepare a P45 and keep it until she asks for it. You should not give it to anyone else unless she authorises you to do so.

(d) Whit Less does not need a new P45. The bonus is paid after deduction of basic rate tax (22%). He should be sent a covering letter giving details of the date of payment, the gross amount (£200) and the deductions made (£44).

Answer 1.7

You need to take the following steps.

(a) Calculate a month's pay and the PAYE due on this in the normal way. **Do not deduct any National Insurance**.

(b) Complete the deduction card.

(c) Complete form P45 in the normal way but remember to put D in the box at the bottom of the form and to put the name and address of Lief's next of kin if you have it in box 11.

(d) Send **all four parts** of the form to the Tax Office.

(e) The salary payment should be made to Lief's **personal representative** – his **executor**, if he left a will. If he did not leave a will, the law lays down who will be his personal representative. If he left a widow, then it would probably be in order to pay the money to her, unless she was separated from him. Your supervisor or manager should establish the proper payee.

(f) Remove him from the current payroll; but remember to keep the records for at least three years after the end of the current tax year.

ANSWERS TO ACTIVITIES

Answer 1.8

If you get all the information below, you should be able to set up her payroll record file.

- Full name and title
- Address
- Sex
- Date of birth (it might be company policy to ask for proof of this)
- Date of appointment
- Rate of pay – basic, overtime etc. } These details would come from personnel, a senior manager or a copy contract of employment
- Holiday pay entitlement
- Building society/bank details (if paying by direct debit)
- Will she be joining the occupational pension scheme (if there is one)?
- Does she have a reduced rate NIC certificate if she is married or widowed?
- Does she have a P45?
- If not, does she have proof of her National Insurance number (eg a P60 from previous employers)? If not, ask NICO to trace it using Form CA6855.
- If she has no P45, you must complete a P46. Depending on her rate of pay, you either send it to the Tax Office to get a tax code calculated, or you keep it on file.
- If a P45 is produced, you need to complete it and send off Part 3 to the Tax Office **after** you have checked it and used the information to start off a P11. File Part 2.
- If you have GAYE, SAYE, season ticket loan schemes, Christmas clubs etc, will she want to participate in any of them? Give her the forms for any in which she expresses an interest.
- Will she be joining a Trade Union? You may have arrangements for deducting subscriptions through the payroll.

Answer 1.9

Note: Even though all four employees have worked for Turnover Ltd before in this tax year you need to start off **new** P11s where necessary.

Job Less

Pay exceeds PAYE threshold of £91 and NIC Lower Earnings Limit of £79. Prepare a P11 and deduct PAYE using Emergency Code (474L in 2004/05) on a Week 1/Month 1 basis.

Hope Less

Since her pay also exceeds PAYE threshold and NIC LEL **and** she has other employment, proceed exactly as above but use Code BR to deduct tax instead of Emergency Code.

ANSWERS TO ACTIVITIES

Grace Less

Her earnings are below the PAYE threshold and the NIC LEL. Do not complete a P11 but record her name, address and amount of pay.

Whit Less

Although he only works for Turnover Ltd for 8 days, he is not a casual employee as far as the Inland Revenue is concerned. You must complete a P46 for him. You would not send it off to the Inland Revenue, however, since his pay has not exceeded the PAYE threshold for the month (£395). He has earned more than the NIC threshold for the month (£343) so you prepare a P11. Enter NI in the tax code box and enter the amount of gross pay and NICs. Keep the P46 and Whit's address on file.

Answer 1.10

None of these students can complete a P38(S). Billie and Lee work for the company during term-time and Pat is not attending a UK university. Remember form P38(S) is for students working during their vacations only.

ANSWERS TO ACTIVITIES

Chapter 2

Answer 2.1

No you do not. Brenda will have to sign a written declaration authorising payroll to make pension deductions from her pay.

Answer 2.2

You can make no deductions until the discrepancy is sorted out. If the scheme rules state 3% contributions, has Brenda made a mistake or does she want to make extra contributions? You need to get back to Brenda to discover her intentions. If she only wants to make the basic 3% contributions, she will have to sign a new mandate to that effect. If she wants to make 5% contributions, she will have to sign **two forms**: one for the basic contributions of 3% and a second for AVCs of 2%.

Answer 2.3

(a) 15% × £100,000 = £15,000
(b) 15% × £102,000 = £15,300

Tutorial note. Remember the earnings cap for tax relief is £102,000 for tax year 2004/05.

Answer 2.4

Payroll records are **confidential**. You can not give information from them to **unauthorised people**. The best thing to do is to refer the query to John Taylor and ask him to contact the trade union to tell them he has resigned. If you wish, you can also reply to the trade union saying that payroll records are confidential, but that you have passed on their query to John Taylor.

Answer 2.5

The first rule is be polite! Check the payroll records and show John Taylor the signed form telling you to stop making contributions to the trade union. Explain that if he wishes to continue to pay contributions, he will have to sign a new mandate.

ANSWERS TO ACTIVITIES

Chapter 3

Answer 3.1

(a) Extremely unlikely. If Biff got these wages every week his or her annual salary would be £56,662.84. Even if Biff earned a huge amount of overtime this week, this seems a very high rate of pay for the job. The only possible explanation is that Biff has received a large amount of back pay and/or a very large bonus this week. It seems most likely, though, that a mistake has been made somewhere.

(b) Yes. £25,000 ÷ 4 = £6,250, so the salary to date of £6,211.67 is reasonable.

(c) No. Her basic salary this month is £1,500 (£18,000 ÷ 12). Her overtime should be £450 (30 hours at £15 per hour). The gross pay total should be £1,950. It looks as if the overtime was calculated as 3 hours, not 30 hours.

Answer 3.2

The form should include the following details.

- Employee's name
- Employee's staff number (if applicable)
- Bank/building society name
- Bank/building society address
- Bank/building society sort code
- Bank/building society account number
- Employee's signature and date

You may have thought of other details, such as the employee's home address. This could be useful, if your organisation does not use staff numbers, in order to differentiate between employees with similar names. The above list represents the **minimum** information needed, the most important being the employee's **signature**.

Answer 3.3

Notice that the form has not been dated or signed. Therefore, you can not make any changes to the payroll records. You need to pass the form back to Michael Jeffries for signature.

Answer 3.4

There is a discrepancy between the form from personnel and the payroll records. You need to contact personnel and inform them that Michael Jeffries' current salary is £24,500 not £20,500 and ask for further instructions.

For the time being, do not implement the salary change.

Chapter 4

Answer 4.1

Remember that skills testing simulates workplace activities. The more real life examples of payroll work you have gathered in your payroll portfolio, the easier it will be to cope with the simulation.

Answer 4.2

If an employee has no contract of employment, then disputes and misunderstandings may arise over entitlement to overtime, holiday entitlement, notice period, etc. This is not only inefficient and bad for staff morale but may leave the employer in a poor position to face an Industrial Tribunal over a serious dispute.

Answer 4.3

(a) Tom's basic pay is 24 × £10 = £240. (The National Minimum Wage would be 40 × £4.85 = £194.)

(b) Asif's basic pay is the higher of his guaranteed minimum wage (£145) and the piecework rate (200 films x 60p = £120). So this week he gets £145. (The National Minimum Wage would be 35 × £4.10 = £143.50.)

(c) Louise's piecework hours produced:

		Hours
Umbrellas	20 × 30 mins	10
Bags	60 × 20 mins	20
Total piecework hours		30

Her basic pay for the week is 30 hours × £4.95 = £148.50 (NMW hourly rate is lower, whatever age she is).

(d) Patrick's basic pay:

	£
First 30 umbrellas: 30 × £2	60
Next 10 umbrellas: 10 × £2.50	25
Last 42 umbrellas: 42 × £3	126
	211

The NMW applies to pensioners. 40 × £4.85 = £194 so Patrick earns well above the NMW.

Answer 4.4

Paula

Overtime in February = one month's salary = £30,000 ÷ 12 = £2,500

Nigel

Hours at time and a half (weekdays, hours in excess of 7 per day):

Date	Overtime hours
2	1
3	2
8	2
9	1
10	1
11	1
12	2
18	1
19	1
22	1
23	2
	15

Hours at double time (weekends):

Date	Overtime hours
6	5
13	7
14	3
	15

Nigel's annual salary = £910 × 12 = £10,920.

His hourly rate is (£10,920 ÷ 52 ÷ 35) = £6.

	£
Overtime at time and a half = 15 × £6 × 1.5	135
Overtime at double time = 15 × £6 × 2	180
	315

Answer 4.5

If you did make the effort to research this, well done! Remember that this is a practical course. You are studying material which will be useful to you in your everyday work. Both your work and your studies will benefit if you relate them to each other.

Answer 4.6

No. You need a signed mandate from Sean.

ANSWERS TO ACTIVITIES

Answer 4.7

	£
Gross salary	750
Less: tax and NIC	200
	550
Less: loan repayment	250
Paid to Sean	300

Answer 4.8

	£
Basic salary backpay June - October (£1,250 – £1,200) × 5	250.00
Overtime backpay (18 + 15 + 16 + 25 + 10) × (£12.50 – £12)	42.00
Total backpay	292.00
November salary	1,250.00
November overtime (21 × £12.50)	262.50
Gross pay in November	1,804.50

Answer 4.9

(a) Natalie should be told that all overtime payments must be authorised and that, since her supervisor has not been at work this week, the payroll department has not received authorisation to pay this amount. It may be that the company's systems have broken down, as another supervisor should perhaps have been asked to provide authorisation by Wednesday lunchtime. Natalie may well have a valid grievance. It is probably too late today to do anything about it but if Natalie is going to be seriously inconvenienced by having to wait until next week for the overtime payment, then the matter could be followed up on Monday. A pay advance may be arranged.

(b) Percy should be told that the payroll department does not have authority to change pay rates. This is only done on the authority of the personnel department. He should ask his supervisor what has happened to the pay increase and find out if there has been a mix-up in the personnel department. You should also talk to personnel, in case a memo has got lost, for example.

Answer 4.10

- Management will want to ensure that the accounts department is adequately staffed at all times, and so the **rules** of the flexitime system will probably state that employees must be at work by a stated hour (such as 10 am) in the morning and must not leave work for the day before, say, 3pm. So the first control would be to ensure that all staff are present between these times.

- **Secondly**, employees should be required to arrange **in advance** the days when they want to work particularly short hours or take a day off. This would be like arranging annual leave.

- **Thirdly**, to keep track of the coming and goings, staff should be asked to sign a **register** or to provide a **record of their hours** on a regular basis (eg weekly). These records should be regularly reviewed by a supervisor or manager to ensure that they seem to be correct and to make sure that staff working flexitime are working the right number of hours. **Timesheets** might also be used, or even a clock card system.

ANSWERS TO ACTIVITIES

Chapter 5

Answer 5.1

Sheree's earnings exceed £79 per week. However she has been sick for only three qualifying days (Thursday, Friday and Monday). As these are waiting days, she is not entitled to any SSP.

Answer 5.2

Sheree's normal working week is Thursday, Friday, Saturday and Sunday. Therefore, she has been sick all 4 days from Thursday 1 July to Sunday 4 July 2004. The first three days are waiting days, so SSP is due for one day.

As Sheree's normal working week is four days, her SSP is £66.15/4 i.e. £16.54.

Answer 5.3

(a) £350 + £345 = £695
(b) £695 × 6 = £4,170
(c) £4,170 ÷ 52 = £80.19

So Simbala still qualifies for SMP.

Answer 5.4

Simbala's average earnings were £80.19. Therefore SMP for the first six weeks is: 90% × £80.19 = £72.17 per week. For the period after the first six weeks, the amount is the **lower** of £72.17 and £102.80, ie £72.17 per week.

Answer 5.5

Recovery: 100% of SMP = £1,000
Compensation: 4.5% of SMP = £45
Total amount recovered: £1,045.

Chapter 6

Answer 6.1

(a)/(b) Mr Dawson and Mrs Mone are both wrong – although you would have to find a more tactful way of expressing that! Directors and pensioners are both covered by the PAYE system. The company could be fined for not making the necessary deductions.

(c) Ms Simmons, as a self-employed person, is not covered by the PAYE system. She will deal with her own tax affairs.

Answer 6.2

(a) Month 3
(b) Month 8
(c) Month 9
(d) Week 3
(e) Week 12
(f) Week 26
(g) Week 41

Answer 6.3

The items which should be included in Louise's pay for the month are:

- Salary
- Bonus, in the month when it is paid
- Commission, when paid

None of the others should be included. The value of her company car and private medical insurance will be taxed, but the Tax Office will see to this (under the benefits rules). The employer's contributions to the pension scheme on Louise's behalf are not taxable at all. The use of the company credit card, if restricted to paying for legitimate business expenses, will not be a taxable benefit.

Answer 6.4

By Month 9 John Jones is entitled to 9/12 of his allowances: £6,000 × 9/12 = £4,500. This is the amount which will be deducted from his total pay to date to arrive at his taxable pay to date.

Answer 6.5

Tyson has presumably just had his 65th birthday. He is now entitled to a higher personal allowance – £6,830 instead of £4,745. So his free pay goes up by £2,085 for the year! He will pay *less* tax, not more. The P at the end of the code simply shows that he is getting the higher personal allowance for those aged 65–74.

ANSWERS TO ACTIVITIES

Answer 6.6

The director's salary from your company is not her main source of income. Her tax allowances have all been used up in working out the tax code to be used by Big plc's payroll department. The code of D0 instructs you that she has no free pay to set against the salary she gets from your company and that it should all be taxed at 40% (as her starting and basic rate bands have been used up on her earnings from Big plc).

Answer 6.7

	£
Gross pay	35,000.00
Less allowances	5,000.00
Taxable pay	30,000.00
Starting rate band: 10% × £2,020	202.00
Basic rate band: 22% × (£30,000 – 2,020)	6,155.60
	6,357.60

Answer 6.8

(a) 541 = 41 + (1 × 500)

Pay adjustment = £104.76 + £1,250.01
= £1,354.77

(b) 709 = 209 + (1 × 500)

Pay adjustment = £524.76 + £1,250.01
= £1,774.77

(c) 3,904 = 404 + (7 × 500)

Pay adjustment = £1,012.26 + (7 × £1,250.01)
= £9,762.33

Answer 6.9

(a) **Robert Bruce**

In Week 8: Column 1 maximum = £311
Column 2 maximum = £4,831

So Robert's tax will be calculated from Table B, as £842 is between £311 and £4,831.

(b) **Shelley Johnson**

In Month 4: Column 1 maximum = £674
Column 2 maximum = £10,467

So Shelley's tax will be calculated from Tables C & D, as £13,967 is above £10,467.

(c) **Garth Wright**

In Week 12: Column 1 maximum = £467

So Garth's tax will be calculated from Table SR, as £282 is less than £467.

Answer 6.10

(a) **Carol Scott**

Carol's pay to date is more than £1,347 and less than £20,934, so use table B to calculate her tax.

	Taxable pay to date £	Total tax due to date £
	2,300	506.00
	50	11.00
	2,350	517.00
Less: starting rate relief Month 8		(161.61)
		355.39
Less: tax paid to end of Month 7		(329.13)
Tax payable at the end of Month 8		26.26

(b) **John Devlin**

John's taxable pay to date does not exceed £28,985, so use Table B and the subtraction tables.

	Taxable pay £	£
Total tax due to date on	16,800	3,696.00
	28	6.16
	16,828	3,702.16
Less starting rate relief to Week 48		(223.76)
Total tax due to date		3,478.40
Less tax paid at end of Week 47		(3,513.45)
Total tax refund due at the end of Week 48		(35.05)

Note: A refund is possible! John Devlin may have worked less hours this period or have had a change in tax code. Either of these could lead to a reduction in his tax due to date and so cause a refund.

ANSWERS TO ACTIVITIES

(c) **Polly Grainger**

Polly's taxable pay does not exceed £18,317, so use Table B and the subtraction tables.

	Taxable pay £	£
Total tax due to date on	15,100	3,322.00
	92	20.24
	15,192	3,342.24
Less starting rate relief to Month 7		(141.41)
Total tax due to date		3,200.83
Less tax paid at end of Month 6		(2,897.33)
Tax payable at the end of Month 7		303.50

Answer 6.11

First check which tax tables to use. £20,000 is above the maximum amounts for Month 5 for Columns 1 and 2 in the pay at monthly rates table, so you need to use Tables C and D.

	£
Total taxable pay to end of Month 5	20,000
Subject to basic and starting rate tax from Table C, Month 5	13,084
Taxable at higher rate – use Table D	6,916

	£	Tax payable to date £
On first £13,084, from Table C		2,777.59
From Table D: On £6,900	2,760.00	
On £16	6.40	
On £6,916		2,766.40
Total tax payable at the end of Month 5		5,543.99

Answer 6.12

Alice Adams

	£
Pay in Month 3	1,250.00
Pay to date as at Month 2	3,750.00
Total pay to date	5,000.00
Free pay to date for 474L, from Tables A (Month 3)	(1,187.25)
Taxable pay to date	3,812.75

Use Table B to calculate tax due to date as £3,812 exceeds £505 (starting rate threshold as at Month 3).

Tax due to date, from Table B:

		£
Tax on:	£3,800	836.00
	£12	2.64
	£3,812	838.64
Less starting rate relief as at Month 3 (subtraction tables)		(60.60)
Tax due to date		778.04
Less tax paid to end of Month 2		605.31
Tax due in Month 3		172.73

Bob Brown

	£
Pay in the month	615.00
Pay to end of Month 2	615.00
Total pay to date	1,230.00
Free pay to date for 370T, from Tables A (Month 3)	(927.27)
Taxable pay to date	302.73

Use Table SR to calculate tax due to date as £302 is less than £505 (starting rate threshold as at Month 3).

		£
Tax due to date, from Table SR:	on £300	30.00
	on £2	0.20
	on £302	30.20
Less tax paid to end of Month 2		NIL
Tax due in Month 3		30.20

Chris Cole

	£
Pay in the month	3,750.00
Pay to end of Month 2	19,565.00
Total pay to date	23,315.00
Free pay to date for 312T, from Tables A (Month 3)	(782.25)
Taxable pay to date	22,532.75

Use Tables C and D to calculate tax due to date as £22,532 exceeds both the starting rate and basic rate thresholds as at Month 3.

	£
Basic and starting rate tax threshold as at Month 3 (from Table C)	7,850
Balance of total taxable pay, taxable at higher rate	14,682
	22,532

		£	£
Tax due to date on first £7,850 (from Table C, Month 3)			1,666.40
From Table D:	on £10,000	4,000.00	
	on £4,600	1,840.00	
	on £82	32.80	
	on £14,682		5,872.80
Total tax payable to date			7,539.20
Less tax paid to end of Month 2			6,704.79
Tax due in Month 3			834.41

ANSWERS TO ACTIVITIES

Chapter 7

Answer 7.1

	Tax code		Amended		~~315T~~		515T				
	~~300T~~		WK/mnth		2		3				
				K codes			K codes			K codes	
Month	Pay in the week	Total pay to date	Total free pay to date	Total additional pay to date	Total taxable pay to date	Total tax due to date	Tax due at end of current period	Regulatory limit	Tax deducted in the week	Tax not deducted owing to the regulatory limit	Tax Credits
	2	3	4a	4b	5	6	6a	6b	7	8	9
1	2,166.67	2,166.67	250.75		1,915.92	401.09			401.09		
2	5,214.67	7,381.34	526.50		6,854.84	1,759.19			1,358.10		
3	1,166.67	8,548.01	1,289.76		7,258.25	1,536.16			(223.03)R		
4	1,166.67	9,714.68	1,719.68		7,995.00	1,678.09			141.93		

Notes

1 Column 4a: £53.00 + £1,666.68 = £1,719.68.

2 Column 5: Column 3 – Column 4a.

3 Did you remember to check which tax table to use? £7,995 (from Column 5) is less than £10,467, so you need Table B **and** the subtraction tables.

		Table B
Taxable pay		£
Tax on: £7,900		1,738.00
£95		20.90
£7,995		1,758.90
Starting rate relief, Month 4		(80.81)
		1,678.09

4 Column 7: Month 4 Column 6 figure less Month 3 Column 6 figure – no refund this month. Tax due instead.

5 Did you remember to complete the details of the tax code amendments in the top boxes?

Answer 7.2

	£
Pay in Month 3	1,166.67
Free pay, Month 1	(429.92)
Taxable pay for the month	736.75

This exceeds the month 1 starting rate relief limit of £169 and so table B is used.

		£
Table B on 700 + 36 (£154.00 + £7.92)		161.92
Starting rate relief, Month 1		(20.21)
Tax payable in Month 3		141.71

So instead of getting a tax refund, Mohammed Ali has to pay tax of £141.71.

Answer 7.3

Tax code	Amended	465T
~~433L W1/M1~~	WK/mnth	3

Month	Pay in the week 2	Total pay to date 3	Total free pay to date 4a	*K codes* Total additional pay to date 4b	Total taxable pay to date 5	Total tax due to date 6	*K codes* Tax due at end of current period 6a	Regulatory limit 6b	Tax deducted in the week 7	*K codes* Tax not deducted owing to the regulatory limit 8	Tax Credits 9
1	3,000		361.59		2,638.41				563.99		
2	3,115	**6,115**	361.59		2,753.41	**1,173.98**			609.99		
3	3,675	9,790	1,164.75		8,625.25	1,976.40			802.42		

Notes

1 Tax is all calculated from Tables C and D.

Month	Table C	Tax due £	Table D	Tax due £	Tax due total £
1	on £2,617	555.59	on £21	8.40	563.99
2	on £2,617	555.59	on £136	54.40	609.99
3	on £7,850	1,666.40	on £775	310.00	1,976.40

2 The figures in Month 2 Columns 3 and 6 have been added in Month 3. They would **not** be filled in while a Month 1 code is in use.

Answer 7.4

			Tax payable £
(a)	Dickie Dawson, as Table D		160.00
(b)	Bryonie Branson, as Table B		22.00
(c)	Naomi Taylor, no tax		NIL
(d)	Mary Wong, as Table SR		10.00

ANSWERS TO ACTIVITIES

Answer 7.5

	Tax code		Amended								
	453L		WK/mnth								
				K codes				K codes			K codes	
Week	Pay in the week	Total pay to date	Total free pay to date	Total additional pay to date	Total taxable pay to date	Total tax due to date	Tax due at end of current period	Regulatory limit	Tax deducted in the week	Tax not deducted owing to the regulatory limit	Tax Credits
	2	3	4a	4b	5	6	6a	6b	7	8	9
51	100.00	5,100.00	4,451.79		648.21	64.80			1.20		
52	100.00	5,200.00	4,539.08		660.92	66.00			1.20		
53	100.00	5,300.00	4,626.37		673.63	67.20			1.20		

Notes

1 Column 4a: £4,539.08 + £87.29
2 Column 5: £660.92 + £(100 − 87.29)
3 Column 7: Week 1 tax due on £12.71, using **Table SR**
4 Column 6: £66.00 + £1.20

Answer 7.6

You can pay the tax refunds due to George Lo and Adelaide Grant. You cannot make a refund to Jez Nielsen until he returns to work or leaves the company. If the strike ends after the tax year ends, then he will not receive his tax refund from the Inland Revenue (see NVQ/SVQ Level 3).

Answer 7.7

Name	K Code	Period	Gross pay £	Additional pay £	Taxable pay £	Tax due £	Regulatory limit £	Tax deducted
Bob Melon	K49	Mnth 3	1,200	124.77	1,324.77	230.68	600.00	230.68
Ann Apple	K150	Wk 3	800	87.06	887.06	181.15	400.00	181.15
Sam Pear	K920	Wk 3	1,000	531.33	1,531.33	322.83	500.00	322.83
Jasmin Grape	K2400	Mnth 3	1,000	6,002.31	7,002.31	1,479.84	500.00	500.00

Answer 7.8

	Tax code		Amended								
	K1200		WK/mnth								
				K codes			*K codes*			*K codes*	
M o n t h	Pay in the week	Total pay to date	Total free pay to date	Total additional pay to date	Total taxable pay to date	Total tax due to date	Tax due at end of current period	Regulatory limit	Tax deducted in the week	Tax not deducted owing to the regulatory limit	Tax Credits
	2	3	4a	4b	5	6	6a	6b	7	8	9
1	250.00	250.00		1,000.76	1,250.76	254.79	254.79	125.00	125.00	129.79	

Notes

1 **Additional pay** (not free pay, of course!)

   (2 × £416.67) + £167.42 = £1,000.76

2 **Tax**: use Table B and subtraction tables.

		Taxable pay £	Tax due £
On		1,200	264.00
On		50	11.00
On		1,250	275.00
Less starting rate relief, Month 1			(20.21)
			254.79

Answer 7.9

	Tax code		Amended		K1200 M1						
	~~K1200~~		WK/mnth		2						
				K codes			*K codes*			*K codes*	
M o n t h	Pay in the week	Total pay to date	Total free pay to date	Total additional pay to date	Total taxable pay to date	Total tax due to date	Tax due at end of current period	Regulatory limit	Tax deducted in the week	Tax not deducted owing to the regulatory limit	Tax Credits
	2	3	4a	4b	5	6	6a	6b	7	8	9
1	250.00	250.00		1,000.76	1,250.76	254.79	254.79	125.00	125.00	129.79	
2	250.00			1,000.76	1,250.76		254.79	125.00	125.00		

Note that the tax is the same as the previous month, but columns 3, 6 and 8 are left blank. Also no account is taken of the £129.79 in column 8 for month 1.

ANSWERS TO ACTIVITIES

Chapter 8

Answer 8.1

(a) **Gary Lennox** is only 15 years old and so is not liable for Class 1 NICs.

   Trevor Owen is aged between 16 and 65 years of age but his earnings are below the Lower Earnings Limit. So he will no pay Class 1 NICs.

   Petra Brown is aged between 16 and 60 and her earnings exceed the LEL but are below the ET, so she will pay no Class 1 NICs. (You will need a P11 for her however.)

   Marsha Lewis had her sixtieth birthday two days before pay day. Therefore, she will pay no Class 1 NICs.

   Dilip Patel is liable to Class 1 NICs on (£1,250 – £395) = £855.

   Sandra Bell earns more than the UEL so she will pay Class 1 NICs at the full rate on the UEL less the ET, (£2,644 – £395) = £2,249, and at 1% on the pay over the UEL (£2,883.33 – £2,644) = £239.33.

(b) Young and Olde Ltd is not liable for employer's NIC on Gary Lennox's earnings because he is under 16, nor on Trevor Owen's or Petra Brown's earnings because they earn less than the ET. It must pay employer's NIC on **all** the earnings above the ET of the other three as there is no upper age limit or UEL for employer's NIC.

Answer 8.2

For NIC purposes, Gabrielle's earnings will comprise:

- Salary, including holiday pay **and before the deduction of her own pension contributions**.
- Overtime payments.
- Bonus, when paid.

Both Gabrielle and Jekyll Ltd will pay NICs on these items.

The employer's pension contributions, season ticket loan (provided that the loan is less than £5,000) and subsidised restaurant are ignored for NIC purposes.

The company car and medical insurance will not give rise to an NIC liability for Gabrielle, but Jekyll Ltd will have to pay Class 1A NICs on this benefit (dealt with in detail at NVQ/SVQ Level 3).

Answer 8.3

Name	Remarks	Table
Jerome Johnstone	Personal pension irrelevant; not contracted-out through employer's scheme	A
Finlay Mackay	Under 65 until 3.6.2005	D
Meredith Anderson		G
Joan Waters	Over 60, so she pays no NICs but Complex plc does	C
Paul Ingle	CA2700	J
Sylvia Chalmers		E
Ursula Wilson-Jones		B
Oliver Barnett	Over 65, so he is not liable for NICs; but Complex plc is	C
Oonagh O'Shaughnessy	Not reduced rate	F

Answer 8.4

Only Piers Smith's NICs involve any calculations. All the other entries are copied straight from Table A (Monthly Table). Did you remember to round *down* gross pay?

Employee	Earnings at the LEL (where earnings reach or exceed the LEL) 1a	Earnings above the LEL, up to and including the Earnings Threshold 1b	Earnings above the Earnings Threshold, up to and including the UEL 1c	Total of employees' and employer's contributions payable 1d	Total of employees' contributions payable 1e
Thomas Taylor	343	36	0	0.00	0.00
Stephanie Cheung	343	52	1,120	267.04	123.42
Lorna Campbell	343	52	204	49.03	22.66
Piers Smith	343	52	2,249	549.89	248.45

Working for Piers Smith

£2,750 – UEL £2,644 = £106 = Additional gross pay

		Total NICs due £	Employees' NICs £
From additional gross pay table, NICs due on	100	13.80	1.00
	6	0.83	0.06
		14.63	1.06
Total NICs due (from Table A)		535.26	247.39
		549.89	248.45

(**Check:** Employees' £248.45 + Employer's (£287.87 + £12.80 + £0.77) = £549.89.)

ANSWERS TO ACTIVITIES

Chapter 9

Answer 9.1

Points you should have spotted at once.

- *Arthur Adams* is over the state retirement age for men, so he has no liability for employees' NICs.
- *Beatrice Blair* is too young to pay NICs. No employer's NIC are due either.
- *Catherine Cross* is paying reduced rate contributions so you use the Table B rate for her NICs.
- *Dilys Dunn* earns too little to be liable for NICs. Her employer has no liability either. Her earnings are below the lower earnings limit.
- *Eric Edwards* and *Frederick Fellowes* are both Table A cases. Frederick's earnings exceed the UEL.

Arthur Adams

Employer's contributions only, Table C rates: (£125 – £91) × 12.8% = £4.35

Catherine Cross

	£
Table B: employees' NICs = (£181 – £91) × 4.85%	4.36
Employer's NICs (£181 – £91) × 12.8%	11.52
Total NICs payable	15.88

Eric Edwards

	£
Employees' NICs at Table A rates:	
(£202 – £91) × 11%	12.21
Employer's NICs (£202 – £91) × 12.8%	14.21
Total NICs payable	26.42

Frederick Fellowes

	£
Employees' NICs at Table A rates on earnings up to	
Upper Earnings Limit (£610 – £91) × 11%	57.09
Above UEL (£625 – £610) × 1%	0.15
Employer's NICs (no UEL): (£625 – £91) × 12.8%	68.35
Total NICs payable	125.59

ANSWERS TO ACTIVITIES

Answer 9.2

	Table	Earnings at the LEL (where earnings reach or exceed the LEL) 1a	Earnings above the LEL, up to and including the Earnings Threshold 1b	Earnings above the Earnings Threshold, up to and including the UEL 1c	Total of employees' and employer's contributions payable 1d	Total of employees' contributions payable on earnings above ET 1e
Bella Thomas	E	343	52	812	113.36	39.48
Muriel Thorne	F	343	52	1,052	222.10	98.25
Peter Abrams	L	343	52	496	48.64	4.15
Darcus Groves	F	343	52	2,249	481.10	210.99

Note. Only Darcus earns more than the UEL. You have to calculate the employees' and employer's NICs payable on the amount he has earned over the UEL.

	£
Total earnings	2,685.30
UEL	(2,644.00)
Additional gross pay	41.30

	Total employer's and employees' contributions £	Employees' contributions £
Per table F	475.44	210.58
Additional contributions on £41:	5.66	0.41
	481.10	210.99

Answer 9.3

	Last Month	This Month
Selina Harcourt	not applicable (not 16)	A
Brian Ellis	not applicable (below LEL)	D
David Deighton	A	D
Louise Wallis	E	B

ANSWERS TO ACTIVITIES

Chapter 10

Answer 10.1

(a) **Week 1**

	£
Net pay	150
Normal deduction	(30)
Leaves	120

This is the protected earnings rate and so the full deduction of £30 is made. Mr Hawk receives:

		£
Net pay		150
DEO deduction	Paid to CSA	(30)
Administrative fee	Kept by Dove Ltd	(1)
Take home pay		119

(b) **Week 2**

	£
Net pay	175
Normal deduction	(30)
Leaves	145

This exceeds the protected earnings rate and so full deduction is made. Mr Hawk receives:

	£
Net pay	175
DEO deduction	(30)
Administrative fee	(1)
Take home pay	144

(c) **Week 3**

	£
Net pay	120

As this is the protected earnings rate, no deduction is made. However, Dove Ltd can still take the administrative fee. Mr Hawk receives:

	£
Net pay	120
Administrative fee	(1)
Take home pay	119

The £30 not deducted is carried forward.

(d) **Week 4**

	£
Net pay	250
Normal deduction	(30)
B/f deduction	(30)
Leaves	190

This exceeds the protected earnings rate and so £60 is deducted this week. Mr Hawk receives:

ANSWERS TO ACTIVITIES

	£
Net pay	250
DEO deduction (weeks 3 & 4)	(60)
Administrative fee	(1)
Take home pay	189

Answer 10.2

	Horatio £	Letitia £
(a)	1,250.00	1,750.00
(b)	62.50	87.50
(c)	125.00	175.00

Answer 10.3

As he will still be under the 15% limit, Max is entitled to pay the extra pension contributions unless he is a very high earner. These will be classified as Additional Voluntary Contributions (AVCs).

He should, however, be aware of the earnings cap, if he is a high earner. This is £102,000 for 2004/05 and the maximum contributions each year which are eligible for tax relief are 15% of this figure.

Lump sum AVCs are also permissible, provided he keeps within the tax limits.

It would be good practice to advise Max:

- That he can also make **free-standing AVCs** to an external provider.
- To seek advice from an **independent financial adviser** or the **pension scheme administrator** so that he gets the full picture.

Answer 10.4

(a) There is no column for FSAVCs as these are private arrangements between the employee and the financial institution he or she deals with. The tax relief on those is obtained by the financial institution itself and the employee (if a higher rate taxpayer).

(b) Separate records of employee's contributions, employer's contributions and AVCs are kept for a number of reasons.

- There is a limit to the amount of tax relief that can be given. If the AVC means that more than 15% of the employee's earnings from employment are being used as pension contributions, the tax relief is restricted.

- Any financial institution to which the employee pays FSAVCs needs information about an employee's payments to operate the scheme.

ANSWERS TO ACTIVITIES

- The employee's basic contributions are noted as deductions on the employee's payslip, as are AVCs. The payroll accounting system might in that case treat each item separately. So that we can see how a total figure is made up, it is helpful to list the items separately.

- Such records are necessary to carry out the correct procedures where people leave the scheme.

- The employer's contributions are an additional payroll cost that needs to be entered in the financial accounts of the employer.

Answer 10.5

The answer is yes. However he must not be a controlling director (or have been one in 2003/04) and must not earn more than £30,000 (in either 2003/04 or 2004/05). Then he can invest a maximum of £3,600 pa gross in a stakeholder pension.

Answer 10.6

(a) Charlotte can pay up to 15% of her salary into the pension scheme. Since she is already paying 6% she can pay up to 9% more of her salary as AVCs. This is £2,160 per annum (£180 per month). The employer's contributions are irrelevant.

(b) The employer's contributions will not be refunded. The employee's contributions will be refunded net of 20% tax.

	£
Contributions	1,200
Less tax at 20%	240
Amount of cheque	960

(c) Marlene has two options:

- Transfer her pension contributions to a personal pension scheme at an agreed **transfer value**.
- **Freeze** the pension until retirement age.

She should seek advice on which option to choose from a financial adviser.

Answer 10.7

P11 box 2 £2,400 (£30,000 ÷ 12 = £2,500: deduct £100 GAYE from this.)

NIC earnings £2,500.

Answer 10.8

There's a lot of information to set out here.

	£
Salary: £27,000 ÷ 12	2,250.00
Less: GAYE donation	(60.00)
Pay in the month, as P11 box 2	2,190.00
Less free pay for month, as Table A	(354.09)
Taxable pay	1,835.91

Tax due this month:
Table B and subtraction table	383.49
NIC – Table A: employees' ((£2,250 – £395) × 11%)	204.05

	£	£
Gross pay		2,250.00
Tax	383.49	
NIC	204.05	
GAYE donation	60.00	
Advance of salary repaid	1,000.00	
SAYE	50.00	
Season ticket loan	50.00	
		1,747.54
Net pay		502.46

Tutorial note. Make sure you understand that taxable pay is £2,190 but NICable pay is £2,250.

Chapter 11

Answer 11.1

	Dr £	Cr £
Gross wages expense, administrative staff	102,531	
Gross wages expense, sales & marketing staff	226,704	
Gross wages expense, production staff	1,067,895	
Wages control		1,397,130
Employer's NIC expense	104,782	
Wages control		104,782
Employer's pension contributions expense	41,728	
Wages control		41,728
Wages control	79,588	
Pension fund creditor (£41,728 + £37,860)		79,588
Wages control	540,437	
PAYE & NIC creditor (£351,826 + £104,782 + £83,829)		540,437
Wages control	10,180	
GAYE creditor		10,180
Wages control	903,893	
Bank (asset)		903,893
Wages control	9,542	
Season ticket loans (asset)		9,542

WAGES CONTROL

	£		£
PAYE & NIC creditor	540,437	Gross wages expense	1,397,130
Pension fund creditor	79,588	Employer's NIC expense	104,782
GAYE creditor	10,180	Employer's pension	
Bank	903,893	contributions expense	41,728
Season ticket loans	9,542		
	1,543,640		1,543,640

Answer 11.2

WAGES CONTROL

	£		£
Inland revenue creditor		Gross wages (W1)	50,661
– tax	2,500	Employer's contributions – NIC	1,500
– NIC	2,500	Pension	1,800
Net pay	48,100	Medical Insurance	500
Pension fund	3,600	Inland revenue creditors	
GAYE	600	– SSP rebate (W2)	675
Medical Insurance	500	– SMP rebate (W2)	3,864
SAYE	1,200		
	59,000		59,000

Workings

1   *Gross pay*

	£
Gross salaries (excluding SSP and SMP)	50,000
SSP	1,000
SMP	4,200
	55,200
Less: SSP and SMP recoveries (W2)	(4,539)
	50,661

2   *NICs due and SSP/SMP recoveries*

	£
Employer's NICs	1,500
Employees' NICs	1,000
	2,500

	£
13% × £2,500	325
SSP paid	1,000
Recovery due	675
SMP recovery due: 92% × £4,200	3,864
	4,539

Note: Amount due to Inland Revenue is only £461 – see account below.

INLAND REVENUE

	£		£
Wages control – SSP recovery	675	Wages control – Tax	2,500
– SMP recovery	3,864	– NIC	2,500
Bal c/f	461		
	5,000		5,000
		Bal b/f	461

ANSWERS TO ACTIVITIES

Answer 11.3

Reasons why employees may prefer to be paid in cash

- It's what they're used to.
- They don't need to have a bank or building society account.
- They can spend some of their money straight away without waiting for a cheque to clear.
- They know how much they have been paid with absolute certainty.
- They can immediately give part of their wages to whoever does the housekeeping, even if that person does not have a bank or building society account.
- They may not trust banks or building societies, and/or perceive them as expensive.
- They get paid weekly (whereas cashless pay is more often monthly) and they find it easier to budget for a week at a time than a longer period.

Answer 11.4

MONARCH BUILDERS LTD												
NAME	NET WAGE		£20	£10	£5	£2	£1	50p	20p	10p	5p	2p	1p
	£	p											
Bigg	120	12	6							1		1	
Little	36	05	1	1	1		1				1		
Large	129	71	6		1	2		1	1				1
Small	87	04	4		1	1						2	
Stout	276	94	13	1	1		1	1	2			2	
Thynne	110	25	5	1					1		1		
Fatt	89	71	4		1	2		1	1				1
Skinnie	122	43	6			1			2			1	1
VALUE	972	25	£900	£30	£25	£12	£2	£1.50	£1.40	10p	10p	12p	3p
NUMBER	—		45	3	5	6	2	3	7	1	2	6	3

Note: As well as calculating each employee's note and coin requirements, you must **check** your calculations by making sure that the totals for each denomination add up to the total of net wages. In this case: £900 + £30 + £25 + £12 + £2 + £1.50 + £1.40 + £0.10 + £0.10 + £0.12 + £0.03 = £972.25.

Answer 11.5

- Gina seems likely to be **self-employed** as she works for several businesses. She should, therefore, be responsible for her own income tax and NICs. However it would be **good business practice** for her to provide an **invoice** with her **business name** and **address** on it. The Inland Revenue would certainly want these details if they ever **investigated** your company's affairs, so that they could ensure that Gina is declaring her income and paying tax. You should recommend this to the accounts department employee who authorises these payments.

- Jo should be asked to **sign a form** expressly authorising the payroll department to deduct the £100 advance from her net pay at the end of the month. It is always best to make arrangements like this crystal clear to avoid disputes.

- Lewis Taylor is a **casual worker**. As he is a full-time student, it is possible that he has no taxable income, but his part-time work may provide him with high enough earnings to be subject to tax and NICs. He should sign a receipt for his earnings, giving his name and address, as this will be needed to complete the year end returns for the Inland Revenue. If he knows his NI number, he should also provide that. His payment is too low to warrant setting up a deduction card for him.

Answer 11.6

This is a small workforce and as the company is new it will want to save as much money as possible on overheads. It will also be looking for a method of payment which will be acceptable to the employees and secure. A software company's employees are likely to be comfortable with new technology; the majority probably already have current accounts with banks or building societies.

Bearing all this in mind:

Payment by	Advantages	Disadvantages
Cash	• Employees get immediate access to pay	• Old fashioned • Time consuming • Expensive • Security risk to company and employees
Cheque	• More secure than cash • Simple system to set up and operate • Not too time consuming to operate in a small company, especially if cheques are printed automatically	• Risk of fraud and theft for company • Cheques can get lost • Delay for employees in getting cleared funds • More payments to follow through on bank statement • Not as modern as direct credit • Could mean high bank charges

ANSWERS TO ACTIVITIES

Payment by	Advantages	Disadvantages
Direct Credit	• Up to date, projects right image for a software company • Quick • Secure • Hardware probably already in use in company • Integrates well with the rest of the accounting system • Helps cashflow management for company • Cleared funds on pay day for employees, even when off sick or on holiday	• Direct access could be expensive because of the cost of the BACSTEL link (a software company would probably have all the hardware needed) and the low number of payments • Indirect access might still be expensive compared with cheques

Assuming that a cost comparison shows that direct credit would be cheaper than cheque payment (or very little more expensive), this seems the best choice for this company. If it would be too expensive, then cheque payment would be much more satisfactory than cash payment.

Tax tables

Appendix I
Taxable pay tables

APPENDIX I: TAXABLE PAY TABLES

Tables SR + B to D (May 2004)

Taxable Pay Tables
Manual method

Keep using
Tables A 1993 issue - Pay Adjustment Tables

Use from 18 May 2004

Try the Calculator Tables — you may find them easier to use

TAX TABLES

Annual Rates

Tax Rates

Starting Rate	10% up to	£2,020	
Basic Rate	22% from	£2,021 to	£31,400
Higher Rate	40% over	£31,400	

Finding out which Table to use

Please ensure that you have disposed of your previous Tax Tables.

Code BR   **always** use Table B on pages 8 and 9.

Code D0   **always** use Table D on page 11.

Week 1/Month 1 Codes **always** use the first line, against '1', in the column headed Week/Month.

The Calculator Tables are printed separately. You may find these easier to use, but you will need a calculator.

You will get both sets of Tables with your *Employer's Budget Pack*, on the Employer's CD-ROM, or you can get them from the Employer's Orderline.

Monthly paid

Month	Column SR Use Table SR on page 5 £	Column B Use Tables B on pages 8 and 9 £
1	169	2617
2	337	5234
3	505	7850
4	674	10467
5	842	13084
6	1010	15700
7	1179	18317
8	1347	20934
9	1515	23550
10	1684	26167
11	1852	28784
12	2020	31400

If you do your payroll on a monthly basis use this table. If it's weekly use the table on page 4.

- Work out which month the pay is for – there is a chart on page 21 of the Help Book E13, *Day-to-day payroll*.
- Pick the month you need from the month column in the table. Look at the figures in Columns SR and B.
- Is your employee's total taxable pay to date **less than or equal to** the figure in Column SR? If so, use Table SR on page 5.
- Is your employee's total taxable pay to date **greater** than the figure in Column SR, **but less than or equal to** the figure in Column B? If it is use Tables B on pages 8 and 9.
- If your employee's total taxable pay to date is **more** than the amount in Column B, use Tables C and D on pages 10 and 11.

Example 1

You are working out the tax due for Month 5. Your employee's total taxable pay to date is £853 which is **more** than £842 in Column SR but **less** than £13084 in Column B. So, as £853 falls between these two figures, use Tables B on pages 8 and 9.

Example 2

You are working out the tax due for Month 7. Your employee's total taxable pay to date is £19720 which is **more** than both £1179 in Column SR **and** £18317 in Column B. So, use Tables C and D on pages 10 and 11.

APPENDIX I: TAXABLE PAY TABLES

Weekly paid

Week	Column SR Use Table SR on page 5 £	Column B Use Tables B on pages 8 and 9 £
1	39	604
2	78	1208
3	117	1812
4	156	2416
5	195	3020
6	234	3624
7	272	4227
8	311	4831
9	350	5435
10	389	6039
11	428	6643
12	467	7247
13	505	7850
14	544	8454
15	583	9058
16	622	9662
17	661	10266
18	700	10870
19	739	11474
20	777	12077
21	816	12681
22	855	13285
23	894	13889
24	933	14493
25	972	15097
26	1010	15700
27	1049	16304
28	1088	16908
29	1127	17512
30	1166	18116
31	1205	18720
32	1244	19324
33	1282	19927
34	1321	20531
35	1360	21135
36	1399	21739
37	1438	22343
38	1477	22947
39	1515	23550
40	1554	24154
41	1593	24758
42	1632	25362
43	1671	25966
44	1710	26570
45	1749	27174
46	1787	27777
47	1826	28381
48	1865	28985
49	1904	29589
50	1943	30193
51	1982	30797
52	2020	31400

If you do your payroll on a weekly basis use this table. If it's monthly use the table on page 3.

- Work out which week the pay is for – there is a chart on page 21 of the Help Book E13, *Day-to-day payroll*.
- Pick the week you need from the week column in the table. Look at the figures in Columns SR and B.
- Is your employee's total taxable pay to date **less than or equal to** the figure in Column SR? If so, use Table SR on page 5.
- Is your employee's total taxable pay to date **greater** than the figure in Column SR, **but less than or equal to** the figure in Column B? If it is use Tables B on pages 8 and 9.
- If your employee's total taxable pay to date is **more** than the amount in Column B, use Tables C and D on pages 10 and 11.

Example 1

You are working out the tax due for Week 14. Your employee's total taxable pay to date is £853 which is **more** than £544 in Column SR but **less** than £8454 in Column B. So, as £853 falls between these two figures, use Tables B on pages 8 and 9.

Example 2

You are working out the tax due for Week 14. Your employee's total taxable pay to date is £19720 which is **more** than both £544 in Column SR **and** £8454 in Column B. So, use Tables C and D on pages 10 and 11.

TAX TABLES

Table SR to work out tax at 10%
Pages 3 and 4 tell you when to use this Table

Look at the Taxable Pay columns, these are shown in black. If your employee's exact amount of taxable pay is shown on it, look across to the figure next to it in brown. This is the tax due.

If the exact amount of taxable pay is not shown (in the black columns), use two of the black figures to reach the amount of taxable pay, rounded down to the nearest £1. Then add together the two brown figures to reach the amount of tax due.

Example

Taxable pay	£1,241.39
Round down to the nearest pound	£1,241
Look up £1200 in the black column 'Tax Due on Taxable Pay from £100 to £1900' =	£120.00
Look up £41 in the black column 'Tax Due on Taxable Pay from £1 to £99' +	£4.10
Total =	**£124.10**

Table SR

Tax Due on Taxable Pay from £100 to £2000		Tax Due on Taxable Pay from £1 to £99			
Total Taxable Pay to date £	Total Tax Due to date £	Total Taxable Pay to date £	Total Tax Due to date £	Total Taxable Pay to date £	Total Tax Due to date £
100	10.00	1	0.10	50	5.00
200	20.00	2	0.20	51	5.10
300	30.00	3	0.30	52	5.20
400	40.00	4	0.40	53	5.30
500	50.00	5	0.50	54	5.40
600	60.00	6	0.60	55	5.50
700	70.00	7	0.70	56	5.60
800	80.00	8	0.80	57	5.70
900	90.00	9	0.90	58	5.80
1000	100.00	10	1.00	59	5.90
1100	110.00	11	1.10	60	6.00
1200	120.00	12	1.20	61	6.10
1300	130.00	13	1.30	62	6.20
1400	140.00	14	1.40	63	6.30
1500	150.00	15	1.50	64	6.40
1600	160.00	16	1.60	65	6.50
1700	170.00	17	1.70	66	6.60
1800	180.00	18	1.80	67	6.70
1900	190.00	19	1.90	68	6.80
2000	200.00	20	2.00	69	6.90
		21	2.10	70	7.00
		22	2.20	71	7.10
		23	2.30	72	7.20
		24	2.40	73	7.30
		25	2.50	74	7.40
		26	2.60	75	7.50
		27	2.70	76	7.60
		28	2.80	77	7.70
		29	2.90	78	7.80
		30	3.00	79	7.90
		31	3.10	80	8.00
		32	3.20	81	8.10
		33	3.30	82	8.20
		34	3.40	83	8.30
		35	3.50	84	8.40
		36	3.60	85	8.50
		37	3.70	86	8.60
		38	3.80	87	8.70
		39	3.90	88	8.80
		40	4.00	89	8.90
		41	4.10	90	9.00
		42	4.20	91	9.10
		43	4.30	92	9.20
		44	4.40	93	9.30
		45	4.50	94	9.40
		46	4.60	95	9.50
		47	4.70	96	9.60
		48	4.80	97	9.70
		49	4.90	98	9.80
				99	9.90

APPENDIX I: TAXABLE PAY TABLES

Step 1 - This is a two step process, **Step 2** is on page 9. For **Code BR** use **Step 1** only.

Table B to work out tax at 22%   *Pages 3 and 4 tell you when to use these Tables*

Table B

Tax Due on Taxable Pay from £100 to £31,400

Total Taxable Pay to date £	Total Tax Due to date £	Total Taxable Pay to date £	Total Tax Due to date £	Total Taxable Pay to date £	Total Tax Due to date £	Total Taxable Pay to date £	Total Tax Due to date £	Total Taxable Pay to date £	Total Tax Due to date £	Total Taxable Pay to date £	Total Tax Due to date £
100	22.00	5600	1232.00	11100	2442.00	16600	3652.00	22100	4862.00	27600	6072.00
200	44.00	5700	1254.00	11200	2464.00	16700	3674.00	22200	4884.00	27700	6094.00
300	66.00	5800	1276.00	11300	2486.00	16800	3696.00	22300	4906.00	27800	6116.00
400	88.00	5900	1298.00	11400	2508.00	16900	3718.00	22400	4928.00	27900	6138.00
500	110.00	6000	1320.00	11500	2530.00	17000	3740.00	22500	4950.00	28000	6160.00
600	132.00	6100	1342.00	11600	2552.00	17100	3762.00	22600	4972.00	28100	6182.00
700	154.00	6200	1364.00	11700	2574.00	17200	3784.00	22700	4994.00	28200	6204.00
800	176.00	6300	1386.00	11800	2596.00	17300	3806.00	22800	5016.00	28300	6226.00
900	198.00	6400	1408.00	11900	2618.00	17400	3828.00	22900	5038.00	28400	6248.00
1000	220.00	6500	1430.00	12000	2640.00	17500	3850.00	23000	5060.00	28500	6270.00
1100	242.00	6600	1452.00	12100	2662.00	17600	3872.00	23100	5082.00	28600	6292.00
1200	264.00	6700	1474.00	12200	2684.00	17700	3894.00	23200	5104.00	28700	6314.00
1300	286.00	6800	1496.00	12300	2706.00	17800	3916.00	23300	5126.00	28800	6336.00
1400	308.00	6900	1518.00	12400	2728.00	17900	3938.00	23400	5148.00	28900	6358.00
1500	330.00	7000	1540.00	12500	2750.00	18000	3960.00	23500	5170.00	29000	6380.00
1600	352.00	7100	1562.00	12600	2772.00	18100	3982.00	23600	5192.00	29100	6402.00
1700	374.00	7200	1584.00	12700	2794.00	18200	4004.00	23700	5214.00	29200	6424.00
1800	396.00	7300	1606.00	12800	2816.00	18300	4026.00	23800	5236.00	29300	6446.00
1900	418.00	7400	1628.00	12900	2838.00	18400	4048.00	23900	5258.00	29400	6468.00
2000	440.00	7500	1650.00	13000	2860.00	18500	4070.00	24000	5280.00	29500	6490.00
2100	462.00	7600	1672.00	13100	2882.00	18600	4092.00	24100	5302.00	29600	6512.00
2200	484.00	7700	1694.00	13200	2904.00	18700	4114.00	24200	5324.00	29700	6534.00
2300	506.00	7800	1716.00	13300	2926.00	18800	4136.00	24300	5346.00	29800	6556.00
2400	528.00	7900	1738.00	13400	2948.00	18900	4158.00	24400	5368.00	29900	6578.00
2500	550.00	8000	1760.00	13500	2970.00	19000	4180.00	24500	5390.00	30000	6600.00
2600	572.00	8100	1782.00	13600	2992.00	19100	4202.00	24600	5412.00	30100	6622.00
2700	594.00	8200	1804.00	13700	3014.00	19200	4224.00	24700	5434.00	30200	6644.00
2800	616.00	8300	1826.00	13800	3036.00	19300	4246.00	24800	5456.00	30300	6666.00
2900	638.00	8400	1848.00	13900	3058.00	19400	4268.00	24900	5478.00	30400	6688.00
3000	660.00	8500	1870.00	14000	3080.00	19500	4290.00	25000	5500.00	30500	6710.00
3100	682.00	8600	1892.00	14100	3102.00	19600	4312.00	25100	5522.00	30600	6732.00
3200	704.00	8700	1914.00	14200	3124.00	19700	4334.00	25200	5544.00	30700	6754.00
3300	726.00	8800	1936.00	14300	3146.00	19800	4356.00	25300	5566.00	30800	6776.00
3400	748.00	8900	1958.00	14400	3168.00	19900	4378.00	25400	5588.00	30900	6798.00
3500	770.00	9000	1980.00	14500	3190.00	20000	4400.00	25500	5610.00	31000	6820.00
3600	792.00	9100	2002.00	14600	3212.00	20100	4422.00	25600	5632.00	31100	6842.00
3700	814.00	9200	2024.00	14700	3234.00	20200	4444.00	25700	5654.00	31200	6864.00
3800	836.00	9300	2046.00	14800	3256.00	20300	4466.00	25800	5676.00	31300	6886.00
3900	858.00	9400	2068.00	14900	3278.00	20400	4488.00	25900	5698.00	31400	6908.00
4000	880.00	9500	2090.00	15000	3300.00	20500	4510.00	26000	5720.00		
4100	902.00	9600	2112.00	15100	3322.00	20600	4532.00	26100	5742.00		
4200	924.00	9700	2134.00	15200	3344.00	20700	4554.00	26200	5764.00		
4300	946.00	9800	2156.00	15300	3366.00	20800	4576.00	26300	5786.00		
4400	968.00	9900	2178.00	15400	3388.00	20900	4598.00	26400	5808.00		
4500	990.00	10000	2200.00	15500	3410.00	21000	4620.00	26500	5830.00		
4600	1012.00	10100	2222.00	15600	3432.00	21100	4642.00	26600	5852.00		
4700	1034.00	10200	2244.00	15700	3454.00	21200	4664.00	26700	5874.00		
4800	1056.00	10300	2266.00	15800	3476.00	21300	4686.00	26800	5896.00		
4900	1078.00	10400	2288.00	15900	3498.00	21400	4708.00	26900	5918.00		
5000	1100.00	10500	2310.00	16000	3520.00	21500	4730.00	27000	5940.00		
5100	1122.00	10600	2332.00	16100	3542.00	21600	4752.00	27100	5962.00		
5200	1144.00	10700	2354.00	16200	3564.00	21700	4774.00	27200	5984.00		
5300	1166.00	10800	2376.00	16300	3586.00	21800	4796.00	27300	6006.00		
5400	1188.00	10900	2398.00	16400	3608.00	21900	4818.00	27400	6028.00		
5500	1210.00	11000	2420.00	16500	3630.00	22000	4840.00	27500	6050.00		

TAX TABLES

Step 2 - Subtraction Tables
to give Starting Rate Relief at 10%.

After you have used Tables B to work out the tax at 22% use the green Subtraction Tables below to give your employee the benefit of the 10% rate band.

Do not use the Subtraction Tables for codes BR and D0.

Find the month or week in which the pay day falls and **subtract** the amount shown to arrive at the tax due.

For Week 1/Month 1 codes subtract the amount shown for Week 1 or Month 1.

Table B
Tax Due on Taxable Pay from £1 to £99

Total Taxable Pay to date £	Total Tax Due to date £	Total Taxable Pay to date £	Total Tax Due to date £
1	0.22	51	11.22
2	0.44	52	11.44
3	0.66	53	11.66
4	0.88	54	11.88
5	1.10	55	12.10
6	1.32	56	12.32
7	1.54	57	12.54
8	1.76	58	12.76
9	1.98	59	12.98
10	2.20	60	13.20
11	2.42	61	13.42
12	2.64	62	13.64
13	2.86	63	13.86
14	3.08	64	14.08
15	3.30	65	14.30
16	3.52	66	14.52
17	3.74	67	14.74
18	3.96	68	14.96
19	4.18	69	15.18
20	4.40	70	15.40
21	4.62	71	15.62
22	4.84	72	15.84
23	5.06	73	16.06
24	5.28	74	16.28
25	5.50	75	16.50
26	5.72	76	16.72
27	5.94	77	16.94
28	6.16	78	17.16
29	6.38	79	17.38
30	6.60	80	17.60
31	6.82	81	17.82
32	7.04	82	18.04
33	7.26	83	18.26
34	7.48	84	18.48
35	7.70	85	18.70
36	7.92	86	18.92
37	8.14	87	19.14
38	8.36	88	19.36
39	8.58	89	19.58
40	8.80	90	19.80
41	9.02	91	20.02
42	9.24	92	20.24
43	9.46	93	20.46
44	9.68	94	20.68
45	9.90	95	20.90
46	10.12	96	21.12
47	10.34	97	21.34
48	10.56	98	21.56
49	10.78	99	21.78
50	11.00		

Tables B   Subtraction Tables

Employee paid at Monthly rates

Month	Amount to subtract £
1	20.21
2	40.41
3	60.60
4	80.81
5	101.01
6	121.20
7	141.41
8	161.61
9	181.80
10	202.01
11	222.21
12	242.40

Employee paid at Weekly rates

Week	Amount to subtract £
1	4.67
2	9.33
3	13.99
4	18.65
5	23.31
6	27.97
7	32.64
8	37.30
9	41.96
10	46.62
11	51.28
12	55.94
13	60.60
14	65.27
15	69.93
16	74.59
17	79.25
18	83.91
19	88.57
20	93.24
21	97.90
22	102.56
23	107.22
24	111.88
25	116.54
26	121.20
27	125.87
28	130.53
29	135.19
30	139.85
31	144.51
32	149.17
33	153.84
34	158.50
35	163.16
36	167.82
37	172.48
38	177.14
39	181.80
40	186.47
41	191.13
42	195.79
43	200.45
44	205.11
45	209.77
46	214.44
47	219.10
48	223.76
49	228.42
50	233.08
51	237.74
52	242.40

APPENDIX I: TAXABLE PAY TABLES

Table C

Pages 3 and 4 tell you when to use this Table

How to use Table C

Example

Employee's code is **431L**
The pay is in **Week 12**

Pay in the week		£745.00
Previous pay to date	+	£9,821.00
Total pay to date	=	£10,566.00
Less Pay Adjustment Table A figure at **Week 12**, code **431L**	−	£996.72
Total taxable pay to date	=	£9,569.28
Round down to the nearest pound		£9,569
Less amount in Column 1 for **Week 12**	−	£7,247
Excess to be taxed at 40%	=	£2,322

Tax due

Tax due on £7,247 per Column 2		£1,538.55
Tax due on £2,322 per Table D	+	£928.80
Total tax due	=	**£2,467.35**

Table C — Employee paid at Monthly rates

Month	Column 1 If total taxable pay to date exceeds £	Column 2 Total tax due to date £
1	2617	555.59
2	5234	1111.19
3	7850	1666.40
4	10467	2221.99
5	13084	2777.59
6	15700	3332.80
7	18317	3888.39
8	20934	4443.99
9	23550	4999.20
10	26167	5554.79
11	28784	6110.39
12	31400	6665.60

Add tax at 40% as shown in Table D on the amount by which the total taxable pay to date exceeds the figure in Column 1.

Table C — Employee paid at Weekly rates

Week	Column 1 If total taxable pay to date exceeds £	Column 2 Total tax due to date £
1	604	128.24
2	1208	256.49
3	1812	384.73
4	2416	512.98
5	3020	641.23
6	3624	769.47
7	4227	897.32
8	4831	1025.56
9	5435	1153.81
10	6039	1282.06
11	6643	1410.30
12	7247	1538.55
13	7850	1666.40
14	8454	1794.64
15	9058	1922.89
16	9662	2051.13
17	10266	2179.38
18	10870	2307.63
19	11474	2435.87
20	12077	2563.72
21	12681	2691.96
22	13285	2820.21
23	13889	2948.46
24	14493	3076.70
25	15097	3204.95
26	15700	3332.80
27	16304	3461.04
28	16908	3589.29
29	17512	3717.53
30	18116	3845.78
31	18720	3974.03
32	19324	4102.27
33	19927	4230.12
34	20531	4358.36
35	21135	4486.61
36	21739	4614.86
37	22343	4743.10
38	22947	4871.35
39	23550	4999.20
40	24154	5127.44
41	24758	5255.69
42	25362	5383.93
43	25966	5512.18
44	26570	5640.43
45	27174	5768.67
46	27777	5896.52
47	28381	6024.76
48	28985	6153.01
49	29589	6281.26
50	30193	6409.50
51	30797	6537.75
52	31400	6665.60

Add tax at 40% as shown in Table D on the amount by which the total taxable pay to date exceeds the figure in Column 1.

TAX TABLES

Table D Tax at 40%. Also to be used for Code D0

Pages 3 and 4 tell you when to use this Table

Table D

Taxable Pay £	Tax £	Taxable Pay £	Tax £	Taxable Pay £	Tax £	Taxable Pay £	Tax £
1	0.40	50	20.00	100	40.00	6100	2440.00
2	0.80	51	20.40	200	80.00	6200	2480.00
3	1.20	52	20.80	300	120.00	6300	2520.00
4	1.60	53	21.20	400	160.00	6400	2560.00
5	2.00	54	21.60	500	200.00	6500	2600.00
6	2.40	55	22.00	600	240.00	6600	2640.00
7	2.80	56	22.40	700	280.00	6700	2680.00
8	3.20	57	22.80	800	320.00	6800	2720.00
9	3.60	58	23.20	900	360.00	6900	2760.00
10	4.00	59	23.60	1000	400.00	7000	2800.00
11	4.40	60	24.00	1100	440.00	7100	2840.00
12	4.80	61	24.40	1200	480.00	7200	2880.00
13	5.20	62	24.80	1300	520.00	7300	2920.00
14	5.60	63	25.20	1400	560.00	7400	2960.00
15	6.00	64	25.60	1500	600.00	7500	3000.00
16	6.40	65	26.00	1600	640.00	7600	3040.00
17	6.80	66	26.40	1700	680.00	7700	3080.00
18	7.20	67	26.80	1800	720.00	7800	3120.00
19	7.60	68	27.20	1900	760.00	7900	3160.00
20	8.00	69	27.60	2000	800.00	8000	3200.00
21	8.40	70	28.00	2100	840.00	8100	3240.00
22	8.80	71	28.40	2200	880.00	8200	3280.00
23	9.20	72	28.80	2300	920.00	8300	3320.00
24	9.60	73	29.20	2400	960.00	8400	3360.00
25	10.00	74	29.60	2500	1000.00	8500	3400.00
26	10.40	75	30.00	2600	1040.00	8600	3440.00
27	10.80	76	30.40	2700	1080.00	8700	3480.00
28	11.20	77	30.80	2800	1120.00	8800	3520.00
29	11.60	78	31.20	2900	1160.00	8900	3560.00
30	12.00	79	31.60	3000	1200.00	9000	3600.00
31	12.40	80	32.00	3100	1240.00	9100	3640.00
32	12.80	81	32.40	3200	1280.00	9200	3680.00
33	13.20	82	32.80	3300	1320.00	9300	3720.00
34	13.60	83	33.20	3400	1360.00	9400	3760.00
35	14.00	84	33.60	3500	1400.00	9500	3800.00
36	14.40	85	34.00	3600	1440.00	9600	3840.00
37	14.80	86	34.40	3700	1480.00	9700	3880.00
38	15.20	87	34.80	3800	1520.00	9800	3920.00
39	15.60	88	35.20	3900	1560.00	9900	3960.00
40	16.00	89	35.60	4000	1600.00	10000	4000.00
41	16.40	90	36.00	4100	1640.00	20000	8000.00
42	16.80	91	36.40	4200	1680.00	30000	12000.00
43	17.20	92	36.80	4300	1720.00	40000	16000.00
44	17.60	93	37.20	4400	1760.00	50000	20000.00
45	18.00	94	37.60	4500	1800.00	60000	24000.00
46	18.40	95	38.00	4600	1840.00	70000	28000.00
47	18.80	96	38.40	4700	1880.00	80000	32000.00
48	19.20	97	38.80	4800	1920.00	90000	36000.00
49	19.60	98	39.20	4900	1960.00	100000	40000.00
		99	39.60	5000	2000.00	200000	80000.00
				5100	2040.00	300000	120000.00
				5200	2080.00	400000	160000.00
				5300	2120.00	500000	200000.00
				5400	2160.00	600000	240000.00
				5500	2200.00	700000	280000.00
				5600	2240.00	800000	320000.00
				5700	2280.00	900000	360000.00
				5800	2320.00	1000000	400000.00
				5900	2360.00		
				6000	2400.00		

Where the exact amount of taxable pay is not shown, add together the figures for two (or more) entries to make up the amount of taxable pay to the nearest £1 below.

APPENDIX I: TAXABLE PAY TABLES

Calculator Tables (May 2004)

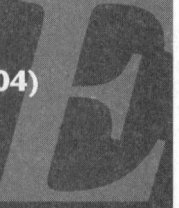

Taxable Pay Tables

Calculator Method

Alternative to Tables SR + B to D

Keep using
Tables A 1993 issue - Pay Adjustment Tables

Use from 18 May 2004

- Open out flat
- Use pages 2, 3 and 4 for weekly paid employees
- Use pages 5 and 6 for monthly paid employees

BS3/04

TAX TABLES

Weekly paid employees - use this side. Monthly paid employees - use pages 5 and 6 on the other side.

Using this booklet - weekly paid

The tables in this booklet will help you work out PAYE tax deductions with a calculator.

Round down taxable pay to the nearest pound.

Throughout these tables, 'Taxable Pay' means any amount of pay after you have used the *Pay Adjustment Tables, Tables A* and entered the amount in Column 5 of the *P11*.
For Codes D0 and BR round down whole pay to the nearest pound.

- For Code **D0** multiply the whole pay by **0.40 (40%)** to find the tax deduction at the Higher Rate.
- For Code **BR** multiply the whole pay by **0.22 (22%)** to find the tax deduction at the Basic Rate.
- For all other Codes follow the sections below in turn to calculate the tax deduction.
- For Codes on a **Week 1** basis, use the Week 1 figures for each calculation if the employee is paid weekly.

The Weekly chart below will help you work out which week number to use.
This is the same as the *P11* week number.

Weekly chart

Period	Week number	Period	Week number	Period	Week number	Period	Week number
6 Apr to 12 Apr	1	6 Jul to 12 Jul	14	5 Oct to 11 Oct	27	4 Jan to 10 Jan	40
13 Apr to 19 Apr	2	13 Jul to 19 Jul	15	12 Oct to 18 Oct	28	11 Jan to 17 Jan	41
20 Apr to 26 Apr	3	20 Jul to 26 Jul	16	19 Oct to 25 Oct	29	18 Jan to 24 Jan	42
27 Apr to 3 May	4	27 Jul to 2 Aug	17	26 Oct to 1 Nov	30	25 Jan to 31 Jan	43
4 May to 10 May	5	3 Aug to 9 Aug	18	2 Nov to 8 Nov	31	1 Feb to 7 Feb	44
11 May to 17 May	6	10 Aug to 16 Aug	19	9 Nov to 15 Nov	32	8 Feb to 14 Feb	45
18 May to 24 May	7	17 Aug to 23 Aug	20	16 Nov to 22 Nov	33	15 Feb to 21 Feb	46
25 May to 31 May	8	24 Aug to 30 Aug	21	23 Nov to 29 Nov	34	22 Feb to 28 Feb	47
1 Jun to 7 Jun	9	31 Aug to 6 Sep	22	30 Nov to 6 Dec	35	1 Mar to 7 Mar	48
8 Jun to 14 Jun	10	7 Sep to 13 Sep	23	7 Dec to 13 Dec	36	8 Mar to 14 Mar	49
15 Jun to 21 Jun	11	14 Sep to 20 Sep	24	14 Dec to 20 Dec	37	15 Mar to 21 Mar	50
22 Jun to 28 Jun	12	21 Sep to 27 Sep	25	21 Dec to 27 Dec	38	22 Mar to 28 Mar	51
29 Jun to 5 Jul	13	28 Sep to 4 Oct	26	28 Dec to 3 Jan	39	29 Mar to 4 Apr	52
						5 April *(use the table on a week 1 basis)*	53

Weekly paid - Calculator Tables

A   10% Starting Rate - weekly paid

Is the taxable pay figure in Column 5 of the *P11* more than the figure shown in Table SR, for the week you are currently working out?

Yes ▶ Go to **B** on page 3.

No ▶ Follow the steps below.

Step 1
Multiply the taxable pay figure in Column 5 on the *P11*, rounded down to the nearest whole pound, by 0.10 (10%).

Step 2
Enter this figure in Column 6 of the *P11*.

You can stop at this section.

Table SR

Week	Pay (£)	Week	Pay (£)	Week	Pay (£)
1	39	19	739	37	1438
2	78	20	777	38	1477
3	117	21	816	39	1515
4	156	22	855	40	1554
5	195	23	894	41	1593
6	234	24	933	42	1632
7	272	25	972	43	1671
8	311	26	1010	44	1710
9	350	27	1049	45	1749
10	389	28	1088	46	1787
11	428	29	1127	47	1826
12	467	30	1166	48	1865
13	505	31	1205	49	1904
14	544	32	1244	50	1943
15	583	33	1282	51	1982
16	622	34	1321	52	2020
17	661	35	1360		
18	700	36	1399		

APPENDIX I: TAXABLE PAY TABLES

B 22% Basic Rate - weekly paid

You should only be using this section if you have been directed here by **A** on page 2.

Is the taxable pay figure in Column 5 of the *P11* more than the figure shown in Table B, for the week you are currently working out?

Yes ▶ Go to **C** on page 4.

No ▶ Follow the steps below.

Step 1
Multiply the taxable pay figure in Column 5 on the *P11*, rounded down to the nearest whole pound, by 0.22 (22%).

Step 2
Then, **deduct** Starting Rate Relief from the table on the right ▶

Step 3
Enter this figure in Column 6 of the *P11*.

You can stop at this section.

Table B

Week	Pay (£)
1	604
2	1208
3	1812
4	2416
5	3020
6	3624
7	4227
8	4831
9	5435
10	6039
11	6643
12	7247
13	7850
14	8454
15	9058
16	9662
17	10266
18	10870
19	11474
20	12077
21	12681
22	13285
23	13889
24	14493
25	15097
26	15700
27	16304
28	16908
29	17512
30	18116
31	18720
32	19324
33	19927
34	20531
35	21135
36	21739
37	22343
38	22947
39	23550
40	24154
41	24758
42	25362
43	25966
44	26570
45	27174
46	27777
47	28381
48	28985
49	29589
50	30193
51	30797
52	31400

deduct Starting Rate Relief

Week	£
1	minus 4.67
2	minus 9.33
3	minus 13.99
4	minus 18.65
5	minus 23.31
6	minus 27.97
7	minus 32.64
8	minus 37.30
9	minus 41.96
10	minus 46.62
11	minus 51.28
12	minus 55.94
13	minus 60.60
14	minus 65.27
15	minus 69.93
16	minus 74.59
17	minus 79.25
18	minus 83.91
19	minus 88.57
20	minus 93.24
21	minus 97.90
22	minus 102.56
23	minus 107.22
24	minus 111.88
25	minus 116.54
26	minus 121.20
27	minus 125.87
28	minus 130.53
29	minus 135.19
30	minus 139.85
31	minus 144.51
32	minus 149.17
33	minus 153.84
34	minus 158.50
35	minus 163.16
36	minus 167.82
37	minus 172.48
38	minus 177.14
39	minus 181.80
40	minus 186.47
41	minus 191.13
42	minus 195.79
43	minus 200.45
44	minus 205.11
45	minus 209.77
46	minus 214.44
47	minus 219.10
48	minus 223.76
49	minus 228.42
50	minus 233.08
51	minus 237.74
52	minus 242.40

TAX TABLES

C 40% Higher Rate - weekly paid

You should only be using this section if you have been directed to **C** by following **B** on page 3.

Table C	
Week	Pay (£)
1	604
2	1208
3	1812
4	2416
5	3020
6	3624
7	4227
8	4831
9	5435
10	6039
11	6643
12	7247
13	7850
14	8454
15	9058
16	9662
17	10266
18	10870
19	11474
20	12077
21	12681
22	13285
23	13889
24	14493
25	15097
26	15700
27	16304
28	16908
29	17512
30	18116
31	18720
32	19324
33	19927
34	20531
35	21135
36	21739
37	22343
38	22947
39	23550
40	24154
41	24758
42	25362
43	25966
44	26570
45	27174
46	27777
47	28381
48	28985
49	29589
50	30193
51	30797
52	31400

Step 1
Deduct the figure in Table C from the taxable pay figure in Column 5 of the *P11* for the week you are currently working out. Round down the result to the nearest whole pound and keep a note of this figure.

Step 2
Multiply the result of **Step 1** by 0.40 (40%). This gives you the tax due on the part of the pay that is taxable at the higher rate.

Step 3
Add to this the tax due at the Starting and Basic Rates for the relevant week, from the table on the right ▶

Step 4
Enter this figure in Column 6 of the *P11*.

Tax due at Starting Rate and Basic Rate tax

Week		£
1	plus	128.24
2	plus	256.49
3	plus	384.73
4	plus	512.98
5	plus	641.23
6	plus	769.47
7	plus	897.32
8	plus	1025.56
9	plus	1153.81
10	plus	1282.06
11	plus	1410.30
12	plus	1538.55
13	plus	1666.40
14	plus	1794.64
15	plus	1922.89
16	plus	2051.13
17	plus	2179.38
18	plus	2307.63
19	plus	2435.87
20	plus	2563.72
21	plus	2691.96
22	plus	2820.21
23	plus	2948.46
24	plus	3076.70
25	plus	3204.95
26	plus	3332.80
27	plus	3461.04
28	plus	3589.29
29	plus	3717.53
30	plus	3845.78
31	plus	3974.03
32	plus	4102.27
33	plus	4230.12
34	plus	4358.36
35	plus	4486.61
36	plus	4614.86
37	plus	4743.10
38	plus	4871.35
39	plus	4999.20
40	plus	5127.44
41	plus	5255.69
42	plus	5383.93
43	plus	5512.18
44	plus	5640.43
45	plus	5768.67
46	plus	5896.52
47	plus	6024.76
48	plus	6153.01
49	plus	6281.26
50	plus	6409.50
51	plus	6537.75
52	plus	6665.60

APPENDIX I: TAXABLE PAY TABLES

Help
We can help you by telephone *(Calls may be recorded for quality and training purposes.)*
- New employers *(less than 3 years)* **0845 60 70 143**   open Mon – Fri, 8am-8pm and Sat – Sun, 8am-5pm.
- More experienced employers   **0845 7 143 143**   open Mon – Fri, 8am-8pm and Sat – Sun, 8am-5pm.
- Deaf or hard of hearing employers *Textphone* **0845 602 1380**

Monthly paid employees - use pages 5 and 6. Weekly paid employees - use pages 2, 3 and 4 on the other side.

Using this booklet - monthly paid
The tables in this booklet will help you work out PAYE tax deductions with a calculator.

Round down taxable pay to the nearest pound.

Throughout these tables, 'Taxable Pay' means any amount of pay after you have used the *Pay Adjustment Tables, Tables A* and entered the amount in Column 5 of the *P11*.
For Codes D0 and BR round down whole pay to the nearest pound.

- For Code **D0** multiply the whole pay by **0.40 (40%)** to find the tax deduction at the Higher Rate.
- For Code **BR** multiply the whole pay by **0.22 (22%)** to find the tax deduction at the Basic Rate.
- **For all other Codes follow the Sections below in turn to calculate the tax deduction.**
- For Codes on a **Month 1** basis, use the Month 1 figures for each calculation if the employee is paid monthly.

The Monthly chart below will help you work out which month number to use.
This is the same as the *P11* month number.

Monthly chart

Period	Month number	Period	Month number
6 April to 5 May	1	6 October to 5 November	7
6 May to 5 June	2	6 November to 5 December	8
6 June to 5 July	3	6 December to 5 January	9
6 July to 5 August	4	6 January to 5 February	10
6 August to 5 September	5	6 February to 5 March	11
6 September to 5 October	6	6 March to 5 April	12

Monthly paid - Calculator Tables

A   10% Starting Rate - monthly paid

Is the figure in Column 5 of the *P11* more than the taxable pay figure shown in Table SR, for the month you are currently working out?

Yes ▶ Go to **B** on page 6.

No ▶ Follow the steps below.

Step 1
Multiply the taxable pay figure in Column 5 on the *P11*, rounded down to the nearest whole pound, by 0.10 (10%).

Step 2
Enter this figure in Column 6 of the *P11*.
You can stop at this section.

Table SR

Month	Pay (£)
1	169
2	337
3	505
4	674
5	842
6	1010
7	1179
8	1347
9	1515
10	1684
11	1852
12	2020

5

TAX TABLES

B 22% Basic Rate - monthly paid

You should only be using this section if you have been directed here by **A** on page 5.

Is the taxable pay figure in Column 5 of the *P11* more than the figure shown in Table B, for the month you are currently working out?

Table B

Month	Pay (£)
1	2617
2	5234
3	7850
4	10467
5	13084
6	15700
7	18317
8	20934
9	23550
10	26167
11	28784
12	31400

Yes ▶ Go to **C** below.

No ▶ Follow the steps below.

Step 1
Multiply the taxable pay figure in Column 5 on the *P11*, rounded down to the nearest whole pound, by 0.22 (22%).

Step 2
Then, **deduct** Starting Rate Relief from the table on the right ▶

Step 3
Enter this figure in Column 6 of the *P11*.

You can stop at this section.

deduct Starting Rate Relief

Month	£
1	minus 20.21
2	minus 40.41
3	minus 60.60
4	minus 80.81
5	minus 101.01
6	minus 121.20
7	minus 141.41
8	minus 161.61
9	minus 181.80
10	minus 202.01
11	minus 222.21
12	minus 242.40

C 40% Higher Rate - monthly paid

You should only be using this section if you have been directed to **C** by following **B** above.

Table C

Month	Pay (£)
1	2617
2	5234
3	7850
4	10467
5	13084
6	15700
7	18317
8	20934
9	23550
10	26167
11	28784
12	31400

Step 1
Deduct the figure in Table C from the taxable pay figure in Column 5 of the *P11* for the month you are currently working out. Round down the result to the nearest whole pound and keep a note of this figure.

Step 2
Multiply the result of **Step 1** by 0.40 (40%). This gives you the tax due on the part of the pay that is taxable at the higher rate.

Step 3
Add to this tax due at the Starting and Basic Rates for the relevant month, from the table on the right ▶

Step 4
Enter this figure in Column 6 of the *P11*.

Tax due at Starting Rate and Basic Rate tax

Month	£
1	plus 555.59
2	plus 1111.19
3	plus 1666.40
4	plus 2221.99
5	plus 2777.59
6	plus 3332.80
7	plus 3888.39
8	plus 4443.99
9	plus 4999.20
10	plus 5554.79
11	plus 6110.39
12	plus 6665.60

Appendix II
NI tables

APPENDIX II: NI TABLES

Inland Revenue

CA38
Not Contracted-out Tables

National Insurance contributions Tables A and J

Use from
6 April 2004 to
5 April 2005 inclusive

TAX TABLES

Earnings limits and NIC rates

Earnings limits	Employee's contribution — Contribution Table letter A	Employee's contribution — Contribution Table letter J	Employer's contribution — Contribution Table letters A and J
Below £79.00 weekly, or below £343.00 monthly, or below £4108.00 yearly	Nil	Nil	Nil
£79.00 to £91.00 weekly, or £343.00 to £395.00 monthly, or £4108.00 to £4745.00 yearly	0%	0%	0%
£91.01 to £610.00 weekly, or £395.01 to £2644.00 monthly, or £4745.01 to £31720.00 yearly	**11%** on earnings above the ET	**1%** on earnings above the ET	**12.8%** on earnings above the ET
Over £610.00 weekly, or over £2644.00 monthly, or over £31720.00 yearly	**11%** on earnings above the ET, up to and including the UEL, then 1% on all earnings above the UEL	**1%** on all earnings above the ET	**12.8%** on all earnings above the ET

APPENDIX II: NI TABLES

Weekly table for not contracted-out standard rate contributions for use from 6 April 2004 to 5 April 2005

Table letter **A**

Use this table for

- employees who are age 16 or over and under State Pension Age (65 for men, 60 for women)
- employees who have an Appropriate Personal Pension or Appropriate Personal Pension Stakeholder Pension.

Do not use this table for

- any year other than 2004-2005
- married women or widows who have the right to pay reduced rate employee's contributions, see Table B, in Leaflet CA41
- employees who are State Pension Age or over, see Table C, in Leaflet CA41
- employees for whom you hold form CA2700, see Table J.

Completing Deductions Working Sheet, form P11 or substitute

- enter 'A' in the space provided in the 'End of Year Summary' box of form P11
- copy the figures in columns 1a-1e of the table to columns 1a-1e of form P11 on the line next to the tax week in which the employee is paid.

If the employee's total earnings fall between the LEL and the UEL and the exact gross pay is not shown in the table, use the next smaller figure shown. If the employee's total earnings exceed the UEL, see page 52.

The figures in the left hand column of each table show steps between the LEL and the UEL. The NICs liability for each step is calculated at the mid-point of the steps so you and your employee may pay slightly more or less than if you used the exact percentage method.

▼ Employee's Earnings up to and including the UEL	Earnings at the LEL (where earnings are equal to or exceed the LEL)	Earnings above the LEL, up to and including the ET	Earnings above the ET, up to and including the UEL	Total of employee's and employer's contributions	Employee's contributions due on all earnings above the ET	▼ Employer's contributions
	1a	1b	1c	1d	1e	
£	£	£ P	£ P	£ P	£ P	£ P
Up to and including 78.99	No NIC Liability, make no entries on forms P11 and P14					
79	79	0.00	0.00	0.00	0.00	0.00
80	79	1.00	0.00	0.00	0.00	0.00
81	79	2.00	0.00	0.00	0.00	0.00
82	79	3.00	0.00	0.00	0.00	0.00
83	79	4.00	0.00	0.00	0.00	0.00
84	79	5.00	0.00	0.00	0.00	0.00
85	79	6.00	0.00	0.00	0.00	0.00
86	79	7.00	0.00	0.00	0.00	0.00
87	79	8.00	0.00	0.00	0.00	0.00
88	79	9.00	0.00	0.00	0.00	0.00
89	79	10.00	0.00	0.00	0.00	0.00
90	79	11.00	0.00	0.00	0.00	0.00
91	79	12.00	0.00	0.00	0.00	0.00
92	79	12.00	1.00	0.35	0.16	0.19
93	79	12.00	2.00	0.59	0.27	0.32
94	79	12.00	3.00	0.83	0.38	0.45
95	79	12.00	4.00	1.07	0.49	0.58
96	79	12.00	5.00	1.30	0.60	0.70
97	79	12.00	6.00	1.54	0.71	0.83
98	79	12.00	7.00	1.78	0.82	0.96
99	79	12.00	8.00	2.02	0.93	1.09
100	79	12.00	9.00	2.26	1.04	1.22
101	79	12.00	10.00	2.49	1.15	1.34
102	79	12.00	11.00	2.73	1.26	1.47
103	79	12.00	12.00	2.97	1.37	1.60
104	79	12.00	13.00	3.21	1.48	1.73
105	79	12.00	14.00	3.45	1.59	1.86
106	79	12.00	15.00	3.68	1.70	1.98
107	79	12.00	16.00	3.92	1.81	2.11
108	79	12.00	17.00	4.16	1.92	2.24

▼ for information only - do not enter on Deductions Working Sheet, form P11

TAX TABLES

Weekly table

Table letter **A**

▼ Employee's Earnings up to and including the UEL	Earnings at the LEL (where earnings are equal to or exceed the LEL)	Earnings above the LEL, up to and including the ET	Earnings above the ET, up to and including the UEL	Total of employee's and employer's contributions	Employee's contributions due on all earnings above the ET	▼ Employer's contributions
	1a	1b	1c	1d	1e	
£	£	£ P	£ P	£ P	£ P	£ P
109	79	12.00	18.00	4.40	2.03	2.37
110	79	12.00	19.00	4.64	2.14	2.50
111	79	12.00	20.00	4.87	2.25	2.62
112	79	12.00	21.00	5.11	2.36	2.75
113	79	12.00	22.00	5.35	2.47	2.88
114	79	12.00	23.00	5.59	2.58	3.01
115	79	12.00	24.00	5.83	2.69	3.14
116	79	12.00	25.00	6.06	2.80	3.26
117	79	12.00	26.00	6.30	2.91	3.39
118	79	12.00	27.00	6.54	3.02	3.52
119	79	12.00	28.00	6.78	3.13	3.65
120	79	12.00	29.00	7.02	3.24	3.78
121	79	12.00	30.00	7.25	3.35	3.90
122	79	12.00	31.00	7.49	3.46	4.03
123	79	12.00	32.00	7.73	3.57	4.16
124	79	12.00	33.00	7.97	3.68	4.29
125	79	12.00	34.00	8.21	3.79	4.42
126	79	12.00	35.00	8.44	3.90	4.54
127	79	12.00	36.00	8.68	4.01	4.67
128	79	12.00	37.00	8.92	4.12	4.80
129	79	12.00	38.00	9.16	4.23	4.93
130	79	12.00	39.00	9.40	4.34	5.06
131	79	12.00	40.00	9.63	4.45	5.18
132	79	12.00	41.00	9.87	4.56	5.31
133	79	12.00	42.00	10.11	4.67	5.44
134	79	12.00	43.00	10.35	4.78	5.57
135	79	12.00	44.00	10.59	4.89	5.70
136	79	12.00	45.00	10.82	5.00	5.82
137	79	12.00	46.00	11.06	5.11	5.95
138	79	12.00	47.00	11.30	5.22	6.08
139	79	12.00	48.00	11.54	5.33	6.21
140	79	12.00	49.00	11.78	5.44	6.34
141	79	12.00	50.00	12.01	5.55	6.46
142	79	12.00	51.00	12.25	5.66	6.59
143	79	12.00	52.00	12.49	5.77	6.72
144	79	12.00	53.00	12.73	5.88	6.85
145	79	12.00	54.00	12.97	5.99	6.98
146	79	12.00	55.00	13.20	6.10	7.10
147	79	12.00	56.00	13.44	6.21	7.23
148	79	12.00	57.00	13.68	6.32	7.36
149	79	12.00	58.00	13.92	6.43	7.49
150	79	12.00	59.00	14.16	6.54	7.62
151	79	12.00	60.00	14.39	6.65	7.74
152	79	12.00	61.00	14.63	6.76	7.87
153	79	12.00	62.00	14.87	6.87	8.00
154	79	12.00	63.00	15.11	6.98	8.13
155	79	12.00	64.00	15.35	7.09	8.26
156	79	12.00	65.00	15.58	7.20	8.38
157	79	12.00	66.00	15.82	7.31	8.51
158	79	12.00	67.00	16.06	7.42	8.64
159	79	12.00	68.00	16.30	7.53	8.77
160	79	12.00	69.00	16.54	7.64	8.90
161	79	12.00	70.00	16.77	7.75	9.02
162	79	12.00	71.00	17.01	7.86	9.15
163	79	12.00	72.00	17.25	7.97	9.28

▼ for information only - do not enter on Deductions Working Sheet, form P11

APPENDIX II: NI TABLES

Table letter A   **Weekly table**

▼ Employee's Earnings up to and including the UEL	Earnings at the LEL (where earnings are equal to or exceed the LEL) 1a	Earnings above the LEL, up to and including the ET 1b	Earnings above the ET, up to and including the UEL 1c	Total of employee's and employer's contributions 1d	Employee's contributions due on all earnings above the ET 1e	▼ Employer's contributions
£	£	£ P	£ P	£ P	£ P	£ P
164	79	12.00	73.00	17.49	8.08	9.41
165	79	12.00	74.00	17.73	8.19	9.54
166	79	12.00	75.00	17.96	8.30	9.66
167	79	12.00	76.00	18.20	8.41	9.79
168	79	12.00	77.00	18.44	8.52	9.92
169	79	12.00	78.00	18.68	8.63	10.05
170	79	12.00	79.00	18.92	8.74	10.18
171	79	12.00	80.00	19.15	8.85	10.30
172	79	12.00	81.00	19.39	8.96	10.43
173	79	12.00	82.00	19.63	9.07	10.56
174	79	12.00	83.00	19.87	9.18	10.69
175	79	12.00	84.00	20.11	9.29	10.82
176	79	12.00	85.00	20.34	9.40	10.94
177	79	12.00	86.00	20.58	9.51	11.07
178	79	12.00	87.00	20.82	9.62	11.20
179	79	12.00	88.00	21.06	9.73	11.33
180	79	12.00	89.00	21.30	9.84	11.46
181	79	12.00	90.00	21.53	9.95	11.58
182	79	12.00	91.00	21.77	10.06	11.71
183	79	12.00	92.00	22.01	10.17	11.84
184	79	12.00	93.00	22.25	10.28	11.97
185	79	12.00	94.00	22.49	10.39	12.10
186	79	12.00	95.00	22.72	10.50	12.22
187	79	12.00	96.00	22.96	10.61	12.35
188	79	12.00	97.00	23.20	10.72	12.48
189	79	12.00	98.00	23.44	10.83	12.61
190	79	12.00	99.00	23.68	10.94	12.74
191	79	12.00	100.00	23.91	11.05	12.86
192	79	12.00	101.00	24.15	11.16	12.99
193	79	12.00	102.00	24.39	11.27	13.12
194	79	12.00	103.00	24.63	11.38	13.25
195	79	12.00	104.00	24.87	11.49	13.38
196	79	12.00	105.00	25.10	11.60	13.50
197	79	12.00	106.00	25.34	11.71	13.63
198	79	12.00	107.00	25.58	11.82	13.76
199	79	12.00	108.00	25.82	11.93	13.89
200	79	12.00	109.00	26.06	12.04	14.02
201	79	12.00	110.00	26.29	12.15	14.14
202	79	12.00	111.00	26.53	12.26	14.27
203	79	12.00	112.00	26.77	12.37	14.40
204	79	12.00	113.00	27.01	12.48	14.53
205	79	12.00	114.00	27.25	12.59	14.66
206	79	12.00	115.00	27.48	12.70	14.78
207	79	12.00	116.00	27.72	12.81	14.91
208	79	12.00	117.00	27.96	12.92	15.04
209	79	12.00	118.00	28.20	13.03	15.17
210	79	12.00	119.00	28.44	13.14	15.30
211	79	12.00	120.00	28.67	13.25	15.42
212	79	12.00	121.00	28.91	13.36	15.55
213	79	12.00	122.00	29.15	13.47	15.68
214	79	12.00	123.00	29.39	13.58	15.81
215	79	12.00	124.00	29.63	13.69	15.94
216	79	12.00	125.00	29.86	13.80	16.06
217	79	12.00	126.00	30.10	13.91	16.19
218	79	12.00	127.00	30.34	14.02	16.32

▼ for information only - do not enter on Deductions Working Sheet, form P11

TAX TABLES

Weekly table

Table letter **A**

Employee's Earnings up to and including the UEL	Earnings at the LEL (where earnings are equal to or exceed the LEL)	Earnings above the LEL, up to and including the ET	Earnings above the ET, up to and including the UEL	Total of employee's and employer's contributions	Employee's contributions due on all earnings above the ET	Employer's contributions
	1a	1b	1c	1d	1e	
£	£	£ P	£ P	£ P	£ P	£ P
219	79	12.00	128.00	30.58	14.13	16.45
220	79	12.00	129.00	30.82	14.24	16.58
221	79	12.00	130.00	31.05	14.35	16.70
222	79	12.00	131.00	31.29	14.46	16.83
223	79	12.00	132.00	31.53	14.57	16.96
224	79	12.00	133.00	31.77	14.68	17.09
225	79	12.00	134.00	32.01	14.79	17.22
226	79	12.00	135.00	32.24	14.90	17.34
227	79	12.00	136.00	32.48	15.01	17.47
228	79	12.00	137.00	32.72	15.12	17.60
229	79	12.00	138.00	32.96	15.23	17.73
230	79	12.00	139.00	33.20	15.34	17.86
231	79	12.00	140.00	33.43	15.45	17.98
232	79	12.00	141.00	33.67	15.56	18.11
233	79	12.00	142.00	33.91	15.67	18.24
234	79	12.00	143.00	34.15	15.78	18.37
235	79	12.00	144.00	34.39	15.89	18.50
236	79	12.00	145.00	34.62	16.00	18.62
237	79	12.00	146.00	34.86	16.11	18.75
238	79	12.00	147.00	35.10	16.22	18.88
239	79	12.00	148.00	35.34	16.33	19.01
240	79	12.00	149.00	35.58	16.44	19.14
241	79	12.00	150.00	35.81	16.55	19.26
242	79	12.00	151.00	36.05	16.66	19.39
243	79	12.00	152.00	36.29	16.77	19.52
244	79	12.00	153.00	36.53	16.88	19.65
245	79	12.00	154.00	36.77	16.99	19.78
246	79	12.00	155.00	37.00	17.10	19.90
247	79	12.00	156.00	37.24	17.21	20.03
248	79	12.00	157.00	37.48	17.32	20.16
249	79	12.00	158.00	37.72	17.43	20.29
250	79	12.00	159.00	37.96	17.54	20.42
251	79	12.00	160.00	38.19	17.65	20.54
252	79	12.00	161.00	38.43	17.76	20.67
253	79	12.00	162.00	38.67	17.87	20.80
254	79	12.00	163.00	38.91	17.98	20.93
255	79	12.00	164.00	39.15	18.09	21.06
256	79	12.00	165.00	39.38	18.20	21.18
257	79	12.00	166.00	39.62	18.31	21.31
258	79	12.00	167.00	39.86	18.42	21.44
259	79	12.00	168.00	40.10	18.53	21.57
260	79	12.00	169.00	40.34	18.64	21.70
261	79	12.00	170.00	40.57	18.75	21.82
262	79	12.00	171.00	40.81	18.86	21.95
263	79	12.00	172.00	41.05	18.97	22.08
264	79	12.00	173.00	41.29	19.08	22.21
265	79	12.00	174.00	41.53	19.19	22.34
266	79	12.00	175.00	41.76	19.30	22.46
267	79	12.00	176.00	42.00	19.41	22.59
268	79	12.00	177.00	42.24	19.52	22.72
269	79	12.00	178.00	42.48	19.63	22.85
270	79	12.00	179.00	42.72	19.74	22.98
271	79	12.00	180.00	42.95	19.85	23.10
272	79	12.00	181.00	43.19	19.96	23.23
273	79	12.00	182.00	43.43	20.07	23.36

▼ for information only - do not enter on Deductions Working Sheet, form P11

APPENDIX II: NI TABLES

Table letter A **Weekly table**

Employee's Earnings up to and including the UEL	Earnings at the LEL (where earnings are equal to or exceed the LEL) 1a	Earnings above the LEL, up to and including the ET 1b	Earnings above the ET, up to and including the UEL 1c	Total of employee's and employer's contributions 1d	Employee's contributions due on all earnings above the ET 1e	Employer's contributions
£	£	£ P	£ P	£ P	£ P	£ P
274	79	12.00	183.00	43.67	20.18	23.49
275	79	12.00	184.00	43.91	20.29	23.62
276	79	12.00	185.00	44.14	20.40	23.74
277	79	12.00	186.00	44.38	20.51	23.87
278	79	12.00	187.00	44.62	20.62	24.00
279	79	12.00	188.00	44.86	20.73	24.13
280	79	12.00	189.00	45.10	20.84	24.26
281	79	12.00	190.00	45.33	20.95	24.38
282	79	12.00	191.00	45.57	21.06	24.51
283	79	12.00	192.00	45.81	21.17	24.64
284	79	12.00	193.00	46.05	21.28	24.77
285	79	12.00	194.00	46.29	21.39	24.90
286	79	12.00	195.00	46.52	21.50	25.02
287	79	12.00	196.00	46.76	21.61	25.15
288	79	12.00	197.00	47.00	21.72	25.28
289	79	12.00	198.00	47.24	21.83	25.41
290	79	12.00	199.00	47.48	21.94	25.54
291	79	12.00	200.00	47.71	22.05	25.66
292	79	12.00	201.00	47.95	22.16	25.79
293	79	12.00	202.00	48.19	22.27	25.92
294	79	12.00	203.00	48.43	22.38	26.05
295	79	12.00	204.00	48.67	22.49	26.18
296	79	12.00	205.00	48.90	22.60	26.30
297	79	12.00	206.00	49.14	22.71	26.43
298	79	12.00	207.00	49.38	22.82	26.56
299	79	12.00	208.00	49.62	22.93	26.69
300	79	12.00	209.00	49.86	23.04	26.82
301	79	12.00	210.00	50.09	23.15	26.94
302	79	12.00	211.00	50.33	23.26	27.07
303	79	12.00	212.00	50.57	23.37	27.20
304	79	12.00	213.00	50.81	23.48	27.33
305	79	12.00	214.00	51.05	23.59	27.46
306	79	12.00	215.00	51.28	23.70	27.58
307	79	12.00	216.00	51.52	23.81	27.71
308	79	12.00	217.00	51.76	23.92	27.84
309	79	12.00	218.00	52.00	24.03	27.97
310	79	12.00	219.00	52.24	24.14	28.10
311	79	12.00	220.00	52.47	24.25	28.22
312	79	12.00	221.00	52.71	24.36	28.35
313	79	12.00	222.00	52.95	24.47	28.48
314	79	12.00	223.00	53.19	24.58	28.61
315	79	12.00	224.00	53.43	24.69	28.74
316	79	12.00	225.00	53.66	24.80	28.86
317	79	12.00	226.00	53.90	24.91	28.99
318	79	12.00	227.00	54.14	25.02	29.12
319	79	12.00	228.00	54.38	25.13	29.25
320	79	12.00	229.00	54.62	25.24	29.38
321	79	12.00	230.00	54.85	25.35	29.50
322	79	12.00	231.00	55.09	25.46	29.63
323	79	12.00	232.00	55.33	25.57	29.76
324	79	12.00	233.00	55.57	25.68	29.89
325	79	12.00	234.00	55.81	25.79	30.02
326	79	12.00	235.00	56.04	25.90	30.14
327	79	12.00	236.00	56.28	26.01	30.27
328	79	12.00	237.00	56.52	26.12	30.40

▼ for information only - do not enter on Deductions Working Sheet, form P11

TAX TABLES

Weekly table Table letter **A**

Employee's Earnings up to and including the UEL	Earnings at the LEL (where earnings are equal to or exceed the LEL)	Earnings above the LEL, up to and including the ET	Earnings above the ET, up to and including the UEL	Total of employee's and employer's contributions	Employee's contributions due on all earnings above the ET	Employer's contributions
		1a	1b	1c	1d	1e
£	£	£ P	£ P	£ P	£ P	£ P
329	79	12.00	238.00	56.76	26.23	30.53
330	79	12.00	239.00	57.00	26.34	30.66
331	79	12.00	240.00	57.23	26.45	30.78
332	79	12.00	241.00	57.47	26.56	30.91
333	79	12.00	242.00	57.71	26.67	31.04
334	79	12.00	243.00	57.95	26.78	31.17
335	79	12.00	244.00	58.19	26.89	31.30
336	79	12.00	245.00	58.42	27.00	31.42
337	79	12.00	246.00	58.66	27.11	31.55
338	79	12.00	247.00	58.90	27.22	31.68
339	79	12.00	248.00	59.14	27.33	31.81
340	79	12.00	249.00	59.38	27.44	31.94
341	79	12.00	250.00	59.61	27.55	32.06
342	79	12.00	251.00	59.85	27.66	32.19
343	79	12.00	252.00	60.09	27.77	32.32
344	79	12.00	253.00	60.33	27.88	32.45
345	79	12.00	254.00	60.57	27.99	32.58
346	79	12.00	255.00	60.80	28.10	32.70
347	79	12.00	256.00	61.04	28.21	32.83
348	79	12.00	257.00	61.28	28.32	32.96
349	79	12.00	258.00	61.52	28.43	33.09
350	79	12.00	259.00	61.76	28.54	33.22
351	79	12.00	260.00	61.99	28.65	33.34
352	79	12.00	261.00	62.23	28.76	33.47
353	79	12.00	262.00	62.47	28.87	33.60
354	79	12.00	263.00	62.71	28.98	33.73
355	79	12.00	264.00	62.95	29.09	33.86
356	79	12.00	265.00	63.18	29.20	33.98
357	79	12.00	266.00	63.42	29.31	34.11
358	79	12.00	267.00	63.66	29.42	34.24
359	79	12.00	268.00	63.90	29.53	34.37
360	79	12.00	269.00	64.14	29.64	34.50
361	79	12.00	270.00	64.37	29.75	34.62
362	79	12.00	271.00	64.61	29.86	34.75
363	79	12.00	272.00	64.85	29.97	34.88
364	79	12.00	273.00	65.09	30.08	35.01
365	79	12.00	274.00	65.33	30.19	35.14
366	79	12.00	275.00	65.56	30.30	35.26
367	79	12.00	276.00	65.80	30.41	35.39
368	79	12.00	277.00	66.04	30.52	35.52
369	79	12.00	278.00	66.28	30.63	35.65
370	79	12.00	279.00	66.52	30.74	35.78
371	79	12.00	280.00	66.75	30.85	35.90
372	79	12.00	281.00	66.99	30.96	36.03
373	79	12.00	282.00	67.23	31.07	36.16
374	79	12.00	283.00	67.47	31.18	36.29
375	79	12.00	284.00	67.71	31.29	36.42
376	79	12.00	285.00	67.94	31.40	36.54
377	79	12.00	286.00	68.18	31.51	36.67
378	79	12.00	287.00	68.42	31.62	36.80
379	79	12.00	288.00	68.66	31.73	36.93
380	79	12.00	289.00	68.90	31.84	37.06
381	79	12.00	290.00	69.13	31.95	37.18
382	79	12.00	291.00	69.37	32.06	37.31
383	79	12.00	292.00	69.61	32.17	37.44

▼ for information only - do not enter on Deductions Working Sheet, form P11

13

APPENDIX II: NI TABLES

Table letter A **Weekly table**

Employee's Earnings up to and including the UEL ▼	Earnings at the LEL (where earnings are equal to or exceed the LEL) 1a	Earnings above the LEL, up to and including the ET 1b	Earnings above the ET, up to and including the UEL 1c	Total of employee's and employer's contributions 1d	Employee's contributions due on all earnings above the ET 1e	Employer's contributions ▼
£	£	£ P	£ P	£ P	£ P	£ P
384	79	12.00	293.00	69.85	32.28	37.57
385	79	12.00	294.00	70.09	32.39	37.70
386	79	12.00	295.00	70.32	32.50	37.82
387	79	12.00	296.00	70.56	32.61	37.95
388	79	12.00	297.00	70.80	32.72	38.08
389	79	12.00	298.00	71.04	32.83	38.21
390	79	12.00	299.00	71.28	32.94	38.34
391	79	12.00	300.00	71.51	33.05	38.46
392	79	12.00	301.00	71.75	33.16	38.59
393	79	12.00	302.00	71.99	33.27	38.72
394	79	12.00	303.00	72.23	33.38	38.85
395	79	12.00	304.00	72.47	33.49	38.98
396	79	12.00	305.00	72.70	33.60	39.10
397	79	12.00	306.00	72.94	33.71	39.23
398	79	12.00	307.00	73.18	33.82	39.36
399	79	12.00	308.00	73.42	33.93	39.49
400	79	12.00	309.00	73.66	34.04	39.62
401	79	12.00	310.00	73.89	34.15	39.74
402	79	12.00	311.00	74.13	34.26	39.87
403	79	12.00	312.00	74.37	34.37	40.00
404	79	12.00	313.00	74.61	34.48	40.13
405	79	12.00	314.00	74.85	34.59	40.26
406	79	12.00	315.00	75.08	34.70	40.38
407	79	12.00	316.00	75.32	34.81	40.51
408	79	12.00	317.00	75.56	34.92	40.64
409	79	12.00	318.00	75.80	35.03	40.77
410	79	12.00	319.00	76.04	35.14	40.90
411	79	12.00	320.00	76.27	35.25	41.02
412	79	12.00	321.00	76.51	35.36	41.15
413	79	12.00	322.00	76.75	35.47	41.28
414	79	12.00	323.00	76.99	35.58	41.41
415	79	12.00	324.00	77.23	35.69	41.54
416	79	12.00	325.00	77.46	35.80	41.66
417	79	12.00	326.00	77.70	35.91	41.79
418	79	12.00	327.00	77.94	36.02	41.92
419	79	12.00	328.00	78.18	36.13	42.05
420	79	12.00	329.00	78.42	36.24	42.18
421	79	12.00	330.00	78.65	36.35	42.30
422	79	12.00	331.00	78.89	36.46	42.43
423	79	12.00	332.00	79.13	36.57	42.56
424	79	12.00	333.00	79.37	36.68	42.69
425	79	12.00	334.00	79.61	36.79	42.82
426	79	12.00	335.00	79.84	36.90	42.94
427	79	12.00	336.00	80.08	37.01	43.07
428	79	12.00	337.00	80.32	37.12	43.20
429	79	12.00	338.00	80.56	37.23	43.33
430	79	12.00	339.00	80.80	37.34	43.46
431	79	12.00	340.00	81.03	37.45	43.58
432	79	12.00	341.00	81.27	37.56	43.71
433	79	12.00	342.00	81.51	37.67	43.84
434	79	12.00	343.00	81.75	37.78	43.97
435	79	12.00	344.00	81.99	37.89	44.10
436	79	12.00	345.00	82.22	38.00	44.22
437	79	12.00	346.00	82.46	38.11	44.35
438	79	12.00	347.00	82.70	38.22	44.48

▼ for information only - do not enter on Deductions Working Sheet, form P11

TAX TABLES

Weekly table Table letter **A**

Employee's Earnings up to and including the UEL	Earnings at the LEL (where earnings are equal to or exceed the LEL) 1a	Earnings above the LEL, up to and including the ET 1b	Earnings above the ET, up to and including the UEL 1c	Total of employee's and employer's contributions 1d	Employee's contributions due on all earnings above the ET 1e	▼ Employer's contributions
£	£	£ P	£ P	£ P	£ P	£ P
439	79	12.00	348.00	82.94	38.33	44.61
440	79	12.00	349.00	83.18	38.44	44.74
441	79	12.00	350.00	83.41	38.55	44.86
442	79	12.00	351.00	83.65	38.66	44.99
443	79	12.00	352.00	83.89	38.77	45.12
444	79	12.00	353.00	84.13	38.88	45.25
445	79	12.00	354.00	84.37	38.99	45.38
446	79	12.00	355.00	84.60	39.10	45.50
447	79	12.00	356.00	84.84	39.21	45.63
448	79	12.00	357.00	85.08	39.32	45.76
449	79	12.00	358.00	85.32	39.43	45.89
450	79	12.00	359.00	85.56	39.54	46.02
451	79	12.00	360.00	85.79	39.65	46.14
452	79	12.00	361.00	86.03	39.76	46.27
453	79	12.00	362.00	86.27	39.87	46.40
454	79	12.00	363.00	86.51	39.98	46.53
455	79	12.00	364.00	86.75	40.09	46.66
456	79	12.00	365.00	86.98	40.20	46.78
457	79	12.00	366.00	87.22	40.31	46.91
458	79	12.00	367.00	87.46	40.42	47.04
459	79	12.00	368.00	87.70	40.53	47.17
460	79	12.00	369.00	87.94	40.64	47.30
461	79	12.00	370.00	88.17	40.75	47.42
462	79	12.00	371.00	88.41	40.86	47.55
463	79	12.00	372.00	88.65	40.97	47.68
464	79	12.00	373.00	88.89	41.08	47.81
465	79	12.00	374.00	89.13	41.19	47.94
466	79	12.00	375.00	89.36	41.30	48.06
467	79	12.00	376.00	89.60	41.41	48.19
468	79	12.00	377.00	89.84	41.52	48.32
469	79	12.00	378.00	90.08	41.63	48.45
470	79	12.00	379.00	90.32	41.74	48.58
471	79	12.00	380.00	90.55	41.85	48.70
472	79	12.00	381.00	90.79	41.96	48.83
473	79	12.00	382.00	91.03	42.07	48.96
474	79	12.00	383.00	91.27	42.18	49.09
475	79	12.00	384.00	91.51	42.29	49.22
476	79	12.00	385.00	91.74	42.40	49.34
477	79	12.00	386.00	91.98	42.51	49.47
478	79	12.00	387.00	92.22	42.62	49.60
479	79	12.00	388.00	92.46	42.73	49.73
480	79	12.00	389.00	92.70	42.84	49.86
481	79	12.00	390.00	92.93	42.95	49.98
482	79	12.00	391.00	93.17	43.06	50.11
483	79	12.00	392.00	93.41	43.17	50.24
484	79	12.00	393.00	93.65	43.28	50.37
485	79	12.00	394.00	93.89	43.39	50.50
486	79	12.00	395.00	94.12	43.50	50.62
487	79	12.00	396.00	94.36	43.61	50.75
488	79	12.00	397.00	94.60	43.72	50.88
489	79	12.00	398.00	94.84	43.83	51.01
490	79	12.00	399.00	95.08	43.94	51.14
491	79	12.00	400.00	95.31	44.05	51.26
492	79	12.00	401.00	95.55	44.16	51.39
493	79	12.00	402.00	95.79	44.27	51.52

▼ for information only - do not enter on Deductions Working Sheet, form P11

15

APPENDIX II: NI TABLES

Table letter A

Weekly table

Employee's Earnings up to and including the UEL ▼	Earnings at the LEL (where earnings are equal to or exceed the LEL) 1a	Earnings above the LEL, up to and including the ET 1b	Earnings above the ET, up to and including the UEL 1c	Total of employee's and employer's contributions 1d	Employee's contributions due on all earnings above the ET 1e	Employer's contributions ▼
£	£	£ P	£ P	£ P	£ P	£ P
494	79	12.00	403.00	96.03	44.38	51.65
495	79	12.00	404.00	96.27	44.49	51.78
496	79	12.00	405.00	96.50	44.60	51.90
497	79	12.00	406.00	96.74	44.71	52.03
498	79	12.00	407.00	96.98	44.82	52.16
499	79	12.00	408.00	97.22	44.93	52.29
500	79	12.00	409.00	97.46	45.04	52.42
501	79	12.00	410.00	97.69	45.15	52.54
502	79	12.00	411.00	97.93	45.26	52.67
503	79	12.00	412.00	98.17	45.37	52.80
504	79	12.00	413.00	98.41	45.48	52.93
505	79	12.00	414.00	98.65	45.59	53.06
506	79	12.00	415.00	98.88	45.70	53.18
507	79	12.00	416.00	99.12	45.81	53.31
508	79	12.00	417.00	99.36	45.92	53.44
509	79	12.00	418.00	99.60	46.03	53.57
510	79	12.00	419.00	99.84	46.14	53.70
511	79	12.00	420.00	100.07	46.25	53.82
512	79	12.00	421.00	100.31	46.36	53.95
513	79	12.00	422.00	100.55	46.47	54.08
514	79	12.00	423.00	100.79	46.58	54.21
515	79	12.00	424.00	101.03	46.69	54.34
516	79	12.00	425.00	101.26	46.80	54.46
517	79	12.00	426.00	101.50	46.91	54.59
518	79	12.00	427.00	101.74	47.02	54.72
519	79	12.00	428.00	101.98	47.13	54.85
520	79	12.00	429.00	102.22	47.24	54.98
521	79	12.00	430.00	102.45	47.35	55.10
522	79	12.00	431.00	102.69	47.46	55.23
523	79	12.00	432.00	102.93	47.57	55.36
524	79	12.00	433.00	103.17	47.68	55.49
525	79	12.00	434.00	103.41	47.79	55.62
526	79	12.00	435.00	103.64	47.90	55.74
527	79	12.00	436.00	103.88	48.01	55.87
528	79	12.00	437.00	104.12	48.12	56.00
529	79	12.00	438.00	104.36	48.23	56.13
530	79	12.00	439.00	104.60	48.34	56.26
531	79	12.00	440.00	104.83	48.45	56.38
532	79	12.00	441.00	105.07	48.56	56.51
533	79	12.00	442.00	105.31	48.67	56.64
534	79	12.00	443.00	105.55	48.78	56.77
535	79	12.00	444.00	105.79	48.89	56.90
536	79	12.00	445.00	106.02	49.00	57.02
537	79	12.00	446.00	106.26	49.11	57.15
538	79	12.00	447.00	106.50	49.22	57.28
539	79	12.00	448.00	106.74	49.33	57.41
540	79	12.00	449.00	106.98	49.44	57.54
541	79	12.00	450.00	107.21	49.55	57.66
542	79	12.00	451.00	107.45	49.66	57.79
543	79	12.00	452.00	107.69	49.77	57.92
544	79	12.00	453.00	107.93	49.88	58.05
545	79	12.00	454.00	108.17	49.99	58.18
546	79	12.00	455.00	108.40	50.10	58.30
547	79	12.00	456.00	108.64	50.21	58.43
548	79	12.00	457.00	108.88	50.32	58.56

▼ for information only - do not enter on Deductions Working Sheet, form P11

TAX TABLES

Weekly table

Table letter **A**

▼ Employee's Earnings up to and including the UEL	Earnings at the LEL (where earnings are equal to or exceed the LEL)	Earnings above the LEL, up to and including the ET	Earnings above the ET, up to and including the UEL	Total of employee's and employer's contributions	Employee's contributions due on all earnings above the ET	▼ Employer's contributions
	1a	1b	1c	1d	1e	
£	£	£ P	£ P	£ P	£ P	£ P
549	79	12.00	458.00	109.12	50.43	58.69
550	79	12.00	459.00	109.36	50.54	58.82
551	79	12.00	460.00	109.59	50.65	58.94
552	79	12.00	461.00	109.83	50.76	59.07
553	79	12.00	462.00	110.07	50.87	59.20
554	79	12.00	463.00	110.31	50.98	59.33
555	79	12.00	464.00	110.55	51.09	59.46
556	79	12.00	465.00	110.78	51.20	59.58
557	79	12.00	466.00	111.02	51.31	59.71
558	79	12.00	467.00	111.26	51.42	59.84
559	79	12.00	468.00	111.50	51.53	59.97
560	79	12.00	469.00	111.74	51.64	60.10
561	79	12.00	470.00	111.97	51.75	60.22
562	79	12.00	471.00	112.21	51.86	60.35
563	79	12.00	472.00	112.45	51.97	60.48
564	79	12.00	473.00	112.69	52.08	60.61
565	79	12.00	474.00	112.93	52.19	60.74
566	79	12.00	475.00	113.16	52.30	60.86
567	79	12.00	476.00	113.40	52.41	60.99
568	79	12.00	477.00	113.64	52.52	61.12
569	79	12.00	478.00	113.88	52.63	61.25
570	79	12.00	479.00	114.12	52.74	61.38
571	79	12.00	480.00	114.35	52.85	61.50
572	79	12.00	481.00	114.59	52.96	61.63
573	79	12.00	482.00	114.83	53.07	61.76
574	79	12.00	483.00	115.07	53.18	61.89
575	79	12.00	484.00	115.31	53.29	62.02
576	79	12.00	485.00	115.54	53.40	62.14
577	79	12.00	486.00	115.78	53.51	62.27
578	79	12.00	487.00	116.02	53.62	62.40
579	79	12.00	488.00	116.26	53.73	62.53
580	79	12.00	489.00	116.50	53.84	62.66
581	79	12.00	490.00	116.73	53.95	62.78
582	79	12.00	491.00	116.97	54.06	62.91
583	79	12.00	492.00	117.21	54.17	63.04
584	79	12.00	493.00	117.45	54.28	63.17
585	79	12.00	494.00	117.69	54.39	63.30
586	79	12.00	495.00	117.92	54.50	63.42
587	79	12.00	496.00	118.16	54.61	63.55
588	79	12.00	497.00	118.40	54.72	63.68
589	79	12.00	498.00	118.64	54.83	63.81
590	79	12.00	499.00	118.88	54.94	63.94
591	79	12.00	500.00	119.11	55.05	64.06
592	79	12.00	501.00	119.35	55.16	64.19
593	79	12.00	502.00	119.59	55.27	64.32
594	79	12.00	503.00	119.83	55.38	64.45
595	79	12.00	504.00	120.07	55.49	64.58
596	79	12.00	505.00	120.30	55.60	64.70
597	79	12.00	506.00	120.54	55.71	64.83
598	79	12.00	507.00	120.78	55.82	64.96
599	79	12.00	508.00	121.02	55.93	65.09
600	79	12.00	509.00	121.26	56.04	65.22
601	79	12.00	510.00	121.49	56.15	65.34
602	79	12.00	511.00	121.73	56.26	65.47
603	79	12.00	512.00	121.97	56.37	65.60

▼ for information only - do not enter on Deductions Working Sheet, form P11

17

APPENDIX II: NI TABLES

Table letter A **Weekly table**

Employee's Earnings up to and including the UEL	Earnings at the LEL (where earnings are equal to or exceed the LEL) 1a	Earnings above the LEL, up to and including the ET 1b	Earnings above the ET, up to and including the UEL 1c	Total of employee's and employer's contributions 1d	Employee's contributions due on all earnings above the ET 1e	Employer's contributions
£	£	£ P	£ P	£ P	£ P	£ P
604	79	12.00	513.00	122.21	56.48	65.73
605	79	12.00	514.00	122.45	56.59	65.86
606	79	12.00	515.00	122.68	56.70	65.98
607	79	12.00	516.00	122.92	56.81	66.11
608	79	12.00	517.00	123.16	56.92	66.24
609	79	12.00	518.00	123.40	57.03	66.37
610	79	12.00	519.00	123.52	57.09	66.43

If the employee's gross pay is over £610, go to page 52

18   ▼ for information only - do not enter on Deductions Working Sheet, form P11

TAX TABLES

Monthly table for not contracted-out standard rate contributions for use from 6 April 2004 to 5 April 2005

Table letter **A**

Use this table for

- employees who are age 16 or over and under State Pension Age (65 for men, 60 for women)
- employees who have an Appropriate Personal Pension or Appropriate Personal Pension Stakeholder Pension.

Do not use this table for

- any year other than 2004-2005
- married women or widows who have the right to pay reduced rate employee's contributions, see Table B, in Leaflet CA41
- employees who are State Pension Age or over, see Table C, in Leaflet CA41
- employees for whom you hold form CA2700, see Table J.

Completing Deductions Working Sheet, form P11 or substitute

- enter 'A' in the space provided in the 'End of Year Summary' box of form P11
- copy the figures in columns 1a-1e of the table to columns 1a-1e of form P11 on the line next to the tax week in which the employee is paid.

If the employee's total earnings fall between the LEL and the UEL and the exact gross pay is not shown in the table, use the next smaller figure shown. If the employee's total earnings exceed the UEL, see page 52.

The figures in the left hand column of each table show steps between the LEL and the UEL. The NICs liability for each step is calculated at the mid-point of the steps so you and your employee may pay slightly more or less than if you used the exact percentage method.

▼ Employee's Earnings up to and including the UEL	Earnings at the LEL (where earnings are equal to or exceed the LEL)	Earnings above the LEL, up to and including the ET	Earnings above the ET, up to and including the UEL	Total of employee's and employer's contributions	Employee's contributions due on all earnings above the ET	▼ Employer's contributions
	1a	1b	1c	1d	1e	
£	£	£ P	£ P	£ P	£ P	£ P
Up to and including 342.99	No NIC Liability, make no entries on forms P11 and P14					
343	343	0.00	0.00	0.00	0.00	0.00
347	343	4.00	0.00	0.00	0.00	0.00
351	343	8.00	0.00	0.00	0.00	0.00
355	343	12.00	0.00	0.00	0.00	0.00
359	343	16.00	0.00	0.00	0.00	0.00
363	343	20.00	0.00	0.00	0.00	0.00
367	343	24.00	0.00	0.00	0.00	0.00
371	343	28.00	0.00	0.00	0.00	0.00
375	343	32.00	0.00	0.00	0.00	0.00
379	343	36.00	0.00	0.00	0.00	0.00
383	343	40.00	0.00	0.00	0.00	0.00
387	343	44.00	0.00	0.00	0.00	0.00
391	343	48.00	0.00	0.00	0.00	0.00
395	343	52.00	0.00	0.00	0.00	0.00
399	343	52.00	4.00	1.43	0.66	0.77
403	343	52.00	8.00	2.38	1.10	1.28
407	343	52.00	12.00	3.33	1.54	1.79
411	343	52.00	16.00	4.28	1.98	2.30
415	343	52.00	20.00	5.24	2.42	2.82
419	343	52.00	24.00	6.19	2.86	3.33
423	343	52.00	28.00	7.14	3.30	3.84
427	343	52.00	32.00	8.09	3.74	4.35
431	343	52.00	36.00	9.04	4.18	4.86
435	343	52.00	40.00	10.00	4.62	5.38
439	343	52.00	44.00	10.95	5.06	5.89
443	343	52.00	48.00	11.90	5.50	6.40
447	343	52.00	52.00	12.85	5.94	6.91
451	343	52.00	56.00	13.80	6.38	7.42
455	343	52.00	60.00	14.76	6.82	7.94
459	343	52.00	64.00	15.71	7.26	8.45

▼ for information only - do not enter on Deductions Working Sheet, form P11

APPENDIX II: NI TABLES

Table letter A **Monthly table**

Employee's Earnings up to and including the UEL	Earnings at the LEL (where earnings are equal to or exceed the LEL)	Earnings above the LEL, up to and including the ET	Earnings above the ET, up to and including the UEL	Total of employee's and employer's contributions	Employee's contributions due on all earnings above the ET	Employer's contributions
		1a	1b	1c	1d	1e
£	£	£ P	£ P	£ P	£ P	£ P
463	343	52.00	68.00	16.66	7.70	8.96
467	343	52.00	72.00	17.61	8.14	9.47
471	343	52.00	76.00	18.56	8.58	9.98
475	343	52.00	80.00	19.52	9.02	10.50
479	343	52.00	84.00	20.47	9.46	11.01
483	343	52.00	88.00	21.42	9.90	11.52
487	343	52.00	92.00	22.37	10.34	12.03
491	343	52.00	96.00	23.32	10.78	12.54
495	343	52.00	100.00	24.28	11.22	13.06
499	343	52.00	104.00	25.23	11.66	13.57
503	343	52.00	108.00	26.18	12.10	14.08
507	343	52.00	112.00	27.13	12.54	14.59
511	343	52.00	116.00	28.08	12.98	15.10
515	343	52.00	120.00	29.04	13.42	15.62
519	343	52.00	124.00	29.99	13.86	16.13
523	343	52.00	128.00	30.94	14.30	16.64
527	343	52.00	132.00	31.89	14.74	17.15
531	343	52.00	136.00	32.84	15.18	17.66
535	343	52.00	140.00	33.80	15.62	18.18
539	343	52.00	144.00	34.75	16.06	18.69
543	343	52.00	148.00	35.70	16.50	19.20
547	343	52.00	152.00	36.65	16.94	19.71
551	343	52.00	156.00	37.60	17.38	20.22
555	343	52.00	160.00	38.56	17.82	20.74
559	343	52.00	164.00	39.51	18.26	21.25
563	343	52.00	168.00	40.46	18.70	21.76
567	343	52.00	172.00	41.41	19.14	22.27
571	343	52.00	176.00	42.36	19.58	22.78
575	343	52.00	180.00	43.32	20.02	23.30
579	343	52.00	184.00	44.27	20.46	23.81
583	343	52.00	188.00	45.22	20.90	24.32
587	343	52.00	192.00	46.17	21.34	24.83
591	343	52.00	196.00	47.12	21.78	25.34
595	343	52.00	200.00	48.08	22.22	25.86
599	343	52.00	204.00	49.03	22.66	26.37
603	343	52.00	208.00	49.98	23.10	26.88
607	343	52.00	212.00	50.93	23.54	27.39
611	343	52.00	216.00	51.88	23.98	27.90
615	343	52.00	220.00	52.84	24.42	28.42
619	343	52.00	224.00	53.79	24.86	28.93
623	343	52.00	228.00	54.74	25.30	29.44
627	343	52.00	232.00	55.69	25.74	29.95
631	343	52.00	236.00	56.64	26.18	30.46
635	343	52.00	240.00	57.60	26.62	30.98
639	343	52.00	244.00	58.55	27.06	31.49
643	343	52.00	248.00	59.50	27.50	32.00
647	343	52.00	252.00	60.45	27.94	32.51
651	343	52.00	256.00	61.40	28.38	33.02
655	343	52.00	260.00	62.36	28.82	33.54
659	343	52.00	264.00	63.31	29.26	34.05
663	343	52.00	268.00	64.26	29.70	34.56
667	343	52.00	272.00	65.21	30.14	35.07
671	343	52.00	276.00	66.16	30.58	35.58
675	343	52.00	280.00	67.12	31.02	36.10
679	343	52.00	284.00	68.07	31.46	36.61

▼ for information only - do not enter on Deductions Working Sheet, form P11

TAX TABLES

Table letter A   **Monthly table**

Employee's Earnings up to and including the UEL ▼	Earnings at the LEL (where earnings are equal to or exceed the LEL) 1a	Earnings above the LEL, up to and including the ET 1b	Earnings above the ET, up to and including the UEL 1c	Total of employee's and employer's contributions 1d	Employee's contributions due on all earnings above the ET 1e	Employer's contributions ▼
£	£	£ P	£ P	£ P	£ P	£ P
903	343	52.00	508.00	121.38	56.10	65.28
907	343	52.00	512.00	122.33	56.54	65.79
911	343	52.00	516.00	123.28	56.98	66.30
915	343	52.00	520.00	124.24	57.42	66.82
919	343	52.00	524.00	125.19	57.86	67.33
923	343	52.00	528.00	126.14	58.30	67.84
927	343	52.00	532.00	127.09	58.74	68.35
931	343	52.00	536.00	128.04	59.18	68.86
935	343	52.00	540.00	129.00	59.62	69.38
939	343	52.00	544.00	129.95	60.06	69.89
943	343	52.00	548.00	130.90	60.50	70.40
947	343	52.00	552.00	131.85	60.94	70.91
951	343	52.00	556.00	132.80	61.38	71.42
955	343	52.00	560.00	133.76	61.82	71.94
959	343	52.00	564.00	134.71	62.26	72.45
963	343	52.00	568.00	135.66	62.70	72.96
967	343	52.00	572.00	136.61	63.14	73.47
971	343	52.00	576.00	137.56	63.58	73.98
975	343	52.00	580.00	138.52	64.02	74.50
979	343	52.00	584.00	139.47	64.46	75.01
983	343	52.00	588.00	140.42	64.90	75.52
987	343	52.00	592.00	141.37	65.34	76.03
991	343	52.00	596.00	142.32	65.78	76.54
995	343	52.00	600.00	143.28	66.22	77.06
999	343	52.00	604.00	144.23	66.66	77.57
1003	343	52.00	608.00	145.18	67.10	78.08
1007	343	52.00	612.00	146.13	67.54	78.59
1011	343	52.00	616.00	147.08	67.98	79.10
1015	343	52.00	620.00	148.04	68.42	79.62
1019	343	52.00	624.00	148.99	68.86	80.13
1023	343	52.00	628.00	149.94	69.30	80.64
1027	343	52.00	632.00	150.89	69.74	81.15
1031	343	52.00	636.00	151.84	70.18	81.66
1035	343	52.00	640.00	152.80	70.62	82.18
1039	343	52.00	644.00	153.75	71.06	82.69
1043	343	52.00	648.00	154.70	71.50	83.20
1047	343	52.00	652.00	155.65	71.94	83.71
1051	343	52.00	656.00	156.60	72.38	84.22
1055	343	52.00	660.00	157.56	72.82	84.74
1059	343	52.00	664.00	158.51	73.26	85.25
1063	343	52.00	668.00	159.46	73.70	85.76
1067	343	52.00	672.00	160.41	74.14	86.27
1071	343	52.00	676.00	161.36	74.58	86.78
1075	343	52.00	680.00	162.32	75.02	87.30
1079	343	52.00	684.00	163.27	75.46	87.81
1083	343	52.00	688.00	164.22	75.90	88.32
1087	343	52.00	692.00	165.17	76.34	88.83
1091	343	52.00	696.00	166.12	76.78	89.34
1095	343	52.00	700.00	167.08	77.22	89.86
1099	343	52.00	704.00	168.03	77.66	90.37
1103	343	52.00	708.00	168.98	78.10	90.88
1107	343	52.00	712.00	169.93	78.54	91.39
1111	343	52.00	716.00	170.88	78.98	91.90
1115	343	52.00	720.00	171.84	79.42	92.42
1119	343	52.00	724.00	172.79	79.86	92.93

▼ for information only - do not enter on Deductions Working Sheet, form P11

APPENDIX II: NI TABLES

Table letter **A**

Monthly table

Employee's Earnings up to and including the UEL	Earnings at the LEL (where earnings are equal to or exceed the LEL)	Earnings above the LEL, up to and including the ET	Earnings above the ET, up to and including the UEL	Total of employee's and employer's contributions	Employee's contributions due on all earnings above the ET	Employer's contributions
	1a	1b	1c	1d	1e	
£	£	£ P	£ P	£ P	£ P	£ P
1343	343	52.00	948.00	226.10	104.50	121.60
1347	343	52.00	952.00	227.05	104.94	122.11
1351	343	52.00	956.00	228.00	105.38	122.62
1355	343	52.00	960.00	228.96	105.82	123.14
1359	343	52.00	964.00	229.91	106.26	123.65
1363	343	52.00	968.00	230.86	106.70	124.16
1367	343	52.00	972.00	231.81	107.14	124.67
1371	343	52.00	976.00	232.76	107.58	125.18
1375	343	52.00	980.00	233.72	108.02	125.70
1379	343	52.00	984.00	234.67	108.46	126.21
1383	343	52.00	988.00	235.62	108.90	126.72
1387	343	52.00	992.00	236.57	109.34	127.23
1391	343	52.00	996.00	237.52	109.78	127.74
1395	343	52.00	1000.00	238.48	110.22	128.26
1399	343	52.00	1004.00	239.43	110.66	128.77
1403	343	52.00	1008.00	240.38	111.10	129.28
1407	343	52.00	1012.00	241.33	111.54	129.79
1411	343	52.00	1016.00	242.28	111.98	130.30
1415	343	52.00	1020.00	243.24	112.42	130.82
1419	343	52.00	1024.00	244.19	112.86	131.33
1423	343	52.00	1028.00	245.14	113.30	131.84
1427	343	52.00	1032.00	246.09	113.74	132.35
1431	343	52.00	1036.00	247.04	114.18	132.86
1435	343	52.00	1040.00	248.00	114.62	133.38
1439	343	52.00	1044.00	248.95	115.06	133.89
1443	343	52.00	1048.00	249.90	115.50	134.40
1447	343	52.00	1052.00	250.85	115.94	134.91
1451	343	52.00	1056.00	251.80	116.38	135.42
1455	343	52.00	1060.00	252.76	116.82	135.94
1459	343	52.00	1064.00	253.71	117.26	136.45
1463	343	52.00	1068.00	254.66	117.70	136.96
1467	343	52.00	1072.00	255.61	118.14	137.47
1471	343	52.00	1076.00	256.56	118.58	137.98
1475	343	52.00	1080.00	257.52	119.02	138.50
1479	343	52.00	1084.00	258.47	119.46	139.01
1483	343	52.00	1088.00	259.42	119.90	139.52
1487	343	52.00	1092.00	260.37	120.34	140.03
1491	343	52.00	1096.00	261.32	120.78	140.54
1495	343	52.00	1100.00	262.28	121.22	141.06
1499	343	52.00	1104.00	263.23	121.66	141.57
1503	343	52.00	1108.00	264.18	122.10	142.08
1507	343	52.00	1112.00	265.13	122.54	142.59
1511	343	52.00	1116.00	266.08	122.98	143.10
1515	343	52.00	1120.00	267.04	123.42	143.62
1519	343	52.00	1124.00	267.99	123.86	144.13
1523	343	52.00	1128.00	268.94	124.30	144.64
1527	343	52.00	1132.00	269.89	124.74	145.15
1531	343	52.00	1136.00	270.84	125.18	145.66
1535	343	52.00	1140.00	271.80	125.62	146.18
1539	343	52.00	1144.00	272.75	126.06	146.69
1543	343	52.00	1148.00	273.70	126.50	147.20
1547	343	52.00	1152.00	274.65	126.94	147.71
1551	343	52.00	1156.00	275.60	127.38	148.22
1555	343	52.00	1160.00	276.56	127.82	148.74
1559	343	52.00	1164.00	277.51	128.26	149.25

24 ▼ for information only - do not enter on Deductions Working Sheet, form P11

TAX TABLES

Monthly table Table letter **A**

Employee's Earnings up to and including the UEL £	Earnings at the LEL (where earnings are equal to or exceed the LEL) 1a £	Earnings above the LEL, up to and including the ET 1b £ P	Earnings above the ET, up to and including the UEL 1c £ P	Total of employee's and employer's contributions 1d £ P	Employee's contributions due on all earnings above the ET 1e £ P	▼ Employer's contributions £ P
2443	343	52.00	2048.00	487.90	225.50	262.40
2447	343	52.00	2052.00	488.85	225.94	262.91
2451	343	52.00	2056.00	489.80	226.38	263.42
2455	343	52.00	2060.00	490.76	226.82	263.94
2459	343	52.00	2064.00	491.71	227.26	264.45
2463	343	52.00	2068.00	492.66	227.70	264.96
2467	343	52.00	2072.00	493.61	228.14	265.47
2471	343	52.00	2076.00	494.56	228.58	265.98
2475	343	52.00	2080.00	495.52	229.02	266.50
2479	343	52.00	2084.00	496.47	229.46	267.01
2483	343	52.00	2088.00	497.42	229.90	267.52
2487	343	52.00	2092.00	498.37	230.34	268.03
2491	343	52.00	2096.00	499.32	230.78	268.54
2495	343	52.00	2100.00	500.28	231.22	269.06
2499	343	52.00	2104.00	501.23	231.66	269.57
2503	343	52.00	2108.00	502.18	232.10	270.08
2507	343	52.00	2112.00	503.13	232.54	270.59
2511	343	52.00	2116.00	504.08	232.98	271.10
2515	343	52.00	2120.00	505.04	233.42	271.62
2519	343	52.00	2124.00	505.99	233.86	272.13
2523	343	52.00	2128.00	506.94	234.30	272.64
2527	343	52.00	2132.00	507.89	234.74	273.15
2531	343	52.00	2136.00	508.84	235.18	273.66
2535	343	52.00	2140.00	509.80	235.62	274.18
2539	343	52.00	2144.00	510.75	236.06	274.69
2543	343	52.00	2148.00	511.70	236.50	275.20
2547	343	52.00	2152.00	512.65	236.94	275.71
2551	343	52.00	2156.00	513.60	237.38	276.22
2555	343	52.00	2160.00	514.56	237.82	276.74
2559	343	52.00	2164.00	515.51	238.26	277.25
2563	343	52.00	2168.00	516.46	238.70	277.76
2567	343	52.00	2172.00	517.41	239.14	278.27
2571	343	52.00	2176.00	518.36	239.58	278.78
2575	343	52.00	2180.00	519.32	240.02	279.30
2579	343	52.00	2184.00	520.27	240.46	279.81
2583	343	52.00	2188.00	521.22	240.90	280.32
2587	343	52.00	2192.00	522.17	241.34	280.83
2591	343	52.00	2196.00	523.12	241.78	281.34
2595	343	52.00	2200.00	524.08	242.22	281.86
2599	343	52.00	2204.00	525.03	242.66	282.37
2603	343	52.00	2208.00	525.98	243.10	282.88
2607	343	52.00	2212.00	526.93	243.54	283.39
2611	343	52.00	2216.00	527.88	243.98	283.90
2615	343	52.00	2220.00	528.84	244.42	284.42
2619	343	52.00	2224.00	529.79	244.86	284.93
2623	343	52.00	2228.00	530.74	245.30	285.44
2627	343	52.00	2232.00	531.69	245.74	285.95
2631	343	52.00	2236.00	532.64	246.18	286.46
2635	343	52.00	2240.00	533.60	246.62	286.98
2639	343	52.00	2244.00	534.55	247.06	287.49
2643	343	52.00	2248.00	535.14	247.33	287.81
2644	343	52.00	2249.00	535.26	247.39	287.87

If the employee's gross pay is over £2644, go to page 52

▼ for information only - do not enter on Deductions Working Sheet, form P11

29

APPENDIX II: NI TABLES

Monthly table for not contracted-out contributions where employee has deferment for use from 6 April 2004 to 5 April 2005

Table letter **J**

Use this table for
employees for whom you hold form CA2700,

Do not use this table for
- any year other than 2004-2005
- employees who are State Pension Age or over, see Table C, in Leaflet CA41

Completing Deductions Working Sheet, form P11 or substitute

- enter 'J' in the space provided in the 'End of Year Summary' box of form P11
- copy the figures in columns 1a-1e of the table to columns 1a-1e of form P11 on the line next to the tax week in which the employee is paid.

If the employee's total earnings fall between the LEL and the UEL and the exact gross pay is not shown in the table, use the next smaller figure shown. If the employee's total earnings exceed the UEL, see page 52.

The figures in the left hand column of each table show steps between the LEL and the UEL. The NICs liability for each step is calculated at the mid-point of the steps so you and your employee may pay slightly more or less than if you used the exact percentage method.

▼ Employee's Earnings up to and including the UEL	Earnings at the LEL (where earnings are equal to or exceed the LEL)	Earnings above the LEL, up to and including the ET	Earnings above the ET, up to and including the UEL	Total of employee's and employer's contributions	Employee's contributions due on all earnings above the ET	▼ Employer's contributions
	1a	1b	1c	1d	1e	
£	£	£ P	£ P	£ P	£ P	£ P
Up to and including 342.99	No NIC Liability, make no entries on forms P11 and P14					
343	343	0.00	0.00	0.00	0.00	0.00
347	343	4.00	0.00	0.00	0.00	0.00
351	343	8.00	0.00	0.00	0.00	0.00
355	343	12.00	0.00	0.00	0.00	0.00
359	343	16.00	0.00	0.00	0.00	0.00
363	343	20.00	0.00	0.00	0.00	0.00
367	343	24.00	0.00	0.00	0.00	0.00
371	343	28.00	0.00	0.00	0.00	0.00
375	343	32.00	0.00	0.00	0.00	0.00
379	343	36.00	0.00	0.00	0.00	0.00
383	343	40.00	0.00	0.00	0.00	0.00
387	343	44.00	0.00	0.00	0.00	0.00
391	343	48.00	0.00	0.00	0.00	0.00
395	343	52.00	0.00	0.00	0.00	0.00
399	343	52.00	4.00	0.83	0.06	0.77
403	343	52.00	8.00	1.38	0.10	1.28
407	343	52.00	12.00	1.93	0.14	1.79
411	343	52.00	16.00	2.48	0.18	2.30
415	343	52.00	20.00	3.04	0.22	2.82
419	343	52.00	24.00	3.59	0.26	3.33
423	343	52.00	28.00	4.14	0.30	3.84
427	343	52.00	32.00	4.69	0.34	4.35
431	343	52.00	36.00	5.24	0.38	4.86
435	343	52.00	40.00	5.80	0.42	5.38
439	343	52.00	44.00	6.35	0.46	5.89
443	343	52.00	48.00	6.90	0.50	6.40
447	343	52.00	52.00	7.45	0.54	6.91
451	343	52.00	56.00	8.00	0.58	7.42
455	343	52.00	60.00	8.56	0.62	7.94
459	343	52.00	64.00	9.11	0.66	8.45

▼ for information only - do not enter on Deductions Working Sheet, form P11   41

TAX TABLES

Table letter J **Monthly table**

Employee's Earnings up to and including the UEL	Earnings at the LEL (where earnings are equal to or exceed the LEL)	Earnings above the LEL, up to and including the ET	Earnings above the ET, up to and including the UEL	Total of employee's and employer's contributions	Employee's contributions due on all earnings above the ET	Employer's contributions
1a	1b	1c	1d	1e	
£	£	£ P	£ P	£ P	£ P	£ P
463	343	52.00	68.00	9.66	0.70	8.96
467	343	52.00	72.00	10.21	0.74	9.47
471	343	52.00	76.00	10.76	0.78	9.98
475	343	52.00	80.00	11.32	0.82	10.50
479	343	52.00	84.00	11.87	0.86	11.01
483	343	52.00	88.00	12.42	0.90	11.52
487	343	52.00	92.00	12.97	0.94	12.03
491	343	52.00	96.00	13.52	0.98	12.54
495	343	52.00	100.00	14.08	1.02	13.06
499	343	52.00	104.00	14.63	1.06	13.57
503	343	52.00	108.00	15.18	1.10	14.08
507	343	52.00	112.00	15.73	1.14	14.59
511	343	52.00	116.00	16.28	1.18	15.10
515	343	52.00	120.00	16.84	1.22	15.62
519	343	52.00	124.00	17.39	1.26	16.13
523	343	52.00	128.00	17.94	1.30	16.64
527	343	52.00	132.00	18.49	1.34	17.15
531	343	52.00	136.00	19.04	1.38	17.66
535	343	52.00	140.00	19.60	1.42	18.18
539	343	52.00	144.00	20.15	1.46	18.69
543	343	52.00	148.00	20.70	1.50	19.20
547	343	52.00	152.00	21.25	1.54	19.71
551	343	52.00	156.00	21.80	1.58	20.22
555	343	52.00	160.00	22.36	1.62	20.74
559	343	52.00	164.00	22.91	1.66	21.25
563	343	52.00	168.00	23.46	1.70	21.76
567	343	52.00	172.00	24.01	1.74	22.27
571	343	52.00	176.00	24.56	1.78	22.78
575	343	52.00	180.00	25.12	1.82	23.30
579	343	52.00	184.00	25.67	1.86	23.81
583	343	52.00	188.00	26.22	1.90	24.32
587	343	52.00	192.00	26.77	1.94	24.83
591	343	52.00	196.00	27.32	1.98	25.34
595	343	52.00	200.00	27.88	2.02	25.86
599	343	52.00	204.00	28.43	2.06	26.37
603	343	52.00	208.00	28.98	2.10	26.88
607	343	52.00	212.00	29.53	2.14	27.39
611	343	52.00	216.00	30.08	2.18	27.90
615	343	52.00	220.00	30.64	2.22	28.42
619	343	52.00	224.00	31.19	2.26	28.93
623	343	52.00	228.00	31.74	2.30	29.44
627	343	52.00	232.00	32.29	2.34	29.95
631	343	52.00	236.00	32.84	2.38	30.46
635	343	52.00	240.00	33.40	2.42	30.98
639	343	52.00	244.00	33.95	2.46	31.49
643	343	52.00	248.00	34.50	2.50	32.00
647	343	52.00	252.00	35.05	2.54	32.51
651	343	52.00	256.00	35.60	2.58	33.02
655	343	52.00	260.00	36.16	2.62	33.54
659	343	52.00	264.00	36.71	2.66	34.05
663	343	52.00	268.00	37.26	2.70	34.56
667	343	52.00	272.00	37.81	2.74	35.07
671	343	52.00	276.00	38.36	2.78	35.58
675	343	52.00	280.00	38.92	2.82	36.10
679	343	52.00	284.00	39.47	2.86	36.61

▼ for information only - do not enter on Deductions Working Sheet, form P11

APPENDIX II: NI TABLES

Monthly table

Table letter **J**

Employee's Earnings up to and including the UEL	Earnings at the LEL (where earnings are equal to or exceed the LEL)	Earnings above the LEL, up to and including the ET	Earnings above the ET, up to and including the UEL	Total of employee's and employer's contributions	Employee's contributions due on all earnings above the ET	Employer's contributions
		1a	1b	1c	1d	1e
£	£	£ P	£ P	£ P	£ P	£ P
683	343	52.00	288.00	40.02	2.90	37.12
687	343	52.00	292.00	40.57	2.94	37.63
691	343	52.00	296.00	41.12	2.98	38.14
695	343	52.00	300.00	41.68	3.02	38.66
699	343	52.00	304.00	42.23	3.06	39.17
703	343	52.00	308.00	42.78	3.10	39.68
707	343	52.00	312.00	43.33	3.14	40.19
711	343	52.00	316.00	43.88	3.18	40.70
715	343	52.00	320.00	44.44	3.22	41.22
719	343	52.00	324.00	44.99	3.26	41.73
723	343	52.00	328.00	45.54	3.30	42.24
727	343	52.00	332.00	46.09	3.34	42.75
731	343	52.00	336.00	46.64	3.38	43.26
735	343	52.00	340.00	47.20	3.42	43.78
739	343	52.00	344.00	47.75	3.46	44.29
743	343	52.00	348.00	48.30	3.50	44.80
747	343	52.00	352.00	48.85	3.54	45.31
751	343	52.00	356.00	49.40	3.58	45.82
755	343	52.00	360.00	49.96	3.62	46.34
759	343	52.00	364.00	50.51	3.66	46.85
763	343	52.00	368.00	51.06	3.70	47.36
767	343	52.00	372.00	51.61	3.74	47.87
771	343	52.00	376.00	52.16	3.78	48.38
775	343	52.00	380.00	52.72	3.82	48.90
779	343	52.00	384.00	53.27	3.86	49.41
783	343	52.00	388.00	53.82	3.90	49.92
787	343	52.00	392.00	54.37	3.94	50.43
791	343	52.00	396.00	54.92	3.98	50.94
795	343	52.00	400.00	55.48	4.02	51.46
799	343	52.00	404.00	56.03	4.06	51.97
803	343	52.00	408.00	56.58	4.10	52.48
807	343	52.00	412.00	57.13	4.14	52.99
811	343	52.00	416.00	57.68	4.18	53.50
815	343	52.00	420.00	58.24	4.22	54.02
819	343	52.00	424.00	58.79	4.26	54.53
823	343	52.00	428.00	59.34	4.30	55.04
827	343	52.00	432.00	59.89	4.34	55.55
831	343	52.00	436.00	60.44	4.38	56.06
835	343	52.00	440.00	61.00	4.42	56.58
839	343	52.00	444.00	61.55	4.46	57.09
843	343	52.00	448.00	62.10	4.50	57.60
847	343	52.00	452.00	62.65	4.54	58.11
851	343	52.00	456.00	63.20	4.58	58.62
855	343	52.00	460.00	63.76	4.62	59.14
859	343	52.00	464.00	64.31	4.66	59.65
863	343	52.00	468.00	64.86	4.70	60.16
867	343	52.00	472.00	65.41	4.74	60.67
871	343	52.00	476.00	65.96	4.78	61.18
875	343	52.00	480.00	66.52	4.82	61.70
879	343	52.00	484.00	67.07	4.86	62.21
883	343	52.00	488.00	67.62	4.90	62.72
887	343	52.00	492.00	68.17	4.94	63.23
891	343	52.00	496.00	68.72	4.98	63.74
895	343	52.00	500.00	69.28	5.02	64.26
899	343	52.00	504.00	69.83	5.06	64.77

▼ for information only - do not enter on Deductions Working Sheet, form P11

43

TAX TABLES

Table letter J　　　　　　　　　　　　　　　　　　　　　　　　　　**Monthly table**

Employee's Earnings up to and including the UEL ▼	Earnings at the LEL (where earnings are equal to or exceed the LEL) 1a	Earnings above the LEL, up to and including the ET 1b	Earnings above the ET, up to and including the UEL 1c	Total of employee's and employer's contributions 1d	Employee's contributions due on all earnings above the ET 1e	Employer's contributions ▼
£	£	£ P	£ P	£ P	£ P	£ P
903	343	52.00	508.00	70.38	5.10	65.28
907	343	52.00	512.00	70.93	5.14	65.79
911	343	52.00	516.00	71.48	5.18	66.30
915	343	52.00	520.00	72.04	5.22	66.82
919	343	52.00	524.00	72.59	5.26	67.33
923	343	52.00	528.00	73.14	5.30	67.84
927	343	52.00	532.00	73.69	5.34	68.35
931	343	52.00	536.00	74.24	5.38	68.86
935	343	52.00	540.00	74.80	5.42	69.38
939	343	52.00	544.00	75.35	5.46	69.89
943	343	52.00	548.00	75.90	5.50	70.40
947	343	52.00	552.00	76.45	5.54	70.91
951	343	52.00	556.00	77.00	5.58	71.42
955	343	52.00	560.00	77.56	5.62	71.94
959	343	52.00	564.00	78.11	5.66	72.45
963	343	52.00	568.00	78.66	5.70	72.96
967	343	52.00	572.00	79.21	5.74	73.47
971	343	52.00	576.00	79.76	5.78	73.98
975	343	52.00	580.00	80.32	5.82	74.50
979	343	52.00	584.00	80.87	5.86	75.01
983	343	52.00	588.00	81.42	5.90	75.52
987	343	52.00	592.00	81.97	5.94	76.03
991	343	52.00	596.00	82.52	5.98	76.54
995	343	52.00	600.00	83.08	6.02	77.06
999	343	52.00	604.00	83.63	6.06	77.57
1003	343	52.00	608.00	84.18	6.10	78.08
1007	343	52.00	612.00	84.73	6.14	78.59
1011	343	52.00	616.00	85.28	6.18	79.10
1015	343	52.00	620.00	85.84	6.22	79.62
1019	343	52.00	624.00	86.39	6.26	80.13
1023	343	52.00	628.00	86.94	6.30	80.64
1027	343	52.00	632.00	87.49	6.34	81.15
1031	343	52.00	636.00	88.04	6.38	81.66
1035	343	52.00	640.00	88.60	6.42	82.18
1039	343	52.00	644.00	89.15	6.46	82.69
1043	343	52.00	648.00	89.70	6.50	83.20
1047	343	52.00	652.00	90.25	6.54	83.71
1051	343	52.00	656.00	90.80	6.58	84.22
1055	343	52.00	660.00	91.36	6.62	84.74
1059	343	52.00	664.00	91.91	6.66	85.25
1063	343	52.00	668.00	92.46	6.70	85.76
1067	343	52.00	672.00	93.01	6.74	86.27
1071	343	52.00	676.00	93.56	6.78	86.78
1075	343	52.00	680.00	94.12	6.82	87.30
1079	343	52.00	684.00	94.67	6.86	87.81
1083	343	52.00	688.00	95.22	6.90	88.32
1087	343	52.00	692.00	95.77	6.94	88.83
1091	343	52.00	696.00	96.32	6.98	89.34
1095	343	52.00	700.00	96.88	7.02	89.86
1099	343	52.00	704.00	97.43	7.06	90.37
1103	343	52.00	708.00	97.98	7.10	90.88
1107	343	52.00	712.00	98.53	7.14	91.39
1111	343	52.00	716.00	99.08	7.18	91.90
1115	343	52.00	720.00	99.64	7.22	92.42
1119	343	52.00	724.00	100.19	7.26	92.93

▼ for information only - do not enter on Deductions Working Sheet, form P11

APPENDIX II: NI TABLES

Monthly table

Table letter **J**

Employee's Earnings up to and including the UEL	Earnings at the LEL (where earnings are equal to or exceed the LEL) 1a	Earnings above the LEL, up to and including the ET 1b	Earnings above the ET, up to and including the UEL 1c	Total of employee's and employer's contributions 1d	Employee's contributions due on all earnings above the ET 1e	Employer's contributions
£	£	£ P	£ P	£ P	£ P	£ P
1123	343	52.00	728.00	100.74	7.30	93.44
1127	343	52.00	732.00	101.29	7.34	93.95
1131	343	52.00	736.00	101.84	7.38	94.46
1135	343	52.00	740.00	102.40	7.42	94.98
1139	343	52.00	744.00	102.95	7.46	95.49
1143	343	52.00	748.00	103.50	7.50	96.00
1147	343	52.00	752.00	104.05	7.54	96.51
1151	343	52.00	756.00	104.60	7.58	97.02
1155	343	52.00	760.00	105.16	7.62	97.54
1159	343	52.00	764.00	105.71	7.66	98.05
1163	343	52.00	768.00	106.26	7.70	98.56
1167	343	52.00	772.00	106.81	7.74	99.07
1171	343	52.00	776.00	107.36	7.78	99.58
1175	343	52.00	780.00	107.92	7.82	100.10
1179	343	52.00	784.00	108.47	7.86	100.61
1183	343	52.00	788.00	109.02	7.90	101.12
1187	343	52.00	792.00	109.57	7.94	101.63
1191	343	52.00	796.00	110.12	7.98	102.14
1195	343	52.00	800.00	110.68	8.02	102.66
1199	343	52.00	804.00	111.23	8.06	103.17
1203	343	52.00	808.00	111.78	8.10	103.68
1207	343	52.00	812.00	112.33	8.14	104.19
1211	343	52.00	816.00	112.88	8.18	104.70
1215	343	52.00	820.00	113.44	8.22	105.22
1219	343	52.00	824.00	113.99	8.26	105.73
1223	343	52.00	828.00	114.54	8.30	106.24
1227	343	52.00	832.00	115.09	8.34	106.75
1231	343	52.00	836.00	115.64	8.38	107.26
1235	343	52.00	840.00	116.20	8.42	107.78
1239	343	52.00	844.00	116.75	8.46	108.29
1243	343	52.00	848.00	117.30	8.50	108.80
1247	343	52.00	852.00	117.85	8.54	109.31
1251	343	52.00	856.00	118.40	8.58	109.82
1255	343	52.00	860.00	118.96	8.62	110.34
1259	343	52.00	864.00	119.51	8.66	110.85
1263	343	52.00	868.00	120.06	8.70	111.36
1267	343	52.00	872.00	120.61	8.74	111.87
1271	343	52.00	876.00	121.16	8.78	112.38
1275	343	52.00	880.00	121.72	8.82	112.90
1279	343	52.00	884.00	122.27	8.86	113.41
1283	343	52.00	888.00	122.82	8.90	113.92
1287	343	52.00	892.00	123.37	8.94	114.43
1291	343	52.00	896.00	123.92	8.98	114.94
1295	343	52.00	900.00	124.48	9.02	115.46
1299	343	52.00	904.00	125.03	9.06	115.97
1303	343	52.00	908.00	125.58	9.10	116.48
1307	343	52.00	912.00	126.13	9.14	116.99
1311	343	52.00	916.00	126.68	9.18	117.50
1315	343	52.00	920.00	127.24	9.22	118.02
1319	343	52.00	924.00	127.79	9.26	118.53
1323	343	52.00	928.00	128.34	9.30	119.04
1327	343	52.00	932.00	128.89	9.34	119.55
1331	343	52.00	936.00	129.44	9.38	120.06
1335	343	52.00	940.00	130.00	9.42	120.58
1339	343	52.00	944.00	130.55	9.46	121.09

▼ for information only - do not enter on Deductions Working Sheet, form P11

45

TAX TABLES

Table letter J   **Monthly table**

Employee's Earnings up to and including the UEL	Earnings at the LEL (where earnings are equal to or exceed the LEL) 1a	Earnings above the LEL, up to and including the ET 1b	Earnings above the ET, up to and including the UEL 1c	Total of employee's and employer's contributions 1d	Employee's contributions due on all earnings above the ET 1e	Employer's contributions
£	£	£ P	£ P	£ P	£ P	£ P
1343	343	52.00	948.00	131.10	9.50	121.60
1347	343	52.00	952.00	131.65	9.54	122.11
1351	343	52.00	956.00	132.20	9.58	122.62
1355	343	52.00	960.00	132.76	9.62	123.14
1359	343	52.00	964.00	133.31	9.66	123.65
1363	343	52.00	968.00	133.86	9.70	124.16
1367	343	52.00	972.00	134.41	9.74	124.67
1371	343	52.00	976.00	134.96	9.78	125.18
1375	343	52.00	980.00	135.52	9.82	125.70
1379	343	52.00	984.00	136.07	9.86	126.21
1383	343	52.00	988.00	136.62	9.90	126.72
1387	343	52.00	992.00	137.17	9.94	127.23
1391	343	52.00	996.00	137.72	9.98	127.74
1395	343	52.00	1000.00	138.28	10.02	128.26
1399	343	52.00	1004.00	138.83	10.06	128.77
1403	343	52.00	1008.00	139.38	10.10	129.28
1407	343	52.00	1012.00	139.93	10.14	129.79
1411	343	52.00	1016.00	140.48	10.18	130.30
1415	343	52.00	1020.00	141.04	10.22	130.82
1419	343	52.00	1024.00	141.59	10.26	131.33
1423	343	52.00	1028.00	142.14	10.30	131.84
1427	343	52.00	1032.00	142.69	10.34	132.35
1431	343	52.00	1036.00	143.24	10.38	132.86
1435	343	52.00	1040.00	143.80	10.42	133.38
1439	343	52.00	1044.00	144.35	10.46	133.89
1443	343	52.00	1048.00	144.90	10.50	134.40
1447	343	52.00	1052.00	145.45	10.54	134.91
1451	343	52.00	1056.00	146.00	10.58	135.42
1455	343	52.00	1060.00	146.56	10.62	135.94
1459	343	52.00	1064.00	147.11	10.66	136.45
1463	343	52.00	1068.00	147.66	10.70	136.96
1467	343	52.00	1072.00	148.21	10.74	137.47
1471	343	52.00	1076.00	148.76	10.78	137.98
1475	343	52.00	1080.00	149.32	10.82	138.50
1479	343	52.00	1084.00	149.87	10.86	139.01
1483	343	52.00	1088.00	150.42	10.90	139.52
1487	343	52.00	1092.00	150.97	10.94	140.03
1491	343	52.00	1096.00	151.52	10.98	140.54
1495	343	52.00	1100.00	152.08	11.02	141.06
1499	343	52.00	1104.00	152.63	11.06	141.57
1503	343	52.00	1108.00	153.18	11.10	142.08
1507	343	52.00	1112.00	153.73	11.14	142.59
1511	343	52.00	1116.00	154.28	11.18	143.10
1515	343	52.00	1120.00	154.84	11.22	143.62
1519	343	52.00	1124.00	155.39	11.26	144.13
1523	343	52.00	1128.00	155.94	11.30	144.64
1527	343	52.00	1132.00	156.49	11.34	145.15
1531	343	52.00	1136.00	157.04	11.38	145.66
1535	343	52.00	1140.00	157.60	11.42	146.18
1539	343	52.00	1144.00	158.15	11.46	146.69
1543	343	52.00	1148.00	158.70	11.50	147.20
1547	343	52.00	1152.00	159.25	11.54	147.71
1551	343	52.00	1156.00	159.80	11.58	148.22
1555	343	52.00	1160.00	160.36	11.62	148.74
1559	343	52.00	1164.00	160.91	11.66	149.25

▼ for information only - do not enter on Deductions Working Sheet, form P11

APPENDIX II: NI TABLES

Monthly table

Table letter **J**

Employee's Earnings up to and including the UEL	Earnings at the LEL (where earnings are equal to or exceed the LEL)	Earnings above the LEL, up to and including the ET	Earnings above the ET, up to and including the UEL	Total of employee's and employer's contributions	Employee's contributions due on all earnings above the ET	Employer's contributions
1a	1b	1c	1d	1e		
£	£	£ P	£ P	£ P	£ P	£ P
1563	343	52.00	1168.00	161.46	11.70	149.76
1567	343	52.00	1172.00	162.01	11.74	150.27
1571	343	52.00	1176.00	162.56	11.78	150.78
1575	343	52.00	1180.00	163.12	11.82	151.30
1579	343	52.00	1184.00	163.67	11.86	151.81
1583	343	52.00	1188.00	164.22	11.90	152.32
1587	343	52.00	1192.00	164.77	11.94	152.83
1591	343	52.00	1196.00	165.32	11.98	153.34
1595	343	52.00	1200.00	165.88	12.02	153.86
1599	343	52.00	1204.00	166.43	12.06	154.37
1603	343	52.00	1208.00	166.98	12.10	154.88
1607	343	52.00	1212.00	167.53	12.14	155.39
1611	343	52.00	1216.00	168.08	12.18	155.90
1615	343	52.00	1220.00	168.64	12.22	156.42
1619	343	52.00	1224.00	169.19	12.26	156.93
1623	343	52.00	1228.00	169.74	12.30	157.44
1627	343	52.00	1232.00	170.29	12.34	157.95
1631	343	52.00	1236.00	170.84	12.38	158.46
1635	343	52.00	1240.00	171.40	12.42	158.98
1639	343	52.00	1244.00	171.95	12.46	159.49
1643	343	52.00	1248.00	172.50	12.50	160.00
1647	343	52.00	1252.00	173.05	12.54	160.51
1651	343	52.00	1256.00	173.60	12.58	161.02
1655	343	52.00	1260.00	174.16	12.62	161.54
1659	343	52.00	1264.00	174.71	12.66	162.05
1663	343	52.00	1268.00	175.26	12.70	162.56
1667	343	52.00	1272.00	175.81	12.74	163.07
1671	343	52.00	1276.00	176.36	12.78	163.58
1675	343	52.00	1280.00	176.92	12.82	164.10
1679	343	52.00	1284.00	177.47	12.86	164.61
1683	343	52.00	1288.00	178.02	12.90	165.12
1687	343	52.00	1292.00	178.57	12.94	165.63
1691	343	52.00	1296.00	179.12	12.98	166.14
1695	343	52.00	1300.00	179.68	13.02	166.66
1699	343	52.00	1304.00	180.23	13.06	167.17
1703	343	52.00	1308.00	180.78	13.10	167.68
1707	343	52.00	1312.00	181.33	13.14	168.19
1711	343	52.00	1316.00	181.88	13.18	168.70
1715	343	52.00	1320.00	182.44	13.22	169.22
1719	343	52.00	1324.00	182.99	13.26	169.73
1723	343	52.00	1328.00	183.54	13.30	170.24
1727	343	52.00	1332.00	184.09	13.34	170.75
1731	343	52.00	1336.00	184.64	13.38	171.26
1735	343	52.00	1340.00	185.20	13.42	171.78
1739	343	52.00	1344.00	185.75	13.46	172.29
1743	343	52.00	1348.00	186.30	13.50	172.80
1747	343	52.00	1352.00	186.85	13.54	173.31
1751	343	52.00	1356.00	187.40	13.58	173.82
1755	343	52.00	1360.00	187.96	13.62	174.34
1759	343	52.00	1364.00	188.51	13.66	174.85
1763	343	52.00	1368.00	189.06	13.70	175.36
1767	343	52.00	1372.00	189.61	13.74	175.87
1771	343	52.00	1376.00	190.16	13.78	176.38
1775	343	52.00	1380.00	190.72	13.82	176.90
1779	343	52.00	1384.00	191.27	13.86	177.41

▼ for information only - do not enter on Deductions Working Sheet, form P11

47

TAX TABLES

Table letter J **Monthly table**

Employee's Earnings up to and including the UEL	Earnings at the LEL (where earnings are equal to or exceed the LEL)	Earnings above the LEL, up to and including the ET	Earnings above the ET, up to and including the UEL	Total of employee's and employer's contributions	Employee's contributions due on all earnings above the ET	Employer's contributions
	1a	1b	1c	1d	1e	
£	£	£ P	£ P	£ P	£ P	£ P
1783	343	52.00	1388.00	191.82	13.90	177.92
1787	343	52.00	1392.00	192.37	13.94	178.43
1791	343	52.00	1396.00	192.92	13.98	178.94
1795	343	52.00	1400.00	193.48	14.02	179.46
1799	343	52.00	1404.00	194.03	14.06	179.97
1803	343	52.00	1408.00	194.58	14.10	180.48
1807	343	52.00	1412.00	195.13	14.14	180.99
1811	343	52.00	1416.00	195.68	14.18	181.50
1815	343	52.00	1420.00	196.24	14.22	182.02
1819	343	52.00	1424.00	196.79	14.26	182.53
1823	343	52.00	1428.00	197.34	14.30	183.04
1827	343	52.00	1432.00	197.89	14.34	183.55
1831	343	52.00	1436.00	198.44	14.38	184.06
1835	343	52.00	1440.00	199.00	14.42	184.58
1839	343	52.00	1444.00	199.55	14.46	185.09
1843	343	52.00	1448.00	200.10	14.50	185.60
1847	343	52.00	1452.00	200.65	14.54	186.11
1851	343	52.00	1456.00	201.20	14.58	186.62
1855	343	52.00	1460.00	201.76	14.62	187.14
1859	343	52.00	1464.00	202.31	14.66	187.65
1863	343	52.00	1468.00	202.86	14.70	188.16
1867	343	52.00	1472.00	203.41	14.74	188.67
1871	343	52.00	1476.00	203.96	14.78	189.18
1875	343	52.00	1480.00	204.52	14.82	189.70
1879	343	52.00	1484.00	205.07	14.86	190.21
1883	343	52.00	1488.00	205.62	14.90	190.72
1887	343	52.00	1492.00	206.17	14.94	191.23
1891	343	52.00	1496.00	206.72	14.98	191.74
1895	343	52.00	1500.00	207.28	15.02	192.26
1899	343	52.00	1504.00	207.83	15.06	192.77
1903	343	52.00	1508.00	208.38	15.10	193.28
1907	343	52.00	1512.00	208.93	15.14	193.79
1911	343	52.00	1516.00	209.48	15.18	194.30
1915	343	52.00	1520.00	210.04	15.22	194.82
1919	343	52.00	1524.00	210.59	15.26	195.33
1923	343	52.00	1528.00	211.14	15.30	195.84
1927	343	52.00	1532.00	211.69	15.34	196.35
1931	343	52.00	1536.00	212.24	15.38	196.86
1935	343	52.00	1540.00	212.80	15.42	197.38
1939	343	52.00	1544.00	213.35	15.46	197.89
1943	343	52.00	1548.00	213.90	15.50	198.40
1947	343	52.00	1552.00	214.45	15.54	198.91
1951	343	52.00	1556.00	215.00	15.58	199.42
1955	343	52.00	1560.00	215.56	15.62	199.94
1959	343	52.00	1564.00	216.11	15.66	200.45
1963	343	52.00	1568.00	216.66	15.70	200.96
1967	343	52.00	1572.00	217.21	15.74	201.47
1971	343	52.00	1576.00	217.76	15.78	201.98
1975	343	52.00	1580.00	218.32	15.82	202.50
1979	343	52.00	1584.00	218.87	15.86	203.01
1983	343	52.00	1588.00	219.42	15.90	203.52
1987	343	52.00	1592.00	219.97	15.94	204.03
1991	343	52.00	1596.00	220.52	15.98	204.54
1995	343	52.00	1600.00	221.08	16.02	205.06
1999	343	52.00	1604.00	221.63	16.06	205.57

▼ for information only - do not enter on Deductions Working Sheet, form P11

CA38 Version 4 - 11/12/03

APPENDIX II: NI TABLES

Monthly table

Table letter **J**

Employee's Earnings up to and including the UEL	Earnings at the LEL (where earnings are equal to or exceed the LEL)	Earnings above the LEL, up to and including the ET	Earnings above the ET, up to and including the UEL	Total of employee's and employer's contributions	Employee's contributions due on all earnings above the ET	Employer's contributions
1a	1b	1c	1d	1e		
£	£	£ P	£ P	£ P	£ P	£ P
2003	343	52.00	1608.00	222.18	16.10	206.08
2007	343	52.00	1612.00	222.73	16.14	206.59
2011	343	52.00	1616.00	223.28	16.18	207.10
2015	343	52.00	1620.00	223.84	16.22	207.62
2019	343	52.00	1624.00	224.39	16.26	208.13
2023	343	52.00	1628.00	224.94	16.30	208.64
2027	343	52.00	1632.00	225.49	16.34	209.15
2031	343	52.00	1636.00	226.04	16.38	209.66
2035	343	52.00	1640.00	226.60	16.42	210.18
2039	343	52.00	1644.00	227.15	16.46	210.69
2043	343	52.00	1648.00	227.70	16.50	211.20
2047	343	52.00	1652.00	228.25	16.54	211.71
2051	343	52.00	1656.00	228.80	16.58	212.22
2055	343	52.00	1660.00	229.36	16.62	212.74
2059	343	52.00	1664.00	229.91	16.66	213.25
2063	343	52.00	1668.00	230.46	16.70	213.76
2067	343	52.00	1672.00	231.01	16.74	214.27
2071	343	52.00	1676.00	231.56	16.78	214.78
2075	343	52.00	1680.00	232.12	16.82	215.30
2079	343	52.00	1684.00	232.67	16.86	215.81
2083	343	52.00	1688.00	233.22	16.90	216.32
2087	343	52.00	1692.00	233.77	16.94	216.83
2091	343	52.00	1696.00	234.32	16.98	217.34
2095	343	52.00	1700.00	234.88	17.02	217.86
2099	343	52.00	1704.00	235.43	17.06	218.37
2103	343	52.00	1708.00	235.98	17.10	218.88
2107	343	52.00	1712.00	236.53	17.14	219.39
2111	343	52.00	1716.00	237.08	17.18	219.90
2115	343	52.00	1720.00	237.64	17.22	220.42
2119	343	52.00	1724.00	238.19	17.26	220.93
2123	343	52.00	1728.00	238.74	17.30	221.44
2127	343	52.00	1732.00	239.29	17.34	221.95
2131	343	52.00	1736.00	239.84	17.38	222.46
2135	343	52.00	1740.00	240.40	17.42	222.98
2139	343	52.00	1744.00	240.95	17.46	223.49
2143	343	52.00	1748.00	241.50	17.50	224.00
2147	343	52.00	1752.00	242.05	17.54	224.51
2151	343	52.00	1756.00	242.60	17.58	225.02
2155	343	52.00	1760.00	243.16	17.62	225.54
2159	343	52.00	1764.00	243.71	17.66	226.05
2163	343	52.00	1768.00	244.26	17.70	226.56
2167	343	52.00	1772.00	244.81	17.74	227.07
2171	343	52.00	1776.00	245.36	17.78	227.58
2175	343	52.00	1780.00	245.92	17.82	228.10
2179	343	52.00	1784.00	246.47	17.86	228.61
2183	343	52.00	1788.00	247.02	17.90	229.12
2187	343	52.00	1792.00	247.57	17.94	229.63
2191	343	52.00	1796.00	248.12	17.98	230.14
2195	343	52.00	1800.00	248.68	18.02	230.66
2199	343	52.00	1804.00	249.23	18.06	231.17
2203	343	52.00	1808.00	249.78	18.10	231.68
2207	343	52.00	1812.00	250.33	18.14	232.19
2211	343	52.00	1816.00	250.88	18.18	232.70
2215	343	52.00	1820.00	251.44	18.22	233.22
2219	343	52.00	1824.00	251.99	18.26	233.73

▼ for information only - do not enter on Deductions Working Sheet, form P11

TAX TABLES

Table letter J **Monthly table**

Employee's Earnings up to and including the UEL ▼	Earnings at the LEL (where earnings are equal to or exceed the LEL)	Earnings above the LEL, up to and including the ET	Earnings above the ET, up to and including the UEL	Total of employee's and employer's contributions	Employee's contributions due on all earnings above the ET	Employer's contributions ▼
1a	1b	1c	1d	1e		
£	£	£ P	£ P	£ P	£ P	£ P
2223	343	52.00	1828.00	252.54	18.30	234.24
2227	343	52.00	1832.00	253.09	18.34	234.75
2231	343	52.00	1836.00	253.64	18.38	235.26
2235	343	52.00	1840.00	254.20	18.42	235.78
2239	343	52.00	1844.00	254.75	18.46	236.29
2243	343	52.00	1848.00	255.30	18.50	236.80
2247	343	52.00	1852.00	255.85	18.54	237.31
2251	343	52.00	1856.00	256.40	18.58	237.82
2255	343	52.00	1860.00	256.96	18.62	238.34
2259	343	52.00	1864.00	257.51	18.66	238.85
2263	343	52.00	1868.00	258.06	18.70	239.36
2267	343	52.00	1872.00	258.61	18.74	239.87
2271	343	52.00	1876.00	259.16	18.78	240.38
2275	343	52.00	1880.00	259.72	18.82	240.90
2279	343	52.00	1884.00	260.27	18.86	241.41
2283	343	52.00	1888.00	260.82	18.90	241.92
2287	343	52.00	1892.00	261.37	18.94	242.43
2291	343	52.00	1896.00	261.92	18.98	242.94
2295	343	52.00	1900.00	262.48	19.02	243.46
2299	343	52.00	1904.00	263.03	19.06	243.97
2303	343	52.00	1908.00	263.58	19.10	244.48
2307	343	52.00	1912.00	264.13	19.14	244.99
2311	343	52.00	1916.00	264.68	19.18	245.50
2315	343	52.00	1920.00	265.24	19.22	246.02
2319	343	52.00	1924.00	265.79	19.26	246.53
2323	343	52.00	1928.00	266.34	19.30	247.04
2327	343	52.00	1932.00	266.89	19.34	247.55
2331	343	52.00	1936.00	267.44	19.38	248.06
2335	343	52.00	1940.00	268.00	19.42	248.58
2339	343	52.00	1944.00	268.55	19.46	249.09
2343	343	52.00	1948.00	269.10	19.50	249.60
2347	343	52.00	1952.00	269.65	19.54	250.11
2351	343	52.00	1956.00	270.20	19.58	250.62
2355	343	52.00	1960.00	270.76	19.62	251.14
2359	343	52.00	1964.00	271.31	19.66	251.65
2363	343	52.00	1968.00	271.86	19.70	252.16
2367	343	52.00	1972.00	272.41	19.74	252.67
2371	343	52.00	1976.00	272.96	19.78	253.18
2375	343	52.00	1980.00	273.52	19.82	253.70
2379	343	52.00	1984.00	274.07	19.86	254.21
2383	343	52.00	1988.00	274.62	19.90	254.72
2387	343	52.00	1992.00	275.17	19.94	255.23
2391	343	52.00	1996.00	275.72	19.98	255.74
2395	343	52.00	2000.00	276.28	20.02	256.26
2399	343	52.00	2004.00	276.83	20.06	256.77
2403	343	52.00	2008.00	277.38	20.10	257.28
2407	343	52.00	2012.00	277.93	20.14	257.79
2411	343	52.00	2016.00	278.48	20.18	258.30
2415	343	52.00	2020.00	279.04	20.22	258.82
2419	343	52.00	2024.00	279.59	20.26	259.33
2423	343	52.00	2028.00	280.14	20.30	259.84
2427	343	52.00	2032.00	280.69	20.34	260.35
2431	343	52.00	2036.00	281.24	20.38	260.86
2435	343	52.00	2040.00	281.80	20.42	261.38
2439	343	52.00	2044.00	282.35	20.46	261.89

50   ▼ for information only - do not enter on Deductions Working Sheet, form P11

APPENDIX II: NI TABLES

Monthly table

Table letter **J**

Employee's Earnings up to and including the UEL	Earnings at the LEL (where earnings are equal to or exceed the LEL)	Earnings above the LEL, up to and including the ET	Earnings above the ET, up to and including the UEL	Total of employee's and employer's contributions	Employee's contributions due on all earnings above the ET	Employer's contributions
▼	1a	1b	1c	1d	1e	▼
£	£	£ P	£ P	£ P	£ P	£ P
2443	343	52.00	2048.00	282.90	20.50	262.40
2447	343	52.00	2052.00	283.45	20.54	262.91
2451	343	52.00	2056.00	284.00	20.58	263.42
2455	343	52.00	2060.00	284.56	20.62	263.94
2459	343	52.00	2064.00	285.11	20.66	264.45
2463	343	52.00	2068.00	285.66	20.70	264.96
2467	343	52.00	2072.00	286.21	20.74	265.47
2471	343	52.00	2076.00	286.76	20.78	265.98
2475	343	52.00	2080.00	287.32	20.82	266.50
2479	343	52.00	2084.00	287.87	20.86	267.01
2483	343	52.00	2088.00	288.42	20.90	267.52
2487	343	52.00	2092.00	288.97	20.94	268.03
2491	343	52.00	2096.00	289.52	20.98	268.54
2495	343	52.00	2100.00	290.08	21.02	269.06
2499	343	52.00	2104.00	290.63	21.06	269.57
2503	343	52.00	2108.00	291.18	21.10	270.08
2507	343	52.00	2112.00	291.73	21.14	270.59
2511	343	52.00	2116.00	292.28	21.18	271.10
2515	343	52.00	2120.00	292.84	21.22	271.62
2519	343	52.00	2124.00	293.39	21.26	272.13
2523	343	52.00	2128.00	293.94	21.30	272.64
2527	343	52.00	2132.00	294.49	21.34	273.15
2531	343	52.00	2136.00	295.04	21.38	273.66
2535	343	52.00	2140.00	295.60	21.42	274.18
2539	343	52.00	2144.00	296.15	21.46	274.69
2543	343	52.00	2148.00	296.70	21.50	275.20
2547	343	52.00	2152.00	297.25	21.54	275.71
2551	343	52.00	2156.00	297.80	21.58	276.22
2555	343	52.00	2160.00	298.36	21.62	276.74
2559	343	52.00	2164.00	298.91	21.66	277.25
2563	343	52.00	2168.00	299.46	21.70	277.76
2567	343	52.00	2172.00	300.01	21.74	278.27
2571	343	52.00	2176.00	300.56	21.78	278.78
2575	343	52.00	2180.00	301.12	21.82	279.30
2579	343	52.00	2184.00	301.67	21.86	279.81
2583	343	52.00	2188.00	302.22	21.90	280.32
2587	343	52.00	2192.00	302.77	21.94	280.83
2591	343	52.00	2196.00	303.32	21.98	281.34
2595	343	52.00	2200.00	303.88	22.02	281.86
2599	343	52.00	2204.00	304.43	22.06	282.37
2603	343	52.00	2208.00	304.98	22.10	282.88
2607	343	52.00	2212.00	305.53	22.14	283.39
2611	343	52.00	2216.00	306.08	22.18	283.90
2615	343	52.00	2220.00	306.64	22.22	284.42
2619	343	52.00	2224.00	307.19	22.26	284.93
2623	343	52.00	2228.00	307.74	22.30	285.44
2627	343	52.00	2232.00	308.29	22.34	285.95
2631	343	52.00	2236.00	308.84	22.38	286.46
2635	343	52.00	2240.00	309.40	22.42	286.98
2639	343	52.00	2244.00	309.95	22.46	287.49
2643	343	52.00	2248.00	310.29	22.48	287.81
2644	343	52.00	2249.00	310.36	22.49	287.87

If the employee's gross pay is over £2644, go to page 52

▼ for information only - do not enter on Deductions Working Sheet, form P11

TAX TABLES

Working out and recording NICs where employee's total earnings exceed the UEL

Where the employee's total earnings exceed the UEL, only the earnings between the ET and the UEL should be recorded in column 1c of form P11

Use the main table to work out the total of employee's and employer's NICs and the employee's NICs due on the earnings up to the UEL.

To work out the total of employee's and employer's NICs and the employee's NICs due on the earnings above the UEL, take the following action:

Step	Action	Example (based on Table A with total monthly earnings of £4544.29)
1	subtract the UEL figure from the total gross pay	£4544.29 - £2644 = £1900.29
2	round the answer down to the nearest whole £	Rounded down to £1900
3	look this figure up in the "additional gross pay table" on page 53	Look up £1900
4	if the figure is not shown in the table, build up to it by adding together as few entries as possible	(see table below)

Amount	Total of Employee's and Employer's NICs payable	Employee's NICs payable
£1000	£138.00	£10.00
£900	£124.20	£9.00
Totals	**£262.20**	**£19.00**

Step	Action		
5	add the further totals of employee's and employer's NICs and employee's NICs worked out on the earnings above the UEL - columns 1d and 1e of the additional gross pay table - to the totals of employee's and employer's NICs and employee's NICs due for earnings at the UEL - columns 1d and 1e of the main table	Total payable by employee and employer £262.20 (further employee and employer NICs) £535.26 (due for employee and employer on earnings at UEL)	Total payable by employee £19.00 (further employee NICs) £247.39 (due for employee on earnings at UEL)
		Totals £797.46	**£266.39**

Step	Action		
6	record the figures resulting from Step 5 in columns 1d and 1e of form P11	On form P11 record	

Col 1a	Col 1b	Col 1c	Col 1d	Col 1e
343	52.00	2249.00	797.46	266.39

52

APPENDIX II: NI TABLES

Additional gross pay table

Earnings on which contributions payable ▼ £	Total of employee's and employer's contributions payable 1d £	Employee's contributions payable 1e £	Employer's contributions payable ▼ £
1	0.14	0.01	0.13
2	0.28	0.02	0.26
3	0.41	0.03	0.38
4	0.55	0.04	0.51
5	0.69	0.05	0.64
6	0.83	0.06	0.77
7	0.97	0.07	0.90
8	1.10	0.08	1.02
9	1.24	0.09	1.15
10	1.38	0.10	1.28
11	1.52	0.11	1.41
12	1.66	0.12	1.54
13	1.79	0.13	1.66
14	1.93	0.14	1.79
15	2.07	0.15	1.92
16	2.21	0.16	2.05
17	2.35	0.17	2.18
18	2.48	0.18	2.30
19	2.62	0.19	2.43
20	2.76	0.20	2.56
21	2.90	0.21	2.69
22	3.04	0.22	2.82
23	3.17	0.23	2.94
24	3.31	0.24	3.07
25	3.45	0.25	3.20
26	3.59	0.26	3.33
27	3.73	0.27	3.46
28	3.86	0.28	3.58
29	4.00	0.29	3.71
30	4.14	0.30	3.84
31	4.28	0.31	3.97
32	4.42	0.32	4.10
33	4.55	0.33	4.22
34	4.69	0.34	4.35
35	4.83	0.35	4.48
36	4.97	0.36	4.61
37	5.11	0.37	4.74
38	5.24	0.38	4.86
39	5.38	0.39	4.99
40	5.52	0.40	5.12
41	5.66	0.41	5.25
42	5.80	0.42	5.38
43	5.93	0.43	5.50
44	6.07	0.44	5.63
45	6.21	0.45	5.76
46	6.35	0.46	5.89
47	6.49	0.47	6.02
48	6.62	0.48	6.14
49	6.76	0.49	6.27
50	6.90	0.50	6.40
51	7.04	0.51	6.53
52	7.18	0.52	6.66
53	7.31	0.53	6.78
54	7.45	0.54	6.91
55	7.59	0.55	7.04

▼ for information only - do not enter on Deductions Working Sheet, form P11

TAX TABLES

Earnings on which contributions payable ▼ £	Total of employee's and employer's contributions payable 1d £	Employee's contributions payable 1e £	Employer's contributions payable ▼ £
56	7.73	0.56	7.17
57	7.87	0.57	7.30
58	8.00	0.58	7.42
59	8.14	0.59	7.55
60	8.28	0.60	7.68
61	8.42	0.61	7.81
62	8.56	0.62	7.94
63	8.69	0.63	8.06
64	8.83	0.64	8.19
65	8.97	0.65	8.32
66	9.11	0.66	8.45
67	9.25	0.67	8.58
68	9.38	0.68	8.70
69	9.52	0.69	8.83
70	9.66	0.70	8.96
71	9.80	0.71	9.09
72	9.94	0.72	9.22
73	10.07	0.73	9.34
74	10.21	0.74	9.47
75	10.35	0.75	9.60
76	10.49	0.76	9.73
77	10.63	0.77	9.86
78	10.76	0.78	9.98
79	10.90	0.79	10.11
80	11.04	0.80	10.24
81	11.18	0.81	10.37
82	11.32	0.82	10.50
83	11.45	0.83	10.62
84	11.59	0.84	10.75
85	11.73	0.85	10.88
86	11.87	0.86	11.01
87	12.01	0.87	11.14
88	12.14	0.88	11.26
89	12.28	0.89	11.39
90	12.42	0.90	11.52
91	12.56	0.91	11.65
92	12.70	0.92	11.78
93	12.83	0.93	11.90
94	12.97	0.94	12.03
95	13.11	0.95	12.16
96	13.25	0.96	12.29
97	13.39	0.97	12.42
98	13.52	0.98	12.54
99	13.66	0.99	12.67
100	13.80	1.00	12.80
200	27.60	2.00	25.60
300	41.40	3.00	38.40
400	55.20	4.00	51.20
500	69.00	5.00	64.00
600	82.80	6.00	76.80
700	96.60	7.00	89.60
800	110.40	8.00	102.40
900	124.20	9.00	115.20
1000	138.00	10.00	128.00
2000	276.00	20.00	256.00

▼ for information only - do not enter on Deductions Working Sheet, form P11

APPENDIX II: NI TABLES

Earnings on which contributions payable ▼ £	Total of employee's and employer's contributions payable 1d £	Employee's contributions payable 1e £	Employer's contributions payable ▼ £
3000	414.00	30.00	384.00
4000	552.00	40.00	512.00
5000	690.00	50.00	640.00
6000	828.00	60.00	768.00
7000	966.00	70.00	896.00
8000	1104.00	80.00	1024.00
9000	1242.00	90.00	1152.00
10000	1380.00	100.00	1280.00
20000	2760.00	200.00	2560.00
30000	4140.00	300.00	3840.00
40000	5520.00	400.00	5120.00
50000	6900.00	500.00	6400.00
60000	8280.00	600.00	7680.00
70000	9660.00	700.00	8960.00
80000	11040.00	800.00	10240.00
90000	12420.00	900.00	11520.00
100000	13800.00	1000.00	12800.00

▼ for information only - do not enter on Deductions Working Sheet, form P11   55

TAX TABLES

Inland Revenue

CA41
National Insurance Contributions Tables

National Insurance contributions Tables B and C

Use from
6 April 2004 to
5 April 2005 inclusive

APPENDIX II: NI TABLES

Earnings limits and NIC rates

Earnings limits	Employee's contribution — Contribution Table letter B	Employee's contribution — Contribution Table letter C	Employer's contribution — Table Letters B and C
Below £79.00 weekly, or below £343.00 monthly, or below £4108.00 yearly	Nil	Nil	Nil
£79.00 to £91.00 weekly, or £343.00 to £395.00 monthly, or £4108.00 to £4745.00 yearly	0%	Nil	0%
£91.01 to £610.00 weekly, or £395.01 to £2644.00 monthly, or £4745.01 to £31720.00 yearly	4.85% on earnings above the ET	Nil	12.8% on earnings above the ET
Over £610.00 weekly, or over £2644.00 monthly, or over £31720.00 yearly	4.85% on earnings above the ET, up to and including the UEL then **1%** on all earnings above the UEL	Nil	12.8% on all earnings above the ET

TAX TABLES

Monthly table for not contracted-out reduced rate contributions for use from 6 April 2004 to 5 April 2005

Table letter B

Use this table for
married women or widows who have the right to pay reduced rate employee's contributions for whom you hold a valid certificate CA4139, CF383 or CF380A.

Do not use this table for
- women aged 60 or over, see Table C
- women for whom you hold form CA2700, see leaflet CA38.

Completing Deductions Working Sheet, form P11 or substitute
- enter 'B' in the space provided in the 'End of Year Summary' box of form P11
- copy the figures in columns 1d and 1e of the table to columns 1d and 1e of form P11. You may copy the figures in columns 1a-1c of the table to columns 1a-1c of form P11 if you wish.

If the employee's total earnings fall between the LEL and the UEL and the exact gross pay is not shown in the table, use the next smaller figure shown. If the employee's total earnings exceed the UEL, see page 52.

The figures in the left hand column of each table show steps between the LEL and the UEL. The NICs liability for each step is calculated at the mid-point of the steps so you and your employee may pay slightly more or less than if you used the exact percentage method.

▼ Employee's Earnings up to and including the UEL	Earnings at the LEL (where earnings are equal to or exceed the LEL)	Earnings above the LEL, up to and including the ET	Earnings above the ET, up to and including the UEL	Total of employee's and employer's contributions	Employee's contributions due on all earnings above the ET	▼ Employer's contributions
1a	1a	1b	1c	1d	1e	
£	£	£ P	£ P	£ P	£ P	£ P
Up to and including 342.99	No NIC Liability, make no entries on forms P11 and P14					
343	343	0.00	0.00	0.00	0.00	0.00
347	343	4.00	0.00	0.00	0.00	0.00
351	343	8.00	0.00	0.00	0.00	0.00
355	343	12.00	0.00	0.00	0.00	0.00
359	343	16.00	0.00	0.00	0.00	0.00
363	343	20.00	0.00	0.00	0.00	0.00
367	343	24.00	0.00	0.00	0.00	0.00
371	343	28.00	0.00	0.00	0.00	0.00
375	343	32.00	0.00	0.00	0.00	0.00
379	343	36.00	0.00	0.00	0.00	0.00
383	343	40.00	0.00	0.00	0.00	0.00
387	343	44.00	0.00	0.00	0.00	0.00
391	343	48.00	0.00	0.00	0.00	0.00
395	343	52.00	0.00	0.00	0.00	0.00
399	343	52.00	4.00	1.06	0.29	0.77
403	343	52.00	8.00	1.76	0.48	1.28
407	343	52.00	12.00	2.47	0.68	1.79
411	343	52.00	16.00	3.17	0.87	2.30
415	343	52.00	20.00	3.89	1.07	2.82
419	343	52.00	24.00	4.59	1.26	3.33
423	343	52.00	28.00	5.29	1.45	3.84
427	343	52.00	32.00	6.00	1.65	4.35
431	343	52.00	36.00	6.70	1.84	4.86
435	343	52.00	40.00	7.42	2.04	5.38
439	343	52.00	44.00	8.12	2.23	5.89
443	343	52.00	48.00	8.82	2.42	6.40
447	343	52.00	52.00	9.53	2.62	6.91
451	343	52.00	56.00	10.23	2.81	7.42
455	343	52.00	60.00	10.95	3.01	7.94
459	343	52.00	64.00	11.65	3.20	8.45
463	343	52.00	68.00	12.35	3.39	8.96
467	343	52.00	72.00	13.06	3.59	9.47
471	343	52.00	76.00	13.76	3.78	9.98
475	343	52.00	80.00	14.48	3.98	10.50
479	343	52.00	84.00	15.18	4.17	11.01

▼ for information only - do not enter on Deductions Working Sheet, form P11

APPENDIX II: NI TABLES

Monthly table for employees who are State Pension Age or over- employer only contributions for use from 6 April 2004 to 5 April 2005

Table letter **C**

Use this table for

employees who are State Pension Age or over, for whom you hold a valid certificate CA4140 or CF384.

Completing Deductions Working Sheet, form P11 or substitute

- enter 'C' in the space provided in the 'End of Year Summary' box of form P11
- copy the figures in column 1d of the table to column 1d of form P11. These figures represent the total of employer only contributions payable.

- you may copy the figures in columns 1a-1c of the table to columns 1a-1c of form P11 if you wish.

If the employee's total earnings fall between the LEL and the UEL and the exact gross pay is not shown in the table, use the next smaller figure shown. If the employee's total earnings exceed the UEL, see page 53.

The figures in the left hand column of each table show steps between the LEL and the UEL. The NICs liability for each step is calculated at the mid-point of the steps so you may pay slightly more or less than if you used the exact percentage method.

▼ Employee's Earnings up to and including the UEL	Earnings at the LEL (where earnings are equal to or exceed the LEL)	Earnings above the LEL, up to and including the ET	Earnings above the ET, up to and including the UEL	Total of employee's and employer's contributions
	1a	1b	1c	1d
£	£	£ P	£ P	£ P
Up to and including 342.99	No NIC Liability, make no entries on forms P11 and P14			
343	343	0.00	0.00	0.00
347	343	4.00	0.00	0.00
351	343	8.00	0.00	0.00
355	343	12.00	0.00	0.00
359	343	16.00	0.00	0.00
363	343	20.00	0.00	0.00
367	343	24.00	0.00	0.00
371	343	28.00	0.00	0.00
375	343	32.00	0.00	0.00
379	343	36.00	0.00	0.00
383	343	40.00	0.00	0.00
387	343	44.00	0.00	0.00
391	343	48.00	0.00	0.00
395	343	52.00	0.00	0.00
399	343	52.00	4.00	0.77
403	343	52.00	8.00	1.28
407	343	52.00	12.00	1.79
411	343	52.00	16.00	2.30
415	343	52.00	20.00	2.82
419	343	52.00	24.00	3.33
423	343	52.00	28.00	3.84
427	343	52.00	32.00	4.35
431	343	52.00	36.00	4.86
435	343	52.00	40.00	5.38
439	343	52.00	44.00	5.89
443	343	52.00	48.00	6.40
447	343	52.00	52.00	6.91
451	343	52.00	56.00	7.42
455	343	52.00	60.00	7.94
459	343	52.00	64.00	8.45
463	343	52.00	68.00	8.96
467	343	52.00	72.00	9.47
471	343	52.00	76.00	9.98
475	343	52.00	80.00	10.50
479	343	52.00	84.00	11.01

▼ for information only - do not enter on Deductions Working Sheet, form P11

TAX TABLES

Table letter C

Monthly table

Employee's Earnings up to and including the UEL	Earnings at the LEL (where earnings are equal to or exceed the LEL)	Earnings above the LEL, up to and including the ET	Earnings above the ET, up to and including the UEL	Total of employee's and employer's contributions
	1a	1b	1c	1d
£	£	£ P	£ P	£ P
483	343	52.00	88.00	11.52
487	343	52.00	92.00	12.03
491	343	52.00	96.00	12.54
495	343	52.00	100.00	13.06
499	343	52.00	104.00	13.57
503	343	52.00	108.00	14.08
507	343	52.00	112.00	14.59
511	343	52.00	116.00	15.10
515	343	52.00	120.00	15.62
519	343	52.00	124.00	16.13
523	343	52.00	128.00	16.64
527	343	52.00	132.00	17.15
531	343	52.00	136.00	17.66
535	343	52.00	140.00	18.18
539	343	52.00	144.00	18.69
543	343	52.00	148.00	19.20
547	343	52.00	152.00	19.71
551	343	52.00	156.00	20.22
555	343	52.00	160.00	20.74
559	343	52.00	164.00	21.25
563	343	52.00	168.00	21.76
567	343	52.00	172.00	22.27
571	343	52.00	176.00	22.78
575	343	52.00	180.00	23.30
579	343	52.00	184.00	23.81
583	343	52.00	188.00	24.32
587	343	52.00	192.00	24.83
591	343	52.00	196.00	25.34
595	343	52.00	200.00	25.86
599	343	52.00	204.00	26.37
603	343	52.00	208.00	26.88
607	343	52.00	212.00	27.39
611	343	52.00	216.00	27.90
615	343	52.00	220.00	28.42
619	343	52.00	224.00	28.93
623	343	52.00	228.00	29.44
627	343	52.00	232.00	29.95
631	343	52.00	236.00	30.46
635	343	52.00	240.00	30.98
639	343	52.00	244.00	31.49
643	343	52.00	248.00	32.00
647	343	52.00	252.00	32.51
651	343	52.00	256.00	33.02
655	343	52.00	260.00	33.54
659	343	52.00	264.00	34.05
663	343	52.00	268.00	34.56
667	343	52.00	272.00	35.07
671	343	52.00	276.00	35.58
675	343	52.00	280.00	36.10
679	343	52.00	284.00	36.61
683	343	52.00	288.00	37.12
687	343	52.00	292.00	37.63
691	343	52.00	296.00	38.14
695	343	52.00	300.00	38.66
699	343	52.00	304.00	39.17

42 ▼ for information only - do not enter on Deductions Working Sheet, form P11

APPENDIX II: NI TABLES

Inland Revenue

CA39
National Insurance Contributions Tables

Contracted-out contributions for employers with Contracted-out Salary Related Schemes

Use from
6 April 2004 to
5 April 2005 inclusive

TAX TABLES

Earnings limits and NIC rates

Earnings limits	Employee's contribution — Contribution Table letter D	Employee's contribution — Contribution Table letter E	Employee's contribution — Contribution Table letter L	Employer's contribution — Table letters D, E and L	Employee's NIC rebate on earnings above the LEL, up to and including the ET (Applies to contribution category letters D and L only)	Employer's NIC rebate on earnings above the LEL, up to and including the ET
Below £79.00 weekly, or below £343.00 monthly, or below £4108.00 yearly	Nil	Nil	Nil	Nil	Nil	Nil
£79.00 to £91.00 weekly, or £343.00 to £395.00 monthly, or £4108.00 to £4745.00 yearly	0%	0%	0%	0%	1.6% on earnings from £79.01, up to and including £91.00 (or monthly or annual equivalents)	3.5% on earnings from £79.01, up to and including £91.00 (or monthly or annual equivalents)
£91.01 to £610.00 weekly, or £395.01 to £2644.00 monthly, or £4745.01 to £31720.00 yearly	9.4% on earnings above the ET	4.85% on earnings above the ET	1% on earnings above the ET	9.3% on earnings above the ET		
Over £610.00 weekly, or over £2644.00 monthly, or over £31720.00 yearly	9.4% on earnings above the ET, up to and including the UEL, then 1% on all earnings above the UEL	4.85% on earnings above the ET, up to and including the UEL, then 1% on all earnings above the UEL	1% on all earnings above the ET	9.3% on earnings above the ET, up to and including the UEL, then 12.8% on all earnings above the UEL		

APPENDIX II: NI TABLES

Weekly table for Contracted-out Salary Related standard rate contributions for use from 6 April 2004 to 5 April 2005

Table letter D

Use this table for

employees in your Contracted-out Salary Related Scheme or the salary related part of your Contracted-out Mixed Benefit Scheme, who are age 16 or over and under State Pension Age (65 for men, 60 for women).

Do not use this table for

- married women or widows who have the right to pay reduced rate employee's contributions, see table E
- employees who are State Pension Age or over, see leaflet CA41
- employees in your Contracted-out Salary Related Scheme or the salary related part of your Contracted out Mixed Benefit Scheme for whom you hold form CA2700, see table L
- employees who have an Appropriate Personal Pension or Appropriate Personal Pension Stakeholder Pension, see leaflet CA38
- employees contracted-out in a Contracted-out Money Purchase Scheme, Contracted-out Money Purchase Stakeholder Pension Scheme or in the money purchase part of a Contracted-out Mixed Benefit Scheme, see leaflet CA43.

Completing Deductions working Sheet, form P11 or substitute

- enter 'D' in the space provided in the 'End of Year Summary' box of form P11
- copy the figures in columns 1a-1e of the table to columns 1a-1e of form P11 on the line next to the tax week in which the employee is paid.

If the employee's total earnings fall between the LEL and the UEL and the exact gross pay is not shown in the table, use the next smaller figure shown. If the employee's total earnings exceed the UEL, see page 79.

The figures in the left hand column of each table show steps between the LEL and the UEL. The NICS liability for each step is calculated at the mid-point of the steps so you and your employee may pay slightly more or less than if you used the exact percentage method.

▼ Employee's Earnings up to and including the UEL	Earnings at the LEL (where earnings are equal to or exceed the LEL)	Earnings above the LEL, up to and including the ET	Earnings above the ET, up to and including the UEL	Total of employee's and employer's contributions	Employee's contributions due on all earnings above the ET	▼ Employer's contributions
	1a	1b	1c	1d	1e	
£	£	£ P	£ P	£ P	£ P	£ P
Up to and including 78.99	No NIC Liability, make no entries on forms P11 and P14					
79	79	0.00	0.00	0.00	0.00	0.00
80	79	1.00	0.00	R 0.07	0.00	R 0.07
81	79	2.00	0.00	R 0.13	0.00	R 0.13
82	79	3.00	0.00	R 0.18	0.00	R 0.18
83	79	4.00	0.00	R 0.23	0.00	R 0.23
84	79	5.00	0.00	R 0.28	0.00	R 0.28
85	79	6.00	0.00	R 0.33	0.00	R 0.33
86	79	7.00	0.00	R 0.38	0.00	R 0.38
87	79	8.00	0.00	R 0.44	0.00	R 0.44
88	79	9.00	0.00	R 0.48	0.00	R 0.48
89	79	10.00	0.00	R 0.54	0.00	R 0.54
90	79	11.00	0.00	R 0.58	0.00	R 0.58
91	79	12.00	0.00	R 0.61	0.00	R 0.61
92	79	12.00	1.00	R 0.33	0.00	R 0.33
93	79	12.00	2.00	R 0.15	0.04	R 0.19
94	79	12.00	3.00	0.04	0.14	R 0.10
95	79	12.00	4.00	0.23	0.23	0.00
96	79	12.00	5.00	0.42	0.33	0.09
97	79	12.00	6.00	0.60	0.42	0.18
98	79	12.00	7.00	0.79	0.51	0.28
99	79	12.00	8.00	0.98	0.61	0.37
100	79	12.00	9.00	1.16	0.70	0.46
101	79	12.00	10.00	1.36	0.80	0.56
102	79	12.00	11.00	1.54	0.89	0.65
103	79	12.00	12.00	1.72	0.98	0.74

▼ for information only - do not enter on Deductions Working Sheet, form P11

TAX TABLES

Weekly table

Table letter **D**

Employee's Earnings up to and including the UEL	Earnings at the LEL (where earnings are equal to or exceed the LEL) 1a	Earnings above the LEL, up to and including the ET 1b	Earnings above the ET, up to and including the UEL 1c	Total of employee's and employer's contributions 1d	Employee's contributions due on all earnings above the ET 1e	Employer's contributions
£	£	£ P	£ P	£ P	£ P	£ P
104	79	12.00	13.00	1.91	1.08	0.83
105	79	12.00	14.00	2.10	1.17	0.93
106	79	12.00	15.00	2.29	1.27	1.02
107	79	12.00	16.00	2.47	1.36	1.11
108	79	12.00	17.00	2.66	1.45	1.21
109	79	12.00	18.00	2.85	1.55	1.30
110	79	12.00	19.00	3.03	1.64	1.39
111	79	12.00	20.00	3.23	1.74	1.49
112	79	12.00	21.00	3.41	1.83	1.58
113	79	12.00	22.00	3.59	1.92	1.67
114	79	12.00	23.00	3.78	2.02	1.76
115	79	12.00	24.00	3.97	2.11	1.86
116	79	12.00	25.00	4.16	2.21	1.95
117	79	12.00	26.00	4.34	2.30	2.04
118	79	12.00	27.00	4.53	2.39	2.14
119	79	12.00	28.00	4.72	2.49	2.23
120	79	12.00	29.00	4.90	2.58	2.32
121	79	12.00	30.00	5.10	2.68	2.42
122	79	12.00	31.00	5.28	2.77	2.51
123	79	12.00	32.00	5.46	2.86	2.60
124	79	12.00	33.00	5.65	2.96	2.69
125	79	12.00	34.00	5.84	3.05	2.79
126	79	12.00	35.00	6.03	3.15	2.88
127	79	12.00	36.00	6.21	3.24	2.97
128	79	12.00	37.00	6.40	3.33	3.07
129	79	12.00	38.00	6.59	3.43	3.16
130	79	12.00	39.00	6.77	3.52	3.25
131	79	12.00	40.00	6.97	3.62	3.35
132	79	12.00	41.00	7.15	3.71	3.44
133	79	12.00	42.00	7.33	3.80	3.53
134	79	12.00	43.00	7.52	3.90	3.62
135	79	12.00	44.00	7.71	3.99	3.72
136	79	12.00	45.00	7.90	4.09	3.81
137	79	12.00	46.00	8.08	4.18	3.90
138	79	12.00	47.00	8.27	4.27	4.00
139	79	12.00	48.00	8.46	4.37	4.09
140	79	12.00	49.00	8.64	4.46	4.18
141	79	12.00	50.00	8.84	4.56	4.28
142	79	12.00	51.00	9.02	4.65	4.37
143	79	12.00	52.00	9.20	4.74	4.46
144	79	12.00	53.00	9.39	4.84	4.55
145	79	12.00	54.00	9.58	4.93	4.65
146	79	12.00	55.00	9.77	5.03	4.74
147	79	12.00	56.00	9.95	5.12	4.83
148	79	12.00	57.00	10.14	5.21	4.93
149	79	12.00	58.00	10.33	5.31	5.02
150	79	12.00	59.00	10.51	5.40	5.11
151	79	12.00	60.00	10.71	5.50	5.21
152	79	12.00	61.00	10.89	5.59	5.30
153	79	12.00	62.00	11.07	5.68	5.39
154	79	12.00	63.00	11.26	5.78	5.48
155	79	12.00	64.00	11.45	5.87	5.58
156	79	12.00	65.00	11.64	5.97	5.67
157	79	12.00	66.00	11.82	6.06	5.76
158	79	12.00	67.00	12.01	6.15	5.86

▼ for information only - do not enter on Deductions Working Sheet, form P11

APPENDIX II: NI TABLES

Monthly table for Contracted-out Salary Related standard rate contributions for use from 6 April 2004 to 5 April 2005

Table letter **D**

Use this table for

employees in your Contracted-out Salary Related Scheme or the salary related part of your Contracted-out Mixed Benefit Scheme, who are age 16 or over and under State Pension Age (65 for men, 60 for women).

Do not use this table for

- married women or widows who have the right to pay reduced rate employee's contributions, see table E
- employees who are State Pension Age or over, see leaflet CA41
- employees in your Contracted-out Salary Related Scheme or the salary related part of your Contracted out Mixed Benefit Scheme for whom you hold form CA2700, see table L
- employees who have an Appropriate Personal Pension or Appropriate Personal Pension Stakeholder Pension, see leaflet CA38
- employees contracted-out in a Contracted-out Money Purchase Scheme, Contracted-out Money Purchase Stakeholder Pension Scheme or in the money purchase part of a Contracted-out Mixed Benefit Scheme, see leaflet CA43.

Completing Deductions working Sheet, form P11 or substitute

- enter 'D' in the space provided in the 'End of Year Summary' box of form P11
- copy the figures in columns 1a-1e of the table to columns 1a-1e of form P11 on the line next to the tax week in which the employee is paid.

If the employee's total earnings fall between the LEL and the UEL and the exact gross pay is not shown in the table, use the next smaller figure shown. If the employee's total earnings exceed the UEL, see page 79.

The figures in the left hand column of each table show steps between the LEL and the UEL. The NICS liability for each step is calculated at the mid-point of the steps so you and your employee may pay slightly more or less than if you used the exact percentage method.

▼ Employee's Earnings up to and including the UEL	Earnings at the LEL (where earnings are equal to or exceed the LEL) 1a	Earnings above the LEL, up to and including the ET 1b	Earnings above the ET, up to and including the UEL 1c	Total of employee's and employer's contributions 1d	Employee's contributions due on all earnings above the ET 1e	▼ Employer's contributions
£ Up to and including 342.99	£	£ P	£ P	£ P	£ P	£ P
	No NIC Liability, make no entries on forms P11 and P14					
343	343	0.00	0.00	0.00	0.00	0.00
347	343	4.00	0.00	R 0.31	0.00	R 0.31
351	343	8.00	0.00	R 0.51	0.00	R 0.51
355	343	12.00	0.00	R 0.71	0.00	R 0.71
359	343	16.00	0.00	R 0.92	0.00	R 0.92
363	343	20.00	0.00	R 1.12	0.00	R 1.12
367	343	24.00	0.00	R 1.33	0.00	R 1.33
371	343	28.00	0.00	R 1.53	0.00	R 1.53
375	343	32.00	0.00	R 1.73	0.00	R 1.73
379	343	36.00	0.00	R 1.94	0.00	R 1.94
383	343	40.00	0.00	R 2.14	0.00	R 2.14
387	343	44.00	0.00	R 2.35	0.00	R 2.35
391	343	48.00	0.00	R 2.55	0.00	R 2.55
395	343	52.00	0.00	R 2.65	0.00	R 2.65
399	343	52.00	4.00	R 1.53	0.00	R 1.53
403	343	52.00	8.00	R 0.78	0.11	R 0.89
407	343	52.00	12.00	R 0.03	0.49	R 0.52
411	343	52.00	16.00	0.71	0.86	R 0.15
415	343	52.00	20.00	1.47	1.24	0.23
419	343	52.00	24.00	2.21	1.61	0.60
423	343	52.00	28.00	2.96	1.99	0.97
427	343	52.00	32.00	3.71	2.37	1.34
431	343	52.00	36.00	4.45	2.74	1.71
435	343	52.00	40.00	5.21	3.12	2.09
439	343	52.00	44.00	5.95	3.49	2.46

▼ for information only - do not enter on Deductions Working Sheet, form P11

21

TAX TABLES

Table letter D **Monthly table**

Employee's Earnings up to and including the UEL	Earnings at the LEL (where earnings are equal to or exceed the LEL)	Earnings above the LEL, up to and including the ET	Earnings above the ET, up to and including the UEL	Total of employee's and employer's contributions	Employee's contributions due on all earnings above the ET	Employer's contributions
	1a	1b	1c	1d	1e	
£	£	£ P	£ P	£ P	£ P	£ P
443	343	52.00	48.00	6.70	3.87	2.83
447	343	52.00	52.00	7.45	4.25	3.20
451	343	52.00	56.00	8.19	4.62	3.57
455	343	52.00	60.00	8.95	5.00	3.95
459	343	52.00	64.00	9.69	5.37	4.32
463	343	52.00	68.00	10.44	5.75	4.69
467	343	52.00	72.00	11.19	6.13	5.06
471	343	52.00	76.00	11.93	6.50	5.43
475	343	52.00	80.00	12.69	6.88	5.81
479	343	52.00	84.00	13.43	7.25	6.18
483	343	52.00	88.00	14.18	7.63	6.55
487	343	52.00	92.00	14.93	8.01	6.92
491	343	52.00	96.00	15.67	8.38	7.29
495	343	52.00	100.00	16.43	8.76	7.67
499	343	52.00	104.00	17.17	9.13	8.04
503	343	52.00	108.00	17.92	9.51	8.41
507	343	52.00	112.00	18.67	9.89	8.78
511	343	52.00	116.00	19.41	10.26	9.15
515	343	52.00	120.00	20.17	10.64	9.53
519	343	52.00	124.00	20.91	11.01	9.90
523	343	52.00	128.00	21.66	11.39	10.27
527	343	52.00	132.00	22.41	11.77	10.64
531	343	52.00	136.00	23.15	12.14	11.01
535	343	52.00	140.00	23.91	12.52	11.39
539	343	52.00	144.00	24.65	12.89	11.76
543	343	52.00	148.00	25.40	13.27	12.13
547	343	52.00	152.00	26.15	13.65	12.50
551	343	52.00	156.00	26.89	14.02	12.87
555	343	52.00	160.00	27.65	14.40	13.25
559	343	52.00	164.00	28.39	14.77	13.62
563	343	52.00	168.00	29.14	15.15	13.99
567	343	52.00	172.00	29.89	15.53	14.36
571	343	52.00	176.00	30.63	15.90	14.73
575	343	52.00	180.00	31.39	16.28	15.11
579	343	52.00	184.00	32.13	16.65	15.48
583	343	52.00	188.00	32.88	17.03	15.85
587	343	52.00	192.00	33.63	17.41	16.22
591	343	52.00	196.00	34.37	17.78	16.59
595	343	52.00	200.00	35.13	18.16	16.97
599	343	52.00	204.00	35.87	18.53	17.34
603	343	52.00	208.00	36.62	18.91	17.71
607	343	52.00	212.00	37.37	19.29	18.08
611	343	52.00	216.00	38.11	19.66	18.45
615	343	52.00	220.00	38.87	20.04	18.83
619	343	52.00	224.00	39.61	20.41	19.20
623	343	52.00	228.00	40.36	20.79	19.57
627	343	52.00	232.00	41.11	21.17	19.94
631	343	52.00	236.00	41.85	21.54	20.31
635	343	52.00	240.00	42.61	21.92	20.69
639	343	52.00	244.00	43.35	22.29	21.06
643	343	52.00	248.00	44.10	22.67	21.43
647	343	52.00	252.00	44.85	23.05	21.80
651	343	52.00	256.00	45.59	23.42	22.17
655	343	52.00	260.00	46.35	23.80	22.55
659	343	52.00	264.00	47.09	24.17	22.92

▼ for information only - do not enter on Deductions Working Sheet, form P11

APPENDIX II: NI TABLES

Monthly table for Contracted-out Salary Related reduced rate contributions for use from 6 April 2004 to 5 April 2005

Table letter E

Use this table for

married women or widows in your Contracted-out Salary Related Scheme or the salary related part of your Contracted-out Mixed Benefit Scheme, and who have the right to pay reduced rate employee's contributions for whom you hold a valid certificate CA4139, CF383 or CF380A.

Do not use this table for

- women aged 60 or over, see leaflet CA41
- women in your Contracted-out Salary Related Scheme or the salary related part of your Contracted-out Mixed Benefit Scheme for whom you hold form CA2700, see table L
- married women or widows in a Contracted-out Money Purchase Scheme, Contracted-out Money Purchase Stakeholder Pension Scheme or in the money purchase part of a Contracted-out Mixed Benefit Scheme, see leaflet CA43.

Completing Deductions Working Sheet, form P11 or substitute

- enter 'E' in the space provided in the 'End of Year Summary' box of form P11
- copy the figures in columns 1b-1e of the table to columns 1b-1e of form P11. You may copy the figures in column 1a of the table to column 1a of form P11 if you wish.

If the employee's total earnings fall between the LEL and the UEL and the exact gross pay is not shown in the table, use the next smaller figure shown. If the employee's total earnings exceed the UEL, see page 79.

The figures in the left hand column of each table show steps between the LEL and the UEL. The NICS liability for each step is calculated at the mid-point of the steps so you and your employee may pay slightly more or less than if you used the exact percentage method.

▼ Employee's Earnings up to and including the UEL	Earnings at the LEL (where earnings are equal to or exceed the LEL) 1a	Earnings above the LEL, up to and including the ET 1b	Earnings above the ET, up to and including the UEL 1c	Total of employee's and employer's contributions 1d	Employee's contributions due on all earnings above the ET 1e	▼ Employer's contributions
£	£	£ P	£ P	£ P	£ P	£ P
Up to and including 342.99	No NIC Liability, make no entries on forms P11 and P14					
343	343	0.00	0.00	0.00	0.00	0.00
347	343	4.00	0.00	R 0.21	0.00	R 0.21
351	343	8.00	0.00	R 0.35	0.00	R 0.35
355	343	12.00	0.00	R 0.49	0.00	R 0.49
359	343	16.00	0.00	R 0.63	0.00	R 0.63
363	343	20.00	0.00	R 0.77	0.00	R 0.77
367	343	24.00	0.00	R 0.91	0.00	R 0.91
371	343	28.00	0.00	R 1.05	0.00	R 1.05
375	343	32.00	0.00	R 1.19	0.00	R 1.19
379	343	36.00	0.00	R 1.33	0.00	R 1.33
383	343	40.00	0.00	R 1.47	0.00	R 1.47
387	343	44.00	0.00	R 1.61	0.00	R 1.61
391	343	48.00	0.00	R 1.75	0.00	R 1.75
395	343	52.00	0.00	R 1.82	0.00	R 1.82
399	343	52.00	4.00	R 0.97	0.29	R 1.26
403	343	52.00	8.00	R 0.41	0.48	R 0.89
407	343	52.00	12.00	0.16	0.68	R 0.52
411	343	52.00	16.00	0.72	0.87	R 0.15
415	343	52.00	20.00	1.30	1.07	0.23
419	343	52.00	24.00	1.86	1.26	0.60
423	343	52.00	28.00	2.42	1.45	0.97
427	343	52.00	32.00	2.99	1.65	1.34
431	343	52.00	36.00	3.55	1.84	1.71
435	343	52.00	40.00	4.13	2.04	2.09
439	343	52.00	44.00	4.69	2.23	2.46

44   ▼ for information only - do not enter on Deductions Working Sheet, form P11

TAX TABLES

Table letter E **Monthly table**

Employee's Earnings up to and including the UEL	Earnings at the LEL (where earnings are equal to or exceed the LEL)	Earnings above the LEL, up to and including the ET	Earnings above the ET, up to and including the UEL	Total of employee's and employer's contributions	Employee's contributions due on all earnings above the ET	Employer's contributions
	1a	1b	1c	1d	1e	
£	£	£ P	£ P	£ P	£ P	£ P
1103	343	52.00	708.00	98.64	34.43	64.21
1107	343	52.00	712.00	99.21	34.63	64.58
1111	343	52.00	716.00	99.77	34.82	64.95
1115	343	52.00	720.00	100.35	35.02	65.33
1119	343	52.00	724.00	100.91	35.21	65.70
1123	343	52.00	728.00	101.47	35.40	66.07
1127	343	52.00	732.00	102.04	35.60	66.44
1131	343	52.00	736.00	102.60	35.79	66.81
1135	343	52.00	740.00	103.18	35.99	67.19
1139	343	52.00	744.00	103.74	36.18	67.56
1143	343	52.00	748.00	104.30	36.37	67.93
1147	343	52.00	752.00	104.87	36.57	68.30
1151	343	52.00	756.00	105.43	36.76	68.67
1155	343	52.00	760.00	106.01	36.96	69.05
1159	343	52.00	764.00	106.57	37.15	69.42
1163	343	52.00	768.00	107.13	37.34	69.79
1167	343	52.00	772.00	107.70	37.54	70.16
1171	343	52.00	776.00	108.26	37.73	70.53
1175	343	52.00	780.00	108.84	37.93	70.91
1179	343	52.00	784.00	109.40	38.12	71.28
1183	343	52.00	788.00	109.96	38.31	71.65
1187	343	52.00	792.00	110.53	38.51	72.02
1191	343	52.00	796.00	111.09	38.70	72.39
1195	343	52.00	800.00	111.67	38.90	72.77
1199	343	52.00	804.00	112.23	39.09	73.14
1203	343	52.00	808.00	112.79	39.28	73.51
1207	343	52.00	812.00	113.36	39.48	73.88
1211	343	52.00	816.00	113.92	39.67	74.25
1215	343	52.00	820.00	114.50	39.87	74.63
1219	343	52.00	824.00	115.06	40.06	75.00
1223	343	52.00	828.00	115.62	40.25	75.37
1227	343	52.00	832.00	116.19	40.45	75.74
1231	343	52.00	836.00	116.75	40.64	76.11
1235	343	52.00	840.00	117.33	40.84	76.49
1239	343	52.00	844.00	117.89	41.03	76.86
1243	343	52.00	848.00	118.45	41.22	77.23
1247	343	52.00	852.00	119.02	41.42	77.60
1251	343	52.00	856.00	119.58	41.61	77.97
1255	343	52.00	860.00	120.16	41.81	78.35
1259	343	52.00	864.00	120.72	42.00	78.72
1263	343	52.00	868.00	121.28	42.19	79.09
1267	343	52.00	872.00	121.85	42.39	79.46
1271	343	52.00	876.00	122.41	42.58	79.83
1275	343	52.00	880.00	122.99	42.78	80.21
1279	343	52.00	884.00	123.55	42.97	80.58
1283	343	52.00	888.00	124.11	43.16	80.95
1287	343	52.00	892.00	124.68	43.36	81.32
1291	343	52.00	896.00	125.24	43.55	81.69
1295	343	52.00	900.00	125.82	43.75	82.07
1299	343	52.00	904.00	126.38	43.94	82.44
1303	343	52.00	908.00	126.94	44.13	82.81
1307	343	52.00	912.00	127.51	44.33	83.18
1311	343	52.00	916.00	128.07	44.52	83.55
1315	343	52.00	920.00	128.65	44.72	83.93
1319	343	52.00	924.00	129.21	44.91	84.30

▼ for information only - do not enter on Deductions Working Sheet, form P11

APPENDIX II: NI TABLES

Monthly table for Contracted-out Salary Related contributions where employee has deferment for use from 6 April 2004 to 5 April 2005

Table letter **L**

Use this table for

employees in your Contracted-out Salary Related Scheme or the salary related part of your Contracted-out Mixed Benefit Scheme, for whom you hold form CA2700.

Do not use this table for

- employees who are State pension age (65 for men, 60 for women) or over, see leaflet CA41
- employees in a Contracted-out Money Purchase Scheme, Contracted-out Money Purchase Stakeholder Pension Scheme, or in the money purchase part of a Contracted-out Mixed Benefit Scheme, see leaflet CA43.

Completing Deductions Working Sheet, form P11 or substitute

- enter 'L' in the space provided in the 'End of Year Summary' box of form P11
- copy the figures in columns 1a - 1e of the table to columns 1a - 1e of form P11.

If the employee's total earnings fall between the LEL and the UEL and the exact gross pay is not shown in the table, use the next smaller figure shown. If the employee's total earnings exceed the UEL, see page 79.

The figures in the left hand column of each table show steps between the LEL and the UEL. The NICS liability for each step is calculated at the mid-point of the steps so you and your employee may pay slightly more or less than if you used the exact percentage method.

▼ Employee's Earnings up to and including the UEL	Earnings at the LEL (where earnings are equal to or exceed the LEL)	Earnings above the LEL, up to and including the ET	Earnings above the ET, up to and including the UEL	Total of employee's and employer's contributions	Employee's contributions due on all earnings above the ET	▼ Employer's contributions
	1a	1b	1c	1d	1e	
£	£	£ P	£ P	£ P	£ P	£ P
Up to and including 342.99	No NIC Liability, make no entries on forms P11 and P14					
343	343	0.00	0.00	0.00	0.00	0.00
347	343	4.00	0.00	R 0.31	0.00	R 0.31
351	343	8.00	0.00	R 0.51	0.00	R 0.51
355	343	12.00	0.00	R 0.71	0.00	R 0.71
359	343	16.00	0.00	R 0.92	0.00	R 0.92
363	343	20.00	0.00	R 1.12	0.00	R 1.12
367	343	24.00	0.00	R 1.33	0.00	R 1.33
371	343	28.00	0.00	R 1.53	0.00	R 1.53
375	343	32.00	0.00	R 1.73	0.00	R 1.73
379	343	36.00	0.00	R 1.94	0.00	R 1.94
383	343	40.00	0.00	R 2.14	0.00	R 2.14
387	343	44.00	0.00	R 2.35	0.00	R 2.35
391	343	48.00	0.00	R 2.55	0.00	R 2.55
395	343	52.00	0.00	R 2.65	0.00	R 2.65
399	343	52.00	4.00	R 2.03	0.00	R 2.03
403	343	52.00	8.00	R 1.62	0.00	R 1.62
407	343	52.00	12.00	R 1.21	0.00	R 1.21
411	343	52.00	16.00	R 0.80	0.00	R 0.80
415	343	52.00	20.00	R 0.38	0.00	R 0.38
419	343	52.00	24.00	0.03	0.00	0.03
423	343	52.00	28.00	0.44	0.00	0.44
427	343	52.00	32.00	0.85	0.00	0.85
431	343	52.00	36.00	1.26	0.00	1.26
435	343	52.00	40.00	1.68	0.00	1.68
439	343	52.00	44.00	2.09	0.00	2.09

▼ for information only - do not enter on Deductions Working Sheet, form P11   67

TAX TABLES

Table letter L   **Monthly table**

Employee's Earnings up to and including the UEL	Earnings at the LEL (where earnings are equal to or exceed the LEL)	Earnings above the LEL, up to and including the ET	Earnings above the ET, up to and including the UEL	Total of employee's and employer's contributions	Employee's contributions due on all earnings above the ET	Employer's contributions
		1a	1b	1c	1d	1e
£	£	£ P	£ P	£ P	£ P	£ P
883	343	52.00	488.00	47.82	4.07	43.75
887	343	52.00	492.00	48.23	4.11	44.12
891	343	52.00	496.00	48.64	4.15	44.49
895	343	52.00	500.00	49.06	4.19	44.87
899	343	52.00	504.00	49.47	4.23	45.24
903	343	52.00	508.00	49.88	4.27	45.61
907	343	52.00	512.00	50.29	4.31	45.98
911	343	52.00	516.00	50.70	4.35	46.35
915	343	52.00	520.00	51.12	4.39	46.73
919	343	52.00	524.00	51.53	4.43	47.10
923	343	52.00	528.00	51.94	4.47	47.47
927	343	52.00	532.00	52.35	4.51	47.84
931	343	52.00	536.00	52.76	4.55	48.21
935	343	52.00	540.00	53.18	4.59	48.59
939	343	52.00	544.00	53.59	4.63	48.96
943	343	52.00	548.00	54.00	4.67	49.33
947	343	52.00	552.00	54.41	4.71	49.70
951	343	52.00	556.00	54.82	4.75	50.07
955	343	52.00	560.00	55.24	4.79	50.45
959	343	52.00	564.00	55.65	4.83	50.82
963	343	52.00	568.00	56.06	4.87	51.19
967	343	52.00	572.00	56.47	4.91	51.56
971	343	52.00	576.00	56.88	4.95	51.93
975	343	52.00	580.00	57.30	4.99	52.31
979	343	52.00	584.00	57.71	5.03	52.68
983	343	52.00	588.00	58.12	5.07	53.05
987	343	52.00	592.00	58.53	5.11	53.42
991	343	52.00	596.00	58.94	5.15	53.79
995	343	52.00	600.00	59.36	5.19	54.17
999	343	52.00	604.00	59.77	5.23	54.54
1003	343	52.00	608.00	60.18	5.27	54.91
1007	343	52.00	612.00	60.59	5.31	55.28
1011	343	52.00	616.00	61.00	5.35	55.65
1015	343	52.00	620.00	61.42	5.39	56.03
1019	343	52.00	624.00	61.83	5.43	56.40
1023	343	52.00	628.00	62.24	5.47	56.77
1027	343	52.00	632.00	62.65	5.51	57.14
1031	343	52.00	636.00	63.06	5.55	57.51
1035	343	52.00	640.00	63.48	5.59	57.89
1039	343	52.00	644.00	63.89	5.63	58.26
1043	343	52.00	648.00	64.30	5.67	58.63
1047	343	52.00	652.00	64.71	5.71	59.00
1051	343	52.00	656.00	65.12	5.75	59.37
1055	343	52.00	660.00	65.54	5.79	59.75
1059	343	52.00	664.00	65.95	5.83	60.12
1063	343	52.00	668.00	66.36	5.87	60.49
1067	343	52.00	672.00	66.77	5.91	60.86
1071	343	52.00	676.00	67.18	5.95	61.23
1075	343	52.00	680.00	67.60	5.99	61.61
1079	343	52.00	684.00	68.01	6.03	61.98
1083	343	52.00	688.00	68.42	6.07	62.35
1087	343	52.00	692.00	68.83	6.11	62.72
1091	343	52.00	696.00	69.24	6.15	63.09
1095	343	52.00	700.00	69.66	6.19	63.47
1099	343	52.00	704.00	70.07	6.23	63.84

▼ for information only - do not enter on Deductions Working Sheet, form P11

APPENDIX II: NI TABLES

Inland Revenue

CA43
National Insurance Contributions Tables

Contracted-out contributions and minimum payments for employers with Contracted-out Money Purchase Schemes

Use from
6 April 2004 to
5 April 2005 inclusive

TAX TABLES

Earnings limits and NIC rates

Earnings limits	Employee's contribution — Contribution Table letter F	Contribution Table letter G	Contribution Table letter S	Employer's contribution — Table letters F, G and S	Employee's NIC rebate on earnings above the LEL, up to and including the ET (Applies to contribution category letters F and S only)	Employer's NIC rebate on earnings above the LEL, up to and including the ET
Below £79.00 weekly, or Below £343.00 monthly, or Below £4108.00 yearly	Nil	Nil	Nil	Nil		
£79.00 to £91.00 weekly, or £343.00 to £395.00 monthly, or £4108.00 to £4745.00 yearly	0%	0%	0%	0%	1.6% on earnings from £79.01, up to and including £91.00 (or monthly or annual equivalents)	1.0% on earnings from £79.01, up to and including £91.00 (or monthly or annual equivalents)
£91.01 to £610.00 weekly, or £395.01 to £2644.00 monthly, or £4745.01 to £31720.00 yearly	9.4% on earnings above the ET	4.85% on earnings above the ET	1% on earnings above the ET	11.8% on earnings above the ET		
Over £610.00 weekly, or over £2644.00 monthly, or over £31720.00 yearly	9.4% on earnings above the ET, up to and including the UEL, then 1% on all earnings above the UEL	4.85% on earnings above the ET, up to and including the UEL, then 1% on all earnings above the UEL	1% on all earnings above the ET	11.8% on earnings above the ET, up to and including the UEL, then 12.8% on all earnings above the UEL		

APPENDIX II: NI TABLES

Monthly table for Contracted-out Money Purchase standard rate contributions for use from 6 April 2004 to 5 April 2005

Table letter **F**

Use this table for

employees in your Contracted-out Money Purchase Scheme or Contracted-out Money Purchase Stakeholder Pension Scheme or the money purchase part of your Contracted-out Mixed Benefit Scheme, who are age 16 or over and under State Pension Age (65 for men, 60 for women).

Do not use this table for

- married women or widows who have the right to pay reduced rate employee's contributions, see Table E
- employees who are State Pension Age or over, see leaflet CA41
- employees in your Contracted-out Money Purchase Scheme or Contracted-out Money Purchase Stakeholder Pension Scheme or the money purchase part of your Contracted-out Mixed Benefit Scheme for whom you hold form CA2700, see Table S
- employees who have an Appropriate Personal Pension, or an Appropriate Personal Pension Stakeholder Pension, see leaflet CA38
- employees contracted-out in a Contracted-out Salary Related Scheme or in the salary related part of a Contracted-out Mixed Benefit Scheme, see leaflet CA39.

Completing Deductions working Sheet, form P11 or substitute

- enter 'F' and the Scheme Contracting-out Number in the space provided in the 'End of Year Summary' box of form P11
- copy the figures in columns 1a-1e of the table to columns 1a-1e of form P11 on the line next to the tax week in which the employee is paid.

If the employee's total earnings fall between the LEL and the UEL and the exact gross pay is not shown in the table, use the next smaller figure shown. If the employee's total earnings exceed the UEL, see page 78.

The figures in the left hand column of each table show steps between the LEL and the UEL. The NICs liability for each step is calculated at the mid-point of the steps so you and your employee may pay slightly more or less than if you used the exact percentage method.

▼ Employee's Earnings up to and including the UEL	Earnings at the LEL (where earnings are equal to or exceed the LEL)	Earnings above the LEL, up to and including the ET	Earnings above the ET, up to and including the UEL	Total of employee's and employer's contributions	Employee's contributions due on all earnings above the ET	▼ Employer's contributions
	1a	1b	1c	1d	1e	
£	£	£ P	£ P	£ P	£ P	£ P
Up to and including 342.99	No NIC Liability, make no entries on forms P11 and P14					
343	343	0.00	0.00	R 0.00	0.00	0.00
347	343	4.00	0.00	R 0.16	0.00	R 0.16
351	343	8.00	0.00	R 0.26	0.00	R 0.26
355	343	12.00	0.00	R 0.36	0.00	R 0.36
359	343	16.00	0.00	R 0.47	0.00	R 0.47
363	343	20.00	0.00	R 0.57	0.00	R 0.57
367	343	24.00	0.00	R 0.68	0.00	R 0.68
371	343	28.00	0.00	R 0.78	0.00	R 0.78
375	343	32.00	0.00	R 0.88	0.00	R 0.88
379	343	36.00	0.00	R 0.99	0.00	R 0.99
383	343	40.00	0.00	R 1.09	0.00	R 1.09
387	343	44.00	0.00	R 1.20	0.00	R 1.20
391	343	48.00	0.00	R 1.30	0.00	R 1.30
395	343	52.00	0.00	R 1.35	0.00	R 1.35
399	343	52.00	4.00	R 0.08	0.00	R 0.08
403	343	52.00	8.00	0.77	0.11	0.66
407	343	52.00	12.00	1.62	0.49	1.13
411	343	52.00	16.00	2.46	0.86	1.60
415	343	52.00	20.00	3.32	1.24	2.08
419	343	52.00	24.00	4.16	1.61	2.55

▼ for information only - do not enter on Deductions Working Sheet, form P11

TAX TABLES

Table letter F **Monthly table**

Employee's Earnings up to and including the UEL	Earnings at the LEL (where earnings are equal to or exceed the LEL)	Earnings above the LEL, up to and including the ET	Earnings above the ET, up to and including the UEL	Total of employee's and employer's contributions	Employee's contributions due on all earnings above the ET	Employer's contributions
1a	1b	1c	1d	1e		
£	£	£ P	£ P	£ P	£ P	£ P
1303	343	52.00	908.00	191.57	84.71	106.86
1307	343	52.00	912.00	192.42	85.09	107.33
1311	343	52.00	916.00	193.26	85.46	107.80
1315	343	52.00	920.00	194.12	85.84	108.28
1319	343	52.00	924.00	194.96	86.21	108.75
1323	343	52.00	928.00	195.81	86.59	109.22
1327	343	52.00	932.00	196.66	86.97	109.69
1331	343	52.00	936.00	197.50	87.34	110.16
1335	343	52.00	940.00	198.36	87.72	110.64
1339	343	52.00	944.00	199.20	88.09	111.11
1343	343	52.00	948.00	200.05	88.47	111.58
1347	343	52.00	952.00	200.90	88.85	112.05
1351	343	52.00	956.00	201.74	89.22	112.52
1355	343	52.00	960.00	202.60	89.60	113.00
1359	343	52.00	964.00	203.44	89.97	113.47
1363	343	52.00	968.00	204.29	90.35	113.94
1367	343	52.00	972.00	205.14	90.73	114.41
1371	343	52.00	976.00	205.98	91.10	114.88
1375	343	52.00	980.00	206.84	91.48	115.36
1379	343	52.00	984.00	207.68	91.85	115.83
1383	343	52.00	988.00	208.53	92.23	116.30
1387	343	52.00	992.00	209.38	92.61	116.77
1391	343	52.00	996.00	210.22	92.98	117.24
1395	343	52.00	1000.00	211.08	93.36	117.72
1399	343	52.00	1004.00	211.92	93.73	118.19
1403	343	52.00	1008.00	212.77	94.11	118.66
1407	343	52.00	1012.00	213.62	94.49	119.13
1411	343	52.00	1016.00	214.46	94.86	119.60
1415	343	52.00	1020.00	215.32	95.24	120.08
1419	343	52.00	1024.00	216.16	95.61	120.55
1423	343	52.00	1028.00	217.01	95.99	121.02
1427	343	52.00	1032.00	217.86	96.37	121.49
1431	343	52.00	1036.00	218.70	96.74	121.96
1435	343	52.00	1040.00	219.56	97.12	122.44
1439	343	52.00	1044.00	220.40	97.49	122.91
1443	343	52.00	1048.00	221.25	97.87	123.38
1447	343	52.00	1052.00	222.10	98.25	123.85
1451	343	52.00	1056.00	222.94	98.62	124.32
1455	343	52.00	1060.00	223.80	99.00	124.80
1459	343	52.00	1064.00	224.64	99.37	125.27
1463	343	52.00	1068.00	225.49	99.75	125.74
1467	343	52.00	1072.00	226.34	100.13	126.21
1471	343	52.00	1076.00	227.18	100.50	126.68
1475	343	52.00	1080.00	228.04	100.88	127.16
1479	343	52.00	1084.00	228.88	101.25	127.63
1483	343	52.00	1088.00	229.73	101.63	128.10
1487	343	52.00	1092.00	230.58	102.01	128.57
1491	343	52.00	1096.00	231.42	102.38	129.04
1495	343	52.00	1100.00	232.28	102.76	129.52
1499	343	52.00	1104.00	233.12	103.13	129.99
1503	343	52.00	1108.00	233.97	103.51	130.46
1507	343	52.00	1112.00	234.82	103.89	130.93
1511	343	52.00	1116.00	235.66	104.26	131.40
1515	343	52.00	1120.00	236.52	104.64	131.88
1519	343	52.00	1124.00	237.36	105.01	132.35

▼ for information only - do not enter on Deductions Working Sheet, form P11

APPENDIX II: NI TABLES

Table letter **F** **Monthly table**

Employee's Earnings up to and including the UEL	Earnings at the LEL (where earnings are equal to or exceed the LEL) 1a	Earnings above the LEL, up to and including the ET 1b	Earnings above the ET, up to and including the UEL 1c	Total of employee's and employer's contributions 1d	Employee's contributions due on all earnings above the ET 1e	Employer's contributions
£	£	£ P	£ P	£ P	£ P	£ P
2623	343	52.00	2228.00	471.41	208.79	262.62
2627	343	52.00	2232.00	472.26	209.17	263.09
2631	343	52.00	2236.00	473.10	209.54	263.56
2635	343	52.00	2240.00	473.96	209.92	264.04
2639	343	52.00	2244.00	474.80	210.29	264.51
2643	343	52.00	2248.00	475.33	210.53	264.80
2644	343	52.00	2249.00	475.44	210.58	264.86

If the employee's gross pay is over £2644, go to page 78

32 ▼ for information only - do not enter on Deductions Working Sheet, form P11

TAX TABLES

Index

INDEX

A
Accounts department	102
Accrued holiday pay for leavers	93
Accuracy	61
Additional pay	220
Additional voluntary contributions (AVCs)	267
Adoption leave	153
Advances of pay	94
Advantages of employment	7
Arrestable earnings	264
Asset	295
Attachable earnings	264
Authorisation	63
Automated payments clearing service	306

B
Backpay	96
BACS	306
Basic pay	78
Basic pay calculations	78
Basic pay errors	99
Bonus	87
BR Codes	215
Budget changes	178
Bureau	307

C
Calculating NICs	234
Cash payment	301
Casual labour	35
Changes during the tax year	256
Cheque payment	305
Cheque signatory	305
Child Support Agency	51, 263
Classes of National Insurance	233
Clock card	103
Commission	89
Completing a P45 for starters	26
Computer bureaux	110
Computerised payroll processing	106
Contracted out earnings and contributions	253
Contracts of employment	76
Contribution records	268
Council Tax orders	52
Court orders	51, 264

D
Codes	214
Data Protection Act 1998	10
Death of employees	23
Deductions working sheet	193
Differential piecework	82
Direct access	307
Direct Credit	306
Documentation	102
Double entry bookkeeping	295

E
Earnings cap	267
Earnings for NIC purposes	237
Electronic transfer	306
Emergency code	31, 176
Employee	5
Employee loans and advances	279
Employee loses his P45	20
Employee master file record	107
Employee or is self-employed	6
Employees paid neither weekly nor monthly	169
Employer's legal responsibilities to collect PAYE	60
Employment law	8
Errors in paye and NIC	281
Errors in tax paid on the P45	31
Exact percentage method	252
Expense claim form	97
Expenses	97
Expenses claims	171

F
Filing and storage	42, 67
Fixed salary	78
Flexible working hours	8
Flexitime	106
Free pay	172
Free standing additional voluntary contributions (FSAVCs)	267

G
Give As You Earn	54, 276
Gross pay	75, 171

H
Holiday pay	91
Holiday pay for employees paid weekly in cash	92
Hourly paid employees	102
Hourly rate	80

INDEX

Indirect access	307
Information flows	101
Joining a company scheme	273
Jury service	91
K Codes	220
Leavers	16
Leaving a company scheme	274
Liability	295
Loans to employees	292
Lump sum	98
Master file	107
Maternity leave	134
National Insurance (NI)	232
National Insurance number	167, 234
National minimum wage	7
National Minimum Wage	77, 82
Net pay	291
NICs and leavers	22
Non-cumulative basis	211
Non-liability for NICs: employees	242
NT Codes	216
Occupational pension scheme	52
Other allowances	86
Overtime	77, 84
Overtime pay	84
P11	178, 193
P2	176
P38(S)	36
P45	18
P46	32
P6(T)	176, 177
Paternity leave	145
Pay Adjustment	220
Pay Adjustment Tables	180
Pay in the week or month	171
PAYE Audit	60
PAYE does not cover self-employed people	166

PAYE reference	234
PAYE reference numbers	167
Payment out of petty cash	304
Payments to an ex-employee after the date of the P45	21
Payroll application package to run on a computer	106
Payroll processing	60
Payroll system input and processing	107
Payroll system output	108
Payslip	282
Pension contributions	52, 265
Pensionable earnings	266
Permanent variations	63
Personal allowance	173
Personnel records	101
Piecework	80
Proforma wages control account	299
Protection from discrimination	8
Record keeping	292
Recovery of overpayments	101
Reduced rate liability for NICs	242
Refunds	40
Regulatory limit	221
Repayment of loans	95
Security	62
Sharesave	54
Sharesave payments	279
Special tax codes	176
Spreadsheets	308
Spreadsheets for the manual calculation of gross pay	158
Stakeholder pensions	271
Starters	25
Starters without a P45	32
Statutory Adoption Pay	149
Statutory Maternity Pay	134
Statutory Paternity Pay	141
Statutory Sick Pay	117
Strike pay	281
Student loan deductions	264
Student Loan Deductions	50
Suffix codes	175
Table A	180

INDEX

Table B	185, 187
Table C	185, 190
Table D	185, 190
Table SR	185, 187
Tax allowances	172
Tax code	174
Tax codes	174
Tax credits	50, 157
Tax months	168
Tax Office	167
Tax rates	179
Tax tables	180
Tax weeks	168
Tax year	167
Taxable pay	178
Taxable Pay Tables	185
Taxable pay tables: Calculator tables	198
Temporary promotions	87
Timesheets	104
Trade disputes	218
Trade union and social club contributions	281
Trade Union subscriptions	54
Transfer value	275
Unclaimed wages	303
Unpaid leave	91
Variations in pay and tax codes	206
Wages analysis book	293
Wages control account	296
Week 1/month 1	210
Week 53 payments	217
Working time regulations	7

INDEX

See overleaf for information on other
BPP products and how to order

AAT Order

To BPP Professional Education, Aldine Place, London W12 8AW
Tel: 020 8740 2211. Fax: 020 8740 1184
E-mail: Publishing@bpp.com Web:www.bpp.com

Mr/Mrs/Ms (Full name) _____
Daytime delivery address _____
_____ Postcode _____
Daytime Tel _____ E-mail _____

	5/04 Texts	5/04 Kits	Special offer	8/04 Passcards	Success CDs
FOUNDATION (£14.95 except as indicated)				Foundation	
Units 1 & 2 Receipts and Payments	☐		Foundation Sage Bookeeping and Excel Spreadsheets CD-ROM free if ordering all Foundation Text and Kits, including Units 21 and 22/23 ☐	£6.95 ☐	£14.95 ☐
Unit 3 Ledger Balances and Initial Trial Balance	☐ (Combined Text & Kit)				
Unit 4 Supplying Information for Mgmt Control	☐ (Combined Text & Kit)				
Unit 21 Working with Computers (£9.95)	☐				
Unit 22/23 Healthy Workplace/Personal Effectiveness (£9.95)	☐				
Sage and Excel for Foundation (Workbook with CD-ROM £9.95)	☐				
INTERMEDIATE (£9.95 except as indicated)					
Unit 5 Financial Records and Accounts	☐	☐		£5.95 ☐	£14.95 ☐
Unit 6/7 Costs and Reports (Combined Text £14.95)	☐			£5.95 ☐	
Unit 6 Costs and Revenues	☐	☐			£14.95 ☐
Unit 7 Reports and Returns	☐	☐			
TECHNICIAN (£9.95 except as indicated)					
Unit 8/9 Core Managing Performance and Controlling Resources	☐	☐		£5.95 ☐	£14.95 ☐
Spreadsheets for Technician (Workbook with CD-ROM)	☐		Spreadsheets for Technicians CD-ROM free if take Unit 8/9 Text and Kit ☐		
Unit 10 Core Managing Systems and People (£14.95)	☐ (Combined Text & Kit)			£5.95 ☐	
Unit 11 Option Financial Statements (A/c Practice)	☐	☐		£5.95 ☐	
Unit 12 Option Financial Statements (Central Govnmt)	☐	☐		£5.95 ☐	
Unit 15 Option Cash Management and Credit Control	☐	☐		£5.95 ☐	
Unit 17 Option Implementing Audit Procedures	☐	☐		£5.95 ☐	
Unit 18 Option Business Tax FA04 (8/04) (£14.95)	☐ (Combined Text & Kit)			£5.95 ☐	
Unit 19 Option Personal Tax FA04 (8/04) (£14.95)	☐ (Combined Text & Kit)			£5.95 ☐	
TECHNICIAN 2003 (£9.95)					
Unit 18 Option Business Tax FA03 (8/03 Text & Kit)	☐	☐			
Unit 19 Option Personal Tax FA03 (8/03 Text & Kit)	☐	☐			
SUBTOTAL	£			£	£

TOTAL FOR PRODUCTS £ _____

POSTAGE & PACKING

Texts/Kits	First	Each extra	
UK	£3.00	£3.00	£
Europe*	£6.00	£4.00	£
Rest of world	£20.00	£10.00	£
Passcards			
UK	£2.00	£1.00	£
Europe*	£3.00	£2.00	£
Rest of world	£8.00	£8.00	£
Success CDs			
UK	£2.00	£1.00	£
Europe*	£3.00	£2.00	£
Rest of world	£8.00	£8.00	£

TOTAL FOR POSTAGE & PACKING £ _____
(Max £12 Texts/Kits/Passcards - deliveries in UK)

Grand Total (Cheques to *BPP Professional Education*)
I enclose a cheque for (incl. Postage) £ _____
Or charge to Access/Visa/Switch
Card Number ☐☐☐☐ ☐☐☐☐ ☐☐☐☐ ☐☐☐☐   CV2 No ☐☐☐ last 3 digits on signature strip

Expiry date ☐☐☐☐   Start Date ☐☐☐☐

Issue Number (Switch Only) ☐☐

Signature _____

We aim to deliver to all UK addresses inside 5 working days; a signature will be required. Orders to all EU addresses should be delivered within 6 working days. All other orders to overseas addresses should be delivered within 8 working days. * Europe includes the Republic of Ireland and the Channel Islands.

See overleaf for information on other
BPP products and how to order

AAT Order

To BPP Professional Education, Aldine Place, London W12 8AW
Tel: 020 8740 2211. Fax: 020 8740 1184
E-mail: Publishing@bpp.com Web:www.bpp.com

Mr/Mrs/Ms (Full name) _____

Daytime delivery address _____

Postcode _____

Daytime Tel _____ E-mail _____

OTHER MATERIAL FOR AAT STUDENTS

	8/04 Texts	3/03 Text	3/04 Text

FOUNDATION (£5.95)
Basic Maths and English ☐

INTERMEDIATE (£5.95)
Basic Bookkeeping (for students exempt from Foundation) ☐

FOR ALL STUDENTS (£5.95)
Building Your Portfolio (old standards) ☐
Building Your Portfolio (new standards) ☐
Basic Costing ☐

AAT PAYROLL

Finance Act 2004
8/04
December 2004 and June 2005 assessments

☐
☐
For assessments in 2005 ☐
☐

Special offer
Take Text and Kit together
£44.95 ☐

£44.95 ☐

Finance Act 2003
9/03
June 2004 exams only

☐
☐
For assessments in 2004 ☐
☐

Special offer
Take Text and Kit together
£44.95 ☐

£44.95 ☐

£ ____

LEVEL 2 Text (£29.95)
LEVEL 2 Kit (£19.95)
LEVEL 3 Text (£29.95)
LEVEL 3 Kit (£19.95)

SUBTOTAL £ ____

TOTAL FOR PRODUCTS £ ____

POSTAGE & PACKING

Texts/Kits	First	Each extra
UK	£3.00	£3.00
Europe*	£6.00	£4.00
Rest of world	£20.00	£10.00

Passcards		
UK	£2.00	£1.00
Europe*	£3.00	£2.00
Rest of world	£8.00	£8.00

Tapes		
UK	£2.00	£1.00
Europe*	£3.00	£2.00
Rest of world	£8.00	£8.00

TOTAL FOR POSTAGE & PACKING £ ____
(Max £12 Texts/Kits/Passcards - deliveries in UK)

Grand Total (Cheques to BPP Professional Education) £ ____

I enclose a cheque for (incl. Postage) ☐
Or charge to Access/Visa/Switch
Card Number ☐☐☐☐ ☐☐☐☐ ☐☐☐☐ ☐☐☐☐ CV2 No ☐☐☐ last 3 digits on signature strip

Expiry date ☐☐☐☐ Start Date ☐☐☐☐

Issue Number (Switch Only) ☐☐

Signature _____

We aim to deliver to all UK addresses inside 5 working days; a signature will be required. Orders to all EU addresses should be delivered within 6 working days. All other orders to overseas addresses should be delivered within 8 working days. * Europe includes the Republic of Ireland and the Channel Islands.

✂

Review Form & Free Prize Draw – AAT Payroll Level 2 Text (8/04)

All original review forms from the entire BPP range, completed with genuine comments, will be entered into one of two draws on 31 January 2005 and 31 July 2005. The names on the first four forms picked out on each occasion will be sent a cheque for £50.

Name: _____ Address: _____

How have you used this Tutorial Text?
(Tick one box only)

- [ ] Home study (book only)
- [ ] On a course: college _____
- [ ] With 'correspondence' package
- [ ] Other _____

Why did you decide to purchase this Tutorial Text? *(Tick one box only)*

- [ ] Have used BPP Texts in the past
- [ ] Recommendation by friend/colleague
- [ ] Recommendation by a lecturer at college
- [ ] Saw advertising
- [ ] Other _____

During the past six months do you recall seeing/receiving any of the following?
(Tick as many boxes as are relevant)

- [ ] Our advertisement in *Accounting Technician* magazine
- [ ] Our advertisement in *Pass*
- [ ] Our brochure with a letter through the post

Which (if any) aspects of our advertising do you find useful?
(Tick as many boxes as are relevant)

- [ ] Prices and publication dates of new editions
- [ ] Information on Interactive Text content
- [ ] Facility to order books off-the-page
- [ ] None of the above

Have you used the companion Assessment Kit for this subject?   [ ] Yes   [ ] No

Your ratings, comments and suggestions would be appreciated on the following areas

	Very useful	Useful	Not useful
Introduction	[ ]	[ ]	[ ]
Chapter contents lists	[ ]	[ ]	[ ]
Examples	[ ]	[ ]	[ ]
Activities and answers	[ ]	[ ]	[ ]
Key learning points	[ ]	[ ]	[ ]
Quick quizzes and answers	[ ]	[ ]	[ ]
Activity checklist	[ ]	[ ]	[ ]

	Excellent	Good	Adequate	Poor
Overall opinion of this Text	[ ]	[ ]	[ ]	[ ]

Do you intend to continue using BPP Interactive Texts/Assessment Kits?   [ ] Yes   [ ] No

Please note any further comments and suggestions/errors on the reverse of this page.

The BPP author of this edition can be e-mailed at: janiceross@bpp.com

Please return this form to: Janice Ross, BPP Professional Education, FREEPOST, London, W12 8BR

Review Form & Free Prize Draw (continued)

Please note any further comments and suggestions/errors below

Free Prize Draw Rules

1   Closing date for 31 January 2005 draw is 31 December 2004. Closing date for 31 July 2005 draw is 30 June 2005.

2   Restricted to entries with UK and Eire addresses only. BPP employees, their families and business associates are excluded.

3   No purchase necessary. Entry forms are available upon request from BPP Professional Education. No more than one entry per title, per person. Draw restricted to persons aged 16 and over.

4   Winners will be notified by post and receive their cheques not later than 6 weeks after the relevant draw date.

5   The decision of the promoter in all matters is final and binding. No correspondence will be entered into.